A Ministry
of Hope:

The Gift
Of
Hope

AUTHOR Sarah Decosimo Jones

DEDICATION

Thank you Susan and Vivian for believing in me when I didn't believe in myself. I also want to thank my family and friends for their love and encouragement.

CONTENTS

ACKNOWLEDGMENTS

Thank you Ruth and Esther for taking me by the
hand and walking me through this process.

Scripture taken from the following sources:

"You are the most arrogant person I know!"

"Sarah, you are the most arrogant person I know." This was a statement from my brother. Since he is my brother and knows me pretty well, the comment had a great impact on me. In fact, it has caused me to begin praying for humility. I had to seek God's help with this, because I didn't really know what he was talking about. Now I do.

Praying for humbling isn't bad; having God answer that prayer is another matter altogether. I don't think there is any part of my life that hasn't been exposed. It reminds me of when I went to the dentist as a little girl. My teeth always looked good to me until he had me chew on a small tablet. Suddenly my teeth were covered by a red stain. The stain simply exposed the plaque that had been there all along. So it has been with my arrogance. It's been there all along, but through prayer God has opened my eyes so that I can see it. YUCK!

Andrew, my son, fixed up a blog site for me when he was home at Christmas. I wanted to share my Bible studies. Why haven't I? I'm too proud. I'm afraid to expose my inability to do it just right—so I haven't done it at all.

One of the main reasons I have been praying for humility is because what I really want is grace. The Bible teaches that God resists the proud, but He gives grace to the humble. The way I see it, I can either live my life in arrogance based on my pride, or I can, in humility, cast my cares on Jesus and live by grace.

To be honest, I'm not there yet. This is really hard. I don't like what I see. This has been a depressing journey, but I'm not finished yet. My encouragement for today is this, "But the eyes of the Lord are on those who fear him, on those whose hope is in his unfailing love, to deliver them from death and keep them alive in famine. We wait in hope for the Lord; he is our help and our shield. In him our hearts rejoice, for we trust in his holy name. May your unfailing love rest upon us, O Lord, even as we put our hope in you" (Psa. 33:18-22 NIV).

So begins my blog about hope. I have put my confidence, my hope, in the unfailing love of my Redeemer. Now I will wait for my transformation through the power of His grace.

Beyond mea culpa

"Mea culpa, mea culpa, maxima mea culpa." "Through my fault, through my fault, through my most grievous fault." I learned about my guilt early in life. I found it to be a constant companion. Often it would awaken me it the night. Suddenly I would think of something I should have done; or, equally as effective in robbing me of sleep, something I shouldn't have done.

I have found guilt to have a paralyzing effect on me. When I am consumed with guilt there is not room for much else. One day it dawned on me that this self absorption was simply just another form of pride. It was as if pride had come in through the back door and was masquerading as humility.

The Bible teaches that you will know the truth and the truth will set you free. The truth that sets me free is the unfailing love of God I find in Jesus Christ. As a child I memorized John 3:16: "For God so loved the world that He gave His only begotten Son, that whosoever believeth in him should not perish, but have everlasting life." As a child I believed and accepted Jesus as my Savior.

That should have been the end of guilt, right? Yet, still I am painfully aware of my faults and failures. Daily I must make the decision of what I will focus on. I also read in Scripture, "I have no greater joy than to hear that my children are walking in the truth" (3 John 4 NIV). The truth is, I am forgiven; I have a Savior, a Redeemer. I have a high priest at the throne of God who understands my struggles and who is interceding on my behalf.

Today I choose to worship my Savior and not my guilt. I lift my eyes away from my fault and to His face. I choose to put my confidence in His grace. Based on the truth of His love, by faith I will rise up and walk. I am humbly aware of my unworthiness, but I am also aware that the hand extended to me bears scars. By those scars I am healed.

Don't bite the thermometer!

I don't remember why I was sitting up on that table at the doctor's office but I do remember the nurse sticking that glass thing in my mouth and ordering me not to bite it. It had never occurred to me to bite it. That is, until she told me not to.

Crunch! Wow, what excitement! No sooner had I bitten the thermometer than little balls of mercy went bouncing all over the room. And if that weren't enough, the nurse seemed to bounce around the room as well. It seemed I was an audience of one. I had caused all this excitement! I had the power! And did I mention I was sick?

"I know how to make her stop," my Grandmother said while producing a small amber colored bottle from behind her back. This was to be the cure for my problem. You see, I was a finger sucker!

"Hold out your hand, Sarah." Being the obedient child I was, I complied with her wishes. She opened the bottle and produced the small brush attached to the top of the bottle. Then she brushed it onto my fingers and said, "Go ahead, Sarah; put your fingers in your mouth." Before my fingers ever found their resting place in my mouth, I could smell the foul odor. The taste matched the smell. When Grandmother saw my reaction she said, "That should cure her, Rachel!"

Oh, but they underestimated the strength of my will. On the outside I was a compliant child, but on the inside...I was my own master! They made the mistake of leaving the bottle unattended. I pulled a chair up to the counter and climbed up until I could reach the offending vial. Then I climbed back down, went outside and emptied it onto the ground. I had the power!

"'You will not surely die,' the serpent said to the woman. 'For God knows that when you eat from it your eyes will be opened, and you will be like God, knowing good and evil'" (Gen. 3:4-5 KJV). Oh, yes, yes. This is just what I always wanted! To be my own God; my own master; nobody will be the boss of me!

Nobody is going to tell me not to bite the thermometer. Nobody is going to keep me from sucking my fingers! Did I mention I had this problem with pin worms? Well, never mind that; back to the important things. I would be my own God—or at least I would worship on my own terms.

"Come, my children, listen to me; I will teach you the fear of the Lord" (Psa. 34:11 NIV). This is how my journey began.

Where time and eternity intersected

There is an orange X on the pavement where it happened. It is the place where time and eternity intersected. This is how it happened...

I was only a few minutes from home when I saw the collision. The impact of the two cars was so great it looked like they met in midair. I had narrowly escaped being a part of the accident myself.

First, I went to comfort the boy whose legs had been crushed when the cars collided. After his mother came, I went to see what I could do for the lady in the van. I saw her body slumped over the steering wheel. She was dead.

Like me, she was only a few minutes from home. It didn't take long for her friends and family to gather. One by one they asked me what had happened. I repeated the story to her mother, her sisters, her children and her husband. The grief was a heavy presence. We were all standing there waiting for the authorities. Until they came, the body remained slumped over the steering wheel.

That was when it happened. The family began to say to each other, "God is good." Each person said this to the one next to them. Finally, the lady next to me looked me in the eyes and said, "God is good. I'm going to pray and ask God that you might not have bad dreams because of what you saw today."

I was stunned! Why would she care if I, a stranger, had bad dreams or not! That night I woke with my heart pounding. I had seen it all in my mind again. I could hear the echo of the boy's screams and the deadly silence of the woman in the van. As I was jolted awake, I also saw again the face of the woman who had promised to pray for me.

I got out of bed and knelt down. I thought of the words of Job when he received word of all he had lost. He too knelt down and worshiped. The family I met at the scene of the accident had shown me what true worship is.

The orange mark has faded, but I will never forget when time and eternity intersected. It was also the day I saw heaven and earth come together in true worship.

"Class, isn't Sarah stupid?"

My teacher was given the almost impossible task of teaching sixty second graders how to read! I became the object of her frustration.

For the life of me, I could not figure out how to decode those letters on the page. They seemed to me to be like little minnows swimming about. This was really a problem for someone whose initials began with an S and ended with a D. My solution was to write one row in one direction and the next in the other direction. My teacher was not impressed by my genius.

One thing we did learn early on was to speak in unison. We had learned to stand and say, "Good Morning, Sister _____." So when my teacher asked, "Class, isn't Sarah stupid," they did a really good job of saying in unison, "Yes, Sarah is stupid"

I may not have learned to read very well in the second grade, but I did learn my place. I longed to not be stupid, but in my mind I saw a bookshelf. I wanted to reach up high, but I knew those book weren't for people like me. They were reserved for only the smart people.

Isn't it funny how, when you have children, you know they should have what you couldn't have? I started reading to my first child before she was born! By the time she was three we had covered all the *Little House on the Prairie* series.

I've been reading children's books now for over thirty years, and I think I'm almost ready to go to the next shelf! My children long ago surpassed me. But I have commissioned them to every now and then come back and tell me what they're learning. What a thrill to be your children's student!

I have a wonderful mystery to share with you. This mystery fills me with wonder and delight. I found a book that was down on my level, a book that contains the living word of God. There are a lot of words in it that I probably don't pronounce right, but that doesn't keep me from reading it.

I started reading it from Genesis to Revelation when I was twelve or thirteen. I'll be sixty in a few years, and you know what? I never get tired of it. It fills my life with wonder and joy. Maybe that is because I am one of those simple people.

I found these verses in the Bible that describe me: "God chose the foolish things of the world to shame the wise; God chose the weak things of the world to shame the strong. He chose the lowly things of this world and the despised things—and the things that are not—to nullify the things that are, so that no one may boast before him" (1 Cor. 1:27-29 NIV).

So, I am satisfied that I am who I am; because through His word I know who He is.

S.A.D.

Oh, Mamas, you must be careful when naming your babies. Stop and think: What will the initials spell? I was given the name Sarah Angeline Decosimo—S.A.D.

I have suffered with depression from my earliest memories. This winter I have felt almost suffocated by it. I looked at its presence in my life in many ways. I see it as my sparring partner. I must wrestle with depression so as not to be overcome by it.

I read in Psalm 139:13, "For you created my inmost being; you knit me together in my mother's womb" (NIV). Because of my depression, I see God choosing deep purple, scarlet and forest green to knit into my being before I was ever born.

I live on a farm now. I have observed that there is something known as fallow time. It happens in the winter. I look across the field and all I can see is barrenness. But that is deceptive, because during this fallow time roots are growing. So it is with me; my depression is my fallow time.

During this winter season of my soul, my roots go deep into the Word of God. I am seeking comfort in His promises. I am waiting for my

Redeemer. I say with the psalmist, "Out of the depths I cry to you, O Lord; O Lord, hear my voice. Let your ears be attentive to my cry for mercy.... I wait for the Lord, my soul waits, and in his word I put my hope" (Psa. 130:1-2, 5 NIV).

This kind of waiting is not done is despair. To hope is to have a confident expectation of good. Because my hope is in Jesus Christ, I am not disappointed. Just as "weeping may last through the night, but joy comes with the morning" (Psa. 30:5 NLT), I have found that winter is always followed by spring!

Guess what. My birthday is March 20, the first day of spring. When the winter is over, I begin to feel within me the stirring of life again. Now I see growth above the ground. Tender colors of green, pink and violet appear. But do not be deceived; they have a strong root system.

My parents gave me the name Sarah Angeline Decosimo. I have discovered that Angeline means messenger. I have begun to ask God to let me be His Angeline. I want to whisper the message of hope to others who are experiencing winter in their soul. If you are reading this, perhaps God has answered my prayer and has let me be His Angeline. That would be redeeming S.A.D. and making it JOY.

If this is true, will you let me know?

The bond of empty arms

"I've had an abortion." It was spoken like a challenge. She was seventeen and homeless. We had taken her in, but she didn't know us and we didn't know her.

When she told me, I wrapped my arms around her and wept. I whispered in her ear, "I am so sorry; my baby died too." When she heard this, her tears flowed freely.

She and I began to share our stories. We found to our amazement that our babies had the same due date. Her room would have been Belle Marie's nursery. I still had the baby clothes that had been given me at her baby shower.

We spent many hours talking and crying. Sometimes we would hold the empty baby clothes and each other as we wept. But something was taking place in both our hearts. Healing came for both of us as we shared our grief.

I talked to her about Jesus and His love. I told her that He is the God who really sees. No one could understand her pain but Him. All of her shame, all of her regret, He was willing to take. At the beginning of His ministry, John had called out when he saw Jesus and said, "Behold, the lamb of God, who takes away the sin of the world" (John 1:29 ESV).

I still miss Belle Marie, but Jesus has redeemed my sorrow; and, even though her life was brief, He gave it meaning.

Get up

"Mom, I want to have more faith." "Well," my Mother said, 'The Bible says faith comes by hearing and hearing comes by the word of God. If you really want to have more faith, I'll wake you up tomorrow at 5 A.M. so you can read the Bible before school." That sounded great to me: a grand adventure, getting an opportunity to really know God! It sounded really good at 5 P.M.; however, at 5 A.M. it didn't sound quite so good.

The next morning my Mother came into my room. She didn't turn on the light; she didn't speak in a loud voice. In fact, she whispered, "Sarah, if you want more faith, get up." Then she quietly left the room.

An amazing thing happened. My bed became alive. The covers became warm arms that wrapped tightly around me. My pillow spoke to me in a warm comforting voice saying, "Stay, Sarah, close your eyes and sleep." I cried out to the Lord for rescue, using the only words that would come to me, "Help, Lord. My spirit is willing, but my flesh is weak!"

To escape my bed, I had to roll onto the floor. I found that at 5 A.M. the gravitational pull on the earth is very strong; therefore, I had to crawl out of my room. I can't remember how many days I went through this process before I conquered the bed and gravity, but I can tell you it was worth it.

Proverbs 8:17: "I love those who love me; and those who diligently seek me will find me" (NAS).

I was thirteen when my mother woke me up so many years ago; now I am approaching sixty. I can hardly wait for the morning to come when I can hear His voice calling me, "Arise, my beloved, and come away." "Oh, yes. Yes, my Lord. I will get up."

Others may, you may not

I just about drove my children crazy. To this day the subject comes up about the things I didn't let them watch on TV. What they don't know is that I am even stricter on myself.

The Bible tells us that, as Christians, we are to be holy because the Lord is holy. This causes many Christians to frown. I think the understanding of holiness has become warped. Most Christians when they hear the word holy think of all the things they are going to have to give up.

Do you want to know what I think about when I read that I am to be holy? I think about Exodus 39, when I read how God set apart the priests. They got to wear sacred garments woven from blue, purple and scarlet yarn. They wore an ephod with gold and jewels on it. Last, but not least, they wore the sacred diadem made from pure gold and engraved on it, like an inscription on a seal, was written, "HOLY TO THE LORD." Did I mention they were in the wilderness?

Maybe I was too strict. But my goal wasn't to take good things away from my children. I just wanted to teach them to prefer the Bread of Heaven over leeks and garlic. I wanted them to crave Living Water more than drinking from the muddy waters of the Nile.

I wanted my children to see the beauty of holiness.

Loraine

"If you don't change your behavior, we will put you into a state mental institution." Loraine smiled, "This is my escape!"

As a child, Loraine had been badly abused. No one at the school realized that the abuse was the root cause of her behavior. Loraine was mean to her peers, and rebellious to all the authority figures at school. The school counselor went to Loraine and her parents with the ultimatum that if Loraine's behavior didn't change she should go to the institution. Loraine's behavior didn't change.

I met Loraine many years later. She had come to a Bible study I was teaching. Loraine had had a spiritual birth. She reminded me of the woman at the well spoken of in the fourth chapter of John. She met Jesus in all her brokenness; He offered her a drink of living water and she took it.

The Scripture teaches us that we hold this treasure in a jar of clay. This was true of Loraine. She and I spent many hours together talking about Jesus. We also talked about her pain. She had been rejected by both her mother and her father. She was alone, but God places the lonely in families. God placed Loraine in mine.

Because Loraine was in my family, she shared holidays with us. Our relationship always seemed a little strange because Loraine was over ten years older than I was, yet she saw me as a mother figure. One Christmas, Loraine asked me to get a song for her Christmas gift. She told me how deeply this song had affected her. She felt it had been God's gift to her and she wanted me to buy it for her. It was "Resurrection" by Nicole Sponberg.

Two months later I found Loraine dead in her apartment.

It was as if the image of her dead body had been burned into my mind. I saw it everywhere I looked. I cried out to Jesus," Help me!" Immediately I heard His voice saying to me, "Sarah, let me tell you what happen. I came to Loraine and called her by name. I told her, "Arise, my beloved, and come away, for the winter is passed and the sound of the turtle dove can be heard in the land" (Song of Solomon 2:10-12 NIV).

I spent days cleaning out Loraine's apartment. The whole time I was there I listened to the song "Resurrection" over and over and over.

Now when I think about Loraine, I think about her in the arms of Jesus.

The KEY

It was a perfect day. I was to be the master of my fate, the captain of my ship. I had the whole day planned and I had made a perfect list. That is when it happened.

My first destination had been Toys R Us°. I felt so efficient as I checked it off my list. But when I got to the car there was a problem. I still had my list, but what I didn't have were keys to my car. Now what was I supposed to do?

That morning I had been studying the sovereignty of God. Suddenly a thought came to me, "How would I respond to this situation if I really believed that God was sovereign and that He loved me?" I decided to go on a Quest.

The first thing I did on my Quest was to offer a sacrifice. Outside Toys R Us° was a garbage can. When I got to it, I lay my hands on it and I prayed, "Lord, it felt so good to be in control of my day. But now I want to know what it feels like to truly believe that You are Sovereign and that You love me." Having said that, I wadded up my list and put it on the altar (which looked a lot like a garbage can, because it was a garbage can).

My Quest had begun. So now what was I supposed to do without keys and without a list? I decided to talk to the Sovereign God who loved me. "Lord, what do I do now?"

I went into the store and explained that I had lost my keys and I needed to use a phone (this was before the day of cell phones). I also told them about my Quest. They gave me a knowing smile and a phone. I called the doctor to cancel the appointment I had had for that day. The receptionist told me she would be happy to come get me. And so the day of miracles began.

I spent that whole day doing two things, telling people about my Quest and praying, "Lord, what am I supposed to do now?" I was amazed at how many people prayed with me and helped me go from place to place. Eventually I ended up at the mall where I was to meet my children. I decided to ask God to send me someone who could tell me what to do about my keyless car.

He answered that prayer too. The woman He sent to me looked at me strangely and said, "Sarah, most people would just call a locksmith." With this information I went to the mall office to see if they had the number of a locksmith.

I told the woman behind the desk what I needed. She smiled at me and said, "Did you lose your keys?" Before I could explain that I hadn't lost them at the mall, she reached out and handed me my keys.

It was then I realized that was one prayer I had not thought to pray: I had not asked God to give me back my keys! I had wanted to know instead what it would feel like to really believe that God was in control and that He loved me. I found out what it feels like. It makes life feel like an adventure. It feels like you are wrapped up in a blanket of peace.

Many people have asked," How did your keys get to the mall"? I don't know. I can simply add that to the long list of things I don't know. But then, I don't have to know everything, because, you see, I'm not in control. However, I belong to the Sovereign Lord of the Universe and He loves me. I am reminded of this every time I use my key.

At the jail at four o'clock on Sunday afternoon

"Lord, I am not going to seek this boy out. If you want me to be part of his life, put him in the middle of my path." I had heard about "Joey." He was only thirteen, yet he had been in and out of reform school, boot camp, and at the present had been suspended from school. I wasn't excited about meeting him, so I left the possibility of our meeting up to God.

After I prayed I went for a walk. Guess who was standing in the middle of the road. That is how my friendship with Joey began. He found out I usually woke up at five in the morning. He would often arrive at my door soon after that and ask me to read the Bible to him.

I met him in the spring of the year; by the fall his mother had died. I became a more constant part of his life. Joey continued to be troubled. He was unable to stay at home. In fact, he spent most of the remainder of his childhood in and out of institutions. I have followed him to all of them. Everywhere he goes, I go. I go to him with the message, "Jesus loves you, and so do I."

Last Sunday afternoon at 4:00 I was at the jail again. I lifted
the receiver and looked through the double-paned glass and said, "Joey,
I love you." He smiled and said, "Sarah, I know you do. You're the only
one who comes to see me." "Joey, I'm here to tell you Jesus loves you.
He will never turn His back on you. Only He really knows you. He
understands your pain. He came to save you. He took on a robe of flesh
so that you could be robed in righteousness." Joey's eyes filled with
tears and he said, "Sarah, will you send me a Message Bible?"

God put Joey in the middle of my path that day and gave me the
assignment to show him the love of Christ. What a privilege.

He was dying of AIDS

I sat beside his hospital bed. He was so sick he could hardly lift his head
from the pillow. I spoke to him about Jesus. He turned his head away.
When he looked back at me, there were tears in his eyes. "It's too late
for that, I'm dying," he said. "You don't know what I've done."

I took his hand and said gently, "I'm not here to talk about what you've
done. I want to tell you what Jesus has done for you." I spoke to "John"
about the love of God; that because of God's love He gave His only son
that, if anyone would believe in Him, he wouldn't perish but have
eternal life.

John told me again that it was too late. He told me he didn't have time
to change. He had lived his life and made his mistakes and now it was
over. That was when I told him about the thief on the cross.

It was the last day of his life and he was impaled on a cross. There
was nothing left for him to do but die. He was aware of the pain, the
remorse, and the mocking crowd. Through the haze of pain and grief, he
became aware of the men on the crosses beside him. One shouted
curses; the other said, "Father, forgive them, for they do not know what
they are doing."

The criminal turned his face toward Jesus; it was all he could do. He
said, "Jesus, remember me when you come into your kingdom." Jesus
answered him, "I tell you the truth, today you will be with me in
paradise" (Luke 23:42-43 NIV).

Jesus, I explained, is the Lamb of God who came to take away the sins of the world. All of humanity is on one side of the cross or the other. We are all like the criminals crucified with Jesus. We either die in our sin cursing the Savior, or by faith we turn our face to Him and cry out for mercy.

John prayed with me that day to accept God's gift of salvation. The next time I saw him was at his funeral, but one day I will see him again in paradise.

Waiting

Waiting, waiting, waiting, waiting for the doctor to call to tell me if my daughter's tumor was malignant. Waiting, waiting, waiting, waiting for a call from the University to find out if my son has been accepted. Waiting, waiting, waiting, waiting to find out if my wayward child will ever come back home to me again.

It doesn't matter what I'm waiting for, in the process I always discover a few things about myself. The first thing that becomes clear is that I am not in control. The next thing I discover is that waiting exposes what I am really putting my confidence in. If I am putting my confidence in anything other than God, waiting will be pregnant with anxiety. If, on the other hand, while I am waiting I am putting my confidence in the Lord, my waiting becomes a time of expectation. Psalm 37:7, "Be still before the Lord and wait patiently for him..." (NIV).

I sat in my friend's living room, the depression so heavy I could hardly breathe."Sarah, what are you doing?" I sat in silence for a while then I whispered, "I am waiting." Susan replied, "Sarah, what are you waiting for?" Slowly the words came, "I am waiting for the Lord."

The next morning while reading my Bible, I found the words that expressed the cry of my heart. "I waited patiently for the Lord; he turned to me and heard my cry. He lifted me out of the slimy pit, out of the mud and mire; he set my feet on a rock and gave me a firm place to stand. He put a new song in my mouth, a hymn of praise to our God. Many will see and fear and put their trust in the Lord" (Psa. 40:1-3 NIV).

No one enjoys waiting; no one enjoys being tested. However,

sometimes at the end of this time of waiting I find a deeper sense of peace than I had known before. I find that, though I am not in control, God is. When I put my trust in Him, I find rest for my soul.

Don't forget the vista

We had just moved into our new house and I guess I got a bit obsessive. Window, windows everywhere. I loved it. Looking out my back window, I had a view of the lake. There were geese on the lake, and from my chair at the breakfast table I could see a blue heron's nest. Looking out my front windows I could see horses grazing in the field, and beyond them were the deer. But there was a problem; I wasn't looking through the window, I was looking at the window.

If you have a house filled with children then you will have windows filled with smudges. On this particular morning all I could see were smudges. In fact, they were driving me crazy. As I sat there murmuring about smudges, I suddenly saw the blue heron perch on his nest and spread his wings. This caught my attention and caused me to look through the glass and not at the glass. That was when the thought came to me, "Life is full of smudges, but don't forget the vista!"

About this time I saw my son coming into the kitchen for breakfast. He took one look at my face and I could almost hear him thinking," Oh, no, Mother has had a revelation!" Maybe I should have waited to share my newfound insight, but I couldn't resist. As he sat there bleary eyed, I poured forth my soul. He didn't say much, just sat there and nodded his head.

After he finished his breakfast, my son went upstairs to his room. When he got to the top to the stairs he yelled down, "Hey, Mom, there's cat vomit up here." Then he paused and added, "But don't forget the vista." My son knew very well how I felt about cat vomit, but this morning, instead of screaming, I laughed and thought, "Perspective, perspective, perspective!"

A tapestry rose

The vase held a single rose. It was the practice of the church where I was going to give a rose to each new mother. The newborn lay in her mother's arms. My eyes suddenly stung with tears. My baby lay in her coffin in the ground. Fighting for composure, I lifted my eyes to the altar. That is when I saw it. Hanging above the altar was a tapestry. Woven into the tapestry was a rose with these words "God's Promise."

My heart reached out and took that rose for my baby. I not only held the tapestry rose in my heart, I also held onto the promises of God. What were the promises that gave me comfort? Jesus said "Blessed are those who mourn, for they will be comforted" (Matt. 5:4 NIV). That's a promise I held on to.

Another promise that sustained me is found in Isaiah 43:1-3: "Fear not, for I have redeemed you; I have summoned you by name; you are mine. When you pass through the waters, I will be with you; and when you pass through the rivers, they will not sweep over you. When you walk through the fire, you will not be burned; the flames will not set you ablaze. For I am the Lord, your God, the Holy One of Israel, your Savior" (NIV).

During this time in my life my sister Rose gave me a poem, "One Day at a Time." I read it over and over. Part of the poem went like this;

One day at a time—but the day is so long
and the heart is not brave and the soul is not strong.
O Thou pitiful Christ, be thou near all the way.
Give courage and patience and strength for the day.
Swift cometh His answer, so clean and so sweet;
"Yea, I will be with thee; thy troubles to meet;
I will not forsake thee, I never will leave."
Not yesterday's load we are called on to bear;
Nor the morrow's uncertain and shadowy care;
why should we look forward or back with dismay?
Our needs, as our mercies, are but for the day.
One day at a time, and the day is His day.

He hath numbered its hour, though they haste or delay.
His grace is sufficient, we walk not alone,
As the day, so the strength that he gives His own.[1]

The mute speak

My daughter-in-law has a very special gift. She helps people find their written voice. When I first heard her speak about this, I only had one thought, "Teach me!"

People have often said to me," Sarah, if you can talk, you can write." Personally, I have never found this to be true. I have no trouble talking—I have addressed large crowds—and yet when I have tried to sit down and capture the thoughts in my mind on paper, there has always been a terrible disconnect.

Because I believe I have the gift of encouragement, I have always wanted to write a devotional. One of my friends even arranged for me to go to a writer's convention. There was a contest that she encouraged me to enter. We were to tell about the greatest obstacle we had to writing. I was embarrassed, wanting to participate, yet not wanting to expose how inadequate I was. I wrote, "My greatest obstacle to writing is adding sweat to a dream and thereby making the dream a reality." I was stunned when they read out my name as a winner.

I have another friend who has shared my dream of capturing thoughts on paper. She said, "Sarah, let's do it together. Maybe we could even write a book together one day." I wanted to, I really did. But every time I sat down to write, the thoughts scattered like leaves in a windstorm. Finally I told her to go without me. I have been reading her devotionals for a year now. She has a book that will be published soon. I rejoice with her! And yet,...

Two weeks ago, I began an in depth study of 1 Corinthians. There I read, "For consider your calling, brethren, that there were not many wise

---

[1] *One Day at a Time*, Annie Johnson Flint. Public domain.

according to the flesh, not many mighty, not many noble; but God has chosen the foolish things of the world to shame the wise, and God has chosen the weak things of the world to shame the things which are strong, and the base things of the world and the despised God has chosen, the things that are not, that He may nullify the things that are, so that no man may boast before God" (1 Cor. 1:26-29 NAS).

Two weeks ago God did a miracle in my life. Just as Jesus made the mute speak, He gave me a written voice. Two weeks ago, with trembling fingers, I began to type my first post.

I hate this!

I was sitting in the church observing as people went down to the altar weeping. I was totally uncomfortable with this outward display of emotion. My husband liked to visit different churches, and, of course, I went with him; but I didn't necessarily like it.

"Don't these people have any self respect?" This is what I was thinking the first time I felt like I heard the Holy Spirit speak to me. This is what I heard Him say, "Sarah, you are pridefully sitting in judgment over my children. I want you to come to the altar and confess your sin of pride."

"No," I thought, "This can't be God." Whenever I feel like the Holy Spirit is directing me to do something, I always try to check it out with my husband. On this occasion I felt surely my husband would agree with me that it had simply been a stray thought. I leaned over and whispered in his ear. When he whispered back, "Sounds like God wants to deal with your pride," I thought , "Oh, no. Steve is deceived too!"

I have no idea what the preacher preached on that day. I was completely caught up in my wrestling match with the idea of going to the altar. Surely, I reasoned, this was not something God wanted me to do. I didn't really belong here. This wasn't my church. This wasn't the way I chose to worship. Finally, I came up with a solution. If I ever came back to this church again, and if God reminded me about going to the altar, then I would know the thought had come from Him and I would obey. I felt safe, since my husband was a preacher with his own church.

Months went by. I had completely forgotten about that church. We had a friend who had been invited to sing. We went to support her. I was stunned when I settled in the pew only to discover that I was back at THAT church and my conversation with God picked up seamlessly where it had ended months before. When this happened, I knew it was no longer a question of "if" I was being prompted by the Holy Spirit, it was now a question of obedience.

Before when I was at the church I had wrestled with the question if what I was thinking was from God; now I was simply wrestling with my pride. Once more I was so consumed with my own struggles that I wasn't paying attention to what was happening around me.

I stepped into the aisle not realizing that there were two young men with trumpets behind me. They began to play and the church began to sing, "We will obey Him, We will obey Him, We will obey Him, Hallelujah." That did it. Full loss of dignity. I ran up to the altar. Suddenly I was surrounded by people praying for me, thanking God I had chosen obedience.

James 4:6: "God opposes the proud but gives grace to the humble."

I lied

"Sarah, are you reading my book." "Yes!" I replied. This would have been the correct response if he had asked, "Do you want to read my book," or "Do you plan to read my book." The problem was, in response to his question, "Are you reading my book," I lied. I was talking to a man I highly respect, who is the author of a book I really want to read. I didn't want to look bad in his eyes, so I sought refuge in a lie.

To this day I remember the first time I found salvation in a lie. I was standing in front of my very angry grandmother. She was holding a broken glass and asking me, "Sarah, did you break this glass?" It was as if I had an out-of-body experience. I thought to myself, "The only thing I have to do to get out of being punished is say 'No'." It seemed like a good plan to me, and it worked! The only problem was, by using this way of escape, I became a liar.

The only way to really understand the problem with lying is to see what

God says about it. Proverbs 12:22 puts it bluntly: "Lying lips are an abomination to the Lord" (ESV). Jesus said, "I am... the truth" (John 14:6). John 8:44 describe the devil's character: "He [the devil] was a murderer from the beginning, and does not stand in the truth because there is no truth in him. Whenever he speaks a lie, he speaks from his own nature, for he is a liar and the father of lies" (NAS).

It seems Satan is always ready to offer me salvation—a way of escape. If I do it his way, I will look good and be able to keep my pride. Jesus offers me Himself as my Savior; His way is the way of truth, humility and righteousness. In fact, Jesus said, "If anyone would come after me [be my disciple], he must deny himself and take up his cross daily and follow me" (Luke 9:23). I see my choices this way: either I follow Jesus or I follow Satan. Because I have chosen to follow Jesus, I have also chosen to write a letter that goes something like this, "Dear _____, I lied...."

There is only one antidote for a lie, and that is the truth.

Finding purpose

"Why am I here?" I was completely frustrated. I had felt compelled to take my children to the mall that morning to have their pictures taken. I was aggravated to find when I arrived that the photography studio was flooded. I walked up and down the mall pushing the stroller with one hand and holding my five-year-old with the other hand, all the while praying, "Lord, why did you bring me here?"

My daughter wanted a drink, but in the process of pushing the stroller, holding her hand, and juggling the cup, the cup fell. I was so frustrated I started to cry. Suddenly a young man came up to help me. When we were settled in a booth he said, "I know how it is, my mother has been crying a lot too. My brother is in the hospital with a broken neck." He went to bring her to talk to me, and I thought, "I am not going to tell him I was crying over a spilt drink."

I found out they were new Christians. She was from out-of-state, and in her hurry to get to her son she had failed to bring the clothing she needed. I told her I would come to the hospital the next day with something she could wear.

At the hospital, I found her in a room filled with men. Her son had been at a Christian boy's home when he fell. The men in the room were kind, but I felt their message was wrong. They were telling her that, now that she was a Christian, she shouldn't cry, because if anything happened to her son he would go to Heaven. Her son had accepted Jesus as his savior, and I too believed he would go to Heaven if he died. But that didn't eliminate her grief. I put my arm around her and wept with her. I told her that the Bible tells us there is a time to cry and that Jesus Himself wept.

God imported me into her story that day. Every time she went to be with her son, I went with her. I watched as she lovingly stroked his face. I listened as she remembered his childhood. I wept as she uncovered his feet and kissed them.

Time passed. My husband was taking me for a ride in the country. I have no sense of direction, so he likes to ask me, "Sarah, do you know where you are?" Usually I don't know; however, this day was different. I told him to pull over and stop the car. In front of us was a Boy's Home. I had never seen it before, but I felt sure that it was the same place where the young man had been when he fell and broke his neck. Suddenly I realized it was the one year anniversary of his death. I prayed all day for his mother and family. The next week I got a letter from his mother. It said, "Today is the anniversary of my son's death. It has been really hard, but God assured me you were praying, and it helped." I wrote her back and told her I was.

Lord Jesus, help me to look for you in everyday events. I want to seek you with all my heart. Show me how to find ways to serve you and find purpose in the ordinary daily happens of my life.

Burn it!

"I'm dying; the doctors have given me six months to live. I want to come visit you and say goodbye." Sometimes you only know the value of something when you realize there is a limited amount of it. My last visit with Debbie was like that.

I first met Debbie when our husbands were going to seminary together. I had been married a month and she had only been married two weeks. I shared with her all the knowledge I had gained; she seemed to appreciate my wisdom. Over the years we developed a deep friendship, and now she was coming to say goodbye.

On our last visit together we shared our memories. Debbie had named her first child after me. She had adopted Sarah from Korea and had invited me to be with her at the airport when the baby arrived. I will never forget watching Debbie hold her little girl for the first time. I stood beside her and cried tears of joy.

We not only shared our joy but our grief. Because we lived in different states we didn't see each other often. I had just finished sharing something with Debbie when she said, "Sarah, your grief over this is so fresh, but I know it happened years ago. Why is that?" I told her that while cleaning the attic I had found one of my old journals. I had printed one word across the front of it, "Sorrow." I told her how I had spent the day sitting in that hot attic reading it. She was silent for a while, and then said, "Burn it!"

After Debbie left, I kept thinking about our conversation. I had worked so hard to forgive the things I'd written about in my journal, yet still I wanted a record of my pain. Debbie's life had been reduced to months. She gave me a perspective I didn't have. Life is too short to hold on to sorrow.

I built a fire and began to burn page after page. Soon there was nothing left but ashes. Forgiveness means you cancel a debt. Not keeping a record of the wrong done to you means you let go of the pain.

Thank you, Debbie, for sharing your wisdom with me. I will see you again in Heaven.

Don't be afraid to grieve

I was standing at the sink washing dishes. The feeling of grief was so strong I just wanted to escape. I found myself wanting to disconnect from the painful emotions. In the background I could hear my children's voices, and I realized that if I emotionally disconnected from my grief I would not be able to be emotionally connected with them. I chose instead to walk through the valley of death with tears in my eyes, but not alone.

I didn't want to grieve, because I don't want to be vulnerable. I liked to be in control; in control of situations and in control of my emotions. The problem was, if I chose not to feel the pain of grief, I would put a wall around my heart; and not only would I not be able to feel my grief, I would also isolate myself from everyone's grief, including my children's.

So where do I turn when I feel this pain? Where can I go for comfort? I turn to Jesus. "He was despised and rejected by men; a man of sorrows, and familiar with suffering....Surely he took up our infirmities and carried our sorrows....But he was pierced for our transgressions, he was crushed for our iniquities; the punishment that brought us peace was upon him, and by his wounds we are healed...For he bore the sin of many, and made intercession for the transgressor" (Isa. 53 NIV).

I grieve, but not without hope. Hope is a confident expectation of good. In my seasons of grieving, I experience comfort. I know that, "weeping may endure for the night, but joy comes in the morning" (Psa. 30:5 KJV). Because I have experienced not only the weeping but the joy, I can share this truth with my children.

I believe this is yours

I saw the small silver heart-shaped pin with a picture of a little girl with my jewelry and decided to wear it. I had breakfast that morning with several of my friends. They commented on how much they liked it. I guess that's why it seemed strange when I felt prompted by the Holy Spirit to give it away.

I am a waitress at a local cafe. While waiting on one of my tables, I felt prompted to give my pin to the woman on whom I was waiting. I didn't do it immediately; instead I prayed, "Lord, do you really want me to do this?" The feeling just wouldn't go away, so I took the pin off and quietly put it at her place and said, "I believe this belongs to you."

I went back to her table to refill her glass. She looked at me and said, "I don't understand." "Oh, great," I thought. "Now I've made a fool of myself." I told her about how I had felt led by the Holy Spirit. She looked at me and began to cry. She stood up and hugged me and then said, "I want to show you something." She opened her wallet and pulled out a picture of her mother taken when she was a little girl. It looked identical to the girl's picture in the pin.

She told me how she would talk to her mother every night while fixing dinner. The first time she was fixing dinner after her mother's funeral, she picked up the phone and her husband asked her what she was doing. She told him she was going to call her mother. He gently took her hand and said, "You don't need a phone to talk to your mother anymore."

I told her how I had been reading in the book of Mark and noticed that every time Jesus encountered a child He would wrap His arms around them. It seemed that when I was prompted to give her that pin, it was like Jesus was wrapping His comforting arms around her. She wept as we embraced.

When God invites you to let go of an earthly treasure He is also inviting you to take hold of an **eternal one.**

Seeing what is unseen

"'Oh, my lord, what shall we do?' the servant asked. 'Don't be afraid,' the prophet answered. 'Those who are with us are more than those who are with them.' And Elisha prayed, 'O Lord, open his eyes so he may see.' Then the Lord opened the servant's eyes, and he looked and saw the hills full of horses and chariots of fire all around Elisha." (2 Kings 6:15-17 NIV)

I put my Bible down sighed and prayed, "Lord, I wish I could see your angels." I identified more with Elisha's servant than I did Elisha. At that time I had a teenage daughter and son and two younger children. Sometimes the world just seemed like a very scary place. And, to be honest, I was afraid for my children.

On this particular morning I had several errands to do. I strapped my two youngest children into their car seats and set off. My first stop was to drop some books off at the library. It was a cold, rainy day in January, so I decided not to get the children out of the van. I got out of the van, put the books into the return slot, turned around, and saw my van rolling away with my screaming children inside it!

I ran after it and yanked the door opened. I was praying all the while, "God, help me!" While trying to stop the van I also thought, "This is how people get run over by their own cars." About that time I got smacked in the face by the door. I fell to the pavement and watched as my van rolled uphill, back into a parking lot, and then back again into a parking place, where it was stopped by a small tree.

After that I had a huge black eye and was rather sore because of my fall. I realized that I could spend the day berating myself for being such a bad mother, or I could spend the day praising God for protecting my children. I choose to do the latter.

I didn't see angels or fiery chariots that day, nor did I see who was steering my van. But I think I know.

I want to increase your faith

The year was 1970. We were sitting in a chicken house we had recently cleaned out and Kay Arthur was teaching us about faith. "I want to increase your faith," she said. She then called our attention to the hill behind the chicken house and added, "One day there will be dormitories on that hill."

I decided to pray for something else that would increase my faith. Every time I went to the Bible study at Reach Out Ranch, I could see the silhouette of a woman advertising the Play Late Club. I began asking God to do something about that place. As time went on, I fine-tuned my prayer and started asking God to use that place to bring Himself glory.

Several years passed. I went off to college, got married, and then moved back to the area. My husband and I decided to attend a Bible study at the Ranch. As we were driving there I suddenly let out a gasp. "What's wrong," my husband asked. I told him about my prayers concerning the Play Late Club. What had startled me was this, in the place where the silhouette had been, there was now a cross. When we arrived for our

Bible study, we met in the dormitories that Kay had spoken of by faith ten years earlier.

What is my prayer of faith today? I look at the barren landscape of people's lives and ask that they might become temples of the Holy Spirit. I see the evidence of sin in the lives of people I love, and pray they would know the redeeming power of the cross.

These are prayers that haven't been answered yet, but I am sure of what I hope for and confident about what I don't see. Isn't that what faith is?

I want to do it MY way

I was offended, but I didn't want to be offended. I know what the Bible teaches, "If your brother sins against you, go and show him his fault..." (Matt. 18:15 NIV). Do you know how awkward that is? I decided it would be much better if I simply worked it out on my own.

I had begun to be obsessive about the offense, so I decided to meditate on scriptures about forgiveness. My problem was that my mind kept going back to Matthew 18:15. I did not want to meditate on that one. I tried praying, but I couldn't focus, because I just kept being mad about what had happened. This went on for an embarrassingly long amount of time.

What I prefer to do when people hurt me is to build a clear plastic wall between me and them. I can see them and they can see me, but they can't hurt me again. There is a problem with this solution: there is also no intimacy. To have inmate relationships I have to be vulnerable. If I am not vulnerable I am isolated. Not to mention the fact that I am also choosing to disobey God's word.

I couldn't stand it any longer; sitting in the grocery store parking lot, I called my friend. I explained how my feelings had been hurt. I wish I could say it was easy, but it wasn't. It was simply obedient. My friend was kind. She understood; the wall was removed.

Would it have mattered if her response had been different? No, this wasn't only about how she responded to me; it was really about how I responded to the Word of God.

"For such a time as this"

I am sure there are some who would think I was only wasting my time. Back then I only had one daughter, and her spiritual life was very important to me. I went to the Christian bookstore and spent a long time looking at all the books, talking to clerk and, of course, praying. I had decided to have a Bible Club for my four-year-old daughter and her two friends.

I spent hours preparing for this little class. I would read the material, plan a game to go with the lesson and gather materials for the craft. I had memory verses each week and take-home pictures to go with the verse. I thought I was ready. But I never knew a five-year-old could ask such hard questions!

Justin always amazed me. When he was just a little boy strapped into a car seat, I would try to entertain him and the other children by pointing out things I thought would interest them. "Children, look. We are going under a bridge!" Then from the back seat came a little voice, "I believe that is called a train trestle." Undaunted, I tried again. "Look at the smoke in the sky," only to be countered with Justin saying, "Isn't that air vapor produced by the plane?" So I gave up and asked him a simple question, "Justin, what do you want to be when you grow up?" He looked up at me and said, "A paleontologist." I confess I had to go home and look it up in the dictionary.

It was many years past the time of our backyard Bible Club when I got a call from Justin. He was to be the valedictorian of his senior high school class. He wanted to know where the verse, "Trust in the Lord with all your heart, lean not to your own understanding; in all your ways acknowledge him, and he will direct your path" (KJV) was in the Bible. Proverbs 3:5-6 had always been some of my favorite verses, and I was delighted to share it with him.

The path that Justin believed God was leading him on took him to Japan. While in seminary, he began studying Japanese. He felt drawn to the language, the people and the culture. Two years ago he married Izumi and moved there.

When I woke up yesterday to the news of the terrible earthquake in Japan, all I could think about was, "Justin is there." He was able to contact his mother and let her know that he and his wife were okay.

I am asking everyone to pray with me for all those in Japan. Pray with me also for Justin who is there, "For such a time as this" (Esther 4:14 KJV).

Remember

I couldn't make it stop. It felt like a hot knife stabbing me in my chest. I thought, "I just need to get my mind off of it," so I tried exercising. Bad idea. My husband suggested I lie down and rest, that didn't work. My daughter called and asked if I could take my granddaughter to ballet. "Ah," I thought. "Cuteness will be the cure!"

Driving home from ballet I could hardly breathe. The fire in my chest made it difficult to drive. When I finally arrived at my daughter's home, I could barely get the words out, "Take me to the hospital!" I spent the next day having tests done. My sister said, "Sarah, maybe God has a message for you in this."

When I got home I looked in my One Year Bible to see what the Scripture was for the day I spent in the hospital. This is what I read:

My heart grew hot within me,
 and as I meditated, the fire burned;
 then I spoke with my tongue:
"Show me, O Lord, my life's end
 and the number of my days;
let me know how fleeting is my life.
You have made my days a mere handbreadth;
the span of my years is as nothing before you.
Each man's life is but a breath. Selah
Man is a mere phantom as he goes to and fro:
He bustles about, but only in vain;
he heaps up wealth, not knowing who will get it.
Psalm 39:3-6 (NIV)

I thought about these verses for several days, then I decided I was making way too much out of my experience. That's when the word came to me, "Remember." "Remember what?" I thought. I sat there trying to think of what I should remember, and then I knew.

Several summers ago I had been coming out of the grocery store when I noticed a man lying under his car. I got to the car at the same time his wife did. She screamed and began shaking him violently. I asked if I could hold his head for her.

When I slipped my arms under him, I realized he was dying. I bent down and whispered, "Jesus is near." He took a last shuddering breath and died. I stayed with his wife until her family arrived. I found out he was in this late forties. This was to have been his last stop, and then they were going on vacation.

I sat there remembering what it was like to be holding a man while he took his last breath. I prayed, "Show me, O Lord, my life's end and the number of my days; let me know how fleeting is my life."

There was nothing I could do

I was sick. I was expecting my fourth child and was so nauseated I could not function. My thirteen-year-old had been through the death of her best friend's father. Now she was sure I was dying as well. She responded with fear, anger and withdrawing from me. My eight-year-old went about seemingly not noticing my absences in his world. My three-year-old was constantly jumping up and down on the bed, desperate for Mommy to get up and do something. The bouncing did cause me to get up, but not like she wanted. My husband had not only all of his responsibilities to take care of, but mine as well.

I wanted desperately to participate in my family's life, but every time I tried I got sick and had to retreat to my bed. It wasn't only being a wife and mother I was failing at, I seemed to be failing at life in general. I had even been told by the doctors that there was a strong possibility that the baby I was carrying would die at birth or have major birth defects.

This was a time when I wanted to find comfort in praying and reading God's word, only there was a problem. Praying and reading made me sick too! I lay on my back in bed, hot tears collecting in my ears. I wanted God's comfort so badly, but I felt too sick to reach out for it. That's when it happened.

Suddenly, in my mind, I could see Jesus on the cross. The message to me was so clear. "For God so loved the world that He gave His only begotten Son, that whoever believes in Him shall not perish, but have eternal life" (John 3:16 NIV). This was not a new idea. I had known it and even believed it. However, it was not until I was fully incapable of doing anything that I experienced the meaning of this verse on a deeper level. Finally I understood it was not about what I did for God, it was what He did for me. I also experienced a peace that passes understanding.

There was nothing I could do but receive the love Jesus freely gave me. That day I began to understand grace.

All I wanted was a Sunday afternoon nap!

I always looked forward to Sunday afternoons. That's when I would take a glorious nap. That's why I didn't respond favorably when my husband said, "Don't you think it would be nice to ask that young couple to start coming home with us after church to spend the afternoon?" I liked the couple, and they had an adorable little baby; but we were talking about giving up my nap! What on earth was wrong with my husband anyway!

I talked to God about it, "Lord, you know you said Sunday was to be a day of rest. I really want to rest. But even more, I want to obey you. So if you want us to have company, I surrender my will to you." We had company. From the first time they came for the day it was obvious that this was God's will.

I became Aunt Sadie to that cute little baby. She took her first steps in my living room. I was in the room when my friend's son was born, and her last child was named after me. I think my friendship has been well worth the sacrifice of a Sunday afternoon nap.

I heard a story once about a little girl who had a necklace made of plastic beads. She loved her necklace and wore it always. She wore it so much that the paint came off the beads and the plastic showed through.

Rather unattractive, but the little girl didn't care; she just wanted her beads.

This little girl was very loved by her father. He noticed how much she liked her beads and decided to do something special for her. He bought her a beautiful strand of genuine pearls. He held the pearls in a velvet bag behind his back. With his other hand he reached out to his daughter and asked her to give him the plastic beads she was wearing.

She clutched at her beads. She didn't want to take them off. He stood there looking at her with love in his eyes. Finally, with tears falling down her face, she removed the plastic. Her father placed in her hands the velvet bag containing the pearls.

What is at the heart of my stories? It is this. Do I really believe that God loves me, and can I trust Him?

Where your treasure is...

I loved my ring. Not only was this ring beautiful, but it had been a gift to me from my father after my baby died. That is why I didn't want to give it away.

She stood before me ready to leave. I was so angry. We had opened our home, shared everything we had, and now she was leaving. So many hours of listening and sharing the message of God's love; had she heard anything? It was then I felt the urge of the Spirit to give her my ring, but I resisted. Later I talked to my husband about it, and he said wait and pray.

The next time I saw her I again felt God asking me to give her my ring. There was a battle going on inside my head. It went like this, "I don't want to. This ring is special to me. It represents people I love!" But what I wanted even more than my ring was to be obedient to God. I gave her my ring.

I wish I could say I felt a surge of joy when I gave my ring away, but the Bible says, "Thou shalt not lie." I missed my ring. I wanted to forget about her, but she had my ring. One day while longing for my ring I felt God's rebuke, "Sarah, you love your ring, but what about my daughter?

Let the ring you love remind you to pray for the person I love and gave my life for." That day my heart began to change. I started to pray for her. I began to think of her in a different way.

Years later I was going through a discouraging time. I was overwhelmed with the feeling that I had lived my life in vain. Suddenly the phone rang. I picked it up and the voice on the other line said, "Sarah, I am calling to tell you that you have not lived your life in vain." I was startled and almost laughed out loud. I hadn't heard from her in so many years. She told me how God had been working in her life, how she read her Bible every day, and how she had begun opening her home to people in need, like Steve and I had opened our home to her so many years before.

Tangible things can reveal intangible truths. Where your treasure is, there your heart will be also.

How dare you treat my daughter like that!

She got on my nerves, and apparently I wasn't the only one who felt that way. I was in a carpool with four other women, and she was one of them. Of course, I was too nice to ever say anything; my feelings were spoken with facial expressions and the rolling of eyes. It is amazing how much bonding can be experienced by excluding just one person.

One night I had a dream; a very vivid dream. In my dream, I went beyond facial communication to the others in the car, and spoke directly to the person irritating me—not in a kind way or a helpful way, but with mean, sarcastic words. She acted in a haughty way, as if my words had no effect on her. I looked at the others and can only express my feeling as satisfied.

My dream then took an unexpected turn, as dreams are prone to do. When she got out of the car I followed her. She began crying as soon as she was in the stairwell going up to her apartment. I was ready to stop the dream but couldn't! "Oh, no,' I thought, 'I don't want to be there when she tells her husband the mean things I said." But it was no use. I couldn't seem to wake myself up; and believe me, I was trying.

She opened the door to her apartment. She ran to where her husband was sitting in a chair with his back to us. She knelt before him and put her head on his lap and cried. I felt sick. Why couldn't I just wake up? I didn't want to see all this pain I had caused, and I didn't want to be confronted by her husband.

Then something happened that causes me to shiver to this day. The man stood up and looked me directly in the eyes. It wasn't her husband. It was Jesus! He looked at me and said, "How dare you treat my child this way!" I woke up.

After my dream, that girl became my friend. My dream had totally changed my view of who she was.

Kneeling in the midst of broken glass

I had not one but two parties back to back. As I washed my crystal, I thought about how much I was enjoying having it. Some of my goblets were family heirlooms. They had been wedding gifts from my husband's grandmother. I pulled a stepping stool close to my china cabinet and was putting a goblet on the top glass shelf when it happened.

I stood there frozen, not able to stop the scene in front of me from happening. As I watched, the top shelf crashed into the second shelf, which in turn crashed into the bottom shelf. I felt like I was watching a horror movie. My beautiful crystal and china was sliding off the shelves and exploding on the hardwood floor. All I could do was to scream, "NO!"

Then there was silence.

I climbed down from the stool and looked around at the dust and shards of broken glass that had moments before been family heirlooms. I got the broom and swept a spot for me to kneel. I thought to myself, "If Job worshiped God when he lost everything, surely I can worship God in the midst of broken glass."

I believe that tangible things can be used to teach us intangible truth, so while I knelt there, I prayed and asked God to speak to me. This is what I heard, "Remember your Creator in the days of your youth, before the days of trouble come and the years approach when you will say, 'I find no pleasure in them'.... Remember him—before the silver cord is severed, or the golden bowl is broken; before the pitcher is shattered at the spring, or the wheel broken at the well, and the dust returns to the ground it came from, and the spirit returns to God who gave it" (Eccl. 12:1, 6-7 NIV).

As if to emphasis this message, the phone rang. It was my sister. "Sarah, we think Dad has had a stroke." I went to see my father at the hospital. His nine children were crowded around him. My father recovered, but I began to understand the meaning of Ecclesiastes that day.

Life is a gift. It is beautiful, precious and fragile. One day dust will return to dust and the spirit will return to the God who gave it.

Just For Me

Hey, this is Faith, Sarah's oldest daughter. Today is my Mommy's birthday, but we're celebrating without her. Mommy is currently on a trip to Romania. For her birthday this year, she is sharing the greatest gift that she's ever been given.

My mom has always been a gifted speaker. She tells this great story about an early experience with public speaking. She was so overcome with stage fright that she burst into tears. But then she worked that into her presentation. She received a perfect score from both her instructor and her peers. I remember as a child that my mother taught a Bible class at Chattanooga Bible Institute. I know she loved it and that it always seemed to be a full class to me. She was starting to be invited to seminars and speaking engagements all over the country. It was kind of impressive, even to a little kid.

I also remember that one day she wasn't teaching at CBI any more. She stopped leaving for weekends. Instead, she was homeschooling, grinding her own wheat to make homemade bread and buying farm cheese in bulk (blech!).

You see, God had closed the screen door to her speaking career and turned her face back toward the inside of her home. This is how important I am to God: He took an amazing, beautiful, powerful speaker and asked her to dedicate 30 years of her life Just.To.Me. If Mommy hadn't paused her career and put us first, there is absolutely no telling how many lives she might have touched. But God gave four (often ungrateful, sniveling, mealy-mouthed, disrespectful, and totally undeserving) children to her and asked her to make us her priority. AND.SHE.DID!

Nearly a year ago, Mom's life changed. Her youngest child was preparing to leave the nest and Mommy was invited to speak—and not in the next county over, either. My mommy went to the Czech Republic. That screen door that God closed when He turned her back towards her home is now being held so wide open that it's like a vacuum sucking her out into the springtime of her career.

I marvel that God deemed me important enough to give me such an awesome Mommy. But then, what can you expect from the kind of God that sacrifices His own son, JUST FOR ME.

At the foot of the mountain a father cried

"Don't be anxious; bring your concerns to God." Yes, yes, I agree completely there is only one problem, I am a mother. I have a confession to make. Sometimes I struggle with being anxious. This often happens about two o'clock in the morning. I love my children and I want to protect them and keep all harmful things away from them, but I can't. In the night as I pray I hear God's voice urging me to place my child in His hands.

The time and place of this story is so important. It happened at the foot of the mountain. The father brought his son to Jesus. No one had been able to help this father. Even as he was talking to Jesus, he saw his son fall to the ground and roll around, foaming at the mouth. I can see the boy in my mind, covered with mud made from his own spit mixed with the dirt he was rolling in.

This was not a casual request for help. This was the cry of a father who was watching his child, his flesh and blood, be destroyed before his very eyes. I know this feeling! At two o'clock in the morning this father's story becomes my story as well. I pray, "Jesus, if you could help, please help my child." I hear the same rebuke the father in the Bible heard. "If I can? Everything is possible for him who believes."

Again my prayer echoes the prayer that father prayed long ago, "I do believe, help me overcome my unbelief" (Mark 9:24 NIV).

However, even though our stories are similar, they are not the same; because I know what happened on that mountain. It was the Mountain of Transfiguration. Jesus' true identity was revealed, and His Father said, "This is my Son whom I love. Listen to Him." The love of every other parent is only a dim reflection of the love the Father has for Jesus. Yet, "God so loved the world that He gave His only begotten son that whoever believes in Him should not perish but have everlasting life" (John 3:16 KJV). God gave His son to be the Savior, the Redeemer, to set both us and our children free.

I can give my child to God because He gave His son to me.

"If just a cup of water I place within your hand..."

"If just a cup of water I place within your hand, then just a cup of water is all that I demand." These words to a song came to me my first morning home from Romania.

Paula had told me as we were preparing to go that she had only been able to think of two songs: "Amazing Grace" and "Jesus Loves Me." This was frustrating for her, because she is an accomplished singer with a library of CDs. Paula was also the team leader for our trip, and I believe God had given her the theme for all that took place on our Romanian trip. All that was said on this trip and all that was done centered on these two truths, God's amazing grace and the love of Jesus.

Again and again we saw these truths played out. When we went to Casa Joseph and met the girls who lived at the orphanage, they listened spellbound as Paula sang these two songs to them. And then they requested they be sung every time we saw them. I cannot count how many times Paula sang about God's grace and Jesus' love at churches at the school and at the nightly Bible study.

On our last day in Romania we were all tired. Paula and I both were fighting a cold. Kara, our teammate, had given her testimony numerous times. We were going to two churches. On the way, I prayed and asked God what I should say. It's not that I hadn't prepared for this trip, but by this time I had already spoken about twenty times. In answer to my prayer I felt the Lord encouraging me to rest in His love and trust in His grace.

Each time I stood to speak, I was given a message for that particular church. On our way home I spoke to my teammates about my experience. They had felt the same way. We had all experienced both God's grace and His love.

"If just a cup of water I place within your hand, then just a cup of water is all that I demand." What a privilege to experience being both called and equipped to serve the Lord

Be still and know

One of my favorite things to do on Sunday afternoon is to find a quiet spot out in the woods. If it's cold I take a blanket and a chair, and then I just sit there. My goal is simple. I want to look until I can see and listen until I can hear. Although this may sound like an easy exercise, it isn't, because it takes time for the buzz of the world to leave my mind and heart so that I can really see what I'm looking at and understand what I'm hearing.

I began this practice in response to the verse, "Be still, and know that I am God" (Psa. 46:10 NIV). When I looked up the Hebrew for "be still," I found the words "relaxes" and "sink." I also got the picture in my mind of a bow where the string is slack. I find this to be a very unnatural state for me, because I often feel like I need to be accomplishing something. Even in my times with God, wouldn't it be better if I were praying, reading my Bible, or doing something godly? Am I allowed to really just sink into His presence and relax?

Then comes the "knowing." When I looked up the meaning for this word, I found it meant "to acknowledge, to be acquainted with." It seemed to carry with it the idea of spending time together. So I sit in the woods listening and looking for God, focused on His gift of creation. When I am finally able to have my bow unstrung, and sink down into His presence, surrendering my weakness to His strength, I am filled with a sense of peace.

This morning, however, my thoughts have taken me in a different direction. What if I applied this not only to my vertical relationship, but also my horizontal relationships? What would it be like if today, when I am with my husband, I really not only listened to his words but tried to understand their meaning? What would happen if I went beyond looking at him and began to really see him? Isn't that what Jesus did?

Today, Lord, please grant me the grace to be still and know that You are God. Please also grant me the grace to be more like Jesus and slow down and listen and seek to understand.

The Lifter of My Head

I didn't know anyone could take up so little space. I noticed her my first night in Romania. I was there to teach a nightly Bible study. She came with her head bent down. Not joining any conversation, she perched on the very edge of the couch.

I have noticed that sometimes songs have a rhythmic beat that reminds me of the beating of a heart. Each Bible study I did had an underling beat that went like this, "Jesus loves you, Jesus loves you, Jesus loves you."

Slowly she began to lift her head. I remember the first time she dared make eye contact. On the third day she wrote her name and gave it to my interpreter. On the fourth day I greeted her by name and saw her smile. We took a picture the last night of the Bible study. I will always be able to pick her out in that picture. She's the one who has her arm around my shoulder.

I never heard her story, but by God's grace I was allowed to write a sentence of it. It went like this, "You are loved; you are loved; you are loved!" I was given the privilege of seeing the love of Jesus lift her head.

"They think I'm the team leader!"

"They think I'm the team leader!"

"That's because you are," I said with a smile. Perhaps she thought I would be the leader because I was almost fifteen years older than she was. But leadership ability does not come with years. Paula proved to be an excellent leader on our Romanian trip.

Several years ago, I was struggling with the obvious gaps in my personality. I lamented the fact that I was not a leader, nor was I an administrator. Trying harder and reading books about the subject didn't seem to help either.

I prayed and asked God for His perspective for my obvious lack, since He was the one who made me the way I am. As I prayed, I began to see myself as a piece of a puzzle. I realized that I only considered the convex parts as valuable. I saw them as my spiritual gifts.

In prayer I felt God showing me that the concave part of the puzzle was as much a gift as the convex. He created me to be part of His body. I realized that, instead of being given all the spiritual gifts within myself, He gave me other people to make me complete. He gave me the gift of relationships.

God gave Paula the gift of leadership, but He gave me the gift of encouragement so I could cheer her on in carrying out the responsibilities of her new role.

You will steer the car in the direction you are looking

"Sarah! Keep your eyes on the road." I remember hearing this a lot when I was learning to drive. Up until they put me in the driver's seat, I had been a passenger and had the liberty to gaze at the scenery. Now I was told that I would steer the car in the direction I was looking.

I have found this to be true in my life in general. When I find myself feeling depressed or angry, I stop and consider what I'm thinking about. I find Philippians 4:8 very helpful, "Finally, brothers [and sisters],

40

whatever is true, whatever is noble, whatever is right, whatever is pure, whatever is lovely, whatever is admirable—if anything is excellent or praiseworthy—think about such things" (NIV). What happens when I choose to think about these things? I find the verse that follows to be true, "And the God of peace will be with you."

Once when I was a little girl and I was full of gloom, an older Christian shared this verse with me: "offer to God a sacrifice of praise" (Heb. 13:15 NIV). I just want to say that if you are feeling depressed, it's really hard to praise God. I guess that is why it would be considered a sacrifice. However, I have found again and again that, just as you steer the car in the direction you are looking, your emotions follow the direction of your thoughts.

Since I have been given a choice today of what to think about, I have decided to rejoice in the Lord!

Telling myself the truth

"Be strong and courageous. Do not be afraid or terrified because of them, for the Lord your God goes with you; he will never leave you nor forsake you" (Deut. 31:6 NIV).

"The Lord himself goes before you and will be with you; he will never leave you nor forsake you. Do not be afraid; do not be discouraged" (Deut. 31:8 NIV).

"Keep your lives free from the love of money and be content with what you have, because God has said, 'Never will I leave you; never will I forsake you.' So we say with confidence, 'The Lord is my helper; I will not be afraid. What can man do to me?'" (Heb. 13:5-6 NIV).

My children are accustomed to seeing 3x5 cards all around the house. I use them to tell myself the truth. Whenever I'm reading the Bible and a verse stands out to me, I copy it onto a 3x5 card. I find my "truth markers" everywhere. Of course I can't keep it to myself, and there are many 3x5's in my children's possessions.

Today the truth I'm carrying with me is that God has gone before me; that He is with me; and that He will never forsake me.

Faithful in prayer

The verse was stamped onto a paper bag. The bag contained a gift to my grandson. However, for me, the gift was the words stamped onto the bag. "Be joyful in hope, patient in affliction, faithful in prayer" (Rom. 12:12 NIV).

I meditated on this verse for days, captivated by the truth. I even woke at 2 A.M. convicted by my lack of joy, which was symptomatic of my lack of hope; aware that, instead of being patient in affliction, I just wanted to be relieved of affliction. But an even deeper awareness that I was not faithful in prayer. No, instead, more often I shrugged my shoulders in defeat and with grim acceptance said, "That's just the way it is."

Why do I stop praying? It's because I lose my focus. I become overwhelmed by the problems in my life. When I fail to rejoice in hope and persevere in suffering, then it is easy to become unfaithful about praying.

When I present my requests to God, I am acknowledging through faith that He loves me; that He is concerned about the struggles I have in this life. When I make my petitions with thanksgiving, I am rejoicing in hope. I am confident that God is at work on my behalf. He is my Redeemer, Savior, High Priest and friend. By His grace He has allowed me to be His child. I have a place in His Kingdom story.

When I am joyful in hope, I can persevere in affliction, because by faith I know I can call out to God in prayer and He is listening.

When times are good be happy

I had just finished teaching "An invitation to a storm," a study on Mark 4:35-41, when she came up to talk to me. She told me about the happy place she was in life. She and her husband were doing well; she had just given birth to her second child; and her family was experiencing a deep sense of peace and harmony. The verse that came to me was "When times are good, be happy; but when times are bad, consider: God has made the one as well as the other" (Eccl. 7:14 NIV).

I understood why she came up to me. I know the feeling I have often had when things seemed to be going well. In my mind the verse could be written, "When things are good you better enjoy it, because you know it's not going to last." This sense of foreboding definitely detracts from my ability to experience joy.

Circumstances change, but God remains the same. When I read the Bible I am keenly aware of an invitation to know who God is. When I read about how God took His children into the wilderness before taking them into the Promise Land, I see God wanting to teach them to trust Him. I remember the first time I saw that God wanted them to "enter into His rest," but they would not. I began to ask Him to let me enter into His rest. I didn't realize that I was asking for a trip into the wilderness.

How does the wilderness become a place to learn to trust God and enter into His rest? I have found the answer in Deuteronomy 32:10-11: "In the desert land he found him, in a barren and howling waste. He shielded him and cared for him; he guarded him as the apple of his eye, like an eagle that stirs up its nest and hovers over its young, that spreads its wings to catch them and carries them on its pinions" (NIV). I see this in God's leading the children of Israel through the wilderness. And I find it true in my own "wilderness."

Because of our relationship with a loving God, we can rest secure in good times and in bad; because He remains the same and He loves us. "Let the beloved of the Lord rest secure in him, for he shields him all day long, and the one the Lord loves rests between his shoulders" (Deut. 33:12 NIV).

From Heavens perspective

I spent yesterday with a friend whose daughter is critically ill. My friend is also my prayer partner. She and I have spent hours before God's throne together. But we have also spent hours together in hospital waiting rooms, grieving the suffering of her child. There is suffering in this world, and simplistic answers bring more insult than comfort. However, I have found deep comfort in God's Word.

When I began to study prophecy, I felt like the curtains of Heaven were pulled back, and I was able to see life and history from an eternal perspective. It was painful to do an in-depth study of Jeremiah and Lamentations. I studied these books inductively using the Precept Bible studies. This meant that for an hour every morning I was studying the "Weeping Prophet." I also have the Bible on CD, so while in my car I listened to the chapters again and again. Sometimes I found myself weeping with Jeremiah as I surveyed through Scripture the devastation brought by sin. I could see, like Jeremiah, how God had told in Deuteronomy the cause and effect of disobedience. Jeremiah not only prophesied the destruction of Jerusalem, he experienced the pain and suffering personally.

How, you might ask, could there be any comfort in the study of Jeremiah's writings? I saw the heart of the Heavenly Father. The discipline for sin was not the end of the story. In the 29th chapter of Jeremiah, I find a letter to the exiles who had been carried into Babylon. "This is what the Lord says: 'When seventy years are completed for Babylon, I will come to you and fulfill my gracious promise to bring you back to this place. For I know the plans I have for you,' declares the Lord, 'plans to prosper you and not to harm you, plans to give you hope and a future. Then you will call upon me and come and pray to me, and I will listen to you. You will seek me and find me when you seek me with all your heart. I will be found by you,' declares the Lord..." (Jer. 28:10-14 NIV).

For me this message in Jeremiah not only shows the heart of the Heavenly Father grieving over the consequence of His children's sin, but it also shows His plan of redemption. Isn't that the story of the whole Bible? There is love; there is disobedience; there are consequences; there is the sacrificial love of God; and there is redemption. Also, in the last chapters of the Bible I read again and again that God will wipe away the tears from our eyes. His plan from the beginning of time was not to harm us but to give us hope and a future, intimate fellowship with our Heavenly Father.

I sit in the waiting room with my friend. Our hearts are heavy with grief, but not devoid of hope.

It would take a miracle for me to forgive

I didn't know I could be so angry. I didn't know that forgiveness was impossible. Why did Jesus teach us to pray, "Forgive us our debts as we forgive our debtors?" I knew the parable Jesus told about the servant whose debt was cancelled but refused to have mercy on a fellow servant and was turned over to the tormentor. "This is how my heavenly Father will treat each of you unless you forgive your brother from your heart" (Matt. 18:35 NIV). I felt like I was being tormented.

Some things are harder to learn than others. Some lessons are learned as we memorize the facts and apply them. Other lessons are learned on our knees through a veil of tears. For me, learning how to forgive was done on my knees. This is a lesson I am still learning.

"'In your anger do not sin': Do not let the sun go down while you are still angry, and do not give the devil a foothold" (Eph. 4:26-27 NIV). "I will never be able to sleep again!" I thought. I didn't want to be angry; I wanted to forgive, but my emotions were holding me hostage. My prayer went something like this, "I don't know what you want me to do! I don't know how to obey you! God, please help me!"

God hears our prayers and answers us in our confusion. First, I began to understand that, in order to cancel a debt, I had to acknowledge that there was a debt. It was okay for me to fully admit that I had been wronged. Next, I had to forgive as God had forgiven me. That's what I found impossible to do.

Philippians 2:12 tells us to "work out [our] salvation with fear and trembling." This is exactly where I found myself in my journey to forgiveness. I didn't want to be the unmerciful servant in Jesus' parable; I didn't want to give the devil a foothold; and I didn't know how to honestly forgive. I knew it would take a miracle, and it did. Verse 13 says, "for it is God who works in you to will and to act according to his good purpose."

There was only one solution. I had to ask God's help. "This is the confidence we have in approaching God: that if we ask anything according to his will, he hears us. And if we know that he hears us— whatever we ask—we know that we have what we have asked of him" (1 John 5:14-15 NIV). He came to my rescue; He answered my prayer.

There are things in this life that it takes a miracle to forgive. But that miracle is available upon request.

The scum is rising to the surface

When I moved to the farm, I began making jam. This was a new experience for me. I added sugar to the fruit, then put it in a pan on the stove and turned up the heat. I was amazed at the amount of scum that would rise to the surface. By the time I scraped all the scum off, I wondered if anything would be left in the saucepan. This is how I felt the first time I took in someone who was homeless.

I always thought I was a nice person. Even when I was a little girl my nickname was "Saint Sarah." I'm not sure if that was meant as a good thing or a bad thing, but I took it as a good thing. I wanted to be good; I wanted to be nice. That's why it was so hard when I began to see a different side of me emerging.

Anger, selfishness, and in general a lack of love began to rise to the surface. I started to look around at other people who were trying to serve God in a self sacrificing manner. How did they do it? How did they keep these bad feelings away? What was their methodology? What I found out was that my problem wasn't feeling, it was being.

God had used the friction of opening my home to expose the sin that was already there. I thought my problem was being caused by having an extra person in my house, but in reality it only exposed the sin that was already in my heart.

I didn't realize it at the time, but I had seen myself as a savior, someone who would come in and make things right. I would redeem a bad situation. Instead, bubbling up to the top was all this sin in my own life. And I, like the saucepan on the stove, could not remove the scum on my own.

I began to pray, "Lord, the scum is rising to the surface; please scrape it off." I needed a Savior and a Redeemer. I wish I could say that it was a once in a lifetime experience, but that would be a lie. Because I have a Savior and a Redeemer, I have this assurance that when the stresses of life expose the sin inside me, He is using it as an opportunity to purity my life.

Now I often pray, "Lord, the scum is rising to the surface; please scrap it off!" And He does.

The Sun always rises

I was appalled at their lack of faith! God had opened the Red Sea for them, drowned their enemies, and three days later they were grumbling?! I was appalled when I first read this as a child. As a middle aged woman, I completely identify with their grumbling. I'm a pro at grumbling. It's not something I'm proud of, it's just something I struggle with.

I had an amazing trip to Romania. I met wonderful people; I was a part of a fantastic team; I got to be a part of something God was doing. Came home and was slammed with jet lag! Lost my balance for about two weeks. I made an emotional U-turn. Do I identify with the children of Israel? Oh yeah!

I have found something in nature that I identify with—day and night. I have observed in my lifetime that there is a pattern that repeats itself over and over and over: day is always followed by night; the darkness of night always has to surrender to the power of the sun.

In my emotional life I have found that "weeping may remain for a night, but joy comes in the morning" (Psa. 30:5 NIV). I have also discovered that the night time of my emotions is a good time for me to examine my heart. "In your anger do not sin; when you are on your beds, search your hearts and be silent" (Psa. 4:4 NIV). Night time becomes a time of reflection for me. "On my bed I remember you; I think of you through the watches of the night" (Psa. 63:6 NIV). Sometimes I have to use my memory, because when I'm depressed I don't feel God's presence—even though He's still there.

This is one thing I am sure of: the sun always rises. One day "the sun of righteous will rise with healing in its wings" (Mal. 4:2 NIV). On that day, all my emotional nights will be over.

Understanding

"There he was transfigured before them. His clothes became dazzling white, whiter than anyone in the world could bleach them" (Mark 9:2-3 NIV). The next day they came down from the mountain and were confronted with chaos: a grieving father, a boy who falls to the ground, foaming at the mouth.

This week I am thinking about why Jesus came. Jesus, "Who, being in very nature God, did not consider equality with God something to be grasped, but made himself nothing, taking the very nature of a servant,… and became obedient to death—even death on a cross!" (Phil. 2:6-8 NIV). I find the reason for Jesus' coming at the foot of the mountain.

I have always identified with the father who was powerless to help his son. This father had faith, but in the midst of his pain he also had doubt. He came to Jesus and humbly prayed, "Lord, I believe, help my unbelief." Jesus met him where he was. He heard his cry, understood his great need and answered his prayer.

Yesterday in church I was remembering this scene. But this time it wasn't the father I identified with, it was the son. I was eighteen again, sitting huddled in the corner of a solitary confinement cell in a state mental hospital. Confused, I sang softly, "But I know whom I have believed and I'm persuaded that He is able to keep what I have committed unto Him against that day" (2 Tim. 1:12 KJV). Just like the boy at the foot of the Mount of Transfiguration, I couldn't save myself.

This week as I celebrate Easter, I am reminded that when Jesus humbled Himself and came down from glory, it was for me. Just as He entered into pain of the father and son at foot of the mountain, He also entered into to my pain and confusion and brought salvation.

Let the day begin!

"And there was evening, and there was morning—the first day" (Gen. 1:5 NIV). Don't you think that should read, "And there was morning and evening—the first day"? This idea of the day beginning in the evening seems odd to me. How can the day begin just as I'm getting ready to go to sleep? The day should begin when I wake up. But maybe there is a message in this order; maybe the message is that I am not the center of the universe.

I have a Franklin Planner. I really like it, but I have noticed that my stress level goes up if what I plan to happen doesn't happen. When I start planning out months, weeks and days in advance, I feel like saying, "It is written; therefore, it must be!" This must be the way the rooster feels when it thinks the sun rises because it crowed. I think a lot of stress is produced when I feel responsible for things I can't control.

Something I have found to help this stress I put on myself is to write across the front of the page, "Man makes his plans, but the Lord controls what happens" (Prov. 16:9 NIV).

Well, it's getting late. I think I'll go to bed. Let the day begin!

Josh met Jesus

I'll never forget the morning they got dropped off at Sunday school. Their mom went into the meeting; they ran out the door, then out of the building. I chased them around the church and caught them in the parking lot.

In order to teach my class that morning, I held Josh and my friend held Joey. It wasn't easy to hold them, either. Their arms were crossed in front of them, their feet restrained, and the whole time I taught I dodged Josh's head as he attempted to head butt me. In the back of my mind I wondered, "Is this legal?" But I knew if we let these boys go, they'd run out into the street.

Their mother brought them for several weeks. It took a while for them to stop trying to kick and bite me, but I began to see a change. One day Josh drew a picture. It was of him and Jesus. I will never forget the smile on his face when he showed it to me. "Jesus loves me!" he said as he looked up at me.

That week I decided to buy Josh a children's Bible. I bought the Bible, but Josh didn't come back to church. I wanted to give it to someone else after several months went by, but the thought kept coming back, "This is Josh's Bible."

His mother showed up at my door one day. Josh was at the hospital having tests done, and she wondered if I'd go visit him. When I got there, he was hiding under his bed. I got down on the floor with him and we talked a while. He was afraid, but he finally got on the bed instead of under the bed. He told me he had moved close to the church, and I told him I'd come visit him at his house.

I kept my promise and went to visit Josh. When I handed Josh the Bible I'd bought for him, he clutched it to his chest and ran up the stairs screaming, "Joey, Joey now we can find out who Jesus really is!" He ran back down the stairs, grabbed my hand, and took me to his room. He had very few toys, but he took the well-loved stuffed animal off his bed and said, "Here, take this to your little girl, and thank you for the Bible."

After that Josh came to church every Sunday. No one else in his family came, just Josh. He told me he tried to get them to wake up, but since they wouldn't, he'd learned to set the alarm clock and come himself. I saw the peace on his face when we talked about Jesus. I understood. I remembered when I was seven and began to hear that Jesus loved me.

One day Josh didn't show up for church. I walked to his house. No one was there. They had moved again. But I knew Josh had met Jesus, and Jesus would never leave him.

Though he stumble, he will not fall

"If the Lord delights in a man's way, he makes his steps firm; though he stumble, he will not fall, for the Lord upholds him with his hand" (Psa. 37:23-24 NIV). "Show us your unfailing love, O Lord, and grant us your salvation" (Psa. 85:7 NIV). "Teach me your way, O Lord, and I will walk in your truth; give me an undivided heart, that I may fear your name" (Psa. 86:11 NIV). These verses all have something in common; they show the psalmist's dependence on God.

"Even though they all fall away, I will not." I like Peter! I don't think I would have said it out loud, but I probably would have thought it. Peter was a man of passion. He loved Jesus, he would never "fall away," he would definitely never deny Jesus...but he did.

When Jesus, in the midst of His suffering, looked at Peter and Peter realized what he'd done, he went out and wept bitterly. When Judas was confronted with the consequences of his actions, he went out and hung himself. Both of these were self-righteous men, but there was a difference. Peter humbled himself and accepted Jesus' forgiveness and salvation; Judas didn't.

I was thinking that when sin is exposed in my life I feel embarrassed, but that's not the same thing as humility. Embarrassment can also be the evidence of my own self-righteousness and pride. Humility is seen in how I deal with my sin. Do I look to myself for the cure or to God?

In the Psalms, I see the man who stumbles, but is not hurled headlong, because God is holding his hand—it doesn't say because he is holding God's hand. The psalmist refers to God's unfailing love for him, not his unfailing love for God. I also appreciate the prayer, "Teach me your way, O Lord, and I will walk in your truth; give me an undivided heart, that I may fear your name" (Psa. 86:11 NIV). I, like the psalmist, need God to teach me His ways so I can walk in His truth. If He doesn't give me an undivided heart, my heart will probably be divided.

Peter tells us in his epistle "God is opposes the proud but gives grace to the humble. Humble yourselves, therefore, under God's mighty hand, that he may lift you up in due time." I always wondered how you were supposed to humble yourself, but Peter explains it in the next verse, "casting all your anxieties on him because he cares for you" (1 Pet. 5:5-7 NIV).

What a comfort to know that Jesus invites me to let go of my self-righteousness, and that, though I stumble, I will not be hurled headlong because He holds my hand. I have a Savior.

Taking refuge under the shelter of your wings!

Sometimes when I am really tired and preparing to sleep, I feel vulnerable. All the things I've done wrong, the stupid, thoughtless things I've said, parade themselves in my mind. Everything I chose not to worry about during the day comes out of hiding to haunt me in the night. Recently a friend asked me how I meditated on Scripture. One of my favorite times to meditate is during the twilight of my consciousness when I am so vulnerable to negative thoughts.

Earlier this week, I was drifting off to sleep when my mind began to wander into the negative zone. I decided to meditate on God's invitation to take shelter under His wing. I wrapped myself in the blanket and thought, "If I was under God's wing, I would also be next to His heart." All through the night, when I woke with haunting thoughts, I would go back to the picture of being near to the heart of God.

"Hear my cry, O God; listen to my prayer. From the end of the earth I call to you, I call as my heart grows faint; lead me to the rock that is higher than I. For you have been my refuge, a strong tower against the foe. I long to dwell in your tent forever and take refuge in the shelter of your wings. Selah" (Psa. 61:1-4 NIV).

The next morning as I was waking up, I saw a scripture reference in my dream. I saw it typed at the bottom of a bookmark. When I got up, I looked for it in the Bible. It was Zephaniah 3:16-17: "Fear not, O Zion; let not your hands grow weak. The Lord your God is in your midst, a mighty one who will save; he will rejoice over you with gladness; he will quiet you by his love; he will exult over you with loud singing" (ESV).

I sought refuge and peace near to the heart of God, beneath His wing, and woke to the sound of His singing.

Ah, Sovereign Lord!

I come from a long line of women who know how to sigh. I remember the long sighs of my grandmother and my mother. The older I get, the more I understand their purpose. Sometimes the pressures of life feel unbearable. That's when I take a deep breath and exhale slowly.

I think the prophet Jeremiah knew how to sigh. Several times I read a prayer in the book of Jeremiah that begins with a sigh. I can just imagine the prophet taking a deep breath and exhaling slowly, saying, "Ahhhhh." But the sigh becomes a prayer when you add the words, "Sovereign Lord."

God had given Jeremiah a hard job. The message he had to deliver was one of inescapable judgment. His ministry was hard; his message wasn't one anyone wanted to hear; but he didn't murmur and complain. He recognized his humanity, but he also recognized his relationship to God.

The title Sovereign shows he knew God was in control. God is above all authority and powers. Jeremiah didn't leave it there. He also called him Lord. When I read in Numbers, I see the children of Israel's rebellion against God. They seem to constantly want to be the lord of their own life. Jeremiah surrendered the lordship to God.

I like this prayer, "Ah, Sovereign Lord!" I often don't understand what God is doing in my life, and it helps me to take a deep breath and exhale slowly. It helps me even more to remind myself that God is Sovereign and that He is my Lord.

Paradigm Shift

I am one of nine children. I have two older brothers and six younger siblings. What that means is that I had a lot of practice in sharing. We were all born within ten years, and, like all children, we wanted attention. My grandmother worked at making us feel special. She had one 8X10 picture frame on her bureau, and she would rotate our pictures in that frame.

The year I turned eleven, I spent the winter with my grandmother. It was a little bit like Heaven getting to be the only child in her house. I had shared her with my siblings all my life, but that year my cousins were coming from Brazil. Sharing my grandmother with my siblings was one thing; sharing her with a whole other family was a lot harder.

Grandmother had never gotten to meet those grandchildren, and as the time got closer she became more and more excited. It was all she could think about; it was all she could talk about; it was the only thing she could focus on. I became very jealous.

I began to pray and ask Jesus to help me with my jealousy. The way He answered my prayer not only had a powerful impact on my childhood, it affected my whole life as well. While struggling with my jealousy, I felt miserable and tormented. After I prayed, I realized I had a choice to love or hate. I asked Jesus to help me love.

My prayer was that I would see my cousins with my grandmother's eyes. I wanted them to be as special to me as they were to her. When God answered this prayer, He gave me a wonderful gift. First, He showed me that He really did answer prayer—that He could change my heart. Then He allowed me to have a wonderful relationship with my cousins.

I looked up a definition of Paradigm Shift and it said "a change from one way of thinking to another. It's a revolution, a transformation, a sort of metamorphism. It just does not happen but rather is driven by agents of change."[2] This seemed to be similar to what I had experienced through prayer.

I don't get to see them very often, but I treasure them very much. This was the first Paradigm Shift of many I have experienced through prayer.

Sandpaper on my soul

"And just look at this view! One thing you can be sure of, you will always have this view." I loved the view out of my picture window. I choose that spot to have my quiet time in the morning. I would wake at dawn wrap myself in a blanket and begin reading my Bible and talking to God.

BANG! BANG! BANG! Something terrible was happening. My neighbor bought the small triangle of land behind our house—the piece of land we had been assured that was too small to build on—and he was building on it! Suddenly my view was completely blocked. The only thing I could see was my neighbor.

I was so angry I couldn't read my Bible, I couldn't focus to pray. He would be working on building his shop at dawn. Since he didn't go to church, he would be out there banging all Sunday. "Hope you don't mind that I've taken you view," he said one day. "No!" I lied. "You bought the land; it's yours."

I kept trying to have my quiet time with God, but it wasn't quiet. It wasn't just the lack of external quiet that bothered me; I didn't have any internal quiet either. I began to pray to find relief. However, the message I heard from God did not bring comfort, it brought conviction.

"Sarah, what is more important to you, your view or your neighbor's

---

[2] http://www.taketheleap.com/define.html

soul." There was no question about it: my view and my comfort were much more important to me than the salvation of my neighbor. In admitting this, I also saw that my comfort was an idol I worshiped.

So now what was I supposed to do? I no longer had my view, and my sin had been exposed. I confessed my sin and asked God for mercy, because I knew I couldn't change on my own. I also knew He didn't want me just to pretend to care now that my lack of love was exposed.

I wish I could say that suddenly I no longer cared that my view was gone, but it still irritated me. As I prayed about it, God spoke to me. "Sarah, I have given you a visual reminder to pray for your neighbor and yourself." So my irritation became a call to prayer.

It was like sandpaper on my soul. I continually prayed that God would change both me and my neighbor and He did.

The first step to being forgiven

"Mimi, you've got to talk to her about stealing!" I looked at my little five-year-old granddaughter, with her head bent as low as her neck would allow. I took her by the hand and led her into the bedroom.

We sat on the bed together; she at one end, and I at the other. "Did I ever tell you about when I stole money from my father?" Her head lifted slightly and she whispered, "No."

"I was about your age when it happened. My daddy always emptied his change from his pockets onto his dresser. I would sneak upstairs to his room and take a handful of change. I always left some, hoping he wouldn't notice. One day, as I was going down the stairs, I met my father coming up. 'Sarah, what is behind your back,' my father asked. 'Nothing,' I said. But my father knew better. He had caught me stealing and lying."

My granddaughter's head lift a little bit more. "Mimi, what did he do to you?" She fully understood my horror at being caught.

"My father took me downstairs, and then he gathered the family together and made me tell them what I had done. I didn't want anyone to know what I'd done, and when everyone gathered all I did was cry. I wanted to run away, but I couldn't. Finally, I whispered what I had done. My father held me and asked if I understood stealing and lying was wrong. 'Yes,' I said through my tears. Then he held me and told me he forgave me, but that I was not to do it again."

My granddaughter moved a little closer and I put my arms around her. "Did you know that the Bible tells us that if we confess our sins God will forgive us and take away all our guilt? 'Confess' means we agree with God that we have done something wrong. Did you steal something?" Silence....

"You know, I'm not a little girl anymore. Now I'm a grandmother, but it is still hard for me tell someone I've done something wrong. I have to ask Jesus to help me. But I know that admitting I did something wrong is the first step to being forgiven. Did you steal something?" A very soft "yes" followed.

"Come with me and let's talk to your mommy." My granddaughter followed me and stood looking so small before her mother. "What do you need to tell your mommy?" Silence.... Waiting.... Silence.... Waiting....

"Mommy, I stole your jellybeans and I lied to you." Her mother bent down and wrapped her in her arms and said, "Do you know stealing and lying are wrong?" "Yes, Mommy," she whispered. The next thing I knew she was wrapped in her mother's embrace. "I forgive you."

Heavenly Father, I don't know why it is so hard for me to admit when I've been wrong; to honestly confess my sin instead of hiding it and holding onto it. I think perhaps it's because part of me doesn't want to give it up. Please help me take the first step to being forgiven and admit, confess, my sin.

I want to love

I guess my lifelong battle with overeating has governed my understanding of what it means to "deny myself." However, the more I think about the context of that verse, the more I realize it has a much deeper meaning, particularly if I put it together with Jesus' "new commandment."

"Then Jesus said to his disciples, 'If anyone would come after me, he must deny himself and take up his cross and follow me" (Matt. 16:24 NIV). "A new commandment I give you, that you love one another: just as I have loved you, you also are to love one another. By this all people will know that you are my disciples, if you have love for one another" (John 13:34-35 ESV).

The thing that made the commandment new wasn't that He said to love others, but to love them in the same way He had loved. That kind of love involves self denial and a cross. Following Jesus' kind of love means making myself nothing, taking the very nature of a servant, and humbling myself to the point of death for another person—not just physical death, but the death of my plans, dreams and goals.

The reason I have trouble with overeating is that I don't want to deny myself. I see the evidence of this when I look in the mirror. My family is another mirror; in it I see how often I selfishly put my agenda before anyone else.

Jesus said if I follow His new commandment people would know I was His disciple. I understand that, because there is no other way I could love like that unless I did it in the power of His Spirit. If I walk in His Spirit, the fruit will be "love, joy, peace, patience, kindness, goodness, faithfulness, gentleness," and last, but not least, "self-control" (Gal. 5:22-23 NIV).

Dear Lord Jesus, I want to follow you. I want to represent you well. I want to love.

This is where I find comfort

The phone rang about 5 A.M. Wednesday morning. It was the warning system for my daughter's school in Alabama. A tornado watch was in effect; the students were told to go to the basement. I found out later that the majority of her day was spent in the basement while the tornadoes hovered above the building.

When the things you take for granted—like the stability of nature—are removed, where do you go for comfort? When you wake up thinking this day will be a carbon copy of the day before—but you end the day without a home—where can you go for comfort? When you see people around you whom you love suffer, where can you go for comfort?

"Have you not known? Have you not heard?
The Lord is the everlasting God,
 the Creator of the ends of the earth.
He does not faint or grow weary;
 his understanding is unsearchable.
He gives power to the faint,
 and to him who has no might he increases strength.
Even youths shall faint and be weary,
 and young men shall fall exhausted;
but they who wait for the Lord shall renew their strength;
 they shall mount up with wings like eagles;
they shall run and not be weary;
 they shall walk and not faint.
   (Isaiah 40:28-31 ESV)

Where is my comfort? It is the same place I have put my confidence. Not in the stability of nature; it is not in my strength or the strength of those around me: I put my hope in the everlasting God—not the creation but the Creator; my Lord and my Savior Jesus who has invited me to find refuge in Him.

I find my comfort trusting in God's word and in His promises that, even though I faint and grow weary, He doesn't. I choose to rest between the shoulders of my God, mounting up with wings like eagles.

The Rock beneath my feet

The accident happened in December and, though there is no evidence of anything being wrong, there is a hidden threat. Because of the car accident, my cousin has a tear in her carotid artery; she lives with the threat of it resulting in a stroke. She was told not to move her head quickly, to carry her medical records with her, to know the location of the nearest ER, to take prescribed medication, and to wait until May 12 for the next scan to see if the tear has healed.

I saw Margaret at Easter. I was amazed by the look of peace that surrounded her. She explained what she was going through by using this picture. She told me it was as if there was a pond in her backyard. Because she was so familiar with it, she knew where all the rocks were, so that she could get from one side to the other by stepping on them. Now, however, since the accident, all the rocks had turned into lily pads. There were no rocks she could stand on that would support her weight. She told me the only security she has is her relationship with Jesus. As I looked at her beautiful face, I thought, "This is what the peace that passes understanding looks like!"

Sunday, after the tornadoes had destroyed many places that were familiar to me, the preacher taught on Isaiah 20 and the different things we put our trust in. I think many times we don't even know what we are trusting in until the storms come. Do I trust in something that will leave me full of anxiety or peace when the foundations of my world are shaken?

"Rejoice in the Lord always. I will say it again; Rejoice! Let your gentleness be evident to all. The Lord is near. Do not be anxious about anything..." (Phil. 4:4-6 NIV).

This was the peace I saw in my cousin as she stood on the solid rock, embraced by the love of Jesus.

Tested at the waters of Meribah

"Lord, I can't believe this has happened! I trusted you." My disappointment was so painful I felt like a cruel joke had been played on me. There was no place to turn but to the Lord. Mine was a cry from a desperate heart, "I will not let you go until you bless me!"

I began the morning after my disappointment with heavy depression and resolve. I was going to read my Bible until I heard the voice of God. Because I try to read through the Bible every year, I started where I had left off the day before. I tried to read, but the words seemed to lie flat on the page. I saw words, but I couldn't hear God's voice.

"This is how Job must have felt." Well, maybe I would understand what God was doing to me if I read the last chapters of Job. I read, but I didn't understand what God was saying to Job either! By now I had been reading for over an hour and still I could only see words on the page. I needed to start work, but I still had a heavy heart and no answers.

As I got ready for the day I continued to pray, "God, please, please help me! I don't understand what you are doing. I want to trust you, but I don't understand!" I began to meditate on the things I had read that morning. I began with what I had read in Job. It was not the comfort I had been seeking, but what was God saying?

As I thought about it, what I saw was God challenging Job with this question, "Will the one who contends with the Almighty correct him? Let him who accuses God answer him!" (Job 40:2 NIV). I realized that was what I was doing. I was contending with the Almighty and accusing Him. Because I didn't understand what God was doing; I felt like He was being cruel to me. This was my starting point.

Next I started thinking about the Psalm I had read that morning, Psalm 81:7. "I tested you at the waters of Meribah" (NIV). Okay, what does that mean? What were the waters of Meribah? I found the answer in Exodus 17:7, where God gave the Israelites water from a rock and they quarreled and said, "Is the Lord among us or not?"

As I meditated on Psalm 81, I began to feel like God was giving me an invitation to trust Him. Psalm 81:10-16: "I am the Lord your God, who brought you up out of Egypt. Open wide your mouth and I will fill it. But my people would not listen to me; Israel would not submit to me.... If my people would but listen to me, if Israel would follow my ways... with honey from the rock I would satisfy you" (NIV)

So I stand thirsty in the wilderness facing a rock. I'm not sure where I am. I'm not sure where I'm going. This is a test—a test of trust. It is the same test Eve had in the garden that I now have in the wilderness. Is God really good? Can I trust Him even if I don't understand Him?

I choose to trust. My soul is satisfied with living water I find sweetness in the hardest places of my life. I have entered into His rest!

What's missing in my life?

What's missing in my life? This was a question I was supposed to answer in my Bible study. I think the correct answer should be nothing. I read in Roman 5:2 "Because of our faith, Christ has brought us into this place of undeserved privilege where we now stand, and we confidently and joyfully look forward to sharing God's glory" (NLT). So my question is, why do I feel so miserable?

I don't always feel miserable, but I did yesterday while I was pondering the question, "What's missing in my life?" It was just one of those days. I was trying to figure out how to get to the point where I was "rejoicing in the Lord" instead of "grumbling and complaining."

I think in pictures. When I think about grace, I think about a bank account. I believe God has placed in my account unfailing love, infinite mercy, redemption and forgiveness for my sin, to name only a few. These things were credited to me as a gift. I did not earn them. I believe the value of what has been placed in my account is beyond anything I could have earned.

When my account was opened for me, I was also given a checkbook called faith. Faith is being sure of what you hope for and confident about what you don't see (Heb. 11:1). My confidence is that, in God's love and provision, I have everything I need. I am lacking nothing. So, back to my original question: Why was I so miserable yesterday?

I have in my account everything I need; I have a checkbook; but now I need something to write with. In my mind I see the pen as prayer. In the book of James it says, "You don't have because you don't ask." Jesus taught that, if we asked according to His will, we would receive. When the blind man came to Jesus, Jesus said, "What do you want me to do for you?"

When I pray in faith, I think of Jesus, "who, although He existed in the form of God, did not regard equality with God a thing to be grasped, but emptied Himself, taking the form of a bond-servant, and being made in the likeness of men. Being found in appearance as a man, He humbled Himself by becoming obedient to the point of death, even death on a cross" (Phil. 2:6-8 NASB). This is what it cost to place the grace in my account. When in prayer I turn my attention away from the frustrations of the world and begin to claim what Jesus died to provide for me, and my heart begins to change.

Through the "pen" of prayer, I fill out the "check" of faith, to access my "account" of grace.

To submit or not to submit

"You were the signet of perfection, full of wisdom and perfect in beauty. You were in Eden, the garden of God; every precious stone was your covering, sardius, topaz, and diamond, beryl, onyx and jasper, sapphire, emerald, and carbuncle; and crafted in gold were your settings and your engravings. On the day you were created they were prepared. You were an anointed guardian cherub. I placed you; you were on the holy mountain of God; in the midst of the stones of fire you walked....Your heart was proud because of your beauty; you corrupted your wisdom for the sake of your splendor" (Ezek. 28:12-17 ESV).

"Have this mind among yourself, which is yours in Christ Jesus, who, though he was in the form of God, did not count equality with God a thing to be grasped, but made himself nothing, taking the form of a servant, being born in the likeness of men. And being found in human form, he humbled himself by becoming obedient to the point of death, even death on a cross" (Phil. 2:5-8 ESV).

"Now the serpent was more crafty than any other beast of the field that the Lord God had made" (Gen. 3:1 ESV). What was the temptation? Wasn't it really to rebel against God's authority? The word submit means to place yourself under authority. Pride responds, "You can't tell me what to do! I am my own boss."

"Then Jesus told his disciples, 'If anyone would come after me, let him deny himself and take up his cross and follow me'" (Matt. 16:24 ESV). Satan shouts, "Rebel!" Jesus invites us to deny ourselves. I have to admit my natural inclination is to rebel. I don't like other people telling me what to do.

Sometimes it's good to know the end of the story, or the consequences of your decision. "By the multitude of your iniquities, in the unrighteousness of your trade you profaned your sanctuaries; so I brought fire out from your midst; it consumed you, and I turned you to ashes on the earth in the sight of all who saw you. All who know you among the peoples are appalled at you; you have come to a dreadful end and shall be no more forever" (Ezek. 28:18-19 ESV).

"Therefore God has highly exalted him and bestowed on him the name that is above every name, so that at the name of Jesus every knee shall bow, in heaven and on earth and under the earth, and every tongue confess that Jesus Christ is Lord, to the glory of God the Father" (Phil. 2:9-11 ESV).

So, in the end, I think it is really just a matter of which one I submit to. Either I choose to submit to "The father of lies, the murderer, the Power of Darkness, the Wicked One," or "Jesus, the way the truth and the life, light of the world, the Good Shepherd, the Prince of Peace."

I choose to submit myself to the authority of Jesus Christ.

Gentleness is the opposite of a control freak

I live on a farm, and we have stables. I have to confess, I'm not an expert on horses; but I have tried to learn a few things. One thing I've learned is that horses are prey animals. Humans are predators. Prey animals are eaten by predators; therefore, they tend to be frightened easily, very much like sheep. However, when a horse learns to trust a human, the horse becomes gentle. When a horse becomes gentle and learns to trust its owner, it yields control to the owner. A horse can panic easily when it is frightened, but when a horse has learned to trust its owner, there is nowhere it will not go. An example of a fearless horse is a warhorse. It is also a beautiful picture of trust.

When I see the word gentle in the Bible, I think of this special relationship of a horse and its owner. I see this relationship in Philippians when it says to, "Rejoice in the Lord. Let your gentleness be known to everyone. The Lord is near; do not be anxious about anything...." (Phil. 4:4-6 ESV). The closeness of the relationship between horse and rider can be measured by the gentleness and fearlessness of the horse. I think that is true of my relationship with Jesus. The more I trust Him, the gentler I become.

I have a confession to make. This is how I want to be, but what happens more often is that, when I feel threatened, I become a control freak. I drive myself and everyone around me crazy. When I enter this panic mode there is no peace in my home, and it ceases to be a safe place for the people around me—very similar to a horse that is panicking. A horse that is panicking can, by accident, kill those closest to him.

What can I do? Again I go to the passage in Philippians. When my eyes are wide with panic and anxiety about things that threaten me but I have no control over, I am instructed to pray. "But in everything by prayer and supplications with thanksgiving let your request be made known to God" (Phil. 4:6 ESV). Prayer shows a correct relationship between the one who is helpless and the one who is protector. The things that cause me to panic, when I humbly bring them to the Lord in prayer, teach me to trust Him. Gentleness and humility are often found together.

I love to go to horse shows where you see a horse that really trusts its master. It seems there is nothing the horse cannot do. This is what I want my relationship with Jesus to look like. "And the peace of God, which surpasses all understanding, will guard your heart and minds in Christ Jesus" (Phil. 4:7 ESV).

Lord Jesus, I yield the reigns of control to You in exchange for your peace. Lord Jesus, make me gentle.

I named my first child Faith

I wanted to share a few mothering tips:

1. If you place your confidence and expectations in yourself and your parenting ability, you will stumble and fall.

2. If you place your confidence and expectations in your children, they will stumble and fall, and then you will trip over them and land on top of them.

3. If you place your confidence and expectations in God and pray without ceasing, He will hear you and give you the wisdom that you need.

4. When the Bible tells you that you cannot judge someone's motives, that applies to your children as well. Just because we gave them birth does not place us in God's position of judging their heart.

5. When removing the splinter from your child's eye, be very careful: it may have splintered off the log in your eye.

6. CHILDREN ARE WITHOUT EXCEPTION A GIFT FROM GOD!

Living with the curtains pulled back

I love to study prophecy! When I study prophecy I feel like the curtains of Heaven are pulled back. I see God at the beginning and the end.

I love the book of Daniel and the picture I find of God there. He is the Ancient of Days seated on the throne. He is the Most High God whose, "kingdom is an everlasting kingdom, and his dominion endures from generation to generation" (Dan. 4:3 ESV).

When I read the book of Ezra I see people who are discouraged. Their enemies are mocking their efforts to obey God. They are living with the consequences of their sin and the sins of their ancestors. They are discouraged and ready to give up. Then God sends two prophets, Haggai and Zechariah. Through these prophets God pulls back the curtains of Heaven and shows them the bigger picture. When they can see their life from the perspective of eternity, they find the courage to do the work God has given them to do.

"For the Lord God does nothing without revealing his secret to his servants, the prophets" (Amos 3:7 ESV). Isn't that amazing? I see this idea repeated over and over: When God said, "Shall I hide from Abraham what I am about to do?" (Gen. 18:17); or when He told Noah about the flood. In so many places in Scripture God reveals what He is about to do, and then invites His servants to be part of it.

Then we come to the ministry of Jesus, and I hear Him say, "No longer do I call you servants, for a servant does not know what his master is doing; but I have called you friends, for all that I have heard from my Father I have made known to you" (John 15:15 ESV). I see this again in the first verse of Revelation, "The revelation of Jesus Christ, which God gave him to show to his servants the things that must soon take place" (Rev. 1:1 ESV). I confess I am very timid at times. Sometimes I'm just scared, I feel like I have no control over my life. However, when I study prophecy, I see the curtains of Heaven pulled back. I see the Ancient of Days seated on the throne. And, miracle of miracles, I hear the message that He loves me. As I study His word I find to my amazement that I have a place in the story He is telling.

Sovereign Lord, as I bow today at your eternal throne, show me how to be a good steward of your revealed mysteries.

Learning to hear the voice of God

I remember my first prayer. I was about four years old and attempting to sweep the sidewalk at my parent's home. Suddenly I was aware that I was not thinking about God. I stopped and prayed, "God, I don't ever want to not think about you again." It was a sincere prayer, and I can still remember the wonder and confidence I felt that God had heard me and would give me the gift I'd asked for.

I love the story of Samuel. Before he knew God, before the word of the Lord had been revealed to him, he heard God call his name. "Samuel!" It did not begin with Samuel pursuing God, but God pursuing Samuel. "Samuel!" Samuel went to the priest for instruction and was told to go back to bed. "Samuel!" Again he goes to the priest. The priest, who had failed to train his own sons to hear the voice of God, realized that the Lord was calling the boy.

So Eli told Samuel, "Go and lie down, and if he calls you, say, 'Speak, Lord, for your servant is listening.'" So Samuel went and lay down in his place. The Lord came and stood there, calling as at the other times, "Samuel! Samuel!" Then Samuel said, "Speak, for your servant is listening" (1 Sam. 3:9-10).

I love to pray this prayer when I open up my Bible. I love the fact that I am simply responding to the love of God. He said, "Open wide your mouth and I will fill it" (Psa. 81:10 ESV).

Eli's sons were not listening to God's voice. Eli honored his sons more than he honored God because he was reaping a benefit from their sin. God was speaking, but His people were not listening. "But my people did not listen to my voice; Israel would not submit to me. So I gave them over to their stubborn hearts, to follow their own counsels. Oh, that my people would listen to me, that Israel would walk in my ways!" (Psa. 81:11-13 ESV).

There have been times in my life when it has seemed God's voice was dim. When this happens I use the words to a song I learned long ago and I sing it to the Lord in prayer. "Lord, to my soul bring back the springtime! Take away the cold and dark of sin. Only hold me now sweet holy Jesus. May I warm and tender be again." [Kurt Kaiser, *Bring Back the Springtime*, © 1970 Word Music.]

Thank You, Jesus, that in love You pursue me, calling me by name. Grant me the grace to respond, "Speak Lord, for your servant is listening," and to always have You in my thoughts.

What mocks the power of God in your life?

When I read a story, I always identify with one of the characters. When I read the story of David and Goliath, I identify with Eliab, David's big brother. David made Eliab angry. Eliab had been on the battlefield for a while. For forty days Goliath had been coming out with his challenge. To fight the war was one thing; to battle Goliath one on one with everyone watching was another. Now here comes David with the question, "Who is this uncircumcised Philistine that he should defy the armies of the living God?" Not content to ask it once, he keeps asking this same question over and over!

I know Goliath personally. He's big. Really big. It's not just me he bothers either. A lot of people are familiar with him. He makes me feel like a failure; his taunts grow louder and louder with each passing day.

He stands in the middle of the road and no progress can be made with him standing there. Behind him are all his mocking buddies, "If your God is so great, come on, let's see it. Fight Goliath."

Along comes David, he's been with the sheep, not fighting Philistines. His perspective is untainted. He calls Goliath an uncircumcised Philistine. In other words, David is pointing out that Goliath doesn't have protection from God. Next he asks the question, "Why is he being allowed to defy the living God?" These questions not only demand an answer, they demand action.

Dear God, sometimes I feel like I've failed before I've even begun. Today give me the grace to run to the battle. Today, Goliath, you are going down!

Worshiping on my knees in the dressing room

"Oh great, all my jeans are worn out!" Not only that, but the shirts I wear to work were stained. I needed to do something about it, but didn't have the resources.

I went to the thrift store and was greeted by an employee that told me today it was a buy one get one free shirt day. I found four shirts all the right color for work and then went to the jeans section. There I found three new pairs of L.L. Bean jeans—in my size!

In the dressing room, I realized I would be able to get four shirts and three new pairs of jeans for less than the regular cost of one pair of jeans. I knelt in the dressing room and thanked God.

I thanked the woman who was checking me out, and then I told her how grateful I was to God for His mercy. There was another woman standing there, breathing with the aid of an oxygen tank. She responded, "The Bible says we have not because we ask not."

I shared with her how I think about God's grace like a bank account that is full. God gave us faith to be the checkbook so that we could access the grace. Prayer is the pen we use to fill out the check. The woman standing at the counter smiled and said, "Praise the Lord!"

When I got to my car, I turned on the radio and heard Fernando Ortega singing, "Grace pouring forth like a fountain flowing, our hearts open wide to sing Your praise." [Odes of Solomon, "Ode 40," *Sing Allelu.* Public domain.] This completed my picture. Because of the sacrifice of Jesus Christ, God has given me abundant grace. I access this grace by faith when I pray. However, when I thank God for His grace, it adds to the blessing.

How to deal with disappointment

I think of Caleb: what he experienced, what he must have felt when he walked on dry ground with the Red Sea piled up on either side of him. He knew desert thirst, but he also knew what it was to have his thirst quenched by water flowing from what had been a dry rock until Moses hit it with his staff. He knew what it was like to have his physical hunger satisfied with the bread from Heaven day after day.

I can only imagine the excitement Caleb must have felt when he was chosen to be one of the twelve to spy out the Promised Land. Caleb's time in the wilderness had taught him to trust God wholeheartedly, and now he was ready to see with his own eyes where God had led him. He went to Hebron where the descendants of Anak the giant lived.

It took two men to carry a single cluster of grapes. Caleb must have been overcome with anticipation. He was 40 years old and in his prime. He was poised to take possession of the land God had promised him. But there was a glitch in the plan. Ten of the spies brought back word that, though the land was everything God had promised, there were giants and fortified cities, and there was no way for the Israelites to take possession of it.

"Then Caleb quieted the people before Moses and said, 'We should by all means go up and take possession of it, for we will surely overcome it'" (Num. 13:30 NAS). Caleb trusted God; Caleb believed God's promise; but Caleb spent the next 40 years, not in the Promised Land, but wandering in the wilderness. Why?

There have been times in my life when the choices of others have altered the course set before me. I have known disappointment. I have discovered time and time again that I am not the captain of my ship or the master of my fate. What to do? How do I respond? To be honest, my first response is usually anger. I have to wrestle with the fact that I do not live an isolated life: it is lived in tandem with those I love; their choices affect my life.

How do I live with disappointment? How did Caleb live with disappointment? There is only one way. When I realize that I am not the captain of my ship or the master of my own fate, I ask myself, "Who is?" Caleb had learned to trust God. He had learned that God could part the Red Sea, provide water from a rock and bread from Heaven. Caleb believed that it was God, not the obedience or disobedience of the people he was with, that was in control.

The question I really have to ask myself when I am disappointed is this, "Does God keeps His promise." My faith is strengthened when I read the request Caleb made when he was 85 years old. "Now then, just as the Lord promised, he has kept me alive for forty-five years since the time he said this to Moses, while Israel moved about in the desert. So here I am today, eighty-five years old! I am still as strong today as the day Moses sent me out; I'm just as vigorous to go out to battle now as I was then. Now give me this hill country that the Lord promised me that day. You yourself heard then that the Anakites were there and their cities were large…. I will drive them out just as he said" (Josh. 14:10-12).

Now, Father, I place my confidence and expectations in You and You alone. When I put my hope in You I will never be disappointed, because, in the fullness of time You always keep Your promise.

Victory over despair

It came in like a suffocating fog, seeping in the cracks. Before I knew it, my mind was blinded by negative thoughts. The negative thoughts became negative words that polluted everything I said and hurt everyone I spoke to. I felt afraid and vulnerable. Nothing seemed safe. I could only think of the worst case scenario in every situation.

There was a battle going on in my mind. Suddenly I remembered a Bible verse, "Let no unwholesome word come out of your mouth…" [Eph. 4:29 NET]. That was the beginning of victory over despair. Next came the verse mingled with my prayer, "Lord, please let the words of my mouth and the meditations of my heart be acceptable in Your sight." A shaft of light, a ray of hope. I would, by God's grace, not be crippled by my depressing thoughts and words.

At 3 A.M., lying in bed physically, mental, emotionally vulnerable, the attack came again. Dark black thoughts shaded everything around and within me. "In the night season I will remember You. I will meditate on You through the watches of the night." I put on my robe and went out to sit on my porch and focus my mind on God. I saw the full moon. I saw in its reflection the beauty of nature. I heard the sound of a whippoorwill. I began to rehearse the many blessings I had received from God. The light came, darkness again was repelled. I went back into the house and fell into a deep restful sleep.

When I woke up this morning, I was thinking about Psalm 22:3. It talks about how God inhabits the praises of His people. In researching this psalm, I found the story of a man who had gone through a bone marrow transplant. He talked about the depression that haunted him in his isolation until he remembered Psalm 22:3. He began to sing praises to God and the grip of despair released its hold on his heart.

Father, today please help me remember that praising You causes prison doors to swing open. Your light and truth gives victory over despair. If the Lord is my shepherd...

If the Lord is compared to a shepherd, then I am compared to sheep. Sheep are known for their "mob instincts," fear and timidity, stubbornness and stupidity. If sheep do well, it is because they have a good shepherd.

Years ago I read the book *A Shepherd Looks at Psalm 23* by Phillip Keller. This book helped me understand some of the things I read in the Psalm. There was one part in particular that stayed with me. It was the part about the shepherd anointing the sheep's head.

In the summertime, sheep are bothered by nose flies that buzz around the sheep's head, hoping to deposit their eggs in the sheep's nose. If they are successful, the eggs hatch into worm-like larvae that work their way up the nasal passages into the sheep's head. This causes the sheep to begin to beat their head against trees, rocks, posts, etc., trying to get relief.

To protect his sheep from the flies, a shepherd will smear an ointment of linseed oil, sulfur and tar over the sheep's nose and head as a protection against nose flies. Once the oil has been applied, the sheep are free from agitation.

I can identify. I get so irritated sometimes by seemingly small things, but they drive me crazy all the same. The thoughts buzz round and round in my mind. I can't seem to get rid of them; and then they begin to multiply, leaving room for nothing else. This is when I need a shepherd.

I cry out to the Shepherd to apply the oil of His Holy Spirit to my mind. I ask Him to anoint the conscious and sub-conscious levels of my thought life so that I can think and react like He would. I am always amazed at the relief I experience in response to this prayer.

I do identify with the problems that sheep have, and I am grateful that I can say, "The Lord is my shepherd, I shall not want."

Finding the words

"I was never allowed to express negative emotions as a child, and now I don't know how." This is what a friend recently told me. I was allowed to express negative emotions as a child, and I still struggle with knowing how to do it. Why?

I think there is the fear that if I really explore how black the darkness is or how deep the brokenness is, I will find no remedy. I think this is why some parents don't allow their children to express their negative emotions. The parents just don't know how to make it right.

I find my relief in God's Word. He verbalized the darkest fears and entered into the deepest brokenness. "My God, my God, why have you forsaken me? Why are you so far from saving me, from the words of my groaning? O my God, I cry by day, but you do not answer, and by night, but I find no rest" (Psa. 22:1-2 ESV).

"Use your words." This is an instruction I have heard parents give little children. But sometimes I can't find the words to express the dark emotions that I feel. I find in these verses God reaching out His hand and inviting me to honestly explore the depths of my fears and giving me words to express my anger and confusion.

I also am amazed to find these words in Jesus' mouth as He hung dying on the cross. Because of His love for me, He entered into my darkness and my brokenness so that I could enter into His light and wholeness.

One of the Psalms I use to comfort myself is Psalm 23, the one that follows Psalm 22. Isn't that interesting? I wonder if the deepest comfort is found only after I explore my deepest fears and brokenness, letting God put the words into my mouth.

Lord Jesus, thank You that when I go into the blackness of the night and face my fears I find I am not alone. You chose to bear my griefs and carry my sorrows. Because of You, though I enter the darkness, I don't stay there.

Finding comfort in the glory of God

When I can't sleep I go outside and sit quietly on my porch in my rocking chair. Embraced by the soft cool air of night, I look at the stars, I listen to the quiet whispers of night. It is peaceful, it is beautiful, it is majestic. When I feel the glory of the night has entered my soul I begin, "Father, who art in Heaven...."

"The heavens declare the glory of God, and the sky above proclaims his handiwork. Day to day pours out speech, and night to night reveals knowledge" (Psa. 19:1-2 ESV). I think the reality of this verse is why I like to pray at night on my porch. I am surrounded by the evidence of the glory of God. I am surrounded by His glory during the day as well, but I get distracted by the artificial lights.

Here, in the majesty of night, I can hear the voice of the Almighty. The creator whose handiwork I see above me invites me to call Him Father. There is a peace and wonder that enters my soul. When my heart and mind are filled with the knowledge declared by the glory of God, there is no room for anxiety.

Now it is time for me to rest. I close my eyes and drift peacefully to sleep, knowing that I have had audience with the God of the Universe. He invited me to come before His throne and lay my worries down... and I did.

The gardener of my soul

Back then the driveway was lined with fruit trees. There were apple trees, peach trees and pear trees. There was so much fruit that sometimes the branches would bend down almost to the ground. So much fruit, but the fruit was small, hard and tasteless.

The reason the trees weren't being pruned was because I had small children at the time. It was a season in my life where I also had a great amount of energy and I was busy doing many projects. I was teaching several Bible studies. I had even been invited to speak at some conferences.

I remember very clearly when it began, the pruning. I was at a national convention. The speaker told us to find a quiet place and to listen to God. I found my quiet place, settled down and was disturbed by what I heard. I felt like God was telling me He was going to retire me from my many activities.

The pruning began on my way home. Several of us were traveling together. The women began to talk about restructuring the class I taught. That was very humbling, because it no longer had me as the teacher. Snip, snip went the pruning shears.

Next came a class I had been teaching for ten years. For the first time since I had been teaching it, no one signed up to take it! Snip, Snip. One by one the classes I taught were eliminated, until the only class left was my children. That was when I decided to home school them.

I poured out on my children all my energy, all my creativity. Morning by morning I shared with them the treasures I found. They didn't necessarily always appreciate this. I caught them rolling their eyes at times. But what a privilege to watch them grow and mature.

I am in a different season of life now. I no longer have boundless energy. I can no longer do several projects simultaneously. I no longer have my children living at home.

Dear Heavenly Father, You who are the gardener of my soul. Thank you for pruning me so that the fruit of my life will have more quality than quantity.

I think I missed the point

"Deny yourself." That seems pretty basic. I've been on enough diets to understand what that means. But it's the words that come after this command that make me think that just maybe I missed the point.

"If anyone would come after me, let him deny himself and take up his cross daily and follow me" (Luke 9:23 ESV). I have a tendency to put myself in the middle of the universe, so I've always thought about denying myself in a positive way, to make me a better me. Taking up my cross daily and following Christ? Well, I thought of that as putting to death the negative things about who I am and being more like Jesus. However, when I examine my thoughts in the context of Jesus' life, I see how self-centered they are.

When I connect Jesus' invitation to follow Him with what I read in Philippians 2, understanding begins to awaken. "So if there is any encouragement in Christ, any comfort from love, any participation in the Spirit, any affection and sympathy, complete my joy by being of the same mind, having the same love, being in full accord and of one mind. Do nothing from rivalry or conceit, but in humility count others more significant than yourselves. Let each of you look not only to his own interests, but also to the interests of others. Have this mind among yourselves, which is yours in Christ Jesus..." (Phil. 2:1-5 ESV). This is not about me being a better me; it's about me loving others like Jesus did. It's about me following Jesus, denying myself, putting to death my flesh in love for others.

This is not about my dying on the mission field either. There is a daily aspect to it. This is a daily choice to love as my life rubs against the lives of others; my choosing to deny myself for them, daily putting to death my flesh so that I might consider others more significant than myself. This simply brings me to my knees and exposes how selfish I really am.

Dear Jesus, I come to You humbled again today by the exposure of Your word. I recognize again how different my thinking is from Yours. No matter how hard I try, I cannot, in my own strength, follow You. Please, Lord, today let me participate in Your Spirit and know You in the power of Your resurrection. By Your grace I want to share in Your sufferings, following the new command You gave, that if anyone wanted to follow You they were to love others as You did. Today, Lord, today grant me this kind of love.

Lemons

"You cut the lemon wrong." Everything within me rises up in my defense. My reputation as a lemon cutter is at stake. "I cut the lemons the way you showed me," I explained. However, the lemons in question had a very thick rind and were lacking in pulp and didn't look right. "No, you cut the lemons wrong." "Perhaps you're right." I walk away in false humility but real anger.

I think of anger like stepping in chewing gun on a hot pavement. Once you step in it, it's stuck to your shoe in a gooey mess and is very hard to get rid of. Seldom—no, I think never is a better word—do I set out to step in melting chewing gum; but it happens all the same. I never choose to be angry. I hate the emotion. But then, suddenly, there it is. And I have to deal with the anger just like I have to deal with the sticky gum on my shoe.

Neither the comment about the lemons nor the person who made it was the real source of my anger. I have heard that anger is a natural emotion we feel when we are threatened. So what in the world was so threatening about being told I cut the lemons wrong? It was a threat to my pride. Don't mess with my pride!

Anger is strong. Anger is powerful. I think of anger like a weed that is able to split the concrete sidewalk. Anger is a warning. It is not in itself wrong, but it is a tool to tell us something is wrong. My problem was not cutting lemons wrong, my problem was with my pride.

Anger is a God-given emotion; it is not a bad thing. How I deal with this emotion is another story. I am uncomfortable with the emotion of anger. I don't know what to do with it. I particularly don't like when it exposes something negative about me: like pride.

Dear Lord, here I am again struggling with the negative feelings I have when my life bumps against the lives of others. Please take this emotion that You created me with, and use it like sandpaper on my soul. Please conform me into the image of Your Son.

A prisoner of hurt or a prisoner of hope

"Return to your stronghold, O prisoners of hope; today I declare that I will restore you double" (Zech. 9:12 ESV). I looked up the definition for the word stronghold and found that it meant a place of refuge or survival.

There are so many things in life, I find, that can take me captive. I can be a prisoner to regret. When I look back over my life and see how some of my bad choices have hurt the people I love, I feel imprisoned by the pain of those choices. I look at David's life and see the grief he and those he loved suffered because of his sin, but he wasn't a prisoner of regret: he was a prisoner of hope. He knew where to run for refuge. The hurt he felt was real, but so was the God who loved him. He endured the pain by putting his confidence in the promise of a Redeemer.

Sometimes I feel like a prisoner of anxiety. It takes me captive in the night as I think about all the things over which I have no control. I see situations that threaten me and the people I love, and suddenly I cry out in fear. I see a reflection of my own tears on the prophet Jeremiah's face. But, like Jeremiah, I return to my stronghold, and say, "Remember my afflictions and my wanderings, the wormwood and the gall! My soul continually remembers it and is bowed down within me. But this I call to mind, and therefore I have hope: the steadfast love of the Lord never ceases; his mercies never come to an end; they are new every morning; great is your faithfulness. 'The Lord is my portion,' says my soul, 'therefore I will hope in him'" (Lam. 3:19-24 ESV).

Lord Jesus, Your love is the key that unlocks the prison of regret because You are the Redeemer. Because You are my Savior, You have set me free from all the fears and failures that bind me. For today I will remain in my stronghold, a prisoner of hope, knowing that the day will come when hope will be exchanged for sight and I will be free.

Well-placed fear produces great courage

I have been looking over the different things I been writing about, and I see a common thread. It's not just a common thread in my writing, it is also a major theme of my life. Day after day, situation after situation, I keep coming back to this question, "God, how do I do this? How am I supposed to live out what I believe?"

I think about the verse in Philippians 2 that says, "...work out your salvation with fear and trembling." I have had this on my mind a lot lately, and so I looked it up to see the context. Because my question is, "How do I work out my salvation with fear and trembling?"

"...work out your own salvation with fear and trembling, for it is God who works in you both to will and to work for his good pleasure" (Phil. 2:12b-13 ESV). I did research on the word fear and found that it meant to be in awe of God, to respect and reverence Him. If I have an awe of God, and believe that He is at work in my life, then I don't have to be afraid of the situations in which I find myself.

As I meditate on what my life would look like if I really lived this way, I think of a man whose name was Tom Jackson. Tom was a quiet man; a man with a deep reverence for God. The reason for Tom's calm was his belief in the sovereignty of God. He believed that if you had a true fear of God you didn't need to be afraid of anything else.

Tom's faith was tested in battle. It was at the battle of Bull Run. Shells and bullets were flying all around him. Jackson stayed on his horse, calm and collected, as if nothing was going on. Brigadier General Bernard Bee saw this and told the troops, "There stands Jackson like a stone wall. Let's determine to die here with him."

Lord Jesus, thank you that I don't have to be anxious about "getting it right." Thank you that You are working in my life to will and do Your good pleasure. Help me to be strong, courageous and faithful.

If there was one thing you could change about yourself, what would it be?

If there was one thing you could change about yourself, what would it be? I don't really have to think about this question too hard before I come up with, not one, but a long list of things. Many of the problems that come to mind have been with me most of my conscious life.

I struggle with my weight, I always have. It never mattered what I looked like on the outside, I was still struggling on the inside. I am one of nine children; I think I have eight of the smartest and most successful people in the world as my siblings. I, on the other hand, used to sit in class and wonder what it would be like to understand exactly what the teacher was talking about, particularly in Latin class. Last, but not least, I have fought depression off and on since I was a small child.

In the ninth chapter of John, Jesus' disciples ask Him, "'Whose fault was it that this man was born blind?' Jesus answered, 'It was not that this man sinned, or his parents, but that the works of God might be displayed in him.'" Could this be true for me as well?

The first miracle done in Jesus' name after His resurrection was done for a man who was over 40 and had been crippled since birth. Acts 3 tells us in the name of Jesus he was healed. This place in his life that had always caused him grief now was the source of amazing joy. Could this be true for me?

Could it be that these weaknesses in my life could become places where God's work could be displayed in me?

Lord Jesus, I come to You just as I am. I can't seem to heal myself, even though I've tried really hard. I bring to You my inadequacies. Shine Your light on me, shine You light in me, shine Your light through me. Let the broken places in my life become the places other people see Your glory!

What's the difference between being used by the Lord and just being used?

I decided to write a Bible study based on the question, "What is the difference between being used by the Lord and just being used?" I did not decide to write this study because I knew the answer, but because I needed to know the answer.

The book of James tells us that if we are lacking in wisdom we can ask God and He will give it to us. So I decided to ask God my question, and then tell others what I found out. What follows is God's answer to my prayer.

"Bear one another's burdens, and so fulfill the law of Christ.... Each will have to bear his own load" (Gal. 6:2, 5 ESV). This scripture became the basis for my study. It also became a subject of prayer, because I could not figure out what it meant. Because I believed God would answer my prayer for wisdom, I continued to study and pray until finally I understood.

When I bear another person's burden, with the aim of fulfilling the law of Christ, it means I love them sacrificially. It means I deny myself and place another person's welfare above my own. It does NOT mean that I take someone's responsibility away from them. To take away someone's responsibility is to take away their dignity and elevate myself above them. Therefore, "each will have to bear his own load."

I have done it wrong so many times, and the results are always the same. When I take someone's responsibly away from them, I end up resenting them. I feel taken advantage of, crippled, because I'm doing their responsibility instead of my own. But I'm not the only one who feels resentful. The person I'm "helping" feels resentment as well. I end up crippling the person I wanted to help, because God-given loads strengthen us. When I try to take that load from someone, I am being arrogant, not loving.

Yesterday I saw a man do it right, and the memory of it has stayed with me like a sweet perfume. I was standing in a checkout line behind a man with his disabled daughter. Her gait was stumbling, her arms seemed to fly about uncontrollably, and her eyes rolled back into their sockets. The father's tone was kind as he asked for her opinion about what she wanted to buy. He gently lifted her burden, but let her carry her own load. What I observed was a man who was fulfilling the law of Christ.

So what's the difference between being used by the Lord and just being used? I think to know the answer to that, I need to ask myself this question, "Is my goal to fulfill the law of Christ or to be someone's savior?" Fulfilling the law of Christ involves deep humility. When I think I can be someone's savior, it is a picture of pride.

Lord Jesus, I come to You again for wisdom. My life is stained by this type of arrogant pride. Please give me the wisdom to fulfill the law of Christ and become the sweet fragrance of You in my world, just like the man I saw yesterday.

The Covenant

"Dearly beloved, we are gathered here in the sight of God, and in the face of this congregation, to join this man and this woman in holy matrimony." Thirty seven years ago today, I entered into a covenant with God and my husband. It wasn't an agreement, it wasn't a contract, it was a covenant.

When I entered into this covenant with God and my husband, I made promises to him and he made promises to me. We promised to, "live together for better or worse, for richer or poorer, in sickness and in health; and forsaking all others, be faithful to each other as long as we live." I was 21, he was 23 when we made this lifetime covenant.

I took a magic marker on our wedding trip. Steve had cancer and was taking radiation treatment. Every time we went swimming together I had to redraw the lines where he needed radiation. On our first anniversary he had completed his chemotherapy. I worked during the day and took care of him at night. The stress and lack of sleep caused me to have a nervous breakdown. He took care of me until I recovered. Our next anniversary was spent working at Yellowstone National Park. "I will live together with you... in sickness and in health."

Steve was with me for the birth of our four children. We shared the miracle of life, and I watched him as he tenderly held his children. We both wept as he dug the grave for Belle Marie here on the farm. I remember his words of comfort as we placed her little coffin in the ground. "Time doesn't heal all wounds, but God will." He comforted me during the loss of two more children. "I will live together with you for better or worse."

If the covenant I made so many years ago had only been with Steve, I don't know if it would have survived. I have failed him often. Our humanity and selfishness have caused us to hurt each other in many ways. However, this covenant was made with God as well. "The steps of a man are established by the Lord, when he delights in his way; though he fall, he shall not be cast headlong, for the Lord upholds his hand"

(Psa. 37:23-24 ESV).

Thirty seven years ago today I was asked, "Do you promise to love, comfort, honor and keep him to be your wedded husband....as long as you both shall live?" I whispered, "I do," but it was loud enough for Steve and God to hear.

A cheerful heart

First, a tree fell on her house. Next, when the plumber was fixing the bathroom that had been messed up by the fallen tree, he failed to hook up the toilet correctly, so the basement flooded. Then, last week, the air conditioner at her business caught on fire. How much stress can one person take?

Knowing all she'd been through, I didn't expect her to be smiling. "Are you alright," I asked. I was surprised by her positive attitude. When she told me about the things that had happen, she told it all from a perspective of God's protection and provision. As I listened, I thought about Proverbs 17:22, "A cheerful heart is good medicine" (NIV).

The other part of the verse says, "but a crushed spirit dries up the bones." My friend could have responded either way. Her cheerful heart was a result of her relationship with a Sovereign God. When someone carries a burden too heavy for them, they are crushed.

The crushing load began in the garden when Satan introduced the idea that man needed to be his own god. Satan told Eve that she couldn't really trust God to have her best interests at heart. In Isaiah 9 we have the remedy. "For to us a child is born, to us a son is given; and the government shall be upon his shoulder, and his name shall be called Wonderful Counselor, Mighty God, Everlasting Father, Prince of Peace" (Isa 9:6 ESV).

We have been given a Savior, and the government of our lives is on His shoulders. To understand this is to have a cheerful heart. To understand this is to be governed by the Prince of Peace.

No longer held captive

She was a prisoner inside her body. My friend had Lou Gehrig's Disease an incurable, fatal neuromuscular disease. I sat with her and talked to her. She was my friend. We were alike in many ways. We both liked to cook; her bookshelves had many of the same books mine did. She and I both had chosen to home school our four children.

Many years ago I had felt like a prisoner inside my body. I had been given strong medicine that made it hard for me to function. I felt like I had lost my personality. It was a painful time in my life, yet whenever I sat with my friend, I felt like God had redeemed that time in my life, because it had opened a window of understanding. When I looked into her eyes, I saw her soul.

She and I had another thing in common. We had both put our faith in Jesus as our Savior. In Luke 12:32, Jesus said, "Fear not, little flock, for it is your Father's good pleasure to give you the kingdom" (ESV). When you have an incurable, fatal disease, this promise becomes an anchor. Hope is a confident expectation of good. Faith is being sure of what you hope for and confident about what you don't see.

I still live daily laying hold of Jesus' promises by faith. But my friend no longer needs to walk by faith. She now walks by sight.

Like a sheep that needs a shepherd

I love Psalm 119. I have attempted to memorize it several times. My problem is that it has 176 verses. Because I've attempted it so many times, I'm pretty good at the first part.

"Blessed are those whose way is blameless, who walk in the law of the Lord! Blessed are those who keep his testimonies, who seek him with their whole heart, who also do no wrong, but walk in his ways! (Psa. 119:1-3 ESV).

I love the passion of this Psalm. When I read it, I hear the conversation between the psalmist and God, and it becomes my prayer. "With my whole heart I seek you; let me not wander from your commandments," verse 10. I like that he makes it a request and not a statement. Another request, "Open my eyes, that I may behold wondrous things out of your law. I am a sojourner on this earth; hide not your commandments from me," verses 18 and 19.

A few more requests that both the psalmist and I make, "Teach me, O Lord, the way of your statutes; and I will keep it to the end. Give me understanding, that I may keep your law and observe it with my whole heart. Lead me in the path of your commandments, for I delight in it.... Let your steadfast love come to me, O Lord, your salvation according to your promise;..." verses 33-35, 41 (ESV).

All through this Psalm I find words to express the cries of my heart. And then I come to the last verse and find, "I have gone astray like a lost sheep; seek your servant, for I do not forget your commandments" (Psa. 119:176 ESV). When I read these verses, I am reminded of Jesus' words, "Fear not, little flock, for it is your Father's good pleasure to give you the kingdom" (Luke 12:32 ESV).

Like sheep need a shepherd, my soul needs a savior. It is not my own striving and struggling to be good enough, but the Father's good pleasure to give a kingdom.

Lessons from Grandma Frizzy

I remember when I first walked into her room. The room had the medicinal smell of a nursing home. She sat in an armchair, small and frail, but with an aura of peace about her. I was a teenager and had volunteered to adopt a grandmother. I was assigned to Grandma Frizzy.

Throughout my life I had been around older people, partly because the church I attended met in a nursing home. I had learned many things from my encounters with those who had a lot more life experiences. Some lessons were very simple: like how to thread a needle. Many times the lessons were about history, or about the different countries they had come from. The lesson Grandma Frizzy taught me was how to deal with depression.

Looking back, I realize my time with her was very short, but the lesson she taught me deeply impacted my life. She would sit in her armchair and I would pull up a chair beside her. Then she would begin to share her life with me. Hers was not an easy life, but she was a woman of great faith, and she shared with me how to be sure of what you hope for and confident about what you don't see.

One day she told me how she would offer to God the sacrifice of praise. She told me about a particularly difficult time in her life. She was suffering from a deep sadness when she read in Hebrews 13:15, "through him then let us continually offer up a sacrifice of praise to God, that is, the fruit of lips that acknowledge his name" (ESV). She told me that when she began to praise God, the sadness lifted and her heart was filled with joy.

After I left her I that day, I continued to think about what she said. I often suffered from depression, and was determined try what Grandma Frizzy had suggested. My first reaction was, "No wonder they call it a sacrifice!" I found that when I was feeling sad or depressed, the last thing I wanted to do was to offer God praise. And yet, as I determined to do just that, something happened. The chains of depression would begin to loosen their grip on me.

The aura of peace I had felt when I first met her had nothing to do with her circumstances, and everything to do with her faith. Hebrews 11 tells us that faith is being sure of what you hope for and confident about what you don't see. She taught me that, by faith, I could praise God regardless of my emotional state.

I am a grandmother now, and these are the lessons I want to teach my grandchildren: how to walk by faith and offer the sacrifice of praise.

Seeking to be understood I understand

My son and I were riding down the street when a car passed on a double yellow line, and he made this observation, "If I do something like that, I have a very good explanation. However, if someone else does it, it's because they are just that kind of person."

I have been praying through the Lord's Prayer, and when I get to the part that says, "Forgive us our sins as we forgive those who have sinned against us," I try to think of someone who has done something similar to me. When I see my own failures or the failures of those I love, I can be compassionate. But I can be very harsh on others.

I find again and again that my weakness, my need for forgiveness, becomes the place where God teaches me to be compassionate. When I am seeking to be understood, God teaches me to understand. Sometimes my mind obsesses about what someone has done to me or someone I love. I play the event over and over in my mind. It's only when I pray and ask God for help that I can get relief. Often God shows me myself in that other person, and, by His grace, I am able to extend to them the forgiveness I seek.

Lord Jesus, I so often come to You seeking forgiveness. Help me extend this same forgiveness to others.

There is no magic fairy dust

When Cinderella needed to have her rags exchanged for a gown, her fairy godmother took the wand, and with the will-o'-the-wisp and a little fairy dust, the transformation took place. I have rags that clothe my soul, rags of anger and bitterness. I am praying, but I'm not seeing any fairy dust.

Sometimes I am haunted by things that anger and embitter me. Sometimes those things are big, like the gashes of a knife; sometimes they are small, like the bite of a flea on a hot summer's night. Big or small, the effect seems the same. My soul is stained with hurt, like fingers stained from berry picking.

It's been like that for me all week. Past wounds, present wounds, wounds intentionally given, wounds unintentionally given, going round and round inside my head. But something else is taking place too. Prayer.

I don't want to be angry; I don't want to be bitter; so I've been praying. But I haven't experienced any fairy dust yet.

I did decide to memorize Psalm 119. I keep deciding to memorize Psalm 119 without success. This time I thought I'd start with verses 153 to 160. I am glad that God chooses the dull and not to bright to be His children, because otherwise I'd have no hope at all. I have spent this whole week on two verses. I repeat them in my head, and then I forget them. If only

I could forget these tormenting thoughts as easily as I can forget God's word.

Yet, as I go back to these verses again and again, they are the basis of my prayer. "Look upon my suffering and rescue me, for I have not forgotten your instruction. Argue my case; take my side! Protect my life like you promised" (NTL). There is no fairy dust, but living in this broken world and calling on my Savior, something is happening. There is a change in the direction of my thoughts.

I wonder, could it be that this might be abiding? Could it be that, because there has been no instant relief, that it has caused me to long for Him at night, and in the morning to yearn for my Redeemer? With my weak mind I cling to His strong words. With my feeble clutching I find I am being held in a strong grip of grace. Could this be what Jesus was talking about when He said for me to abide in Him and He would abide in me?

At first this week all I could think about was the hurt, the disappointment, the things I wanted to change but couldn't. Truly, I wanted some magic answer to my prayer that would take away the stain of disappointment in my soul. What God gave me was a struggle that brought me to Him. I feel the light of His presence taking residence within me. Abiding yes, yes this is abiding!

There is no magic fairy dust but I think the abiding will bear fruit!

You can't fight flesh with flesh

I saw myself more clearly portrayed in the family movies then I ever have in my reflection in my mirror at home. There I was, eating a big piece of cake. Was it really me? Did I really look like that? Next was the scene of a hike my sisters and I had taken. My sisters are in good shape and, though the path was steep, they were obviously taking it in their stride. Then the camera looked back to where I was. It was not an easy walk for me. One sister had decided to keep me company, but she didn't want to lose the benefit of her power walk so she was walking back and forth in front of me. By the time we reached the top of the hill she had probably walked twice or even three times as far as I had, yet I was the one out of breath. It was a funny family movie...well... kind of funny.

Have you ever heard of a besetting sin? It's mentioned in Hebrews 12:1b: "Let us also lay aside every weight, and sin which clings so closely, and let us run with endurance the race that is set before us" (ESV). I have a sin like that. The reason it clings so closely is that I don't fully want to give it up. My sin of gluttony springs from my sin of rebellion. Joy is a fruit of the Spirit, but there is a counterfeit called pleasure. Just as joy is produced from my union with the Spirit, I find a fleshly pleasure in my gluttony. How bad can it be, really? "To set the mind on the flesh is death, but to set the mind on the Spirit is life and peace" (Rom. 8:6 ESV).

I find a parallel idea in the Old Testament. Over and over I find the phrase, "He did what was right in the eyes of the Lord.... The high places, however, were not removed, and the people continued to offer sacrifices and burnt incense there." These were good kings that just held back a little. Then there was Hezekiah, "And he did what was right in the eyes of the Lord.... He removed the high places.... He trusted in the Lord, the God Israel.... For he held fast to the Lord. He did not depart from following him.... And the Lord was with him; wherever he went out, he prospered" (2 Ki. 18:3-7 ESV).

Do you want to know why this sin still clings to me? Because I have a hard time letting it go. I have tried over and over. When I fail I give up and sigh, "At least I tried." What does it take to get rid of this besetting sin? What does it take to remove this high place in my life?

When I look at Hebrews I find the answer. In fact, it's in the same sentence that talks about the sin that clings to me. "And let us run with endurance the race that is set before us, looking to Jesus, the founder and perfecter of our faith" (Heb. 12:1-2 ESV). My problem is I've tried to fight flesh with flesh. Another book, another program, if I try a little harder I'll get it this time. I need faith, not flesh.

I think God allows these struggles in our lives to showcase our desperate need for a savior. My sin of gluttony constantly brings me to a place of humility. I need help. I am comforted by the words I find in Romans 8:11: "If the Spirit of him who raised Jesus from the dead dwells in you, he who raised Christ Jesus from the dead will also give life to your mortal bodies through his Spirit who dwells in you" (ESV).

Lord Jesus, here I am again. I don't want to hold back. I want to give myself to You completely. I want to be like the cloud of witnesses spoken of in Hebrews 11 who walked by faith. Help me to be like Hezekiah who fully obeyed You. Help me to walk in Your Spirit. Meet me now in this place of weakness and show me Your strength!

I just wanted to help!

I was just trying to help! Why was it so hard? My husband and I had decided to have people who didn't have anywhere else to go come live with us. It sounded very noble to me to first. What it really was was exposing.

I thought I was a pretty good person, but shortly into my hospitable adventure I saw myself in a different light. I thought I was selfless, but discovered I was selfish. I thought I was kind, but found instead it was only a mask. I thought I wanted to introduce others to the Savior, but found instead I wanted to BE the savior.

How could this have happened to me? As a child I had always enjoyed reading saint stories. I guess that would be the Catholic equivalent of reading missionary stories. From the comfort of home I would daydream about sacrificing for Jesus. However, when the opportunity came, I found that I valued my comfort more than I knew.

The painful realization of my inadequacy drove me to my knees. I could not by will or determination be the person I really wanted to be. I was confused and disillusioned. What I found was that that was a good place to start. If you don't jump in the water, you will never learn how to swim. If you never leave your comfort zone, you will not encounter The Comforter.

I just wanted to help, and in the process I found that I was the one who needed help. In my attempt to, "Deny myself, take up my cross and follow Him," I found it could only be done if I was empowered by His Spirit. I guess the pain I encountered could be considered growing pains.

The experiment

"Let no corrupting talk come out of your mouths, but only such as is good for building up, as fits the occasion, that it may give grace to those who hear" (Eph. 4:29 ESV). Okay, I won't. That was to be my new law: I would not allow any corrupting, unhealthy, unwholesome words out of my mouth.

You would think by now I'd get it: the law doesn't correct sinful behavior, it just exposes it. My experiment with only saying things that were good for building people up, etc., was very exposing. I found myself confronted again and again with my unkind words. Sometimes the unkindness were veiled, but they were destructive nonetheless.

When I determined to practice guarding my tongue, I exposed my heart. This became a place of confession and surrender. What the law exposes, grace can correct. Once more I found myself totally dependent on God's Spirit; dependent and determined to obey God's word. I must add that this is a very humbling process.

Since my words exposed my heart, I thought it might be a good idea to apply Philippians 4:8: "Finally, brothers, whatever is true, whatever is honorable, whatever is just, whatever is pure, whatever is lovely , whatever is commendable, if there is any excellence, if there is anything worthy of praise, think about these things" (ESV). Do you know what a verse like this does to your social life! Have you ever tried to apply this to a movie or a television show or a book you're reading?

Just picture this scene: you're enjoying an evening while watching a show, and you begin to be aware that you are entertaining yourself with impurity, and there is little or nothing honorable or commendable about the show either. This drives me crazy. I just want to amuse myself, I don't want to think. The problem is, I am thinking, but not about the things listed in this verse. The problem is magnified if I am with other people, because then I'm afraid I will come across as "holier than thou."

Back I go to that place of confession and surrender.

Lord, You know me. However, I really don't know myself. I think I'm a good person until I try to obey Your word, and then I find out how sinful I really am. When I see my true self in the light of Your word, I also see my true need for a Savior. When I determine to walk according to Your word, I find my determination is inadequate. Then I remember You not only gave me Yourself as a Savior, but You gave me Your Spirit as well. Take me, Lord, to a deeper surrender; a place where my tongue reflects a heart and mind controlled by the love of Christ. In this place I find the peace that passes understanding.

She walked!

Freshman year: "Mrs. Jones, your daughter's blood count is low. We want to give her a transfusion." "Mama, I'll be alright. I want to keep going." She did.

Sophomore Year: "The tumor is malignant. The biopsy shows cancer." "Mama, I can do it. I don't need to drop out this semester!" She was too sick to keep going. She had to lose that semester. She went back for the second semester. She was sick, but she went back.

Junior Year: Two weeks before the end of the second semester, "Mama, I'm so sick. I'm so sick, I can't stay awake." The words were spoken through her tears. I drove four and a half hours, trying to see through my tears. "Mrs. Jones, your daughter has mono. I smiled. It wasn't cancer. "Mama, I can finish the semester. Let me try." But she was too sick. She tried, but she was too sick. She lost another semester.

The summer between her Junior and Senior Year, we wait for the results of the CT Scan. I watch my daughter go from pale to gray. She is so sick. She is having trouble staying awake. "Mama, I feel so close to God. This has been worth it, because I know He is real!" The results come back negative. I weep with gratitude.

Senior Year, "Mama, I want to walk with my class!" I feel the tears sting my eyes. She's a full year behind her class now. She is still sick, but she is so determined. "O, Lord, have mercy on my child. O, Lord, have mercy on my child!"

Yesterday, I watched my daughter walk with her class. She walked across the stage and got her college diploma. She graduated cum laude with a degree in Biology. I cried.

O, Lord, thank You for Your mercy and Your grace! Thank You for showing me what walking by faith looks like. Thank You for letting me see my child become a beautiful woman. Thank You for letting her walk with her class.

My prayer

Lord, help me care more about understanding other people and less about trying to make people understand me. This doesn't come natural to me. I need Your help.

Lord, Your word says to be quick to hear, slow to speak, and slow to angry; but I've got it all turned around. First I get angry, then I'm quick to respond in anger. Often I've never even heard what the other person was trying to say. I want desperately for people to look beyond my words and care enough to look into my heart. Please Lord; show me how to do that when I'm with other people.

Lord, show me how to care about others more than I do myself. Help me to love them so much that I'm willing to speak when to keep silent would be to keep safe. But, Lord, help me to keep silent when to speak is just to justify myself or promote my own agenda. And Lord, I desperately need to know the difference.

Help me to be humble except in one area of life. When I come before You in prayer, I ask for holy boldness. You have promised that if I ask anything in Your name, You would give it to me. You told me that I didn't have because I didn't ask. Lord, I don't want to miss out on anything You have for me, so in this area make me bold!

And last of all, Lord, thank You in advance.

Freed from worry free to wonder

It was the winter of 1960. It was the year of the ice storm. All the trees were sheathed in ice. There was no electricity because of the storm. This meant my whole family was camping in the living room, including my baby brother who was born during the storm. The fireplace provided both heat and a place to cook meals. How much fun can one child have!

I'm not sure my mother would remember the storm as pleasantly as I do. When the fireplace caught fire, I remember the excitement of all of us slipping and sliding down the stairs; Mother gingerly navigated the frozen stairs carrying her newborn son while her other seven children, ranging from age nine and younger, laughed and slid in front of her. Most of our neighbors had left their mountain homes during the storm to find shelter where they could have electricity. Luckily, Mother found a neighbor who had come to check on her home and was able to help Mother contact the fire department.

I considered both the storm and even the fire to be a grand adventure. I was a child. I had total confidence in my parents to take care of me. It didn't matter if I had a lot or a little, because I always had enough. I was able to marvel at the way the trees looked, sparkling with ice. Everything around me caused me to be filled with wonder and delight.

My adult daughter came home for a visit and she woke me in the middle of the night. The cares of the world were heavy on her mind. "Mom, will you come and sit with me a while?" We sat together, my arm around her shoulder. Then I reminded her of what she already knew. "Look at the birds of the air; they do not sow or reap or store away in barns, and yet your heavenly Father feeds them. Are you not much more valuable than they?... See how the lilies of the field grow. They do not labor or spin. Yet I tell you that not even Solomon in all his splendor was dressed like one of these" (Matt. 6:26-29 NIV).

As we sat together, wrapped in the quiet of the night, we both remembered the words of Jesus. "Do not worry, saying, 'What shall we eat?' or 'What shall we drink' or 'What shall we wear?' For the pagans run after all these things, and your heavenly Father knows that you need them. But seek first his kingdom and his righteousness, and all these things will be given you as well. Therefore, do not worry about tomorrow, for tomorrow will worry about itself. Each day has enough trouble of its own" (Matt. 6:31-34 NIV).

Whenever I begin to worry, I lose my sense of wonder. When I allow anxiety to paralyze me, I am no longer free to do the tasks that lay before me. When I forget I have a heavenly Father who loves me, I forget to seek His kingdom and His righteousness and I get lost in the storm around me.

Lord Jesus, I want to walk in childlike faith. Help me to let go of worry and take hold of wonder. Fill me today with the wonder of Your love. Let me seek Your kingdom and Your righteousness today with the heart of a child who knows she's loved and cared for. And one more thing: let me share this joy with others!

There was a warrant for my arrest!

There was a warrant out for my arrest!

Let me start at the beginning. Once, when I was a new driver, I failed to recognize that I was in a school zone. I saw the blue lights flashing. I started crying. I did not get a speeding ticket, I got a reckless driving ticket!

Because I got a reckless driving ticket, I had to go to court. Did I mention I was a new driver? I was still trying to figure out how to maneuver all the one-way streets in town. I didn't know how to get to the courthouse. I panicked as I drove round and round town, trying to find where I was supposed to go. When I finally found where I was supposed to be, the lady behind the desk told me coolly," You missed your court date and there is now a warrant out for your arrest." Once more the tears came.

They rescheduled my court date. I was there early. I was terrified! A man sat beside me and I began to pour out my story. After listening, he told me to sit there and wait for him. I had no plans of moving. When he came back, he told me he was a lawyer and had gone back and talked to the judge on my behalf and I was free to go.

I was the kind of kid that wanted to follow the rules. I wanted to do things right. However, that didn't keep me from getting a reckless driving ticket. Even though I didn't realize I was in a school zone, it didn't change the fact that I was in a school zone. I didn't mean to miss my court date, but that didn't change the reality that I did miss it and ended up with a warrant for my arrest. Sometimes no matter how I tried I'm just not good enough.

"I will ask the Father, and he will give you another Advocate, who will never leave you" (John 14:16 NLT). One definition for advocate is to speak, plead, to argue in favor of. I experienced that in the courtroom so very long ago. In some ways I experience this on a daily basis. No matter how hard I try, I still mess up. What a comfort to know I have an Advocate.

Lord Jesus, thank You so much for sending me Your Spirit.

Behold the extravagance of God!

I was shocked when I came into her hospital room. She looked so weak. I knew she had had surgery, but I wasn't expecting to see her so weak.

After greeting me, she directed my attention to the beautiful flower arrangement that had been sent to her. I have never forgotten the words she said, "Behold the extravagance of God! God created this beauty whether anyone saw it or not." What my aunt was doing was what she has always done for me. She wasn't just directing my attention to the flowers, but to the Creator.

Together my aunt and I looked at the beautiful flowers. Until she called my attention to them, they had simply been part of the hospital room. Suddenly, while looking at these beautiful flowers, my heart was lifted. I would not have taken the time to notice the beauty that God had created if she hadn't pointed it out. Yet the flowers would have been there with or without my appreciation. I realized that day that I was surrounded not only by the extravagant beauty God has created, but also by the extravagant love He has given me.

"Be still, and know that I am God" (Psa. 46:10 NIV). God is God whether I see it or not. Sometimes I get so caught up in what I'm doing that I lose sight of Him. This usually causes me anxiety. When I become overwhelmed, I go sit in the woods and quiet myself. My goal is simple. I look until I can see; I listen until I can hear. "His invisible attributes, namely, his eternal power and divine nature, have been clearly perceived, ever since the creation of the world, in the things that have been made" (Rom. 1:20 ESV). When I take the time to enjoy the beauty God has created, I rest in His love for me as well.

Last night I had trouble sleeping. There are so many things I have no control over. Sometimes in the night I feel so vulnerable. Last night was one of those nights. I got up and went to sit on my front porch. There was a quiet, but not a silence. I could hear nature singing. Next, my eyes began to focus on the silhouette of the trees that surrounded me. One by one the stars came into view. "The heavens declare the glory of God, and the sky above proclaims his handiwork. Day to day pours out speech, and night to night reveals knowledge. There is no speech, nor are there words, whose voice is not heard" (Psa. 19:1-3 ESV). I went to bed at peace, knowing that all this beauty was here whether I saw it or not. I rested in the extravagant love of God.

"Be angry and do not sin." HOW?

Have you ever stepped into a wad of slightly melted gun? It sticks to your shoe and every time you take a step the gum sticks. This is how I feel about the emotion of anger.

I know anger is a God-given emotion for our own protection. I also know sometimes I get stuck and can't seem to move on. "Be angry and do not sin" (Eph. 4:26 ESV). I remember when I first learned this. I found it very confusing. It left me with this basic question: How? How am I supposed to be angry and not sin?

I smiled when I looked it up and read the context it was in. It is always helpful to me to see where a verse fits in. When I looked up Ephesians 4, what I found is that the first verse gives me a clue to where the 26th verse fits in. "I therefore, a prisoner for the Lord, urge you to walk in a manner worthy of the calling to which you have been called, with all humility and gentleness, with patience, bearing with one another in love, eager to maintain the unity of the Spirit in the bond of peace" (Eph 4:1-3 ESV). Not getting stuck in anger means that my focus is not just on my rights but on, "maintaining the unity of the Spirit in the bond of peace."

I sometimes suffer from chronic niceness. What that means is that, in order to maintain a form of peace, I am not honest with how I feel. How interesting it is to find that the verse that precedes the one on anger states, "Therefore, having put away falsehood, let each one of you speak the truth with his neighbor, for we are members one of another" (Eph. 4:25 ESV). Chronic niceness is a form of falsehood. Sometimes to speak truth you risk making someone angry. But it goes both ways. Sometimes when someone tells me the truth about my fault, it makes me angry. This is messy, messy, messy.

I really see how important it is for me not to sin in my anger when I read the verse that follows the one about anger, "and give no opportunity to the devil" (verse 27). When I allow anger to stick in my mind, I open the door to the one whose mission is to, "steal, kill, and destroy." Farther down in the paragraph I read that I am not to grieve the Holy Spirit. I am to "let all bitterness and wrath and anger and clamor and slander be put away from [me], along with all malice. Be kind to one another, tenderhearted, forgiving one another, as God in Christ forgave [me]" (Eph. 4:31-32 ESV).

My question of how is answered as I read and meditate on Ephesians 4. Sometimes I need more than a verse lifted from its context. Sometimes I need to go back and find where the verse is and seek to understand what the full counsel of God is. "All Scripture is breathed out by God and profitable for teaching, for reproof, for correction, and for training in righteousness, that the man of God may be competent, equipped for every good work" (2 Tim. 3:16-17 ESV).

Lord Jesus, thank You for Your word that teaches me, rebukes me, corrects me, and trains me. Thank You for not only telling me how to live but giving me Your Spirit to enable me.

Jack's Pilgrim's progress

"Please come, Mimi!" It is really hard for an eight-year-old boy to be in a house full of adults who are content to simply talk. My grandson had been playing in the woods and wanted to show someone what he had created, but no one was willing to leave the comfort of air conditioning and go. Finally I said, "Yes."

He took me by the hand into the woods. What he had been doing in the woods was to recreate the story he had been told this summer of *Pilgrim's Progress*. He showed me what he dubbed "Vanity Fair." It was the fire pit we have in the woods. "I decided this would be Vanity Fair because this is an easy place to just sit and do nothing." Next, he drew me further into the woods than I really wanted to go.

It wasn't an easy path. I was worried about the possibility of getting ticks or chiggers. "How much longer, Jack," I asked, trying not to show how impatient I really felt. "Oh, Mimi, it will be worth it when we get to the wicket gate and you see Heaven." I had to smile; he was so excited about showing me "Heaven." On and on we went. My mind was torn between my "*Pilgrim's Progress* journey" and my great desire to get back to the air conditioner.

Suddenly, I looked up. Jack was standing by a fallen tree. He had a mimosa branch in each hand waving it. He explained that the fallen tree was supposed to be the wicket gate. The branches were supposed to make me think of angels. "Look, Mimi, look." I peered through an opening in the trees and got a glimpse of the lake with geese floating peacefully on it. "Doesn't it look like Heaven, Mimi?" My smiling grandson was waving "angel wings," sharing a hidden place he considered Heaven. Suddenly the comfort of the air conditioned house and adult conversation didn't seem so important.

Thinking back over my *Pilgrim's Progress* journey with Jack, I was struck by the lessons my grandson taught me. At Sunday school we had talked about spiritual formation. We talked about how the Scriptures teach us that we have a part to play in our spiritual growth. We are to be doers of the Word and not hearers only. We are to walk in the truth and to put to death the deeds of the flesh. I am often very content to stay in my comfort zone and not go on the *Pilgrim's Progress* journey at all. I like comfort and choose it over progress. Once on the journey, sitting around the fire pit and simply talking about the journey is the next best thing.

I don't think I will ever forget the expression of joy on my grandson's face as he stood there waving the mimosa branches and showing me a glimpse of Heaven. It was worth the journey.

"The dream" or soul rest?

The pilgrimage took place every summer. My father had moved to the South when he married, but the rest of his family lived up North. Often these trips began at night when it was cooler and the children would, hopefully, be asleep.

I was young, and my soul was at rest. I would wake to the low murmur of my parents talking in the front seat. Looking out the windows all I could see was the flicker of an occasional car on the road. I didn't have to ask where we were, my Daddy was in the driver's seat and I had complete trust in him. Sometimes the car would break down. We may have even gotten lost a time or two, but I wasn't worried. My Daddy was in control.

As I began to grow older, I began to have "the dream." "The dream" goes something like this: I am behind the steering wheel. I am a child and my feet don't touch the pedals. I'm not sure which is the brake and which is the gas. Suddenly I wake up in a panic. I found out this was a universal dream when my daughter was five and woke me up screaming. She told me what she had dreamed and I held her in my arm with perfect understanding.

"Come to me, all who labor and are heavy laden, and I will give you rest. Take my yoke upon you, and learn from me, for I am gentle and lowly in heart, and you will find rest for your souls. For my yoke is easy, and my burden is light" (Matt. 11:28-30 ESV). When I was a young child I trusted Jesus, but as I became older I began to have "the dream." "The dream" went like this: I am behind the steering wheel. All my family is in the back seat. I am in control. The problem is, I don't really know where I am going, or even how to work the car. I have no rest for my soul, but, instead, a deep sense of anxiety. Then from somewhere in the recesses of my memory I hear a voice calling to me "Come to me, Sarah, and I will give you rest for your soul."

Lord Jesus, I come to You. I want rest for my soul. I want Your yoke; mine is killing me. I want Your burden; mine is crushing me. I want You.

The effects of childlike faith

Her laugh was contagious. I was honored when she choose me to be her prayer partner. That was when I learned her story.

My friend had heart surgery in her early twenties. Life had not been easy for her, yet she had a childlike faith in God. She explained to me that facing her mortality at such a young age had given her a deeper understanding that God was in charge. She had learned to rest in His love. The evidence of her trust was her ability to laugh

My friend lived life to the fullest. Her passion caused others to want to be with her. We were at a party she was giving when I made the statement, "I guess we'll just have to wait till heaven to finally get a visit in." From the way she looked at me I was afraid I had offended her. I never saw her again. She died just a few days later. I think she knew her end was near.

At her funeral the preacher read a letter she had written for the occasion. I will never forget the opening line. She said, "I'll bet you never thought you'd ever really be sitting here at my funeral." It was true. Even though we all knew she had suffered with a weak heart, she was so alive.

A stained glass window for the church was given in her memory. Sitting in the church, with the sun shining through the glass casting its colorful shadow, I remember my friend. She lived her life with childlike faith. Sitting there warmed by the light coming through the window, I remember the words from Psalm 131: "O Lord, my heart is not lifted up; my eyes are not raised too high; I do not occupy myself with things too great and too marvelous for me. But I have calmed and quieted my soul, like a weaned child with its mother; like a weaned child is my soul within me" (Psa. 131:1-2 ESV).

Lord Jesus, I too want to trust You with childlike faith. I want to rest in You. I want Your light to shine through me and cast joyful colors all around. Oh, yes, and I want to laugh.

Severe honesty

Doctors are good at it. I think that's why a lot of people don't go to the doctor. They are afraid of the truth.

My neighbor had been sick for a while. Her daughter urged her to seek medical attention, but she refused. She confided in me that she was afraid she had cancer and just didn't want that fear confirmed. By the time she went to the doctor it was too late. I saw the pain and devastation her death caused, and couldn't help but wonder if it could have been prevented.

I realize there are areas in my life where I am not really honest with myself. I don't want to look at the truth, because I don't want to deal with the truth. I would rather be comforted by a lie rather than to be disturbed by the truth. I have also found that, when I am not honest with myself, a cloud of confusion begins to form. This cloud of confusion distorts reality.

Jesus taught that Satan is the father of lies. He also taught that Satan comes to steal, kill and destroy. To comfort myself with a lie is the same as comforting myself with a murder, a robbery, or destruction. Jesus also taught that I could know the truth and the truth would set me free. Jesus came to give me abundant life. So I must ask myself again and again, "Why am I afraid of the truth?"

Lord Jesus, show me the truth. Show me where I have allowed myself to be deceived by the enemy. Jesus, I believe you are the great physician. I come to you and ask for severe honesty. I also come to You for healing.

It's His responsibility, not mine

My husband and I were sitting on the porch swing in the cool of the evening, visiting. I began talking about how anxious I feel sometimes when I read the story of Eli the priest. He didn't correct his sons, and the results were disastrous. We rocked silently a few moments, then my husband spoke, "Sarah, consider this. In the book of 1 Samuel, you have Eli's sons, Samuel's sons, King Saul's son, King David's sons. Which one was the most godly?"

Jonathan, the son of King Saul, was the answer. Three chapters before I read about David and Goliath, there is a similar story of Jonathan and the Philistines. In order to reach the Philistine outpost, Jonathan and his armor-bearer had to climb a cliff using hands and feet. His armor-bearer was behind him. The Philistines were above him mocking, "The Hebrews are crawling out of the holes they were hiding in." Jonathan's initial response to the situation shows his faith in God: "Come, let's go over to the outpost of those uncircumcised men. Perhaps the Lord will act in our behalf. Nothing can hinder the Lord from saving, whether by many or by few" (1 Sam. 14:6 NIV). Just like with David, Jonathan's bravery caused the whole army to take courage and have a victory over the Philistines.

When I really see the heart of Jonathan is when David is hiding from King Saul who is trying to take his life. Jonathan finds him and encourages him with these words, "Don't be afraid…. My father Saul will not lay a hand on you. You will be king over Israel, and I will be second to you" (1 Sam. 23:17 NIV). Usually, the son of the king is next in line for the position.

What made Jonathan the courageous, godly man he was? I think it was because he anchored his plans in the purposes of God. Jonathan had a good grasp of God's faithfulness. He had a zeal for God's glory, not his own.

As I meditate on these things, it brings me back to my anxiety. Why do I feel anxious? I think it's because I have become more focused on my efforts and less focused on God's faithfulness. I often seek my own glory, my agenda, my success, and forget God has a bigger plan.

Lord Jesus, You alone are the author and finisher of my salvation. You alone are the author and finisher of the salvation of those I love. Help me by faith to be courageous and to leave the results to You.

True intimacy and the intimacy of truth

The first blog I wrote was, "Sarah, you are the most arrogant person I know." Hearing those words spoken by one of my brothers sent me on a journey. My first question was, "How dare he say something like that to me?" My next thought was, "Is there truth in what he said?"

In response to my brother's words, I have begun to pray for humility on a regular basis. It has been an interesting journey. One of the things I have discovered is that my intimacy with another person can be measured by the level of truth in our relationship.

Several times since I have been consciously praying for humility, people have said very hurtful things to me. My first response is always the same, ANGER. My next response is that I want to defend myself, and point out something I don't like about them in the process. Lastly, I want to put distance between myself and that other person so they won't be close enough to hurt me again.

What I am finding is that pride causes me to put walls around my heart so that people can't hurt me. The end result is that I am safe at last! I am safe: safe and very much alone. I think God created me with a desire to know and to be known. I think I was created with a desire to be understood and to understand. I think I was created for intimacy; yet intimacy is very risky.

One of the byproducts of praying for humility this year is that I have found my relationships with the people around me deepening. At times it has been painful, yet in the end it has been worth it. I realized that not only had I ceased to hear truth about myself, I had also stopped caring enough to risk telling the truth. The end result was that my relationships had become superficial.

Lord Jesus, please teach me to be humble. Open my heart to give and receive the truth.

The healing touch of truth

She woke up, but she didn't want to. She had been having her favorite dream. In it she was a wife and mother; she was loved and respected. She was awake now, and it was hot. There were chores to do. In her dream she was loved and respected, but in her reality she felt a deep sense of failure and shame. It was late; she was thirsty; her escape of sleep would have to wait till later.

The book of Isaiah says, "He Himself took our infirmities and bore our sickness" (Matt. 8:17, NIV, quoting Isa. 53:4). Throughout the Scriptures, I see Jesus healing by reaching out His hand and touching the one who is sick. When the leper came to Jesus in Mark 1:40, he knelt before Jesus and said, "If you will, you can make me clean." Jesus was moved with compassion and He reached out and touched him and said, "I will, be clean" (Mark 1:40-41 ESV).

Blindness, deafness, leprosy, these were not the only infirmities Jesus bore. There is also an infirmity of the heart and a sickness of the soul. It is often hidden from the eye, but it cripples just the same.

When she reached the well, she saw Him there. She was startled when He asked for a drink. Jews didn't talk to Samaritans. Then He offered her the gift. He said, "If you knew the gift of God, and who it is that is saying to you, 'Give me a drink,' you would have asked him, and he would have given you living water." She was intrigued, "Sir, give me this water, so that I will not be thirsty or have to come here to draw water" (John 4:10, 15 ESV).

She was surprised when He told her to get her husband. She replied honestly, "I don't have one." That's when His words touched her wounded soul. "You are right in saying, 'I have no husband;' for you have had five husbands, and the one you now have is not your husband. What you have said is true" (John 4:17-18 ESV). That was too personal, so she asked a question about religion. However, Jesus kept it personal when He referred to God as Father. "The Father," said Jesus, "is seeking people to worship him in spirit and in truth."

Her heart was pounding now; she could hardly form the words, "I know the Messiah is coming. When he comes, he will tell us all things." Jesus said to her, "I who speak to you am he" [John 4:25-26 ESV]. Her wounded soul was touched; her thirst was quenched.

Lord Jesus, You know my wounded, thirty soul as well. You alone see the hidden hurts; Your word reaches in to touch what only You can see. Your words of truth bring healing and the refreshment of living water.

Jack's door

"Jack, why do you have a shoe hanging on your door?"

Jack pointed out the other things he had hung on his door. At church they had talked about the armor of God. He had made a shield of faith out of cardboard; it hung on the door. He also had a wooden sword stuck in his backpack hanging on the door. As Jack pointed out the different items and why they were there, I smiled.

Doors lead somewhere. Jack's door reminds me of the truth of Ephesians 6:10-20. We are to be strong in the Lord and in the strength of His might. The strength of the Lord is something I put on or forget to put on. If I fail to put it on, I fail to stand against the schemes of the devil.

I had trouble with this yesterday. I forgot that I wasn't just wrestling with flesh and blood. I forgot that my real battle was with rulers, against authorities, against the cosmic powers over this present darkness. I forgot that Scripture tells me that there are spiritual forces of evil in the heavenly places. I left my armor hanging on the door and went into the world unarmed.

Lord Jesus, help me to be strong in the strength You give me. You have provided everything I need to be more than a conqueror through You. Oh, yes, and please help Jack to remember to always wear Your armor.

The key to the dungeon

I can't believe it happened again! This time Jack wanted not only me to go on his *Pilgrim's Progress,* but his mother as well. Once more I was reluctant to leave the comfort of the couch for the journey into the woods.

Jack had been excited to see that I had written about my last journey with him, and he wanted to do it again. Into the woods we went. Deeper and deeper into the woods we went. "I added more," Jack said. "I can tell," I responded.

Suddenly, Jack stopped. "You are now in the dungeon of Giant Despair. Pretend it's dark and you feel hopeless and you can't see a way out." It wasn't that hard to pretend. I had been feeling that way all week. I did feel I was being held captive by something bigger than me, and I was having a hard time getting free.

Jack bent down and picked up a stick."This is the only key that can get you out of the giant's dungeon. This key is God's promises." I had forgotten. I had forgotten that I needed to meditate on God's promises. I had just been drifting with the situations that overwhelmed me. It took my eight-year-old grandson holding up a stick to set me free.

That night I was tucking Jack into bed. "You've been going through some hard things, haven't you?" Suddenly Jack looked very vulnerable and nodded his head yes. "Remember what you told me in the woods today about the key? It's true." I told him I would bring him a box of promises I had from God's word. "We can read one every night. It will help all of us stay out of Giant Despair's dungeon."

Lord Jesus, I keep forgetting the things You've told me. I keep finding myself imprisoned by fear and doubt. Thank You for sending me an eight-year-old grandson who knew where to find the key.

When the yellow jackets swarm

All I knew was pain. I ran without direction, driven by terror. I had stepped into a yellow jackets' nest.

That was many years ago when I looked down and saw my legs covered with yellow jackets, but the memory still causes me to shiver. I was reminded of this yesterday when I felt like bees were buzzing around my head. They weren't literal bees, they were negative thoughts. Fear, anger, hopelessness, stung my mind. I am no longer a child. I have learned what to do when I am tormented by negative thoughts.

In the book of Ezra, God's people are rebuilding the temple after they came back from captivity. The people around them set out to discourage them and make them afraid. They wrote letters to the king accusing them. They succeeded at bringing the work to a standstill. That is, until Haggai the prophet and Zechariah the prophet came on the scene.

It was as if these two prophets took the curtains of Heaven and pulled them back, revealing God on the throne. Once they saw themselves with an eternal perspective, they were filled with courage. The people set to work, and the prophets of God were with them, helping them.

What I have learned over the years is that I am not at the mercy of the painful, hurtful things that happen in my life. Do they happen? Yes. Still, I am not at their mercy. I have a choice. One of the promises Jesus made was that He would send a Helper. He promised to send His Spirit and He did.

Haggai and Zechariah caused God's people to refocus. I too must choose daily to focus my mind on the truth of what God has done for me. I find new mercy every morning as I renew my mind according to His Word. I see the yellow jackets stinging my legs; I feel the pain; but with the hand of faith I knock them off.

Lord Jesus, here I am again. I am weak but You are strong. Show me today how to be strong with Your strength. Please redeem my sorrow and use it for Your glory.

Perspective, perspective, perspective

It wasn't about my honor, it was about His honor.

I woke up, but I didn't want to get out of bed. I had discovered that someone at our church had used our absence to gossip about us. The hurt I felt was so deep. I didn't want to face the day, and I didn't want to face anyone else either.

I lay there hurting, but trying to pray. I was struggling to find the words. I decided to just say the words Jesus used when He taught His disciples to pray. "Our Father, who art in Heaven." The reality of these words intersected my pain. For a moment I just lay there letting the truth of having access to the throne of Heaven penetrate my mind. But Jesus didn't just give me access, He gave me permission to approach the throne with the relationship of a child to her father.

"Hallowed be Thy name." Because of the gossip and slander that had occurred, I felt dishonored. Suddenly, as I prayed, I became aware of the truth: I wasn't praying "Hallowed be MY name," I was praying" Hallowed be Thy name." Suddenly the focus of my prayer shifted. I began to pray that God would redeem the situation and use it to bring Himself honor.

In the Bible there are sacrifices that are put on the altar and God sends down fire to consume them as a sign that He has accepted what was offered. I had, in prayer, laid my humiliation on the altar and asked my Heavenly Father to redeem it and use it for His glory. I felt as if a ray from Heaven came down and my prayer was accepted.

When I saw the day through the lens of faith, my view was altered. When I bowed in prayer before my Heavenly Father, I received the courage I needed to face the day.

An eclipse can only hide the light, it can never extinguish it

Thinking back, I can remember several eclipses.

The eclipses of my life have included times when the darkness surrounding me felt as if it would smother me. During these times of darkness I have sat in silence. I have sat in silence waiting, waiting, waiting. The Bible says that faith is being sure of what you hope for and confident about what you don't see. An eclipse is an invitation to experience God by faith. The darkness of the eclipse invites me to base my relationship with God not on what I can see, but what I believe.

"For whoever would draw near to God must believe that he exists and that he rewards those who seek him" (Heb. 11:6b ESV). Difficult times force me to draw near to God or away from Him. When faith is required I have to seek God, because sometimes I don't feel His presence. When light is hidden by the darkness and my soul reaches out to God in faith, something happens.

Often, in the silent stillness of the dark, all my brokenness becomes apparent. By faith and not sight, my heart cries out, and my cry is answered by the One who came to bind up the brokenhearted. When light is hidden from my view and I draw near to God by faith, I find in Him the One who gives rest to my soul.

He gives, "beauty for ashes, and the oil of gladness instead of mourning, the garment of praise instead of a faint spirit" (Isaiah 61:3 ESV). The reward I find when I seek God during the eclipses of my life is that, sometime during the darkness, my weakness has been exchanged for His strength. When my heart has sought by faith what my eye cannot see, I am given the privilege of bringing glory to my Lord.

Lord Jesus, sometimes the path You lead me on is flooded with such glorious light. Sometimes I walk in darkness. Thank You for Your promise to never leave me or forsake me. In the light or in the darkness, let me always walk with you.

Love is a verb

When I was a little girl, I liked to read books about saints. This is probably because I went to a Catholic school. The books had an effect on me. I wanted to be like the people I read about. I remember getting up to clean the kitchen when everyone had gone to bed because that's what a saint would do. I also would get up early and help Mother make lunches for everyone. That was no small job since there were nine children in my family. Of course, sometimes I'd forget to put the meat in the sandwich, and someone would get two slices of bread for lunch. Oops.

What I learned from this was that often feelings followed actions. However, I was a teenager in the 1960's, and the message was just the opposite. As a teenager, I was bombarded with the message that love is a warm fuzzy feeling. I have to confess that these two opposing ideas of love have been somewhat like a tennis game in my life, with the ball going back and forth from one side of the court to the other.

When I got married, I remember having a conversation with my husband. He made a statement I thought was helpful. He said, "Love is a verb." This made sense to me. When I read 1 Corinthians 13, I see what love does and doesn't do. When I read about God's love in John 3:16, I read God so loved the world He gave. In Jesus I see the one who came to seek and to save the lost.

One time a man told me that part of his wedding vows were, "I promise to stay with you till love grows cold." If that had been my vow, I would be long gone. My feeling of love can be as unstable as the weather in Georgia. The basis of my love has to come from the source of love. First John tells me that God is love. When I base my action on the source, the feelings follow.

Lord Jesus, thank You for loving me. You are the manifestation of the love of God. Please let Your love be manifested in my life as I choose to love others by my actions.

I think God does give us more than we can handle

"God will never give me more than I can handle!"

I have lost count of how many times I've heard this statement. It has, more often than not, been followed by, "That's what the Bible teaches." Sometimes I just want to let it go, but I can't. So I say, "Actually, that verse is about temptations: 'God is faithful; he will not let you be tempted beyond what you can bear'" (1 Cor. 10:13 NIV).

I believe that the difficult things I encounter draw me into the love of God. The overwhelming circumstances of life cause me to seek a God outside myself. If God never gave me more than I could handle, I would be God, wouldn't I?

What I believe is that nothing can separate me from the love of God. "Who shall separate us from the love of Christ? Shall tribulation, or distress, or persecution, or famine, or nakedness, or danger, or sword?... No, in all these things we are more than conquerors through him who loved us. For I am sure that neither death nor life, nor angels nor rulers, nor things present not things to come, nor powers, nor heights nor depth, nor anything else in all creation, will be able to separate us from the love of God in Christ Jesus our Lord" (Rom. 8:35-39 ESV). I believe this, because I have asked Jesus to be my Savior.

The difficulties of this life do not show my independence, but instead they show my dependence. God often gives me more than I can handle, but never more than He can handle. When I encounter difficulties, I also encounter a loving God. "When we were utterly helpless, Christ came at just the right time and died for us sinners. Now, most people would not be willing to die for an upright person, though someone might perhaps be willing to die for a person who is especially good. But God showed his great love for us by sending Christ to die for us while we were still sinners" (Rom. 5:6-8 NLT).

Lord Jesus, thank You for coming to me when I was utterly helpless. Thank You for letting the trials of this life press me deeper and deeper into Your love. Thank You that neither death nor life can separate me from Your love.

Humility in the cockpit

"Sometimes it is not so easy in bad weather at this airport to see the runway." A transcript from the Korean Airlines shows the second officer saying something like this to the captain right before the plane crashed into the side of a hill.

The Korean Airlines had been plagued with a high number of airplane crashes. The problem was traced back to the fact that the pilots were responding to the strongly hierarchical nature of Korean culture. Once Korean Airlines realized what was going on, they were able to retrain their Korean pilots, and their crash rate immediately declined to typical industry-wide levels.

"Where there is no guidance, a people falls, but in an abundance of counselors there is safety" (Prov. 11:14 ESV). This isn't the only proverb that talks about how important it is to have counselors. However, sometimes it's hard to hear them, because it involves humility. I often find, when someone dares to tell me they think I'm doing something wrong, a strong sense of pride arises from within me. It's as if they have wakened a sleeping giant.

It's not only receiving counsel I have trouble with, I also have trouble giving it. Ephesians 4:15 says we are to speak the truth in love. Yet I often hesitate, because I am more uncomfortable with someone's displeasure than I am concerned with their wellbeing. This self protection shows a lack of love on my part.

When I look at the teaching of Scripture, I see how God choose to put me in a community of believers. As part of this community, I need the counsel of others. I also need to care enough to give counsel when it's appropriate. Above all, I need humility to receive what is said to me. I also need wisdom and courage to know when to speak and when to be silent.

Lord Jesus, Your word teaches that both safety and victory are found where there is an abundance of counselors. Please help me be humble enough to hear wise counsel and loving enough to give it.

Making wise the simple

It all began with a statement I made to my mother when I was thirteen. "Mom, I want to have more faith." "That's easy, Sarah, faith comes by hearing and hearing by the word of God. I'll wake you up tomorrow and you can begin reading your Bible with me."

It was 45 years ago I began this journey of reading God's word. Mother was right: it has increased my faith. It has become my passion: "For the word of God is living and active, sharper than any two-edged sword, piercing to the division of soul and of spirit, of joints and of marrow, and discerning the thoughts and intentions of the heart" (Heb. 4:12 ESV). I have discovered that while I was reading God's word, it was reading me.

Often when friends come over, I see them checking out my bookshelves. I sometimes feel a little embarrassed. My friends are avid readers. I have heard them say that you can tell a lot about a person by the books they have in their library. My problem is that I am dyslexic, and reading isn't easy for me. That's why I am so amazed when it comes to reading the Bible. This seems to be the exception. I plan my day around when I will be able to read it. I resonate with the verses in Psalm 19: "The law of the Lord is perfect, reviving the soul; the testimony of the Lord is sure, making wise the simple; the precepts of the Lord are right, rejoicing the heart.... More to be desired are they than gold, even much fine gold; sweeter than honey and drippings of the honeycomb" (Psa. 19:7-8, 10 ESV).

My life has been shaped by my reading of God's word. "All Scripture is breathed out by God and profitable for teaching, for reproof, for correction, and for training in righteousness, that the man of God may be competent, equipped for every good work" (2 Tim. 3:16-17 ESV). When I read, I inhale deeply of the breath of God.

Nine years ago, I drove my son to college. "Mom, you ought to write." I smiled, because I know that, if you are going to be a writer, you can't be someone like me; you need to be smart. I knew I could speak, and I knew I wanted to share the treasures I had discovered from God's word, but I also knew I couldn't write. Nine years later, my son set up this blog for me and said, "Mom, you ought to write."

When Andrew set up the blog for me, I was studying 1 Corinthians.

That's why I am writing this blog. What I read was, "For consider your calling, brothers: not many of you were wise according to worldly standards, not many were powerful, not many were of noble birth. But God chose what is foolish in this world to shame the wise; God chose what is weak in this world to shame the strong" (1 Cor. 1:26-27 ESV). When I read these verses, I felt qualified.

Lord Jesus, I come to You in all my simplicity. By faith I want to share the treasures of Your word.

Divine appointments

I don't believe in chance. I do believe in a Sovereign God. I guess that's why I believe in Divine appointments.

Divine appointments don't come with trumpets announcing them, but sometimes with a simple prayer, "Lord, what do You want me to do?" Once I was trying to get a photograph of my children at the mall. The photography kiosk was closed, so I started praying for guidance. That's when I met a woman from out of town who was a new Christian. Her son was dying in the hospital. I ended up spending the next day at the hospital with her, simply being her Christian sister. I sat with her, prayed with her, cried with her. I was with her when she said goodbye to her son for the last time. It was a Divine appointment.

Another time I was at the grocery store. My groceries were in the trunk, I was driving away when I saw him: a man lying under his car. I got there the same time his wife did. She began shaking him violently. I was concerned that this might hurt him, and ask if I could help. I was there as he took his last breath. The couple had been from out of town. I spent the rest of the day with man's widow as we waited for the rest of the family to come. She was a Christian, and I sat at the hospital with her, praying with her, crying with her, simply being her Christian sister. It just seemed like my assignment for that day.

Once I met my Divine appointment in the form of a thirteen-year-old boy standing in the middle of my path. I was talking a walk in my neighborhood. From that simple meeting came a deep friendship. Over the course of years, he became part of my life. I was there when his son was born. I have been with him through his times of joy and times of deep sorrow. It all began with a prayer. I had met his mother the day before, and she told about her son. The next morning I had written in my prayer journal, "Lord, if you want me to be part of this boy's life, put him in the middle of my path." So God did, literally, put him in the middle of my path.

Father, I do believe that You are the Sovereign Lord. Please help me live my life with an open heart. Show me how to serve You in my generation; not seeing the interruption of my plans as an irritation, but instead an invitation to a Divine appointment.

Trust the instrument panel

"He thought his plane was horizontal, but in reality it was plunging toward the ocean." A pilot of a major airline was explaining to our class the meaning of the expression "flying by the seat of your pants." The pilot explained how a person's instincts can tell them one thing while the instrument panel gives them a completely different picture of the position of the plane. He suggested that, when the two are contradictory, trust the instrument panel.

Sometimes I get confused about very basic things. It's almost embarrassing, but I wonder if it's true for other people as well. One of the most basic instincts I can be confused about is how to express love. Maybe it's because I was a child in the 1960's when this was a hot topic.

Sometimes what I feel is right and what the Bible teaches don't line up. I can be going in the opposite direction of biblical teaching and feel like I'm going in the correct direction. It's times like these when I need to stop and look carefully and prayerfully at my instrument panel and change my course accordingly.

This happens almost every time I read 1 Corinthians 13. This morning I was looking at the part that says love "always protects, always trusts, always hopes, always perseveres" (1 Cor. 13:7 NIV). I had memorized it a little differently, "love bears all things." Either way, the truth of the matter is, I didn't know what it meant.

In trying to gain a better understanding, I looked the Greek word and found, "Beareth all things—*panta stegei*. This word is also variously interpreted: to endure, bear, sustain, cover, conceal, contain" [*Clarke's Bible Commentary*, accessed at godrules.net]. It went with 1 Peter 4:8 where it says, "love covers a multitude of sins." It was a picture of a roof that keeps the rain out, or of a ship that keeps its cargo safe. I see this picture of love as a vessel where something is safe and protected, as opposed to Plato's picture of a fool's soul, which he said was like a sieve.

One of the translations I found said, "She knows how to be silent." The "she" was love. Love seems so simple, but when I look at its description in 1 Corinthians 13, I see that love is so much more than an instinctual feeling!

Lord Jesus, when what I feel is right conflicts with what Your word says is right, grant me the grace to obey Your word.

The Dark Shadow versus the Light

I'm reading the book of Job again. Every year at this time in my One Year Bible I come to the book of Job. This book brings up the question we all ask, "How do I interpret the things that happen to me?" Things happen, bad things happen, but then how do we process them as Christians?

There was a song I heard when I was younger. It was a funny song, but the chorus reflects a way I often interpret the things that happen in my life. "Gloom, despair, and agony on me, deep, dark depression, excessive misery,..." [*Gloom, Despair and Agony on Me*, © The Grand Ole Opry]. We live in a fallen world; bad things happen; but when I let this chorus interpret my life, I am listening to a Dark Shadow.

The Dark Shadow tells me that there is no hope. In the darkness of that shadow, things look bleak. A shadow is cast when something is blocking the light. This is exactly what happens when I let the enemy of my soul block the light of truth, and cast his shadow on the events of my life. "What you see is what you get," he whispers in the cold darkness. "Nothing will ever change. There is no hope. Things will only get worse." What happens when I listen to the Dark Shadow's interpretation of my life is that I feel sucked into the vortex of gloom.

here is another voice that calls to me. It is the voice of light. In Psalm 36:9 I read, "For with you is the fountain of life; in your light do we see light" (ESV). I think about this when I think about Jesus on the Mountain of Transfiguration, bathed in light. Jesus was transfigured before Peter, James and John. His face shone like the sun, and His clothes became white as light. However, when He came off the mountain, He encountered a man wrapped in grief who had brought his demon-possessed son to be healed. The father was consumed with the plight of his son and did not see who Jesus really was.

Third John 4 says, "I have no greater joy than to hear that my children are walking in the truth" (3 John 4 ESV). So what is it to walk in the truth? I believe walking in the truth is to live my life interpreting all the parts of my life, both the good and the painful parts, in the light. The father who brought his son to Jesus did not see Jesus for who He was. When all the broken pieces of my life are spread out in the presence of Jesus, they are spread before the Savior and the Redeemer. When I see my life interpreted though the light of who Jesus is, I can gain true understanding.

Lord Jesus, help me today, by faith, to listen to the truth and walk in the light. Help me remember that, although the Dark Shadow can hide the light, he can never extinguish it!

HELP! There is a tick on my shoulder blade

I felt something biting or stinging, but when I looked I couldn't see anything. It was my left shoulder blade, and I couldn't reach it. First, I tried with my right hand reaching down behind my head. No luck. Next, I tried to reach my left hand back and up, but to no avail. No matter how I twisted or contorted my body, I could neither see nor reach the spot. Finally, I asked my husband for help, and within moments the tick was removed.

Sometimes, in my spiritual life, I feel like something is wrong. I can't tell exactly what, but something just seems out of place. That's when I go to one of my brothers or sisters in Christ and ask for help. When I look at the scriptures, I see that God chose to put me in a community of believers.

There are at least 59 "one another" verses in the Bible. Here are some of them:

"Wash one another's feet," John 13:14 (NIV)

"Instruct one another," Romans 15:14 (NIV)

"Carry each other's burdens," Galatians 6:2 (NIV)

"Admonish one another," Colossians 3:16 (NIV)

"Encourage one another," Hebrews 3:13 (NIV)

"Spur one another on toward love and good deeds," Hebrews 10:24 (NIV)

Community can be messy, but community is necessary. Sometimes I just need the people around me to help me understand what's going on. It is humbling to need other people. I would prefer to have all the answers and not need anyone, but that's my pride. And I've learn over and over again, "Pride goes before destruction, and a haughty spirit before a fall" (Prov. 16:18 ESV).

Lord Jesus, thank You for not leaving me down here all by myself on this pilgrim's journey. Thank You for letting me be part of a family of believers.

My sparring partner

From my earliest memories, depression has been my sparring partner. These are a few things I have learned along the way.

One of my first lessons in dealing with depression was taught me by my mother. When mother saw me becoming depressed, she would send me on a walk to a nursing home that was near where I lived. Getting outside, walking, focusing on someone else, all these things helped me as a child.

While visiting at a nursing home one day, an elderly lady told me how she handled depression. She told me the verse about offering to God the sacrifice of praise and thanksgiving (Heb. 13:15). I confess, it is a sacrifice to praise and thank God when your mind is overcome with gloomy thoughts. However, over the years I have learned that I have a choice. Depression and I meet face to face; the wrestling match begins. "You have no hope," he whispers in my ear. I combat the lie with the truth, and thank Jesus that He promised to never leave me or forsake me. On and on it goes, until at last I have the victory!

Another tactic my sparring partner uses is to try and attack me as I'm falling asleep. Sometimes he even wakes me in the middle of the night. Usually in the night he comes and tries to bind me with fear. He reminds me at these times of my weakness and my failure. He is so good at this. He's like a ventriloquist who throws his voice into my mind. I counter this attack with the verse that says, "I will remember you on my bed, I will meditate on you through the watches of the night" (Psa. 63:6 ESV).

Not long ago, I found a weapon he was using against me to pull me down into depression. It was my own tongue! I was letting his words come out of my mouth. This has been a very effective weapon in his arsenal. Again, I turned to the Word of God to gain victory. "Let no corrupting talk come out of your mouths, but only such as is good for building up, as fits the occasion, that it may give grace to those who hear" (Eph. 4:29 ESV).

Would you believe he has even grabbed the weapons I'm using against him and tried to turn them against me? "You are such a failure, he whispers in my ear. "Look at what you believe and look at yourself. You don't measure up, and you never will." This attack can really cripple me, because I see the truth of my sin. With tears in my eyes I go to 1 John 1:9 and whisper back, "If we confess our sins, he is faithful and just to forgive our sins and to cleanse us from all unrighteousness" (ESV).

I have had a genetic dispossession towards depression since my earliest memories, and there have been times I have felt like I lost the battle. There have been times I didn't think I could hold on anymore, and I was falling into a dark slimy pit that had no bottom. That is when I discovered my greatest weapon against depression. "If the Lord delights in a man's way, he makes his steps firm; though he stumble, he will not fall, for the Lord upholds him with his hand" (Psa. 37:23-24 NIV). Did you get that? It's not me holding His hand, it's Him holding my hand. His grip is strong and sure and loving. With Him on my side, holding my hand, the victory is mine.

Lord Jesus, I thank You for my weakness because in my weakness I see Your strength manifested again and again and again.

"...but not without hope"

Her grandson sat beside her, weeping. Her voice was weak, but her words were strong. She was dying, and she was saying goodbye. She told him he didn't have to hold back the tears; it was okay for him to cry. She gently explained that her body was worn out and the time had come for her to die. Then she turned to me and said goodbye.

As I sat there, the words of Ecclesiastes 3 flooded my mind. "For everything there is a season, and a time for every matter under heaven: a time to be born, and a time to die... a time to weep, and a time to laugh; a time to mourn..." (Eccl. 3:1-4 ESV). Yesterday, we got the call that Anne had died, and it was time to weep and time to mourn.

The sorrow is real, the grief is real, and yet we don't grieve like those who have no hope. When I think about the last time I saw Anne, and her parting words to me knowing this would probably be our last meeting here on earth, I also think about how Jesus prepared His disciples for His death. "Let not your hearts be troubled. Believe in God; believe also in me. In my Father's house are many rooms. If it were not so, would I have told you that I go to prepare a place for you? And if I go and prepare a place for you, I will come again and will take you to myself, that where I am you may be also" (John 14:1-3 ESV).

Last year I taught a Bible Study on Heaven. Anne was in the class. We talked about the mystery and the victory of what God has prepared for us. We talked about how the perishable body must put on the imperishable, and how this mortal body must put on immortality. Anne is the first of the class to graduate. She now knows the victory that is hers in our Lord Jesus Christ. For Anne, "Death is swallowed up in victory" (1 Cor. 15:54).

I stand on this side of eternity peering through a veil of tears. I see dimly, but I believe that Anne now beholds her Savior face to face.

Lord Jesus, You are the Resurrection and the Life, yet You stood at Lazarus' tomb and wept. Thank You that Your plans for us go beyond the grave.

Truth that goes beyond the circumstances

"Let me tell you what the truth is!" Then the list of circumstances began. This had begun when I made the comment that it sounded like spiritual warfare, and the first piece of armor is the belt of truth.

Sometimes it's confusing when you read in the Bible about putting on the belt of truth, or, "you will know the truth, and the truth will set you free" (John 8:32 ESV). This word truth is misunderstood as the undeniable things that are happening in our life. But I don't believe that is what it means.

Sometimes the very real circumstances of my life trip me up and make me feel anything but free. In fact, they can make me feel in bondage. For instance, when I have sinned against God and the consequence of my sin has changed the landscape of my life, the truth goes beyond what I see and what I feel. I'm sure the children of Israel must have felt that they were hopeless when they were on their way to Babylon. They had disobeyed God. Not only had they not listened to the prophets, they killed them! Now they were getting what they deserved. I would have felt that way if it were me. Yet, this is where I find God's reassurance, "For I know the plans I have for you, declares the Lord, plans for wholeness and not for evil, to give you a future and a hope" (Jer. 29:11 ESV). So, what is the truth here? God is bigger than my failures.

Sometimes I'm not only living with my own brokenness, but the brokenness of those I love. I keep going back to the story of the father who brought his son to Jesus. What was the reality that the father was living with? Over and over and over again the father witnessed his son foaming at the mouth, becoming rigid, rolling into the fire or water. The father had tried everything. He had even brought his son to Jesus' disciples, but they hadn't been able to help. This was his reality. But what was the truth Jesus confronted him with? "All things are possible for one who believes" (Mark 9:23 ESV).

Sometimes the circumstances of my life bind me and make me feel helpless. Sometimes my circumstances cause me to trip and lose my confidence of ever being able to succeed. But the Scripture teaches me that truth should be worn like a belt to keep me from tripping, and that truth is something that sets me free. The truth I read in James 4:2 is, "You do not have, because you do not ask" (ESV). Sometimes my payer reflects the prayer of the father who responded to Jesus by saying, "Lord, I believe; help my unbelief." The truth is, He hears my prayers and He understands my human weakness.

Whenever I need to see people who based their life on truth, not circumstances, I turn to Hebrews 11. There I read that the fact that Sarah and Abraham were past childbearing years did not keep them from the truth that He who had promised is faithful and is able to keep His promises. What I see in this chapter is that people who base their life on the truth of God are made strong out of weakness. I want to be like them and live beyond my circumstances and take hold of the truth of God.

Lord Jesus, the truth is, I have this treasure in a jar of clay. Sometimes I am hard pressed, but never crushed. Sometimes I am perplexed, but not in despair. The truth is that the all surpassing power to live this Christian life is not from me but from You, and You have promised to never leave me or forsake me. I choose to live by this truth regardless of how difficult my circumstances are.

Reflections on prayer

Maybe it was just a bad place for a mirror. I couldn't help but notice that whenever we were eating and my guests caught a glimpse of their reflection in the mirror, they would have a hard time looking anywhere but at themselves. Then I tried sitting opposite the mirror and I understood; I was captivated by my own reflection.

I think this is sometimes true when I come to God in prayer. My prayers are often more reflective of how I see myself than how I see God. Often, when I have sinned, that is where I want to start. "Dear God, please forgive me!" But this is not how Jesus taught us to pray. He taught us to begin with, "Our Father, who art in Heaven." The focus isn't on me or my sin, the focus is on a relationship with a father who is in Heaven. I am to be a child going into the presence of her father, and not a criminal going into the presence of a judge.

"My soul is cast down within me; therefore, I remember you" (Psa. 42:6 ESV). The next psalm continues with this focus on God and not self. "Send forth your light and your truth, let them guide me; let them bring me to your holy mountain, to the place where you dwell. Then will I go to the altar of God, to God, my joy and my delight. I will praise you with the harp, O God, my God. Why are you downcast, O my soul? Why so disturbed within me? Put your hope in God, for I will yet praise him, my Savior and my God" (Psa. 43:3-5 NIV).

When I reflect only on myself, I become downcast. When I remember that I have access to the throne of Heaven, and I let God's light and truth guide me to my Heavenly Father, my heart is filled with hope. There is a place for confession of sin; it is important to confess my sin; however, I believe that, before I reflect on my sin, I should spend time looking intently at my Heavenly Father.

Lord Jesus, thank You for giving me a pattern for prayer. Thank You also for showing me the heart of the Father to whom I pray.

"This Is It." Or is it?

My children would be shocked if they knew I was watching a DVD left behind by my younger daughter, but I was. It was a DVD titled "This Is It," by Michael Jackson. I was amazed at his talent, and saddened by the title, "This Is It."

I am reading Ecclesiastes, and I keep thinking of Michael Jackson. He was so talented; he won so many honors; yet I wonder if he would have agreed with Solomon when he said, "I denied myself nothing my eyes desired; I refused my heart no pleasure. My heart took delight in all my work, and this was the reward for all my labor. Yet when I surveyed all that my hands had done and what I had toiled to achieve, everything was meaningless, a chasing after the wind; nothing was gained under the sun" (Eccl. 2:10-11 NIV).

At the beginning of the DVD there were talented people from all over the world who wanted to perform with Michael. One of the young men being interviewed made this statement, "Life is hard, and I've been looking for something to shake me up a bit. I've been looking for meaning, a reason to live. This is it." Less than three weeks before "This Is It" was to open, Michael died. For the young man who looked to Michael as a savior, this must have been devastating. Ecclesiastes asks the question, "What does man gain from all his labor at which he toils under the sun?" (Eccl. 1:3 NIV). If this life is all there is, then I agree with Solomon, "Meaningless! Meaningless!" says the Teacher. "Utterly meaningless! Everything is meaningless" (Eccl. 1:2 NIV).

Today I am going to a memorial service for my friend. The majority of the world does not know her. The news of her death did not make the headlines of all the major newspapers of the world. Yet all of us who knew her were impacted by her life and her faith. "Now faith is the assurance of things hoped for, the conviction of things not seen" (Heb. 11:1 ESV). My friend Anne lived her life well. Amidst difficulty and hardship she was an overcomer. I believe the secret to her strength was that she didn't look at life and say, "This is it." She had the "assurance of things hoped for, and the conviction of things not seen." Today, we will celebrate, though our hearts are sad and our eyes fill with tears. We will celebrate a life well-lived. Hebrews also tells us that we are surrounded by a great cloud of witness, those who put their faith in something beyond what they could see. Anne put her faith in Jesus Christ. He is her Savior and she is with Him today.

Always!

It was just a little after two A.M when I heard it whispered in my ear, "Rejoice in the Lord always. I will say it again: Rejoice!" (Phil. 4:4 NIV). With that sounding in my ears and in my heart, I woke up.

I have this "thing" that happens when the seasons change. I don't want it to happen, but it does anyway. I begin to struggle with a sense of sadness. So I felt it creeping in on me yesterday like a dark mist seeping in under the door. It began to shroud my thoughts and my emotions. My prayer was as simple as that of a child; it was all I could muster, "Lord, show me Yourself!" Over and over I prayed this simple prayer as wave after wave of sadness swept over me.

Then I heard the command, "Rejoice in the Lord always. I will say it again: Rejoice!" I had been sound asleep, but suddenly I was wide awake. I got out of bed and I began to think about what that verse in Philippians means. I began to think about who my Lord is. As I meditated on who my Lord is, I began to rejoice. I couldn't help it. The reality that He is not only the Lord but the lover of my soul simply caused me to rejoice.

Recently I looked online for advice for people, like me, who want to write devotionals. The advice I found was that you must define your audience. As soon as I read that, I knew who my audience was: it's me. I am my audience. Like David in 1 Samuel, I seek to daily comfort myself in the Lord. I find the comfort that I seek, and then I just want to share it with others who are on this pilgrim's journey with me.

Lord Jesus, day by day I look for You. Sometimes I can see You clearly, sometimes You seem hidden from my view. But always, always You are there, the same yesterday, today and forever. And by faith I will rejoice. I want to turn and say to those around me, "Be encouraged, be comforted, rejoice! He is Lord!"

A view through the window

I have often viewed life like a big comfortable room; a room where all my needs are met. In this room there is a window, but there was no need to look out the window as long as I have everything I need. Yet when the comfort provided in that room begins to diminish, my attention is drawn to the window. Climbing up on a chair, standing on tiptoe, I peer out that window. Suddenly my whole perceptive is changed.

It was the year King Uzziah died that Isaiah saw the Lord. Uzziah had reigned for 52 years. His had been a prosperous reign. I think we as humans like to find security in what is familiar. When Uzziah died the question hung in the air, "What will happen now?" This is when Isaiah got a view through the window. "I saw the Lord seated on a throne, high and exalted, and the train of his robe filled the temple" (Isa. 6:1 NIV).

For Ezekiel, his vision of God happened while he was among the exiles who had been taken into Babylon. He had been from a priestly background. Ezekiel had been taken away from his home and I can only imagine the uncertainty he would feel about what would happen next. That is when God gave him a view through the window. "Above the expanse over their heads was what looked like a throne of sapphire, and high above on the throne was a figure like that of a man.... Like the appearance of a rainbow in the clouds on a rainy day, so was the radiance around him" (Ezek. 1:26, 28 NIV).

John was the last of the disciples, and according to the historian Tertullian he survived being boiled in oil before he was exiled to the island of Patmos. In his own words he was a companion in the suffering and patient endurance that was his because he belonged to Jesus. But he also received a view through the window, and this is what he saw, someone "like a son of man, dressed in a robe reaching down to his feet and with a golden sash around his chest. His head and hair were white like wool, as white as snow, his eyes were like blazing fire. His feet were like bronze glowing in a furnace, and his voice was like the sound of rushing waters.... His face was like the sun shining in all its brilliance" (Rev. 1:13-16 NIV).

I really like to be comfortable, but when that comfort is taken away, I am drawn to the window. When I look through the window of prophecy, I gain perspective.

The exchange

Once upon a time there was a little girl who owned a beautiful necklace. It was the most beautiful necklace in all the world—well, in her eyes it was. She wore it day and night. She loved her necklace so much she refused to take it off. It became part of her identity.

This little girl had a father who loved her dearly. He knew that the necklace his daughter wore was really a string of painted plastic beads. He watched as the paint chipped, but she couldn't see it. He wanted to show his love for her. When he saw the time was right, he bought her a string of pearls. He didn't choose just any pearls; these pearls were to show his love. The pearls he chose were flawless; they had a rare, brilliant sheen and a soft inner glow. They were both distinctive and precious, just like his love for his daughter.

"I have a gift for you." That was all he said as he held out the box. She opened the box, then stood looking up into his eyes. She saw reflected in his eyes a rare, brilliant sheen, a soft inner glow. From that day on, her identity became not plastic beads, but one who was loved by her father.

Lord Jesus, You once told a parable about the kingdom of heaven. You said it was like a merchant in search of fine pearls, who, on finding one pearl of great value, went and sold all that he had and bought it. Lord Jesus, I have been holding on to a string of plastic bead. I ask You, by Your Spirit let me see Your Kingdom clearly. Then it will be easy for me to let go of these beads. Let my identity be found in Your love.

Spreading out my concerns before the King of Glory

I learned to pray this way from two stories in the Bible, one in the Old Testament, the other in the New Testament.

The Israelites had been captured and carried away to Assyria. Now Assyria turned its hungry eyes to neighboring Judah. Surely this would be an easy conquest: Judah was smaller than Israel. Assyria used the tactic that had worked so well in other countries; first came the terror, and then the attack.

Hezekiah received a letter filled with threats. The letter listed all the nations that had been conquered. The letter listed the kings of those nation that had fallen to Assyria. Hezekiah was well aware of the reality of the threat. However, his response to the threat has become one of my examples of prayer in the Old Testament. Hezekiah received the terrifying letter and went up to the house of the Lord and spread it before the God of Heaven.

There have been things in my life that terrify me. When I become stunned by the events of life, I simply go before the throne of God and spread out my concern before Him. What I learned from Hezekiah is that prayer is sometimes simply spreading out before the Lord the circumstances over which you have no control.

I saw this pattern for prayer repeated in the New Testament when Mary

and Martha sent Jesus word that, "The one that you love is ill." No more needed to be said. They felt no need to instruct Jesus, but instead simply brought their concern before Him. However, I doubt they expected Him to wait till their brother was dead to come.
They probably thought Jesus would heal Lazarus, not raise him from the dead!

In both these stories there were situations over which the people had no control. I have learned from both Hezekiah and Martha and Mary that there are times when my prayer is simply to bring before God the things of this life that overwhelm me. But I have learned something else as well. I have learned that sometimes God allows painful things in my life to grant me the honor of bringing Him glory.

Lord Jesus, today there are many things over which I have no control. Like Hezekiah, I spread them out before You. Like Martha and Mary, I wait expectantly for You to respond. I lift my eyes to You and ask that You would be glorified.

Take away the chaff and leave the grain!

"Look at her! She is so serene, so saintly, so Sarah." About that time I wake up from my daydream.

In my daydreams I am very forgiving, no matter what the offenses are. In my daydreams I have no fear, but instead only respond to fearful situations with faith. In my daydreams I trust only in the Lord. I have no secret idols to which I go for comfort. But the pain and pressure and reality of this world wake me up from my daydream, and I find the true condition of my heart exposed.

The pain and pressures of this life show me the truth of where I am. My irritability is really a manifestation of my fear concerning the situation I'm in that I can't control. My overeating isn't just a bad habit, it's an idol I turn to for comfort. I believe God uses these broken places in my life to draw me closer to Him.

I really, really want to be forgiving. I want to be a woman of faith. I don't want to turn to anything but Jesus. Yet, when my life feels like it is careening out of control, I see a different me than the me of my daydreams. I also realize how prideful my daydreams really are. In my daydreams, I am the star. The truth is, I am in desperate need of my Savior every day.

My brokenness causes me to cry out for mercy and grace. It's not always pretty; sometimes the scene is downright messy. Like an operating table differs from a formal dining table, so my reality of who I am differs from my dreams. Yet I find again and again that I am grateful that the Lord exposes me.

"Surely God is my salvation; I will trust and not be afraid. The Lord, the Lord, is my strength and my song; he has become my salvation" (Isa. 12:2 NIV). When God allows the pressures of my life to expose the conditions of my heart and I cry out for mercy, I find Him faithful to be my strength and the theme of my song. Pride is broken and a true sense of stability is found on the Rock of my Salvation.

Lord Jesus, You alone know my heart. I am so much like Peter who vowed he would never forsake You. Yet, when he was sifted, he saw who he really was. I feel like I am being sifted. Lord, take away the chaff and leave the grain. Thank You for new mercies every morning!

Removing grave clothes

I was reminded by a friend recently that the Christian life is to be lived in community. I have a tendency to withdraw sometimes. If I am struggling with something, I will often disappear into my cocoon while I try to figure out what is wrong. Why? Maybe because I feel vulnerable; maybe because I have an image I'm trying to protect. To be honest, I don't always know why I retreat, but I know I retreat.

My friend reminded me of the story of Lazarus. Lazarus, who had been dead for four days, was called to life when Jesus "cried out with a loud voice, 'Lazarus, come out.' The man who had died came out, his hands and feet bound with linen strips, and his face wrapped with a cloth. Jesus said to them, 'Unbind him, and let him go'" (John 11:38-44 ESV). Jesus, who called Lazarus from death to life, could also have released him from the grave clothes, but He chose not to.

As I have meditated on how this looks in my life, I have thought about Ephesians 4, where it talks about unity in the Body of Christ. Just as Jesus called Lazarus to life, He has called me to life. Just as Lazarus was alive but bound with grave clothes that needed to be removed by the hands of others, so it is with me. The "calling" I see in Ephesians is a calling of community. I am called to "walk… with all humility and gentleness, with patience, bearing with one another in love" (Eph. 4:1-2 ESV). Others, while operating in their spiritual gifts, speaking the truth in love, remove from me the grave clothes that bind me. Then I, in turn, use the spiritual gifts God has given me to help set them free.

Part of me wants to be independent. I simply want to be complete within myself. I don't want to need anybody. Jesus has called me from death to life; isn't that enough? Yet what I see is not a call to independence but a call to interdependence. "Rather, speaking the truth in love, we are to grow up in every way into him who is the head, into Christ, from whom the whole body, joined and held together by every joint with which it is equipped, when each part is working properly, makes the body grow so that it build itself up in love" (Eph. 4:15-16 ESV).

Lord Jesus, You have called me from death to life. You have also called me to walk humbly before You in community. Oh, Lord, I choose to humbly submit to others out of reverence for You—letting other people's hands remove my grave clothes; willing also to help remove the grave clothes of those You've called to life.

Be alert!

It was just a simple cotton thread that I wrapped round and round and round about him. He was a strong young man in his twenties, and had volunteered to help me with my illustration. As I encircled him with the thread, I talked about how Satan whispers to us concerning our sin, "You can quit any time you choose; and, after all, what you're doing isn't really that bad." At first the young man was smiling; but as I continued to talk, he began to panic. By the time I finished with my second spool of thread, he was desperately trying to break free. There was something that Satan was using to bind him, and suddenly he became aware of the truth of my illustration.

I pulled out my scissors and explained, "The weapons of our warfare are not of the flesh but have divine power to destroy strongholds" (2 Cor. 10:4 ESV). He was struggling to break the threads I'd wrapped him in, but it took the scissors to set him free. I explained that strongholds were not destroyed by our willpower, but by the work Christ did on the cross. We are victorious when we, by faith, access the grace provided for us.

Again and again in Scripture we are told to be alert. Why? I believe it is because, "we do not wrestle against flesh and blood, but against the rulers, against the authorities, against the cosmic powers over this present darkness, against spiritual forces of evil in the heavenly places" (Eph. 6:12 ESV). I believe that one of our enemy's greatest schemes is to lull us into complacency, like a spider wraps its victim in thin silken thread until he is immobilized.

Lord Jesus, thank You that we are not powerless victims. Thank You for making us more than conquerors by Your love for us. Thank You "that neither death nor life, nor angels nor rulers, nor things present nor things to come, nor powers, nor height nor depth, nor anything else in all creation, will be able to separate us from the love of God" in You, our Lord (Rom. 8:38-38 ESV). But, Lord Jesus, help us to be alert against the schemes of our enemy!

Because You are worthy of my trust, I wait

"Wait for me!" Waiting for someone implies that you trust them.

When I see my children struggling with painful circumstances, I embrace them and whisper, "Trust in the Lord with your whole heart. Do not lean on your own understanding. In all your ways acknowledge Him and He will direct your path" (Prov. 3:5-6). What I am saying is, "Wait. I know right now things seem really bad, but wait. God is faithful. He will come through for you."

As I watch my children struggle, my heart is filled with pain. I want to take all their hurt away, but I am their mother, not their savior. As I watch and pray, I am embraced by the Holy Spirit who whispers to my spirit, "You must trust Me with your whole heart; do not lean on your own understanding." So I join my children in watching and waiting expectantly to see God's faithfulness in every situation.

In our family we have a saying that the first sign of maturity is delayed gratification. I believe this is true in spiritual maturity as well. How could the psalmist say, "**I waited patiently for the Lord**" (Psa. 40:1 NIV)? It was because he had experienced God's faithfulness to him in the past.

This kind of waiting and trusting also shows that I am looking for something outside myself to meet my needs. This is the encouragement I give my children, because I have known the faithfulness of the Lord. Like the psalmist, I have experienced what is like to have my cry heard. I too have been lifted from the pit and have had my feet set on a rock and my steps made secure. Yet, watching my children go through this period of waiting is hard. It takes me to another level of maturity.

Lord Jesus, I come to You watching and waiting and trusting. I join with the psalmist and say, "O my Strength, I watch for you; you, O God, are my fortress, my loving God" (Psa. 59:9-10 NIV).

Honey or Hurt?

Many years ago I went to a writer's convention at Moody Bible Institute. I learned a lot that week, but there is an incident that sticks out in my mind. At one session I had shared that I wanted to write devotionals. One of the women in the class told me later she had a Bible verse to share with me. Every time she saw me during that week she would say, "I must give you that Bible verse before this week is over." Finally, as I was packing up the car to leave, she came running up to me and handed me a slip of paper. I opened it and read, "The Lord God has given me the tongue of those who are taught, that I may know how to sustain with a word him who is weary. Morning by morning he awakens; he awakens my ear to hear as those who are taught" (Isa. 50:4 ESV).

This is what I experience morning after morning: An idea will come to me, a Bible verse, and illustration, sometimes a problem I am struggling with. And then, throughout the night, I feel like I am being taught. And when I wake up in the morning, I share what I've been taught in the night by writing it as a devotional.

I experienced it again this morning. Yesterday I read about the healing properties of honey. I read how it was used in the past as an antibiotic and would be put on wounds to bring healing and keep out infections. Last night I spoke unkindly to my husband. How do these two things fit together? When I woke up this morning I was thinking, "Gracious words are like a honeycomb, sweetness to the soul and health to the body" (Prov. 16:24 ESV).

In James 3:8 I read how my tongue can be a "restless evil, full of deadly poison," and yet if my words are gracious they can have the healing properties of honey. What's makes the difference whether my words bring wounds or healing? Jesus said it was a matter of the heart; that it's from the heart that the mouth speaks.

Lord Jesus, I want my words to sustain the weary. I want my words to bring healing. I want this not only for those who read the words I write, but for those who hear my words day by day. Lord Jesus, create in me a pure heart.

I was good, but not good enough

I just wanted to be good. Even as a little girl I wanted to obey my parents. I craved their approval and to have them smile on me. Can anything be wrong with that?

My grandmother gave me stickers for memorizing Bible verses. She began with, "All have sinned and come short of the glory of God" (Rom. 3:23 KJV). Next came, "All we like sheep have gone astray; we have turned every one to his own way" (Isa. 53:6 KJV). Then, "There is none righteous, no not one" (Rom. 3:10 KJV). I wanted to be good; I wanted to please my grandmother; I wanted those stickers. I memorized the verses, got my stickers, and saw the stickers as proof that I truly was a good girl, a very good girl. However, I totally missed the point.

I will never forget the day I stood before my grandmother ready to yet again be awarded another sticker for memorizing John 3:16, "For God so loved the world that He gave His only begotten Son, that whosoever believeth in Him should not perish but have everlasting life." I said it word for word; I was ready for my reward. But this time, Grandmother didn't give me a sticker. She began to ask me questions. Her questions revealed what I really believed.

What did I really believe? I believed I was not only good, but I was good enough for God. Grandmother reviewed all the Scriptures she had had me memorize. When we talked about what they meant, it became clear that, although I memorized them, I didn't believe them. Although I thought they were true for others, they were not true for me. Not only was I good, good enough for God, I was also better than anyone else. And so the Pharisaical heart of a little girl was revealed.

Grandmother kept going back to John 3:16. She asked me again and again, "How do we get eternal life?" I reluctantly bowed my knee before the Lord. I remember walking home and thinking, "I'm just a little girl; surely, if given enough time, I could be good enough." Yet, God's word that I had memorized was at work in my heart.

I am no longer a little girl. If you ask my grandchildren, they would tell you I am ancient. Over the years and through meditating on God's word, I have learned the truth of who I am. I now realize that there is no sin I am not capable of committing. Even the goodness I was so proud of as a child was a mantle of pride. Yet I am loved by God and all my sins were atoned for by the blood of Christ. This truth brings me to my knees and fills me with an overwhelming sense of gratitude.

Lord Jesus, when I read the gospels, I see myself as one of the Pharisees who stood in opposition to You because You pointed out their need for something greater than themselves. Thank You for not leaving me where You found me. Thank You for lovingly showing me who I was so that I could see who You are.

Only one author

There have been some dark chapters in my story. There are places I've been that I would never have chosen to go. Sometimes I've felt like God led me into my deepest fears. There is a verse in Hebrews that says that Jesus is the author of our faith, and I confess there have been times I wanted to take the pen and be the author of my own story.

I have found that every time I have been led to a place I would never have chosen to go, I find Jesus waiting for me there. There are lessons I learn in the darkness I could have never learned in the light. In Hebrews 12 it says, "Let us run with endurance the race that is set before us, looking to Jesus, the founder [author] and perfecter of our faith" (Heb. 12:1-2 ESV). Faith grows as I face my deepest fears, but live my life based not on what I see or feel, but believe. I surrender the pen; I am not the author of my story. Jesus is not only the author of my faith, He is the perfecter of it as well.

I think of the three Hebrew boys whose "race" led them into a fiery furnace. They were in the furnace, but they were not alone. When they came away from the flame, only the ropes that bound them were burnt. This has been my experience as well. I think I have faith, but when I experience His presence in the midst my pain, my faith is strengthened.

I have known this in my own life, but sometimes as a mother I want to shield my children. I don't want them to know the heat of the fire. But I must ask myself, "From what do I want to shield them?" I have to remind myself I am not the author and perfecter of their faith any more than I am of my own. In faith I watch and pray as Jesus takes them into places where He will reveal Himself to them, healing and releasing them from their fears, even as He has released me from mine. This I have found is simply another part of the race set before me.

Lord Jesus, You are faithful. Again and again You told me not to be afraid. Thank You for all the times You have redeemed my sorrows and changed them into places where I encountered You in a more intimate way. Thank You that You are at work in my children's lives as well.

What makes a person valuable or significant?

Do I have value? Am I significant? This is a question that often comes to my mind, and I don't think I'm alone. When I was growing up, I dreamed of doing great things for God. I listened to a radio program called, "Heroes of Faith." I was determined that one day I would be included in that lineup. Looking back, I recognize that part of my desire was to be seen as valuable and significant.

What makes a person valuable? I read in Psalm 139, "For you formed my inward parts; you knitted me together in my mother's womb. I praise you, for I am fearfully and wonderfully made. Wonderful are your works; my soul knows it very well. My frame was not hidden from you, when I was being made in secret, intricately woven in the depths of the earth. Your eyes saw my unformed substance; in your book were written every one of them, the days that were formed for me, when as yet there were none of them" (Psa. 139:13-16 ESV).

Where can I find my significance? "Because of his great love for us, God, who is rich in mercy, made us alive with Christ even when we were dead in transgressions—it is by grace you have been saved. And God raised us up with Christ and seated us with him in the heavenly realms in Christ Jesus.... For we are God's handiwork, created in Christ Jesus to do good works, which God prepared in advance for us to do" (Eph. 2:4-6, 10 NIV).

I see this illustrated when the disciples encountered the man who was blind from birth and they asked, "Who sinned, this man or his parents, that he was born blind?" Jesus told them that this blindness was not a result of sin but so that the glory of God could be displayed. Surely, God does not count value the way we do. I again read in 1 Corinthians 1:26-31, "God chose what is foolish in this world to shame the wise; God chose what is weak in the world to shame the strong; God chose what is low and despised in the world, even things that are not, to bring to nothing the things that are..." (ESV).

Again I ask myself, how can I know if I have value or significance? I find my answer in God's word, "Since you are precious and honored in my sight, and because I love you... everyone who is called by my name, whom I created for my glory, whom I formed and made" (Isa. 43:4, 7 NIV). I find my significance and value when I, by grace, do the works God planned in advance for me to do, sometimes by simply offering to Him my weakness to be a place where His glory can be displayed.

Lord Jesus, in Your love I find who I really am. Help me see others through Your eyes as well.

Neither do I condemn you

When they put her in her mother's arms, it was just a little taste of heaven here on earth. She was loved. Yet this world has a way of stripping joy from the heart, and so it was for her. Somewhere along the way she got confused; she got lost; and found herself face down in the dirt.

She knew she was guilty. She spoke not a word in her own defense but simply waited for the stones. She heard their accusations; they had found her committing adultery and had dragged her to the feet of Jesus. Her shame was great. She had gone with her mother to hear Jesus. She had longed to be His follower but she had failed. And now she was being presented to Him, not as one who followed His teachings, but as one who was deserving of death.

She knew the law. Leviticus 20:10, "If a man commits adultery...both the adulterer and the adulteress shall surely be put to death" (ESV). And so she waited, almost welcoming an end to her shame. The beating of her heart was deafening, and yet she heard His words. "Let him who is without sin cast the first stone." One by one she heard the stones drop. Then once more His voice penetrated her pain. "Woman, where are they? Has no one condemned you?" For the first time she spoke, "No one, Lord."

She called Him Lord. She had wanted to call Him Lord from the first time she ever heard Him speak when she'd been with her mother. But the world and her flesh got in the way. Now she stood before Him in her guilt and shame, hearing Him say, "Neither do I condemn you; go, and from now on sin no more." But she knew the law. She deserved to die, but accepted His forgiveness. (John 8)

There is more to her story. It is found in Romans 3:21-25, "But now the righteousness of God has been manifested apart from the law, although the Law and the Prophets bear witness to it—the righteousness of God through faith in Jesus Christ for all who believed...for all have sinned and fall short of the glory of God, and are justified by his grace as a gift, through the redemption that is in Christ Jesus, whom God put forward as a propitiation by his blood, to be received by faith" (ESV). She didn't know how He could forgive her, but she put her faith in Him.

The Law was the Law, and Jesus paid the price on the cross. "In this is love, not that we loved God, but that he loved us and sent his Son to be the propitiation for our sins" (1 John 4:10 ESV). This is the rest of the story. That day when she stood before Him guilty and covered in shame, He didn't simply say, "I don't condemn you." He took her shame upon the cross. He carried her guilt on His shoulders. He paid the price for her righteousness. That's propitiation!

Lord Jesus, I see myself. Your word says, "All have sinned and fall short." Oh, Jesus, I see myself. But I see You dying on the cross, carrying in the robe of flesh my sin, so that I can be draped in the robe of Your righteousness. May I never forget the price You paid.

Bound...but not by fear

"Rejoice in the Lord always; again I will say, Rejoice!" (Phil. 4:4 ESV). How? How can I rejoice when my heart is broken? Am I to pretend? Am I supposed to be a fake? Isn't that what the Bible calls a hypocrite? Is this verse telling me to be a hypocrite?

I need the next verse to help me understand how I can "Rejoice in the Lord always." "Let your gentleness be known to everyone." A horse is gentled when he submits to his master. My gentleness can be known to others when I submit to Jesus and become a "prisoner of hope." As a "prisoner of hope," I am bound by the love of Christ. Just as a horse can be taken onto a battlefield when their master is near, so I can face life's situation that cause my eyes to sting with tears and rejoice. It is because my savior and the lover of my soul is near.

Isn't this hypocrisy? A lack of honesty? No, because in this passage I am told not to be anxious but to pray (Phil. 4:6), and my prayers often overflow with tears. "Weeping may tarry for the night, but joy comes with the morning" (Psa. 30:5 ESV). I am not a prisoner of my circumstances, but I am a prisoner: a prisoner of hope. I have put my confidence in the person and promises of Jesus Christ, so in faith I cry out.

I find great freedom in God's word to grieve, to mourn, to lament. However, it is not grief that defines me, but joy. The sun always rises. I find that His mercy is new every morning. I wake bound to the truth that, "This is the day that the Lord has made, [I will] rejoice and be glad in it" (Psa. 118:24 ESV).

Lord Jesus, I am Your prisoner of hope, bound fast by Your unfailing love. By the power of Your Holy Spirit, grant that I might live by faith and not by what I see. Let my life be defined by Your promise: "'Though the mountains be shaken and the hills be removed, yet my unfailing love for you will not be shaken nor my covenant of peace be removed,' says the Lord, who has compassion on you" (Isa. 54:10 NIV). Thank You, Jesus, that the peace of God, which surpasses all understanding, will guard my heart and my mind. Gladly do I surrender myself to You to be gentled by Your love. When you are near, I can rejoice—always.

He dwells with the brokenhearted

"For this is what the high and lofty One says—he who lives forever, whose name is holy: 'I live in a high and holy place, but also with him who is contrite and lowly in Spirit, to revive the heart of the contrite'" (Isa. 57:15 NIV). What does this mean?

For years, I have read through the Bible, and my mind has been blinded by the glory of God as I read the first chapters of Ezekiel. I have tried to picture the cherubim, the chariots of fire, the likeness of a throne, in appearance like sapphire, the likeness of an expanse, shining like awe-inspiring crystal. I have tried, but could not truly grasp the glory of God and His dwelling place. Truly this awe-inspiring place is a fitting dwelling for a holy God, yet He also dwells with "him who is contrite and lowly in spirit."

Sometimes my vision is equally dimmed by the sin and suffering all around me. I see no glory; only darkness shrouds my vision. Then I hear the word of God penetrating my pain, "Surely the arm of the Lord is not too short to save, nor his ear too dull to hear" (Isa. 59:1 NIV). "The Lord looked and was displeased that there was no justice. He saw that there was no one, he was appalled that there was no one to intervene; so his own arm worked salvation for him, and his own righteousness sustained him" (Isa. 59:15-16 NIV).

Isn't this the picture that I saw in the gospel at the foot of the mountain of transfiguration? Jesus stood on the mountain in His glory, yet didn't stay there. He came into the valley and met a man whose heart and spirit were broken. Jesus showed that His arm was not too short to save, nor was His ear deaf to the cries of one who was lowly in spirit. No one else could set the demon-possessed child free, so Jesus did it Himself.

Lord Jesus, please give me the spirit of wisdom and of revelation in the knowledge of You. Open the eyes of my heart and let me know the hope to which You've called me. Please show me the glorious inheritance You have for me. Let me see the immeasurable greatness of Your power towards me; You who dwell in glory and with those who have a lowly spirit.

The Master and the canvas

"Are you willing to be the canvas upon which I paint my glory?" This is the question I hear as I pray. My response is simple, "Yes, Lord."

The picture to be painted on the canvas was predetermined in the heart of God before the world began. The painting is a picture of redemption and forgiveness. The colors gloriously reflect His rich and lavish grace. There is mystery and insight as each stroke of His brush reveals His love and His glory.

To be a canvas for God's glory is to begin to know His heart. As I begin to see the picture unfold, I count everything else as loss because of the surpassing worth of knowing Him. When I relinquish the right to make the painting of my life glorify me, and instead choose to bring glory to God, I also begin a quest to know what the glory of God is.

Part of the glory that I see is the resurrection of Jesus. And so I pray, "Oh, Lord, yes, paint my life's story with the power of Your resurrection." So the Master takes His brush and I see the splashes of color that represent life. The painting on the canvas is full of light and color and joy. It is a painting of victory. But there is more.

To be a canvas surrendered to the Master means I also share in His sufferings. These are the colors of a darker hue. Each stroke is placed with a gentle touch. These are not the colors I would choose if I were the one who held the brush, but I have chosen to relinquish my earthly perspective to His heavenly one.

It is hard sometimes for me to appreciate the artwork of the Master. Just as it is hard to fully appreciate any art if you stand too close to the canvas. The only way I can interpret what is being created is to look at it through the lens of His word.

Lord Jesus, I ask that Your redeeming love be clearly seen in my life. Please let the canvas of my heart be a place where Your glory is fully displayed.

Before I knew your name

I was getting ready to pick my children up from school when the phone rang. "Mrs. Jones, we're sorry to tell you, but the tests show a problem with your baby."

It was my sixth pregnancy. I had three children, two children had died. The news made my heart ache. I dropped to my knees and prayed, using Psalm 139: "All the days of my baby's life have been written in Your book before any of them came to be. Lord, You give and take away. I choose to trust You." I knew what it was like lose a baby. I had been bleeding for days, and now the tests showed a problem.

I got into the car and mindlessly shoved the cassette tape into the player. My car was filled with the voice of Sandi Patty singing "Masterpiece." The song was being sung to an unborn child who didn't even have a name. She spoke of the baby being formed in seclusion in God's safe and hidden place. After she finished singing, she quoted from Psalm 139, "For you formed my inward parts; you knitted me together in my mother's womb. I praise you, for I am fearfully and wonderfully made. Wonderful are your works; my soul knows it very well. My frame was not hidden from you, when I was being made in secret, intricately woven in the depths of the earth. Your eyes saw my unformed substance; in your book were written every one of them, the days that were formed for me, when as yet there were none of them" (Psa. 130:13-16 ESV).

I lost count of how many times I listened to that song. My children complained because it was their tape, "The Friendship Company," however, I felt I needed it more than they did and I promised to give it back after the baby was born.

I had picked out the name Stephen Christopher for my baby, yet by the time I got to my ninth month I decided it might be a good idea to have a girl's name as well. I began making lists, but nothing sounded right, so I enlisted the aid of my two prayer partners. On Father's Day I was at my parent's home and my mother asked, "Sarah, have you considered the name Abigail Divine? It is a family name." The next day one of my prayer partners called and said, "Sarah, have you considered the name Abigail Divine? My husband was preaching about Abigail in the Bible. The name means the delight of the father. Abigail would mean the delight of the Heavenly Father. On Tuesday my second prayer partner called, "Sarah, have you considered the name Abigail Divine?" I didn't need an ultrasound. I knew I was going to have a little girl and name her Abigail Divine.

When I came to the last week of my pregnancy I found it hard to sleep. I kept hearing the doctor's warning. "The baby could die at birth or be born with profound birth defects." I wanted to hear the song "Masterpiece" again, so I put the cassette in and found that I had broken it by playing it so often. I was desperate. I pulled it out of the player, lifted it up and prayed, "Lord, you are the Healer please let me hear this song again." I put the cassette back in the player and heard. "Miracles still happen for those who love the Lord. Trust in the Lord with all your heart. His miracles you'll behold." The next song was "Masterpiece." That week a healthy baby girl was born.

Lord Jesus, thank You for Your tender mercies. Thank You for lavishing Your love and grace on me. Oh yes, and thank You for giving me Abigail. May she always be the masterpiece you created her to be.

With hands held open

She gave me a picture of her hands, her open hands. Then she told me the story.

Her firstborn son was born with a cleft lip. When he was three months old he had plastic surgery, but the incision began to scar within a matter of weeks. She made continual visits to the hospital to deal with the scarring. Her baby was often sick, running fevers for no apparent reason. The effect on my friend was understandable; she became an anxious mother.

When her son was ten months old she was reading Psalms 127. She read, "Lo, children are the heritage of the Lord and the fruit of the womb is His reward" (Psa. 127:3 KJV). As she meditated on the truth of these words, her eyes were drawn to the preceding verses. "Except the Lord build the house, they labor in vain that build it…. It is vain for you to rise up early, to sit up late, to eat the bread of sorrows: for so He gives His beloved sleep" (Psa. 127:1-2 KJV). Her heart was convicted and she held her hands open as she relinquished her children to God. But that is not the end of the story.

Less than a week later she was back at the hospital. This time it was because her son had spinal meningitis. She was told that he might not make it through the night. God had prepared her heart, and she prayed, knowing that she did not have control over the life of her son. Her son lived, and my friend learned a deep lesson. She told me how, over the years, in many situations, God taught her to acknowledge that she had no control over people or situations. She learned that, with open hands, she is to relinquish everything to God.

Ah Sovereign Lord, how I struggle with this! Thank You for giving me friends who teach me by their lives to trust You. Grant me the grace to worship You with hands held open.

What does it take to see God's Glory?

It's been about a year since I began praying daily that God would allow me to have a humble heart. Most people who hear about my prayer ask if I'm crazy. Humility isn't like a package found under the tree Christmas morning; instead it comes from choosing to put pride to death. I was talking to a friend of mine this weekend about the things that have happened this year and their effect on me. They were not pleasant things, and yet God has used them in my life to humble me.

I woke up the next morning, after our conversation thinking about Isaiah 28:27-29 (ESV), "Dill is not threshed with a threshing sledge, nor is a cartwheel rolled over cumin, but dill is beaten out with a stick, and cumin with a rod. Does one crush grain for bread? No, he does not thresh forever; when he drives his cart wheel over it with his horses, he does not crush it. This also comes from the Lord of hosts; he is wonderful in counsel and excellent in wisdom." What I see is that God does what is necessary to make me useful. We have walnut trees. I use the walnuts, but only if I remove the hull. In the same way I believe that I am only useful to God with a humble heart. Sometimes it's a painful process, but I trust God because He is, "wonderful in counsel and excellent in wisdom."

Somewhere during the year my prayer changed. My focus shifted. I began to say, Lord, glorify Yourself." My prayer was a reflection of John the Baptist when he said, "He must increase and I must decrease." When I go outside on a dark starry night I can see the stars best if there is no artificial light shining. This is what I am finding as I pray for humility. When the artificial light of my own pride is taken out of the way, others have a better opportunity of seeing Christ in me.

Lord Jesus, I want my life to be useful for Your Kingdom. I want to decrease and have You increase. I want to see Your glory!

Shattered or Healed?

I was at a funeral yesterday, and someone quoted a Jewish proverb. It went something like this: When sorrow upon sorrow is piled on a heart, one of two things will happen. The heart will shatter and break and send out shards that will pierce and wound all those around, or the pressure will cause the heart to break open and it will be filled with the love of God.

As I have pondered this, my mind has been drawn to what the scripture says about the brokenhearted. "The Lord is near to the brokenhearted and saves the crushed in spirit" (Psa. 34:18 ESV). "He heals the brokenhearted and binds up their wounds" (Psa. 147:3 NIV). I have both seen and experienced the nearness of the Lord when the sorrows of this life have broken my heart and crushed my spirit. Yet, I have seen the other as well.

When my husband and I began opening our door to people in distress someone told me, "Be careful, hurting people hurt people." What makes the difference? I think I can find the answer in the same psalms that talk about God healing the brokenhearted. Psalm 34 and Psalm 147 talk about someone who is humble in heart. Someone who is humble in heart is someone who is seeking the Lord and crying out to Him when life becomes unbearable. Someone who is humble in heart is someone who hopes in the steadfast love of God. The opposite of that is someone who raises their fist then turns their back on God in times of distress.

Lord Jesus, when You began Your ministry here on earth, You said You came to bind up the brokenhearted. Lord, let me be one who always turns towards You and not away from You when the sorrows of life threaten to break my heart and crush my spirit.

A Prayer for those Overwhelmed by Life

The task was overwhelming! I felt like was being crushed by the load I was being asked to carry. It was then I remembered the prayer.

This prayer begins with a deep breath. When I was in labor with my children, this kind of breath was called a cleansing breath. The purpose of a cleansing breathing in childbirth was to give me an extra boost of oxygen in order to help me relax and focus. So I take a deep breath through my nose and then exhale slowly through my mouth while saying, "Ah."

The next part of this prayer has to do with worship. If I really believe that God is sovereign and deserving of my trust, how should I respond to this situation that I have no control over? My first response is usually to murmur and complain. I find this pattern in the Scriptures, but the problem is, the people murmuring and complaining are also rebelling against a Sovereign God who loves them. I sigh deeply, relinquishing the control that I don't have, bow my knees and focus on God's sovereignty.

The next part of my prayer has to do with my relationship with God. When my children were little, occasionally they would look at me defiantly and say, "You're not the boss of me!" I would always correct this misconception of our relationship. However, this form of rebellion against authority started in the Garden when the serpent told Eve, "Don't let God tell you what you can and can't have. Eat the fruit and be your own boss." This attitude didn't work any better for my children than it did for Eve. Again, after my deep breath, I bow my knees and then humble my heart. I acknowledge my relationship with the Sovereign God and call Him Lord.

Ah, Sovereign Lord! I am overwhelmed by what I see ahead of me. I feel crushed by the responsibilities I face, and so I humbly bow before You. As I pour out my heart to You, I am reminded of what Paul said in Colossians when he said that he toiled, struggling with all the energy of Christ that was working powerfully within him. May Your strength be manifested in my weakness. As I approach the difficulties of my life with humility, may You be glorified!

When the Valley of Tears becomes a place of refreshment

I was talking to my daughter after she had gone through her treatment for cancer, and she spoke about how close she felt to God. It reminded me of the Valley of Baca.

"Blessed are those whose strength is in you, who have set their hearts on pilgrimage. As they pass the Valley of Baca, they make it a place of springs..." (Psa. 84:5-6 NIV). Another interpretation for the Valley of Baca is the Valley of Tears. What can change the Valley of Tears into a place of springs and refreshment?

I have seen it go both ways. I have watched people go through heartbreak and become people who encourage others who are going through similar grief. I have also known those who became bitter from their difficult experiences and pass that bitterness to all they meet. The difference can be found in the preceding verse. "Blessed are those whose strength is in you, who have set their hearts on pilgrimage."

My daughter told me how she lay on the table waiting for her treatment and meditating on God. She found what she was looking for. She found her strength in God. But there is more to it than that; there is also "setting their hearts on pilgrimage." To set your heart on pilgrimage means you understand that this life is not all there is.

Lord Jesus, You have loved me, and by Your grace You have given me eternal encouragement and good hope. You have encouraged my heart and strengthened me and shown me how the Valley of Tears becomes a place of refreshment. Thank You for letting me see this transformation in my children's lives as well.

Dealing with Anger

I was so angry yesterday that I really wanted to hurt someone. And I think I would have if it hadn't been for my husband. Jesus said, "If anyone would be my disciple, he must daily deny himself, take up his cross, and follow me" (Matt. 16:24). I needed my husband's help with the crucifying of my flesh yesterday.

Anger is such a strong emotion. It's not a sin, it's an emotion. It's part of the way God chose to create us. I think it plays an important role in our lives. Anger is meant to protect us and the people we love from danger. When someone does something that hurts my children, I really get angry! Then what?! How am I supposed to respond as a Christian?

When my children were younger, I had them memorize several Bible verses about anger. I'm reviewing those verses, because I need to remind myself how to control this emotion. "A fool gives full vent to his anger, but a wise man keeps himself under control" (Prov. 29:11 (NIV). I think this goes back to what Jesus said about being His disciple. If I choose to daily follow Christ, I also choose to let Him be in control, and not my anger.

Proverbs also says that someone who is quick to anger acts foolishly. On the contrary, another verse says that "Whoever is slow to anger is better than the mighty, and he who rules his spirit than he who takes a city" (Prov. 16: 32 ESV). When I think about this, I think about how mighty rushing waters can cause great destruction. However, if that energy is harnessed, it can be of great value.

Lord Jesus, sometimes I feel so mad I just want to give full vent to my anger. But more than giving vent my emotions, I truly want to be Your disciple. I surrender to Your Spirit. Help me to be quick to hear, slow to speak, and slow to anger.

Let my people go!

When I was a little girl I would listen to the Negro spiritual "Let My People Go" over and over. I woke up in the middle of the night thinking about the words.

> When Israel was in Egypt land, Let My people go!
>
> Oppressed so hard they could not stand, Let my people go!
>
> Go down, Moses, way down to Egypt's land;
>
> Tell old Pharaoh to let My people go!"
>
> [Anonymous, *Let My People Go*, Public domain]

In thinking about the passion flowing from those deep, rich voices, I feel like I can hear the voice of God: "Let My people go!" God had heard the cry of His people and He sent Moses to Pharaoh to boldly demand that he let God's people go. But it took the blood of Pharaoh's firstborn son for him relinquish his hold on God people.

I see the parallel to Jesus' ministry. He came to seek and save the lost. When Jesus wept at the grave of Lazarus, I see the heart of God. When Jesus cried, "Lazarus, come forth!" I hear an echo of "Let My people go!" Death was the ultimate consequence for the fall of man. Satan comes to kill steal and destroy, but Jesus came that we might have abundant life. God heard the moaning and the cries of His people and He sent Jesus to say, "Let My people go!"

Jesus came. He came to seek and to save the lost. He came to those who were bound by Satan. He heard the cries of mothers and fathers who brought their demon-possessed children to Him, and He set them free. Jesus entered the poverty of the poor. He entered into the suffering and sorrows of His broken and bound creation. He came on a mission—to "let His people go!"

Just as it took the blood of Pharaoh's son to get the children of Israel out of Egypt, it took the blood of Jesus to set us free from Satan's grip. "For God so loved the world that he gave his only begotten son that whosoever believes in him should not perish but have eternal life" (John 3:16). God the Father sent Jesus with this message to Satan, "Let My people go!"

My response is:

Jesus, I Come

Out of my bondage, sorrow and night,
Jesus, I come, Jesus, I come;
Into Thy freedom, gladness, and light,
Jesus, I come to Thee;
Out of my sickness, into Thy health,
Out of my want and into Thy wealth,
Out of my sin and into Thyself,
Jesus, I come to Thee.

Out of my shameful failure and loss,
Jesus, I come, Jesus, I come;
Into the glorious gain of Thy cross,
Jesus, I come to Thee;
Out of earth's sorrows, into Thy balm,
Out of life's storms and into Thy calm,
Out of distress to jubilant psalm,
Jesus, I come to Thee.

Out of unrest and arrogant pride,
Jesus, I come, Jesus, I come;
Into Thy blessed will to abide,
Jesus, I come to Thee;
Out of myself to dwell in Thy love,
Out of despair, into raptures above,
Upward for aye on wings like a dove,
Jesus, I come to Thee.

Out of the fear and dread of the tomb,
Jesus, I come, Jesus, I come;
Into the joy and light of Thy home,
Jesus, I come to Thee;
Out of the depths of ruin untold,
Into the peace of Thy sheltering fold,

Ever Thy glorious face to behold,
Jesus, I come to Thee.
[William True Sleeper, *Jesus, I Come*, Public domain]

A cross stitched picture hanging on my friend's wall

The words were cross stitched and hung in a frame on my friend's wall. God's word is alive and powerful, it is good for teaching, rebuking, correcting, and training in righteousness—even if you simply read it on a friend's wall.

"We continually remember before our God and Father your work produced by faith, your labor prompted by love, and your endurance inspired by hope in our Lord Jesus Christ" (1 Thess. 1:3 NIV). When I read this verse, I thought about when I was expecting my first baby. Physically I was miserable. I had a terrible case of nausea through much of my pregnancy, yet I was filled with joy. Why?

"Faith is to be sure of what you hope for and confident about what you don't see" (Heb. 11:1). In some ways this would describe my pregnancy. I couldn't see my baby, but I knew she was there. I spent the whole time I was expecting getting ready for her arrival. My work was "produced by faith."

Then came the labor. Although I had been to classes to tell me what to expect while giving birth, I was stunned by the pain. The most helpful advice I had been given was to focus on my baby and not on the pain. With every contraction I would envision my baby coming into the world. My labor was "prompted by love."

Raising my children has been a privilege. It has been the best and hardest work I've ever done. Being a mother takes endurance; it takes patience. Many times I have had to look beyond what my physical eyes could see. I have often been discouraged but I haven't given up, because I believe that Jesus Christ will do for my children what I cannot. My endurance as a mother has been "inspired by hope in our Lord Jesus Christ."

There is a sense of wonder and joy that I always had when I was expecting and raising my children. As I have meditated on this verse, I have felt the Holy Spirit inviting me to live my whole life this way. Perhaps living a life filled with the sure promises of God's love is what it means to rejoice in the Lord always.

Lord Jesus, thank You for drawing me back to the truth. Sometimes I get distracted and discouraged by life. Thank You for the power of Your word even found cross stitched on a friend's wall.

Where Wisdom Dwells

My grandfather was a coal miner. He sank into the deep shadows forgotten by foot. The path he took into the heart of the earth was one no bird of prey knows. The falcon's eye never caught sight of what my grandfather saw. The proud beasts that walk upon the earth never walked the path my grandfather took beneath the earth. Even the fiercest lion could never go where my grandfather went. As a little girl, I knew my grandfather was the mightiest man alive.

When I was twelve, my grandfather had a stroke. That summer I sat on a stool beside his wheelchair, my head on his lap. The love I had for that mighty man only increased as I saw the strength of his heart. My grandfather would have me read the Gospels to him. He never tired of hearing the stories of Jesus over and over and over.

One day I found my grandfather crying. I now know that depression often comes when people have had a stroke. My grandfather had been a shepherd in Italy in his youth. I found a picture of Jesus holding a little lamb and brought it to him. "Granddaddy, you are like this little lamb Jesus is holding in His arms. When you were young and strong, you were like the other lambs in this picture, running all over the field. But now Jesus holds you close to His heart."

I often think of my grandfather when I read Job 28. It talks about men going into the heart of the earth and overturning the mountain at its base. The question that is being asked is, "Where then does wisdom come from? And where is the place of understanding?" (Job 28:12). The search for wisdom takes us to the heights of the heavens and the heart of the earth. Yet where can wisdom be found, and where is the place of understanding?

A twelve-year-old girl with her head on the lap of
her paralyzed grandfather found the place where wisdom dwells.
Wisdom dwells in the heart of God: When all other things are taken
away and what you crave most is to hear the love of God read to you
over and over and over again; when you finally rest in the arms of your
shepherd as the one He came to seek and to save.

With Perspective Comes Comfort

My friend and I were talking about how our understanding of people
and events changed as we matured. I was thinking about this
in respect to my study of scripture as well.

I am at an age where I am beginning to understand what my
grandfather meant when he would read from the last chapter of
Ecclesiastes, "Remember also your Creator in the days of your youth,
before the evil days come and the years draw near of which you will say,
'I have no pleasure in them;' before the sun and the light and the moon
are the stars are darkened and the clouds return after the rain, in the
day when the keepers of the house tremble, and the strong men are
bent, and the grinders cease because they are few, and those who look
through the window are dimmed...." (Eccl. 12:1-3 ESV). When I was
younger this was simply poetry; now I see it drawing nearer as reality.

As my physical eyes dim, my spiritual eyes are drawn to the prophets. I
have no desire to argue about the different views of eschatology. I have
no desire to draw a chart and explain to anyone exactly what God
is planning to do and exactly when He is planning to do it. What my
heart is longing for as I study prophecy is to see God's glory! As I read
the prophets, my heart is overwhelmed by His love and His eternal
plans.

As I stand with my loved ones who are at the brink of eternity, I find
comfort in Isaiah 25:8, "He will swallow up death forever; and the Lord
God will wipe away tears from all faces, and the reproach of his people
he will take away from all the earth, for the Lord has spoken" (ESV).

When I was younger, I felt I had a greater sense of control than I do
now. As I look into the prophets, I see more clearly the heart of God. I

no longer rest in my power to control the circumstances of my life, but rest instead in the steadfast love of a Sovereign God. "'For the mountains may depart and the hill be removed, but my steadfast love shall not depart from you, and my covenant of peace shall not be removed,' says the Lord, who has compassion on you" (Isa. 54:10 ESV).

Lord Jesus, I believe Your words are trustworthy and true. I believe You have not hidden Yourself or Your plans from those who are willing to seek You like hidden treasure. You have told us, "'Behold, I am coming soon. Blessed is the one who keeps the words of the prophecy of this book'…. The Spirit and the Bride say, 'Come.' And let the one who hears say, 'Come.' And let the one who is thirsty come; let the one who desires take the water of life without price" (Rev. 22:7, 17 ESV).

Lord Jesus, I am thirsty, and I am watching, and I am praying, "Come."

Untangling the Golden Chain

I knew exactly what necklace I wanted to wear, but when I looked at it in my hand it was a tangled golden mess. It was very valuable, but useless in that condition.

"Love is patient…love never fails." "God is love." I have been reading through the Bible now for over forty years, and this is the message I see. In the beginning, the God of love looked at all He had created and behold it was very good. But the serpent, full of hatred and lies, spoke doubt to God's creation, "He doesn't really love you, you can't trust Him. You can be in control of your own destiny; you can be your own god." And so the golden chain became a tangled mess.

This could easily have been the end of the story—except for the fact that God is love, patient, kind and unfailing. To fully understand the scope of God's redemptive plan it is important to understand that this is not a story of time, but of eternity. When the sin of rebellion entered the heart of man, the story of God's salvation began.

I never fully understood anger, much less wrath, until I became a mother. When someone hurt or wounded my child, my heart burned with wrath to protect and defend them against anyone or anything that would harm them. I would gladly die in their defense. I believe this is but a dim reflection of the passionate love of God. Part of God's redemptive plan is to restore His creation to a correct relationship with Himself. "As I live, declares the Lord God, surely with a mighty hand and an outstretched arm and with wrath poured out I will be king over you" (Ezek. 20:33 ESV). He was unwilling to allow what He valued to be discarded or remain useless.

When I read this verse, I see Jesus hanging on the cross, the sign above His head reading "King of the Jews." All around Him are mocking crowds, jeering at His suffering. The love of God comes from a God of love. "In this the love of God was made manifest among us, that God sent his only Son into the world, so that we might live through him. In this is love, not that we have loved God but he loved us and sent his Son to be the propitiation for our sins" (1 John 4:9-10 ESV). He untangled the mess we made with the tenderness of His love.

When sin was introduced into God's creation, sorrow and suffering came as well. When I turn to the last chapters of the story of God's redeeming love, I find these words, "Behold, the dwelling place of God is with man. He will dwell with them, and they will be his people, and God himself will be with them as their God. He will wipe away every tear from their eyes, and death shall be no more, neither shall there be mourning, nor crying, nor pain anymore, for the former things have passed away" (Rev. 21:3-4 ESV).

Lord Jesus, I praise You because You have made all things new. You have completed the task of redemption. You are the Alpha and the Omega, the beginning and the end. You have taken the tangled mess of my life and made into something beautiful for both time and eternity.

What About the Other Babies?

Have you ever compared baby Moses and baby Jesus?

Moses was born when a decree had gone out from the King of Egypt that the midwives were to kill all the male children born to the Hebrew women. They were to be cast into the Nile. God turned this around and used a baby floating on the Nile to be the one to lead His people out of captivity. Pharaoh's own daughter brought up this child in Pharaoh's household as a prince of Egypt. God's power is displayed in our weakness. Yet, my heart asks the question, "What about the other babies?"

The God of the Universe chose a young poor Jewish maiden to be the mother of the Messiah. Herod the King sent out a decree that all the male children in Bethlehem two years old or under were to be killed. Joseph, Mary and the baby fled to Egypt, fulfilling the prophecy of Jeremiah, "Out of Egypt I called my son." Once more the power of the mighty to destroy a baby is thwarted by the power of the Almighty. Yet, my heart asks the question, "What about the other babies?"

It was during a difficult dark chapter of my life when I discovered I was expecting a baby. Yet, as the weeks turned into months, I began to welcome the thought that there was another heart that beat beneath my heart. My mind began to thrill at the thought that I was carrying another life within me. Because of all the turmoil around me, I kept my baby a secret.

In the third month something went wrong. I drove myself to the doctor's office. In retrospect, I realize what a bad decision that was. They took me to have an ultrasound. That was when I knew my baby had died. I sat in the hallway, surround by pregnant women, my mind blurred by pain. My husband came and took me to the hospital. Then it was over. My baby was gone.

I don't know if it was a dream or a vision, but somehow, in the depth of my sorrow, when the labor was over and the life of my baby ended, I saw Jesus. He was standing at the foot of my bed holding a baby. He had two other children at His side. "Thank you, Sarah, for being faithful to carry these children for all the days I had written in My book for them." I was comforted.

When I was a young girl, I told my mother I wanted to have more faith. She told me that faith would grow as I began to read God's word. As I began to read God's word, I began to see God's power. But I saw something else: I saw God's love. I began to see that faith is really resting in the power and love of God even when I do not understand the direction He is leading.

Lord Jesus, long ago I learned that there are times when the plans that You have are beyond my ability to understand. I have found that there are times that my heart is so blinded by pain I can't see You. But most of all, as I have read Your word and learned to rest in Your power, I have found I can always trust Your heart.Living in the Middle of a Trilogy

I can still see her kneeling by the bed, her long gray hair flowing down her back like a veil. I would listen to my grandmother calling out the names of all who were dear to her, and I knew she was talking to God. At night I would climb into the bed beside her, wrapped in the safe, warm comfort of her love. I would rest my head on her chest, listening to her heartbeat as she would read God's word aloud so that I could learn to know His voice like she did. At church she lifted her voice in joyful songs of praise. She held nothing back; I stood so close to her I could feel her whole body vibrating with passionate praise.

When I was thirteen, my grandmother came to live with us. I stood in the doorway peering into the dark room. Grandmother's hair hung limp about her face. She was weeping as she sat rocking in the darkness. I went in and wrapped my arms around her to comfort her. Grandmother's voice was full of mournful sorrow. She was suffering from dementia. Although the disease dimmed my grandmother light, it could not extinguish it.

My grandmother taught me many things. I listened to her prayers, and as I grew I watched them be answered one by one. I saw my mother pick up the torch of faith and hold it high for all her children and grandchildren to see. Though I was a child, I recognized that God was using even my grandmother's illness in answer some of the prayers I heard her pray. I learned that people die, but prayers never die.

Sometimes I feel like I am living in the middle book of a trilogy. The first part of the trilogy is full of promise; the last part is full of glorious victory; but the middle part of the story is full of tension. When I was a little girl, wrapped up in the warmth of my grandmother's love, listening to her heartbeat, she was listening to the heartbeat of her Heavenly Father. It was in His word I heard the rest of the story. This is what He said, "Behold, I am coming soon."

Lord Jesus, You told us that in this world we would have tribulation, but that in You we would have peace. Sometimes this world is not a friendly place, but You told us to take heart, because You have overcome the world. Lord Jesus, I am living my life full of anticipation, watching for You with tear-filled eyes.

A View of Heaven from the Brink of Eternity

"Sarah, sorry I haven't kept in touch much. Haven't been feeling as well the past few months. Five months ago, the oncologist said I had a maximum of six months to live. They see cancer all through my skeleton."

This note fell out of *The Father's House* [C. H. Spurgeon, *The Father's House*, Fox River Press, 2002]. My friend Diane Dew had been asked to write the foreword to this book, which is a collection of Spurgeon's sermons on Heaven. She sent me a copy shortly before she went there. I thought I'd share with you some of her reflections after she was told she only had a short time to live:

"What's heaven like," my son asked me from his hospital bed in the cancer ward. Caught off guard, I realized I knew next to nothing about the subject. I thought for a moment, then told him, "Heaven will have all of the good things and none of the bad."

After searching the Scriptures, I found that was not such a bad answer. Much of what God's Word reveals regarding heaven is about what's not there. There will be no more pain, no more death, no more sorrow, no crying, no violence, no darkness, no hunger, no thirst, etc., (Isa. 65:19-25; Rev. 7:17; 21:4).

I personally became interested in heaven after the passing of my dear mother. I wanted to learn everything the Bible says about the subject. So, when the doctors told me I had only a few months to live, I was not devastated by the news.

We prepare in great detail when making plans for vacation of just a few days' duration. When planning to relocate to a new community, we research the climate, socioeconomic, real estate prospects, employment opportunities, etc.

However, when it comes to the place of our abode for eternity, many Christians make no preparation, but live as though this earth were our permanent home. They spend every spare moment shopping or pursuing vain entertainment.

Then, after spending so much time, money, and effort decorating their homes within and without, they leave to their loved ones the task of ridding their lives of the burden of all that "stuff" accumulated.

Jesus told about a man who spent his entire life accumulating many possessions—who, when he had no more room to store his goods, made plans to build yet another structure in which to store it all. Then one day he was called away to meet his Master. Jesus' response was, "Then whose shall these things be?"

"Lay not up for yourselves treasures upon earth," Jesus said. Our treasures should be in heaven. That's where our investments should be held, for true security.

While sharing Diane's view of heaven, I received word that another dear friend of mine died during the night.

Lord Jesus, the grief and sorrow of losing the ones we love to death is very real. Thank You for preparing a place for us in Your Father's house. Help me not to become so preoccupied with the stuff of this life that I lose sight of eternity.

A Promise Made Before Time Began

"He has made everything beautiful in its time. He has also put eternity into the hearts of man; yet they cannot fathom what God has done from beginning to end" (Eccl. 3:11 NIV). When I was a little girl, I wanted to have more faith. My mother pointed me to the Bible. What I have learned about faith through reading the Bible is to look at life through the lens of eternity. Reading from Genesis to Revelation year after year, I have begun to see the heart of God, and I have begun to glimpse eternity.

When you live your life based on eternity, it changes the way you live. I think about Daniel in the Bible. He had seen his home destroyed. He was probably from a royal linage, but in captivity they changed his name. Daniel resolved that he would not defile himself; they could change his name, but they could not change his heart. Daniel, from the time of his youth, even in captivity, was someone who based his life not on temporal circumstances, but a view of eternity.

"The knowledge of the truth that leads to godliness—a faith and knowledge resting on the hope of eternal life, which God, who does not lie, promised before the beginning of time" (Titus 1:1-2 NIV). Hope is the confident expectation of good. When our hope is anchored in the promises of God, it changes how we live. Why did Daniel resolve not to defile himself? He realized that he was an alien and stranger on this earth. He based how he chose to live on the promises of a God who does not lie.

"Blessed be the God and Father of our Lord Jesus Christ, who has blessed us in Christ with every spiritual blessing in the heavenly places, even as he chose us in him before the foundation of the world, that we should be holy and blameless before him" (Eph. 1:3-4 ESV). How shall I live my life today? In what will I choose to invest my time and energy? Will I allow the enemy of my soul to mar the image of God in me, or will I let the knowledge of truth lead me to godliness so that I can stand blameless before the God of love at the end of this day?

Lord Jesus, in Your word I see the promises made before time began. Enlighten my eyes and heart to know the hope to which You have called me. Show me the riches of Your glorious inheritance, and let that be what I use to chart my course in life. Let my life so shine with the light of eternity that it causes others to look to You.

The Sophomore and the Shepherd

"Have you declared your major?" "What are you going to do with the rest of your life?" In the sophomore year of college you are expected to know this. This will determine your future. This is also a major reason why many sophomores in college suffer from depression and anxiety attacks!

I am one who likes to make plans. For many years I have had planners where I charted my course for the year, planning what I wanted to do and when I wanted to do it. This is not a bad thing—unless somewhere in the charting of my course I begin to feel like I am in control of my future. Many years ago I found Proverbs 19:21; I write it at the top of my planner, "Many are the plans in the mind of a man, but it is the purpose of the Lord that will stand" (ESV).

When I am with "sophomores" who are planning what to do with their lives, I tell them what I tell myself, "It is good to make plans, but don't forget who is in control. 'Trust in the Lord with your whole heart; don't lean on your own understanding. In all your ways acknowledge him and he will direct your path'" (Prov. 3:5-6).

I have sat beside several people at the end of their lives, and I see no planners beside their bed. But there is something I have consistently encountered. "Sarah, will you say Psalm 23 with me?" And I do, "The Lord is my shepherd, I shall not want." In some ways, they are like sophomores getting ready to take their place in an unknown world. When they have put their trust in the Lord and know Him as their Shepherd, they are at peace.

Lord Jesus, You are the Good Shepherd. Help me to daily relinquish to You the burden of being the one who is in control of all that happens in my life and the lives of those I love.

A Measure of Success

I felt like I had poured all of myself into my children. Now the success or failure of my life rested on their shoulders; at least, that's how I felt. I watched as one of my children made choices that were contrary to what I had taught them. I began to fall into a depression. Over and over I heard, "All you have done has been in vain!" That's when I got a telephone call from someone who had lived with us many years earlier. I picked up the phone and heard, "I just called you to tell you that you have not lived your life in vain."

Upon what should I base the success or failure of how I've lived my life? I realize now how unfair it was for me to place that heavy burden on the back of my child. The girl who called to tell me that my life had not been lived in vain was someone in whom I had invested much of my life, yet when she left my home I could not see that anything I had done or said had been of value. God put her back in my life just when I needed her to teach me how to measure success.

If I measure the success or failure of my life by how it affects those around me, then I must count the lives of Isaiah, Jeremiah, Ezekiel and most of the prophets to be utter failures. I read in Ephesians 2:10, "For we are his workmanship, created in Christ Jesus for good works, which God prepared beforehand, that we should walk in them" (ESV). To measure the success or failure of my life, I can't look around me; I must look to God. If God is responsible for preparing the good works He has for me to do, then He is also responsible for the outcome.

The main ingredient in understanding this is faith. Not faith in my abilities or in the outcome of my efforts; because I have surrendered to the Lordship of Jesus Christ, my success or failure is found in Him. When I read about the people listed in Hebrews 11, I see some of them experiencing miracles while others are suffering "mocking and flogging, and even chains and imprisonment...of whom the world was not worthy." I see people who have chosen to live their lives here on earth, but with their eyes fixed on the promises of God. And I want to be one of them.

Lord Jesus, thank You for letting me have a part in the work You are doing in my generation. Thank You that the measure of the success of my life is not found in who I am, but in who You are. And, oh yes, thank You for putting friends in my life to help me when I get tangled up in my own importance.

Bowing Down with Eyes Uplifted

"Sweet hour of prayer, sweet hour of prayer, That calls me from a world of care and bids me at my Father's throne make all my wants and wishes known!" [William W. Walford, *Sweet Hour of Prayer*, Public domain] I was a young woman caught up in the beautiful idea of this song. I decided I would take an hour and go before the throne of Heaven. It only took about five minutes before I found myself checking my watch to see if an hour was up. Something wasn't right, but what was it?

In all the other spiritual disciplines I find myself doing something. Bible reading, study, meditation, etc., all these involve effort on my part. But what I find when I pray is that it requires humility. When I look at the meaning of the word humility, I find that it means to be close to the ground. In prayer, the posture is often to kneel or even to prostrate yourself before the Lord. Maybe this is why I don't have as much trouble with next phrase of the song.

"In seasons of distress and grief, my soul has often found relief, and oft escaped the tempter's snare by thy return, sweet hour or prayer." I find it much easier for me to humble myself in prayer when I am in seasons of distress and grief. I think this is because the situation has already done the job of humbling me. In these times I become like a child who recognizes her need for her father.

"And since He bids me seek His face, believe His word and trust His grace, I'll cast on Him my every care, and wait for Thee, sweet hour of prayer." Again, in these word I see humility; acknowledging that I am not the master of my own fate, but that I need to trust His grace. "Do not be anxious about anything, but in everything by prayer and supplications with thanksgiving let your requests be made known to God" (Phil. 4:6 ESV). The opposite of humbly calling on God in prayer is to carry with anxiety the weight of my own worries.

Lord Jesus, thank You for giving me this gift of communion with You in the form of prayer. Although I count it sweet, I look forward to the day when, "I view my home and take my flight: This robe of flesh I'll drop and rise to seize the everlasting prize; and shout, while passing thro' the air, 'Farewell, farewell, sweet hour of prayer.'"

The Church that Had No Door

Was I wrong to expose my children to Jennifer?

When Jennifer's family moved into the neighborhood an alert was sounded to all the other families. The family had a bad reputation in town. In an attempt to find her place among the children of the neighborhood, Jennifer shared with them all the bad words she knew. She knew a lot of them. All the mothers felt that their fears had been confirmed.

The edict was given by all the good mothers of the neighborhood that Jennifer was not allowed to play with their children. They further sought to protect their children by saying that no child that played with Jennifer would be allowed to play with their children. They wanted to protect their children's innocence. I understood their concern, but I was conflicted.

I brought Jennifer into my living room and sat beside her. "Jennifer, what do you think Jesus would say to you if He was here in the room with us?" Without hesitation she responded, "He would tell me to go away and leave everyone alone." She spoke with conviction about her unworthiness to be around the "good" children. I knew then that I my response to this child was to show her the love of God.

I monitored the conversations she had with my children; I took her with us when we went to church and other programs for children. She began to eat daily at my table; she ate as if she were starving. The Department of Children's Services came to my home one day asking about Jennifer. When I told them about her ravenous appetite, they told me she probably was starving.

For her birthday that year I gave her a children's Bible that had questions to answer at the end of each chapter. She brought it to me two weeks later with a big smile on her face. She had read it all the way through. She showed me how she had answered all the questions. She said she read it every chance she got. Then one day her family moved away.

During the last two months of Vincent Van Gogh's life he painted The Church at Auvers. The problem with the church is that it appears to have no door. When I opened my door to Jennifer, I also tried to show her that she was not shut out from the love of God. I wanted her to know the church had a door and it was opened for her.

Lord Jesus, show me how to represent You correctly to a hurting world.

A Secret for Survival and Success

I remember the first time I heard it said.

It was a season in my life when I felt overwhelmed. I didn't want to get out of bed. Everything I did took more energy than I had. I just wanted to quit. That's when an elderly man in our church told me his secret of survival. "Sarah, you don't have to be responsible for doing everything, just the next right thing."

I think that's what faith looks like. You choose to do the next right thing not because that's what you feel like doing, but because you trust something outside yourself. I think that's what humility looks like too. In 1 Peter 5 it says to humble yourself under the mighty hand of God by casting all your anxieties on Him. Pride can cause me to be paralyzed, feeling the weight of the world crushing me. When I humble myself and cast my anxieties on God, then I am free to simply do the next right thing and leave everything else to God.

I've heard that one of the reasons a lion roars at his prey is because it terrifies them and causes them to not be able to run away. First Peter 5 tells us that our adversary is like a roaring lion, seeking someone to devour. But we are told to resist him, firm in our faith. Faith isn't simply what I believe; it's how I act because of what I believe. Because I believe God is in control, I can do the next right thing and leave the outcome to Him.

Sometimes the reason I have trouble functioning is because I'm suffering. I'm suffering emotionally; I'm suffering because of choices I've made or the choices someone else has made. In times like this, I choose again to do the next right thing, because I believe God has called me in Christ to something beyond what I am experiencing right now.

Lord Jesus, You never promised a life without trouble. What You did promise was that You would restore, confirm, strengthen, and establish me. Because I trust You, I will continue to do the next right thing.

My Path is Hidden from Me but not from Him

I turned seven the week my Aunt Sally got married. She was the heroine of all my childhood dreams. Soon after she married she left to be a missionary and live with a primitive tribe of Indians on a tributary of the Amazon River. My grandmother would read long letters about her adventures, written on paper as thin as the peel of an onion. It was through the stories written in those letters I began to learn what it looks like to trust the Lord.

While with the Indians Aunt Sally's baby Margaret developed cerebral malaria. In an effort to save her baby's life, she needed to get her to Belem. The only way to get there was by canoe. Holding her feverish baby in a canoe on a tributary of the Amazon River, she was invited by God to a deeper level of trust. She was reminded of these words, "Never doubt in the dark what God has revealed in the light."

While in Belem, she received two letters from Margaret's grandmothers. Each grandmother told how they had been awakened in the middle of the night with an urgent need to pray for Margaret. In retrospect, Aunt Sally realized they were praying at the very time Margaret's fever was raging.

Trust in the Lord is not perfected in times of ease. It is perfected when the way is hidden from us; when we choose to trust God with all our hearts even when He takes us or those we love on paths we do not understand.

When you are a child, the direction of your life is dictated by adults who have authority over you. My childhood perspective was that one day I would be in charge of my own destiny and, like my Aunt Sally, I would chart my own course. But what I learned from the letters written on onionskin paper is that our life is directed by the Lord when we trust Him with all our hearts.

Lord Jesus, thank You for the example of those who have gone before me who taught me by their lives what it looks like to trust You: A grandmother who trusted You to direct the lives of her daughter and granddaughter in a foreign land; a young mother who chose not to doubt in the dark what you revealed in the light. Oh, Lord, let my life be an example of one who trusts in You, not leaning on my own understanding. Truly my path is hidden from me but not from You; therefore, let me trust You with my whole heart

To Be Set Free

I'm sure it is a universal desire. When I became a mother I wanted to be the perfect mother. There was one major thing that stood in my way. It was me. I couldn't be the perfect mother because I was flawed. As a result of my imperfection, I inflicted all my faults on my children.

When my oldest daughter came to live with me, she invited me to watch several movies with her. Each movie had a similar theme. They depicted daughters who began to understand who their mother really was. Watching these movies together opened up communication between us. It gave me an opportunity to ask my daughter to forgive me. Our bond of love deepened as she gave me the gift of understanding. In her forgiveness I was set free to become who I had wanted to be—someone who loved her.

One piece of advice I offer to all who stand on the threshold of adulthood is to forgive their parents. When you are a child, your parents are godlike in their relationship to you. They have control. And in my childlike mind they were to be all-knowing and all-powerful. However, because they were not God, they failed. If a child refuses to forgive their parents, the relationship between the child and the parents is crippled.

When I think about the prayer Jesus taught His disciples to pray, I think it is interesting that the one part He illustrated was that of forgiveness. The warning that we would be forgiven as we forgive is strong. I often see children who have been hurt by the flaws of their parents. If there is no forgiveness, the parents' flaws become the children's flaws as well. When someone becomes a mother or father and is bitter towards their parents, the pattern of bitterness is reproduced in their children even if they go into parenting with resolve to be perfect.

Lord Jesus, thank You for knowing me and loving me. Thank You for setting me free from my sins by Your forgiveness. Please help me to set the ones I love free and not to bind them and myself by unforgiveness.

To Know and to be Known

"I never struggled with vanity." About that time my sister almost choked. "Sarah, don't forget we shared a room growing up. If you never struggled with vanity, why exactly did you sleep with those huge prickly curlers in your hair?" Sometimes your family understands you better than you do yourself.

"Love is patient." When the Bible describes love, this is the first word used in the definition. One dictionary definition for patience is the ability to endure provocation, annoyance, misfortune, or pain with calm and strength [Dictionary.com]. Where better to experience this than in a family? It began at birth. When my parents took me home from the hospital, they began having to endure provocation, annoyance, misfortune and pain with calm and strength. This is love. They responded lovingly to me because there was understanding.

Growing up in a large family, I was constantly being provoked and annoyed. I was also learning to love. I was learning to understand people who were different from me. Whenever I would come home, I was safe to be who I was. I was safe to let down my guard.

I think a basic need for all people is to know and be known; to have a place where you feel like the people around you understand who you are and accept you. I think this is why God created families. Even when Jesus taught us to pray, it began, "Our Father who art in Heaven"—the family relationship of a child approaching their father.

Sometimes it's hard for a child to understand their parents. Yesterday my friend told me about something that happens in autumn. It's called fall turnover. It's when the cool water on the bottom of a lake changes places with the warm water on top. When this happens, the lake becomes very clear and you are able to see all the way to the bottom of the lake. I have seen this happen in the autumn of my life as I look at my parents. As I see them with clearer understanding, my love grows.

Lord Jesus, thank You for placing me in a family. Thank You for adopting me into Your family as well. Help me to love; to give the gift of knowing and receive the gift of being known.

•

Rejoicing in Hope

As we sat eating lunch, my sister told me about giving her testimony the day before. The theme of her story was one of hope of joy and of worship. As she spoke, my mind went back to the day her husband died.

Two weeks before my sister turned 30 her husband died, leaving her a widow with three little boys four and under. That day the colors of the world blurred and the earth tilted, throwing everything off its base. Coming home from the hospital, I watched as she picked up a card that someone had sent her. On it were printed the words of Jeremiah 29:11, "I know the plans I have for you, declares the Lord, plans for welfare and not for evil, to give you a future and a hope" (ESV). I held my breath, wondering how she would respond.

In a whisper, her words choked with tears, she said, "The good plan God had for Steve was Heaven." Her response was one of faith and worship.

Hope that is seen is not hope. During her time of intense grief my sister often repeated the verse, "I would have despaired if I had not believed that I would see the goodness of God in the land of the living" (Psa. 27:13 NASB). "We hope for what we do not see; we wait for it with patience. Likewise the Spirit helps us in our weakness" (Rom. 8:25-26 ESV). I watched as my sister grieved deeply but not without hope, upheld in her weakness by the Spirit of God.

The passage my sister used in her testimony was 1 Thessalonians 5:16-19, "Rejoice always, pray without ceasing, give thanks in all circumstances; for this is the will of God in Christ Jesus for you. Do not quench the Spirit" (ESV). This is the essence of worship: To submit your life in hope to the love of God; to trust that if He chooses to crush the grape, it is to produce the wine of joy; to believe that His plans are good and not evil even when worship involves a broken heart. This is true worship; this is pure joy.

Lord Jesus, I know that through You I obtain by faith grace to stand in all situations. Because of Your grace I am able, like my sister, to rejoice in hope. I believe that our suffering produces endurance. I have watched as this endurance produced character in my sister's life. Thank You, Lord, that the hope my sister had in You did not put her to shame. You have been faithful to shed Your love abroad in her heart and mine through the power of Your Holy Spirit.

How to Begin the Day with Strength and Courage

I opened my eyes, but it was still dark. The darkness felt like a heavy cold blanket wrapped around my heart. As my hand reached for the light switch, my heart reached for the light as well. With spiritual light came spiritual truth, "This is the day the Lord has made, I will rejoice and be glad in it" (Psa. 118:24 NIV). I made the declaration; I spoke the word of God; and suddenly I saw a scene in my mind.

As a young man, Joshua had been one of the twelve spies to go into the Promised Land. What he saw confirmed the promises God had made; it was indeed a land flowing with milk and honey. He also had seen the giants and the walled cities. With Moses at the lead, he had encouraged the people to believe that God was able to keep His promises. That was 40 years ago. Moses was gone now; it was his job to lead the people into a land inhabited with giants. It was his job to take possession of the walled cities.

How did he overcome his sense of inadequacy? Joshua was called by God to trust Him. With the calling came the promise, "Just as I was with Moses, so I will be with you. I will never leave you or forsake you" (Josh. 1:5 ESV). With the promise came the command, "Be strong and very courageous" (v. 6). Strength and courage were byproducts of Joshua's belief that God would keep His promises.

When it came time for the first battle, Joshua encountered a man standing before him with a drawn sword in his hand. "Whose side are you on? Are you for us or our adversary?" The problem was, Joshua was asking the wrong question. Joshua was not only given an answer, he was given perspective. "No; but I am the commander of the army of the Lord. Now I have come."

Lord Jesus, I often begin my day weighed down with a heavy heart, unsure that I have what it takes to face the day. Yet Your word says to rejoice because it is a day You have made. You also promised that You would not leave or forsake me. My eyes do not see the "commander of the army of the Lord." But you said that the Father would send the Helper, the Holy Spirit, to teach and to guide. Lord Jesus, You have given me Your peace, and with a heart of faith I receive it. Knowing You are worthy of my trust and Your promises are true, I begin the day with courage and rejoicing.

To Be Somebody

Maybe it's because I was one of nine children born within ten years. Maybe it's just human nature. Maybe it's the reason Jesus' disciples kept the argument going about which one of them was the greatest. It is the haunting question, "Am I significant?"

As I wrestled with this question again this morning, I started thinking about Jesus' example. "Have this mind among yourselves, which is yours in Christ Jesus, who, though he was in the form of God, did not count equality with God a thing to be grasped, but made himself nothing, taking the form of a servant, being born in the likeness of men" (Phil. 2:5-7 ESV). Why? Why would Jesus humble Himself to the point of death, even death on a cross? It wasn't because of my love for Him, it was because of His love for me. If the one who calls forth the day from the womb of the dawn has chosen to love me, can I find my significance in His love?

Again, I think of Jesus, "When Jesus knew his hour had come to depart out of this world to the Father, having loved his own who were in the world, he loved them to the end" (John 13:1 ESV). This verse is followed by Jesus laying aside His outer garment, taking a towel, tying it around His waist, and beginning to wash His disciple's feet. In their quest for greatness, none of them would have thought to stoop before the others and wash their feet. Yet Jesus said, "For I have given you an example, that you also ought to wash one another's feet." Can I find my significance in taking up the basin and the towel and following Jesus' example of being a servant?

Lord Jesus, forgive me for my pride. I identify with Your disciples, desperately wanting to be recognized for being somebody. Thank You, Lord, for loving me. Thank You, Lord, for knowing who I am. Thank You, Lord, for seeing me. It's so easy to get lost these days in the shuffle and the noise. Please help me to find my identity in Your love and service.

What Does it Mean to be Heard?

It is a character flaw that drives my husband crazy. I am a bad listener. I think of it every time I read in James that we are to be quick to hear and slow to speak. My problem is that I get it backwards: I am quick to speak and slow to hear.

I was thinking about this yesterday. What is my core problem that causes me to be more apt to speak than to listen? It didn't take too much pondering before the truth bubbled to the surface. It is my old nemesis Pride. Because of my pride, I want to be heard. I am more interested in expressing what I have to say than in patiently listening to what others say.

How different this is from the way Jesus was when He encountered the people who came to Him. Over and over He would ask, "What do you want me to do for you?" Their needs seemed obvious me when I read the Gospels. If someone is blind, give them their sight; if someone is paralyzed, get them on their feet and move them on. But Jesus wasn't doing assembly line healing. His healing touch went deeper than their physical needs.

"What do you want me to do for you?" I picture Jesus pausing and looking at the person who had been brought to Him. In Jesus' presence, each person was heard. Time no longer mattered. By His penetrating question they were invited to let their deepest pain be heard. When one responded, "Lord, that I might receive my sight," I wonder what kind of sight He gave them. I think that after He healed them it wasn't just their physical blindness that was removed.

When I read in James, "You have not because you ask not," I feel Jesus inviting me to be heard. It takes time to unravel the tangled mess in my soul. For what should I ask when I am invited before the throne of God? Some things seem so obvious, but there are other things that are buried so deep within my soul I can't put words to them.

What does it take for me to be heard? I have the invitation, but it takes more than the invitation, it takes time. By faith I come into His presence morning by morning. I read His word, I meditate on it and I wait. I wait for His Holy Spirit that comes like a warm anointing oil; a penetrating oil, bringing clarity where once there was nothing but confusion. When my quiet time with God is over, I know I have been heard.

Lord Jesus, I want to be more like You. This morning, again, I hear You inviting me to bring before You the deepest requests of my heart. Please grant me the grace to put to death my pride so that I can hear what others around me are really saying.

How Can I Tell You Why I Believe What I Believe?

"Think fast!" These were words I heard shortly before the ball smashed into my body. I was never good at thinking fast as a child, nor am I good at it now. When I am put on the spot and asked to give a defense of what I believe, my brain stutters and my tongue sticks to the roof of my mouth. Why? Maybe it's because sharing my faith and what I believe is about more than just quickly spewing words.

The teacher in a class on apologetics helped me a great deal. He did it by giving directions on how to share what you believe using a pattern found in 1 Peter 3:15-16. Looking at my problem through the corrective lens of God's word, some things became clearer to me.

As I meditated on these verses, I saw the place to begin was in my own heart. I was to "regard Christ the Lord as holy." Jesus said of Himself, "I am the way, the truth, and the life, no one comes to the Father except by me" (John 14:6). In this statement, Jesus proclaimed His holiness. If in my heart I regard Him as Lord and as holy, it means I place myself under the authority of His word.

"Always being prepared to make a defense to anyone who asks you for a reason for the hope that is in you." Hope is an anchor for the soul. It is a confident expectation of good. Hope often becomes evident to others when we go through suffering. Hope in Christ causes us to endure. Endurance changes our character to be more like the one we've put our trust in. When people see joy in the midst of suffering, they want to know its source.

There is more to it. The teaching of the Bible often clashes with our culture. We are told to share what we believe with gentleness and respect. I remember as a child being bludgeoned with the knowledge of children older than I was. The result wasn't that I leaned what they knew. The result was that my ignorance became a spectacle. To share what I believe with gentleness is to be respectful of the one with whom I am speaking. Respect also means I am not doing all the talking. I have often shared what I believe with others as if I'm shooting at them with a machine gun, never giving them a chance to say a word.

If I just stop with these thoughts, I would be taking these verses out of context. I think the context of these verses helps explain why I get nervous when I share the things I believe that are politically incorrect. The next verse says, "when you are slandered." It doesn't say "if" it says "when." I don't really want to be slandered. I want people to like me. I want people to think I'm smart. Yet being slandered, in this passage of 1 Peter 3, goes with being zealous for what is good and regarding Christ in my heart as holy.

Lord Jesus, You came as the Lamb of God who takes away the sins of the world. You came that I might have life and have it abundantly. You gave me this great gift, this anchor that holds my soul secure during the greatest storms of life. You also commissioned me to go into a hurting, dying world with words of truth, comfort and salvation. You also said that no servant was greater than his master, and if they persecuted You, I should not expect to be treated differently. Jesus, grant me the grace to love You more that I love myself and share what I believe with gentleness and respect.

The Secret of Contentment

The very idea that there was a secret to being content made me angry!

When I was 18, I knew that my life would begin when I left home and went to college. At college I was restless and longed to be married. Once I was married, I knew if only I had a child I would be satisfied. After the birth of my first child, I waited for more children to make my family complete. Then I knew it was having a house that would bring contentment to my life. I didn't ask for much, just a little bit more and a little bit better.

One Christmas morning, I observed as one of my children opened gifts with their head turned. This child was completely unaware of the gift they had received, because all the attention was on the gift a sibling was unwrapping. That was a picture of my discontent. I was totally unaware of the value of what I had received, but I was keenly aware of what the people around me were receiving. However, that was only part of my problem.

During one particularly dissatisfying chapter of my life I encountered Philippians 4. It was in this chapter that I found that Paul had learned the secret of contentment. I was puzzled. If God wanted me to be content, why would He choose to make it a secret? I decided to go on a quest to find out what this secret was. It began with prayer followed by study and meditation on Philippians 4. This is what I discovered.

First, Paul wrote Philippians while he was imprisoned in Rome; therefore, his contentment wasn't based on his circumstances. Paul wasn't looking at the gifts others had been given; he wasn't even rejoicing in the gifts he had received. He was rejoicing in the Giver. Because his joy was in the Lord, he had learned to rejoice in hope. From the things he suffered he received the gift of endurance. With the gift of endurance came the gift of character. Focused on God's faithfulness, he experienced joy. Suffering with Christ, he began to know the power of the resurrection. Going through both plenty and hunger, he found that he could do all things through Jesus who strengthened him.

Lord Jesus, forgive me. Not only have I been like a spoiled child who didn't appreciate Your gifts, I have not appreciated the Giver of every good and perfect gift. The secret wasn't that hard to understand when I finally looked up and saw that everything I had ever received I received from Your loving hands. When my heart surrenders to the love of Your heart, I knew contentment.

Removing the Labels

Labels are something you begin receiving in childhood. The first label I got was when I was in the first grade and riding the school bus. The older children gave the label "cute" to some of the first grade girls, I wasn't one of them. My label was "not cute." In class I received my next label. I had difficulty reading, so I was given the label "not smart." Although these labels hurt, there was a label that was far worse than any label I received; it was "not wanted."

When I became an adult, I opened my home to children who bore the label "not wanted." I understood what labels do. They hang invisible over your head and become a prison for your heart. They limit your hopes and dreams. No matter where you go, you believe that everyone knows the label that has been placed above your head. I welcomed the "not wanted" children into my home; I wanted to share with them what I had learned about how to remove the labels.

The way I received my labels was when I saw myself reflected in the eyes of other people. I accepted their assessment of me as truth. Then I learned to see myself reflected in the eyes of a loving God. In the words of Jeremiah 31:3, God says, "I have loved you with an everlasting love: therefore with loving kindness I have drawn you." God's love gave me value. This is the same value I tried to share with the children who came into my home with their heads bowed low with the burden of the "not wanted" label.

From the perspective of my peers and my teachers, I was "not cute," I was "not smart." But when I read God's word I received a different perspective. I learned in Psalm 139 that God formed my inward parts; that He knit me together in my mother's womb. I was made in secret, intricately woven in the depths of the earth. The knowledge that I was a reflection of God's creativity gave me value. This was the value I longed to impart to the children who came into my home. I whispered it to them in the morning and tucked them in bed with it at night.

Lord Jesus, in Your word I find that I am God's workmanship, created in You for good works, which God prepared beforehand that I should do. Thank You for redeeming the pain of the labels I received in my childhood. Dear Lord, please let me help others see themselves reflected in Your loving eyes.

Lessons Learned in the Storm

I picture the scene as I read the words. "When the ship was caught and could not face the wind, we gave way to it and were driven along" (Acts 27). I can picture it because I have experienced it. Not a storm on the sea, but surely in the storms of life. In the storms of life I discovered how vulnerable I really am.

"Since we were violently storm tossed, they began the next day to jettison the cargo." In my mind's eye I can see an ark surrounded by a watery darkness. There is no light to indicate if it is day or night. There are no stars to guide East or West. The ark is tossed by the hands of a monster awakened by the storm. What once seemed precious is now just cargo to be jettisoned in hope of survival.

When all hope was extinguished, Paul spoke and said, "Do not be afraid." How could he say that? He too was experiencing the storm. His words were based on his faith in a Sovereign Lord. Storms often seem to expose a contest of strength. Who will win? To whom will we bow as victor?

In the first chapter of James I read, "Count it all joy, my brothers, when you meet trials of various kinds, for you know that the testing of your faith produces steadfastness." What is steadfastness? The definition I found was, "Fixed, unchanging, steady." This is the quality I see in Paul when he says during the storm, "Do not fear." A storm will not only show you how vulnerable you are, it will show you how strong God is when you put your faith in Him.

"And let your steadfastness have its full effect, that you may be perfect and complete, lacking in nothing." What is valuable, what is real. The enemy of my soul comes with darkness. Shrouded by the storm-produced confusion, I lose my way. "You are lost and at my mercy," fear whispers in my ear. By faith my spirit seeks what my eye cannot see. I call out in faith for wisdom! God gives it generously without reproach. He knows my frame, that I am weak.

Lord Jesus, I call to You in faith when the storms have caused me to lose my way. I do not want to be like the waves of the sea, tossed by the wind. Please create in me a steadfast heart. And please let my life be a beacon of light to others who struggle in the dark night of the storm, a light that points to You.

God Loves a Cheerful Giver

The smell of bread being baked filled the house. Every week my grandmother would bake 12 loaves of bread. How much bread could three people eat in a week?

In my mind those loaves of bread were symbolic of my grandmother's generous heart. On the days Grandmother baked, I would be sent out all over the patch (the neighborhood) delivering her gifts of fresh baked bread. The Bible teaches that God loves a cheerful giver, and I never doubted that God loved my grandmother.

Grandmother remembered everyone's birthday. For some of her friends, she would be the only one to remember. Grandmother delighted in writing letters. What joy it was as a little girl to receive a letter from my grandmother, written with her phonic spelling that expressed her French accent. I never received a letter where she wouldn't write at the bottom, "P.S. I joint you a hanky," or "I joint you a dollar."

Grandmother's life had not been a life of great wealth and ease. She was born in France on November 10, 1891. When she was eight years old her mother died. Every year she would send me for her box of treasures. She would take out the postage stamp size picture of her mother and kiss it. She was a young woman during World War I. It was during this time that she met and married my Italian grandfather. Her infant son died in Italy.

She came to America and became a citizen. While her husband worked in the coal mines, my grandmother worked at home raising her family during the lean years of the depression. When World War II started, her two sons enlisted. Grandmother fully understood a life of sacrifice. Grandmother, however, didn't spend her time focused on what she gave, but on what she'd been given.

When I reflect on the lessons my grandmother taught me, I think about the joy she found in giving. It was in her last years, however, that I discovered the secret of her generosity. She had sold her home and was living with her daughter. A hospital bed had been placed in the downstairs living room. When I would visit, she was always overflowing with joy and would tell me that she was the richest woman alive because she had all she needed. Her life of giving had been an overflow of a grateful heart.

Lord Jesus, thank You for the example my grandmother gave me. Thank You for letting me see a life that overflows with gratitude for what You have done for them by giving to others. Thank You for the lesson Grandmother taught me: that no one is ever poor who has something to give.

Humility

"You are not the boss of me!" These words were spoken with great conviction by my three-year-old son. However, at that time I was the boss of him. His statement represented a clear lack of understanding about our relationship.

I have begun the practice of daily asking God to give me the spirit of humility. Many people think I am crazy for doing that. When I pray for humility what I am really seeking is to live my life with a correct view of my relationship to God. The first time I heard humility explained to me was in connection with 1 Peter 5:6-7, "Humble yourselves, therefore, under the mighty hand of God so that at the proper time he may exalt you, casting all your anxieties on him, because he cares for you" (ESV). If

I am relating correctly with God, I am resting in Him. This for me is a picture of humility.

I also see humility as having a correct relationship with the gifts God has given me. When humility is spoken of in 1 Peter and in James 4, there is a warning to resist the devil. Why? "You were the signet of perfection, full of wisdom and perfect in beauty. You were in Eden, the garden of God; every precious stone was your covering.... You were an anointed guardian cherub.... You were blameless in your ways from the day you were created, till unrighteousness was found in you." What was the unrighteousness? "Your heart was proud because of your beauty; you corrupted your wisdom for the sake of your splendor" (Ezek. 28:12-17 ESV). Pride is the opposite of humility. Whenever I focus on what God has given me instead of focusing on God, pride enters my heart.

When I clash with those around me, it is often because I find it more natural to be prideful than to relate to others with humility. I see their problems clearly while I find my own more difficult to detect. I'm quick to tell others what I think, but slow to hear what they are trying to say.

Lord Jesus, I find in Your word that I am to clothe myself with humility. Help me to live my life based on Your grace, casting my cares on You. Help me to have a heart of gratitude and not pride, and help me to consider others more than I do myself.

I Can't Protect Them

Suddenly I was awake! What I had seen was so clear that even now, almost thirty years later, I can recall every detail. I saw a car with my daughter looking out at me from the rear window driving away from me. With my mind washed with adrenaline I stumbled as quickly as I could in the dark to her bedroom, where she lay sleeping peacefully. She was asleep, but I was wide awake.

The dream represented the truth that I was not sovereign in my child's life. I could not protect her from all evil. I also realized that God does allow painful things into the lives of those who belong to Him. It wasn't only the reality of my inability to protect my child that kept me awake most of the night, it was my inability to trust God.

That night I paced the floor for hours, praying. My mind was reviewing the horrors children and their parents endure. Children are kidnapped, abused, and suffer with terminal illness. I believe in a Sovereign God; how could I reconcile this in my mind? What if the child who suffered these things was my child? My prayer was basic, "Lord, I want to trust You. Show me how!"

The truth was that in my own strength I was unable to trust God. As I wrestled with my lack of faith, I realized that faith is a gift of God. I asked God for the grace to trust Him with the possible harm that could come to my child. What I heard in response was, "I will give you the grace you need for the trials you will face today. I will give you the grace to trust Me for the future."

I was finally able to sleep when I began to turn my focus away from the "what ifs" to look at who God is. The anxiety I was experiencing was about things over which I had no control. In prayer, I was able to bring it all into the presence of a loving God. The assurance I received was that, not only was there grace for today, but for every tomorrow I would face.

My children are all grown and have left my home. I have experienced the grace of trusting God on their behalf many times. I have learned that God doesn't give grace for the "what ifs;" for that He gives me faith. Being a mother has taught me time and time again that only God is sovereign and He is worthy of my faith. I have also learned I can trust God to give me the grace I need for each day.

Lord Jesus, thank You that Your mercy is new every morning; great is Your faithfulness. Please help me rest in Your love for both myself and my family. Thank You that when I am blindsided by anxiety I can bring it to You in prayer, and find the grace that leads to peace.

The Gift of Gratitude

There are different ways to open and receive gifts. I have observed both. I have watched children rip through a pile of beautifully wrapped, expensive gifts and then sit amongst the littered paper with an expression of disappointment and ask, "Is that all?" I also had the privilege of watching a woman whom my family adopted, Aunt Loraine, open gifts.

Aunt Loraine took her time opening gifts. We would gather around her and be her audience as she would carefully examine each package. Each child wrapped their own gift to her. She would compliment them on the wrapping paper, noticing how they thoroughly covered the gift with tape, making it shine. When she got to the gift itself she would fully explore all its benefits. Aunt Loraine savored the gifts she was given and showered the giver with gratitude.

"Give thanks in all circumstances, for this is God's will for you in Christ Jesus" (1 Thess. 5:18 NIV). I have discovered in life that, until I receive gifts with a grateful heart, I don't fully receive them at all. If my heart is full of gratitude, not only do I look, I also see; not only do I touch, I am able to feel; I not only listen to what is being said, I am able to hear what is meant; not only do I eat the feast before me, I also am able to taste and savor the flavors.

From my earliest memories I have struggled with depression. One of my weapons in the battle is gratitude. "Through Jesus, therefore, let us continually offer to God a sacrifice of praise—the fruit of lips that confess his name" (Heb. 13:15 NIV). Sometimes being grateful is a sacrifice. I find it's not a feeling as much as it is a decision. There are other verses in this chapter that help me make this decision. "Never will I leave you; never will I forsake you. So I say with confidence, The Lord is my helper, I will not be afraid...." Through the sacrifice of praise and thanksgiving my spirit is able to see more clearly the gifts that surround me.

Lord Jesus, thank You for all You have given me. Help me to take the time today to fully appreciate Your gifts.

The Hidden Problem

They were everywhere! A swarm of little fruit flies suddenly appeared in my kitchen. They were unwelcome guests, and I was determined to get rid of them. So my quest began.

I got out my computer and typed "how to get rid of fruit flies." There were many creative solutions. There was only one problem; they didn't seem to work. My husband came to my rescue; he got out the vacuum and in a short time he vacuumed up most of them. Then a week later, there was another swarm.

This battle seemed to go on forever until I decided I needed to find the source. I started in the laundry room, totally cleaning everything. That's when I found "it." "It" at one time had been a bag of potatoes, but had fallen behind a box. The potatoes had changed into a black, gooey incubator for fruit flies.

As I was vacuuming up the remaining flies, I thought about how this parallels something that happens in my spiritual life as well. I am often disturbed or bothered by things in my life that aren't the way I want them to be. Self improvement becomes almost a hobby, but it seems that no sooner do I clear up one bad habit than another one appears.

One of the names given to Satan is Beelzebub. It means lord of the flies. Flies are drawn to dead and rotten things, and they can be so irritating that they become the focus. What I have discovered over the years is that I need more than self improvement: I need a Savior. When I humble myself before God and pray with the words of the psalmist, I find relief, "Search me, O God, and know my heart! Try me and know my thoughts! And see if there be any grievous way in me, and lead me in the way everlasting!" (Psa. 139:23-24 ESV).

Lord Jesus, thank You for coming as the "Lamb of God who takes away the sins of the world." Thank You also that, in my daily battle with the world the flesh and the devil, You are there as my Savior. Help me to continually humble myself before You in prayer. Expose my secret sins and set me free.

Trust

She wore sorrow like a mantle. Her eyes were cast down. She was a picture of hopelessness. How could someone so young see herself with no future?

I listened to her story; my heart felt her sadness. I realized what she needed was hope. She needed to know there was something to look forward too. I wanted to help her lift her downcast eyes to the horizon and see the rays of the sun. I longed to share that God is good and worthy of her trust.

I shared the Scripture that been an encouragement to me so many times. "Trust in the Lord with all your heart, and do not lean on your own understanding. In all your ways acknowledge him, and he will make straight your paths" (Prov. 3:5-6 ESV). There was an angry flash of light in her eyes. "This has nothing to do with trusting God," she said.

What does it mean to "Trust in the Lord with all your heart?" For me, this has been at life long journey. When I have faced disappointment, "trusting in the Lord" meant to let go of my dreams and believe that the Sovereign Lord, who was my shepherd, had a better plan than I could see. When I have looked at the future with fear and anxiety, "trusting the Lord" caused me to remember Jesus' promise to never leave me or forsake me.

My concern for the people I love takes me to a whole different level of trusting God. I have learned the peace this trust brings with it, and I want them to have it as well. However, I cannot make someone else choose to trust God. This reality brings me to the question; do I believe God will teach them to trust Him the way He has taught me?

Lord Jesus, You have taught me to trust You by the difficulties You've taken me through. Trusting You has taught me how to rejoice in hope and be patient in affliction. Help me to be faithful in prayer as I walk with others who are learning to trust You.

Victory Over the Darkness

There is an old faded photo of a little girl sitting on concrete stairs. Her eyes are dark; her hair is short; but the most distinguishing feature about her is the halo of sadness that surrounds her. That little girl was me.

From my earliest memories, I struggled with depression. I would feel it coming like a case of the flu. One moment, everything looked wonderful; the next moment I would experience an eclipse. Darkness would shroud my thoughts. I look back at the picture of that sad little girl and am reminded of the lessons I have learned in the dark.

Because of my struggle with darkness and depression, I began to seek the light. I read in James 1:2-3, "Count it all joy, my brothers, when you meet trials of various kinds, for you know that the testing of your faith produces steadfastness" (ESV). I do consider my struggle with depression to be a trial, but I also count it as a blessing. The battle with darkness has caused me to crave the light. Jesus said, "I am the light of the world. Whoever follows me will not walk in darkness, but will have the light of life" (John 8:12 ESV).

I cannot say that I no longer struggle with depression, but I can say that I do not walk in darkness. Morning by morning I wake before the sun rises. I open the Word of God and I open my heart, my spirit, and my soul to the light of the world. I write verses on 3X5 cards to carry with me. I take each dark and negative thought captive to the obedience of Jesus Christ. In the night, when anxiety threatens to suffocate me, I remember the One who came to save me. In His light the darkness cannot remain.

James also says, "and let steadfastness have its full effect, that you may be perfect and complete, lacking in nothing" (James 1:4 ESV). The trial of darkness sends me seeking Light. In His light I see truth; I find wisdom; I find healing; I find joy. I see the faded picture of the sad little girl and I whisper, "Don't be afraid, your Redeemer lives. The light of the world has come to take away the darkness."

Lord Jesus, because of You there is victory over darkness. May Your redemption of my struggle be to the glory of "the only Sovereign, the King of kings and the Lord of lords, who alone has immortality, who dwells in unapproachable light" (1 Tim. 6:15-16 ESV)

Far as the Curse is Found

I noticed this year that all the figures in my nativity scene seem to be looking down at the baby in the manger. I was trying to arrange them, but I had a problem: the animals got in the way. I didn't know where to put them. I began to wonder what they really had to do with the story of the Savior's birth anyway.

Often I see cattle, lambs, and perhaps a dove in the rafters as part of the manger scene. As I pondered the animal's presence at Jesus' birth, I thought about why He had come. When Jesus began His ministry, John the Baptist announced Him by saying, "Behold the lamb of God who takes away the sins of the world." I moved the lambs a little closer to the manger.

When sin entered the world, the curse entered the world as a result. God saw what He had made at creation and it was very good. When man sinned, the ground was cursed; thorns and thistles were brought forth. Man was clothed with a garment of skins. It was the first sacrifice made to atone for sin.

This sacrifice was a picture of something innocent dying for one who was guilty. Leviticus shows that sacrifices were not done in an impersonal way. The one who brought the sacrifice had to lay his hands on the head of the animal to be sacrificed. All of creation was waiting for the Savior, the one who came to take away the sins of the world. I found a place for all the animals; they too are part of the story of Christmas.

While setting up the Nativity scene, a verse of a carol was going through my mind. "No more let sins and sorrow grow, Nor thrones infest the ground; He comes to make his blessings flow far as the curse is found, far as the curse is found.... And heaven and nature sing." [Isaac Watts, *Joy to the World*, Public domain.]

Love I Didn't Initiate

The words that were being sung on the radio as I woke up reminded me that it wasn't I who had found Christ, it was He who found me. As I prepare myself for Advent, I wrap myself in this truth like a warm cloak on a winter's day.

This truth of a love that was initiated not from me but from the heart of God is all through the Scriptures. The book of Jeremiah was written to a rebellious nation. They refused to obey God's precepts; they would not heed His law; they refused to pay attention to the prophets God sent to cause them to repent. God pronounced judgment on them and they were sent into exile to Babylon. Yet that wasn't the end of the story.

Jeremiah 31:3 talks about God's everlasting love, "Yea, I have loved thee with an everlasting love: therefore with loving kindness have I drawn thee (KJV)."

One of my favorite psalms is Psalm 119. In it I hear the heart of someone who is truly seeking God. "I rejoice in following your statutes as one rejoices in great riches" (verse 162). "I meditate on your precepts and consider your ways. I delight in your decrees; I will not neglect your word" (verse 15). My heart echoes the rejoicing and delight in the word of God. I also fully identify with the last verse of this Psalm, "I have strayed like a lost sheep. Seek your servant, for I have not forgotten your commands" (verse 176). My relationship with God is not because I have a tight grip on Him, but because He has loved me with a love that doesn't let go.

Sometimes, when I come to God in prayer for the ones I love, my heart is heavy. I see hopeless situations. I see people who seem to be straying so far from God, and I see no chance that they can ever find their way back. Then I am reminded of the words of Jesus, "If a man has a hundred sheep and one of them has gone astray, does he not leave the ninety-nine on the mountains and go in search of the one that went astray?" (Matt. 18:12). Who is seeking whom? It is not the lost sheep that is seeking the shepherd; it is the shepherd that seeking the sheep. If that shepherd is also the Sovereign Lord of the Universe, I can trust He is able to find what He looks for.

What Were the Chances?

When I was younger, I often saw my life like a smooth stone cast upon the still waters. I erroneously thought I had control over the number and direction of the ripples that would be formed. Now I stand on the shore, watching the ripples cover the face of the water; all illusion of control is gone.

There is great comfort in knowing that God who loves me is in control. One of the ways I know He is in control is when I ponder the probabilities of the prophecies of Jesus' first coming being fulfilled. The Old Testament, written over a 1,000-year period, contains 300 references to the coming Messiah. All of these were fulfilled in

Jesus. One web site I visited said that,

> "By using the modern science of probably—in reference to just eight of these prophecies—the chance that any man might have lived to fulfill all eight prophecies is one in one hundred trillion!

> "To illustrate this: If we take 100 trillion silver dollars and lay them on the face of Texas, they would be two feet deep. Now we mark one of these silver dollars and stir the whole mess thoroughly—all over the state. Now blindfold a man and let him travel as far as he wishes, but he must pick only one silver dollar. What chance would he have of picking the right one? The same chance that the prophets would have of writing just eight of these prophecies and having them all come true for any one man—if they had written them without God's inspiration!" [http://home.surewest.net/dfrench/evidence/prophecy.htm, emphasis in original]

What were these prophecies about? They were about a God who loved us so much that He sent His son to be our Savior. This is the Sovereign God of the Universe who wanted to leave no doubt that this was not done by chance.

Lord Jesus, again and again You tell me not to be afraid. Yet fear comes so naturally to me. I am constantly aware that I am not in control of my life, or the lives of those I love. During this Advent season, help me to rest in the truth that You have left nothing to chance.

A Prayer For Mercy

"We do not make requests of you because we are righteous, but because of your great mercy. O Lord, listen! O Lord, forgive! O Lord, hear and act!" (Dan. 9:18-19 NIV). This was a prayer of Daniel. Maybe it's because I read these verses on the first day of December that it seemed to me God answered this prayer on Christmas.

Daniel was a prophet who sought the mercy of God. In the Christmas story there is another prophet who was sent to proclaim God's mercy. "And you, child, will be called the prophet of the Most High; for you will go before the Lord to prepare his ways, to give knowledge of salvation to his people in forgiveness of their sins, because of the tender mercy of our God, whereby the sunrise shall visit us from on high to give light to those who sit in darkness and in the shadow of death, to guide our feet into the way of peace" (Luke 1:76-79 ESV). These were the words of Zechariah concerning his son John.

There was darkness the night of Jesus' birth. I know this because the Scriptures teach that the shepherds were out in the field, keeping watch over their flocks by night. I wonder if any of these would have been used as a sacrifice for the sins of the people? A Christmas carol portrayed it this way: "Hark! the herald angels sing, Glory to the new-born King; Peace on earth, and mercy mild; God and sinner reconciled." [Charles Wesley, *Hark, the Herald Angels Sing*, Public domain.] This came to pass, not because we were righteous, but because of God's mercy.

I know many people suffer from depression this time of year. My prayer for them is similar to Zechariah's. I pray that they would become aware of the tender mercies of God. I pray that those who sit in darkness would be visited with the sunrise from on high and be given light. Again, using the words of a Christmas carol: "All ye, beneath life's crushing load, Whose forms are bending low, Who toil along the climbing way with painful steps and slow, Look now! for glad and golden hours come swiftly on the wing: O rest beside the weary road, and hear the angels sing!" [Edmund H. Sears, *It Came Upon a Midnight Clear*, Public Domain.]

Lord Jesus, truly it was not our righteousness that brought You to be our Savior, it was Your tender mercy. My heart sings with the angels. You, O Lord, listened! O Lord, You forgave! You heard and You acted! You are Emmanuel; You are with us! You are Jesus who takes away the sins of the world!

That is Mercy!

Free To Be Who God Created You To Be

Sarah, will you upholster my car?

A little background check on this question would reveal two facts. One, I had never upholstered anything in my life, and two, the question was asked by my young husband who believed I could do anything. There is something about knowing you are loved that enables you to do more than you ever imagined you could do. I did upholster his car, and when it was finished it looked pretty good.

Love has a transforming power. When I saw myself through the eyes of my husband I was able to do things I would have never otherwise tried, like upholstering a car. This transformation is something I have seen in my life and the lives of others when we encounter the love of Jesus.

Who did Jesus chose for His companions? Not the wealthy, highly educated people of His day; He went to the ordinary. But when they were exposed to the love of God, they were never the same. In John 8, Jesus said, "If you abide in my word, you are truly my disciples, and you will know the truth, and the truth will set you free." Again he said, "So if the Son sets you free, you will be free indeed." This truth of the saving love of God sets the captive free.

Down through the ages this amazing transformation has taken place in those who have accepted the love of God: Ordinary people doing extraordinary things. How? "God is love. Whoever lives in love lives in God, and God in him" (1 John 4:16 NIV). What an extraordinary truth! It is a truth that sets you free to be the person God created you to be.

Lord Jesus, as I meditate on the gift of Christmas I am full of wonder. You are the perfect gift of love from the Father. Your love sets me free. Your love gives power and meaning to my life. Bv

And Then What?

My sister rides bicycles. She rides them up and down mountains!

My sister and I have the same parents. We share the same genetic background. We have the same number of muscles in our bodies. But we are not the same. What's the difference? My sister has disciplined her body and exercised her muscles so that she is able to do things I wouldn't even try.

I have another sister who gave me an amazing electronic reading device. It wasn't my birthday. It wasn't Christmas. There was no occasion that would make me think I deserved this gift. It was given to me simply because I have an extraordinarily generous sister. Now the gift is mine, and I am trying to figure out how to use it.

I see a parallel between my sister who has exercised and used her the muscles to the point that she is able to ride up and down mountains and what Paul teaches about athletes in 1 Corinthians 9:24-26: "Every athlete exercises self-control in all things." This is true of my sister with her bike riding. But there is also the athlete of the spirit who exercises spiritual discipline. What difference does it make? I think that just as the physical muscle is strengthen by physical exercise, the spiritual life is strengthened by spiritual exercises.

I have a confession. When my sister first gave me the electronic reader, I was intimidated by it. It took me a while to begin to even figure out a little of its capacity. This reminded me of Paul's instruction to Timothy, "Do not neglect the gift you have, which was given you... practice these things, devote yourself to them, so that all may see your progress." When I became a Christian, I was given spiritual gifts. I have the option of developing my spiritual gifts or neglecting my spiritual gifts.

Lord Jesus, all I have I have received by Your grace. Please help me be an athlete of the spirit so I can develop spiritually. Help me not neglect the spiritual gifts You have given me, but to learn to use them for Your glory.

This Wasn't What I Expected

The year was 1988. I was expecting a baby Christmas week. As I thought about getting into the car for a 45 minute drive to church, I groaned. That was when I began to imagine a conversation between Mary and God. This is what came to mind:

Go to Bethlehem? What is he talking about Lord! I'm about to have a baby. Everything seems so confusing! It's not at all like I had planned. Yet the message You have given me again and again through these nine months has remained the same. You have said, "As you go, step by step,

I will open the way before you."

O Lord, it was such a short time ago I heard your angel telling me that I was most blessed among women because I had been chosen to be the mother of the Son of God. I knew from that moment on my life would never be the same, but I could not fathom at that time the changes that were to come.

When I first told my family, I thought they would share my joy; but instead it was shame I read on their faces. They didn't understand it was the Son of God I was carrying within me. I cried out to You in prayer and heard Your gentle reply.

> *"Child of my love, fear not the unknown morrow. Dread not the new demand life makes of you. Your ignorance holds no cause for sorrow, since what you do not know is known to Me."*

With Your words of assurance I went to my cousin Elisabeth's. At last I found someone who understood the miracle that was taking place within me. Oh, the joy of praising You together for what You had done in each of our lives.

I wanted to stay with Elisabeth, but the time came when I had to go back to Nazareth. Would they understand now that the child within me was from God? I cried out to You for direction. I did not understand all that happening to me. You didn't explain, but Your answer sustained me.

> *"Child, you do not see today the hidden meaning of my command, but you will gain light. You must walk on in faith leaning on my promises. You can only see one step now that is far enough for faith to see. Take that step and you next duty will be shown you. It is step by step that I am leading you."*

But Lord, I was so sure that even if all my family had misunderstood surely Joseph would know I was carrying Your child. It was shortly after my return home that I heard Joseph was planning to put me away quietly. Oh, how I cried that night to You. Thinking I was all alone with such a large task ahead of me. It was during that long night I heard Your encouraging words.

> *"My child, do not stand in fear, counting your adversaries. You must dare every peril except to disobey. You will march on, all*

obstacles surmounting. For I, the Strong, will open up the way."

How overjoyed I was to find the next morning that You had revealed to Joseph that this baby was from God. The wonder and the joy that Joseph and I have shared knowing that we are part of Your plan has filled me with delight. Now I knew everything was going to be okay. Except— expect now the word has come that we must go to Bethlehem. How can I travel so far feeling the way I do? Where will this child, Your son, be born? Once again I hear Your voice.

> *"My daughter, go gladly to the task I have assigned you. Having My promise, needing nothing more, than just to know, wherever the future finds you. In all your journeys I go before."*

It was twenty three years ago that I wrote this. Life has been full of unexpected twists and some heartbreaking turns. Yet I still find it true that following God requires faith to believe that He is leading me step by step. I have the same assurance that Mary had—that wherever the future finds me in all my journeying, He has gone before.

[Poetry excerpts from Frank Exley, *Step by Step*. Public domain.]

A Truth That Cannot Be Hidden

A truth that cannot be hidden, a light that cannot be extinguished and a thirst that cannot be denied. These were the things I thought of while I listened to her story.

I listened as a beautiful young woman from China told me her story. She had been taught that all things could be accomplished by hard work. She had been taught that there was no spiritual truth: that it was all a myth. She said with 80 percent of her mind she agreed, yet there was 20 percent of her that wondered. The truth could not be hidden. When it found her, it set her free. I saw pure joy on her face; she had experienced a spiritual birth.

I meet a young man on a university campus in the Czech Republic. "Tell me how you became a Christian." He told me that he had been raised in a Communist home. He had been taught that Christianity was foolishness. Yet, when he came to the University, he saw something different in the lives of those who followed Jesus. He was drawn to the light and the warmth that he found when he was around them. The light shone in the darkness and the darkness could not extinguish it. He came to the light and experienced a spiritual birth.

I knew she would be my friend from the moment I met her. She had been part of the Romanian Communist party. She told me how she had come to know Jesus as her Savior and, in doing so, a deep thirst in her soul had been satisfied. She had a passion to share Jesus with any who would listen. Being with her reminded me of Isaiah 55:1, "Come, everyone who thirsts, come to the waters; and he who has no money, come, buy and eat!" (ESV).

When Nicodemus came to Jesus at night with his questions, Jesus responded by saying, "Truly, truly, I say to you unless one is born again he cannot see the kingdom of God." Nicodemus found this very illogical, and Jesus went on to say, "That which is born of the flesh is flesh, and that which is born of the Spirit is spirit." Jesus drew the parallel between the Spirit and the wind. "The wind blows where it wishes, and you hear its sound, but you do not know where it comes from or where it goes. So it is with everyone who is born of the Spirit" (John 3). My friends had been told to ignore the wind—that it didn't exist; yet they found they could not deny its reality.

Lord Jesus, when I meet those to whom the truth has been reveal, upon whom the light of Your glory shines, and who have experienced the quenching of their thirst, my heart sings the words from Hosea 6:3, "Let us know; let us press on to know the Lord; his going out is sure as the dawn; he will come to us as the showers, as the spring rains water the earth" (ESV).

Who Controls the Trajectory of Your Life?

"Surely the Sovereign Lord does nothing without revealing his plan to his servants the prophets" (Amos 3:7 NIV). But did he know this sitting alone in his cell? His brothers had betrayed him; when he had responded to temptation righteously he had been slandered; and now

he sat in his cell forgotten. But was he truly forgotten?
Could Joseph have known that the course he was on had been chosen
for him from the beginning of time?

"Know for certain that your offspring will be sojourners in a land that is
not theirs and will be servants there, and they will be afflicted for four
hundred years. But I will bring judgment on the nation that they serve,
and afterward they shall come out with great possessions" (Gen. 15:13-
14 ESV). God had determined the trajectory of Abraham's descendants
before any had been born. He knew they would go to Egypt, how long
they would stay, and that He would deliver them.

In the fullness of time, Joseph stood before Pharaoh. His trust in God
had been fully tested. What Pharaoh saw before him was a man in
whom the Spirit of God dwelt. Because Joseph had chosen to trust God,
he had entered into a place of rest in the midst of turmoil. It was rest for
his soul. A place of surrender to a Sovereign Lord.

After four hundred years, just as God had foretold, Israel called out to
Him in their distress and He delivered them. According to Psalm 81, He
answered them in the secret place of thunder; and tested them at the
waters of Meribah. He tested them to see if they would trust Him.
He brought them out of slavery and promised them that, if they would
only open wide their mouth, He would fill it. But they wouldn't listen,
they wouldn't submit, they chose their own counsel over God's counsel.
The path God had chosen for them would have led them to enter into
His rest. In their rebellion, they chose a different way.

Lord Jesus, sometimes life is hard and I do not understand what I see.
Please help me be like Joseph and put my faith in You. I do believe it is
Your will to bring honey from the rock, sweetness from the hardest
places of my life. Lord, please don't let me, by lack of faith, alter the
trajectory You have chosen for my life.

Power Made Perfect in Weakness

She is many years my senior, yet she is my friend. I have walked beside
her as the light in her eyes dimmed and her vision faded. Her world has
become closed in by silence. Her brilliant mind can no longer retain

the information given her, and she asks the same questions again and again. Her body has become frail, and like a child she needs help with simple tasks. In all of her frailty she has taught me the truth of power made perfect in weakness.

When her strength first began to fail, she shared with me her prayer. "I have prayed and told the Lord, if He could use my weakness to bless my family, that I am willing to be weak." Truly this prayer of surrender is a prayer of love. "Greater love has no one than this, that someone lays down his life for his friends" (John 15:13 ESV). I have seen a reflection of the love of God in her sacrifice for her family and those who know her. Grace and been poured out, and many have been blessed.

Recently her son received a call in the night; she had fallen. I watched as he gently lifted her in his arms. He placed her lovingly in her bed, then sat beside her, his arm wrapped around her frail shoulders. I couldn't help but ask myself, "Who lifted whom?"

When the Bible describes love, it begins this way, "Love is patient and kind" (1 Cor. 13). In an attempt to define patience I found, "Bearing or enduring pain, difficulty, provocation, or annoyance with calmness" [thefreedictionary.com]. When I read this definition, it made me smile, because it reminded me of becoming a mother and taking care of my newborn children. God used my children to teach me how to love. Now I also see it in reverse. I see a mother who is willing to be used by God to teach her children how to love.

In attempting to understand kindness, I found that kindness means to do good to others in thought, word or deed. If I am kind, then my goal is to be an instrument of God in the lives of others. This is the lovingkindness I have seen in my friend. By surrendering her weakness to the grace of God, she has taught us, one by one, to learn in turn to treat her with lovingkindness as well.

Lord Jesus, thank You for putting people in my life that light the path that leads to You. Thank You for giving me an example of what power made perfect in weakness looks like.

I Can't Do This!

I can't do this! It's just too hard! I feel overwhelmed!

These are feelings I am very familiar with. I have felt them at every stage of my life. When I was a student and exams were approaching, I would often feel panicked and overwhelmed. As a mother, it started when I was in the delivery room and the contractions became seemingly impossible to bear. Then, surrounded by my children, I was constantly confronted with situations where I was supposed to be in charge, and I didn't know what to do.

"I can't do this! It's just too hard! I feel overwhelmed." I always see pictures of Mary as being calm and serene, but God used real people, not actors. When Mary's honor was brought into question because of the pregnancy; when she had to go to Bethlehem when it was time to give birth; when she had to flee to Egypt in the night to save the life of her child; I think she was stressed. She was a young woman given a task that was too big for her to do.

What was it the angel had said to her? "Greetings, you who are highly favored! The Lord is with you." As I meditate on this I wonder, is this true for Mary alone? Hasn't God also promised to be with me? When Mary wondered how the things the angel told her could happen, the angel said, "The Holy Spirit will come upon you, and the power of the Most High will overshadow you." God was not calling Mary to accomplish this task apart from Him, but empowered by Him. This isn't really different from the things God is calling me to do.

When Jesus was preparing to leave His disciples, He gave them this promise, "If you love me, you will keep my commandments. And I will ask the Father, and he will give you another Helper, to be with you forever, even the Spirit of truth, whom the world cannot receive, because it neither sees him nor knows him. You know him, for he dwells with you and will be in you" (John 14:15-17 ESV). This is the same Spirit that overshadowed Mary and made the impossible possible.

The last words the angel said to Mary were, "For nothing is impossible with God." Mary humbled herself and responded, "I am the Lord's servant. May it be to me as you have said." This reminds me of Ephesians 2:8-10 (ESV), "For by grace you have been saved through faith. And this is not your own doing; it is the gift of God, not a result of works, so that no one may boast. For we are his workmanship, created in Christ Jesus for good works, which God prepared beforehand, that we should walk in them." So, I choose to say with Mary, "I am the Lord's servant. May I walk in the good deeds you prepared in advance for me to do."

Lord Jesus, You know that when I am faced with tasks that overwhelm me, my human response is to panic. When I feel my children are in harm's way, I feel frightened. I think Mary must have shared these human emotions as well. Help me to look at the responsibilities You've given me with eyes of faith and not with eyes of flesh. When my flesh screams, "I can't do this! It's just too hard. I feel overwhelmed!" Help me to anchor my hope in Your promise that You have given me Your Holy Spirit, and with You nothing is impossible.

Clinging to God's Kindness or Clinging to Worthless Idols

The call came at 3 A.M. My daughter's car had a flat tire, and she was pulled over on the side of the interstate. My husband was attempting to explain over the phone what she needed to do, but she was tired, cold and frightened. That's when he showed up. An older man stopped to help her, and within minutes he had changed the tire for her and she was on her way. I thanked God for the kindness of a stranger.

"I expect to pass through this world but once; any good thing therefore that I can do, or any kindness that I can show to any fellow creature, let me do it now; let me not defer or neglect it, for I shall not pass this way again," [often attributed to Ettiene (Stephen) de Grellet]. I believe kindness is a reflection of the love of God and a gift of the Holy Spirit.

This morning I read the book Jonah. In it I saw the precious lovingkindness of God inviting all men to take refuge in the shadow of His wings. Jonah was to be God's messenger of kindness, but he didn't want the job. He rebelled against God and received the judgment he thought the people of Nineveh deserved. But in the midst of judgment, God extended kindness to Jonah, the kindness He also wanted to show to the people of Nineveh. I learn from Jonah that when I extend mercy to others, I position myself to receive mercy from God.

"In my distress I called to the Lord, and he answered me. From the depths of the grave I called for help, and you listened to my cry.... To the roots of the mountains I sank down; the earth beneath barred me in forever. But you brought my life up from the pit, O Lord my God." The mercy God extended to Jonah was a picture of the kindness He wanted to share with the people of Nineveh as well.

I wonder sometimes how I represent the God I serve. Do I neglect or defer opportunities to show kindness to those around me? The truthful answer is yes. I am often like Jonah, passing judgment on others. I am often self centered and cling to my agenda like a god, and do not want to interrupt my plans to be bothered by the needs of others; not just the needs of strangers, but the needs of those I supposedly "love."

Lord Jesus, Your word teaches that love is patient and kind. I confess I lack this kindness, but I also believe that it is a gift of Your Holy Spirit. Your word also teaches that, "Those who cling to worthless idols forfeit the grace that could be theirs" (Jonah 2:8 NIV). Lord Jesus, I confess my sin of clinging to the idol of my time, my things, my value. I lay them down before You and ask that I might receive the grace to show kindness to my fellow creatures today, for I shall not pass this way again.

The One Who Holds the Scepter Rules

"I am the master of my fate and the captain of my ship!" [William Ernest Henley, *Invictus*] That sounds nice, but the truth looks more like this, "I am stressed out; I have too many options; and I don't really know what I should do." "The serpent said to the woman, 'You will not surely die. For God knows that when you eat of it your eyes will be opened, and you will be like God, knowing good and evil'" (Gen. 3:4-5 ESV). What really happened was their eyes were opened and they realized they were naked and they hid themselves from God and death entered the world on every level. Blessing was replaced by a curse. But even then there was a promise of redemption; a promise that was to come in the form of a child.

This promise is spoken of again in Isaiah 9:2-7, "The people who walked in darkness have seen a great light; on them has the light shined.... For to us a child is born, to us a son is given; and the government shall be upon his shoulder." I remember the first time it was explained to me that it wasn't only the government of the nations but the government of my life that was to be placed upon His shoulders. I was invited to relinquish the burden I was never intended to carry. I felt I had been invited back into the garden in the cool of the day, and I could hear the sound of God walking towards me, inviting me to let Him be the master of my fate and the captain of my ship.

"And his name shall be called Wonderful Counselor." On this side of eternity I still get stressed, and I am confused about what I'm supposed to be doing; but I have access to the Wonderful Counselor. I no longer have to sit in the darkness of confusion. "Mighty God, Everlasting Father." When I read this, I am reminded of how Jesus taught me to pray, "Our Father, who art in Heaven." When Jesus died on the cross He cried out, "It is finished!" The curse was broken, and now I have an Everlasting Father whom I approach knowing the government of my life is on His shoulders.

"Prince of Peace." Some synonyms for peace are calmness, quiet, tranquility and rest. If the Prince of Peace is governing my life and he is the Wonderful Counselor, Mighty God, and Everlasting Father, it makes sense that all the synonyms for peace could be used to describe me, right? So why do I wake up in the middle of the night anxious, stress out and afraid? The snake in the garden still comes to me with his lies that I can be my own god. However, when I am awakened in the darkness by a wash of anxiety, I now can focus on the light of truth: that the government of my life has been placed on the shoulders of Jesus Christ. The curse has been broken!

Lord Jesus, when I meditate on the way You came to earth as a baby and fulfilled the promise made in the garden, my heart is filled with joy and I sing, "No more let sins and sorrows grow, nor thorns infest the ground; he comes to make his blessings flow far as the curse is found." [Isaac Watts, *Joy to the World*. Public domain.] In grateful humility I bow before You and relinquish to You the government of my life.

Songs in the Night

The day had been long and I was tired. I welcomed the night.
I climbed into bed ready to relinquish my conscious state
for blissful sleep. My head sank into the pillow; I was cocooned in the
warmth of my blankets as I drifted into the restful night. Then suddenly
I was awake.

There was no light; the night was black. My mind and body were
exhausted, but I was awake. The blankets now felt like chains that
bound me. The pillow was suffocating, like my thoughts. A parade
of worrisome and anxious thoughts trooped into my mind. The darkness
and my fatigued state accentuated the reality that I was not in control.

Many years ago I learned the verse, "when I remember you upon my
bed, and meditate on you in the watches of the night; for you have
been my help, and in the shadow of your wings I will sing for joy. My
soul clings to you; your right hand upholds me" (Psa. 63:6-8 ESV). When
I was a little girl and would wake up with night terrors, I would call out
for my father. There is something about being awaken in the night that
makes you seek out someone stronger than yourself. Now, as a
grandmother and mother, I still cry out in prayer to one who is stronger
than I am.

"By day the Lord commands his steadfast love, and at night his song is
with me, a prayer to the God of my life" (Psa. 42:8 ESV). My song in the
night is a song about the unfailing love of God. My spirit sings it loudly
to drown out the voices of despair. The theme of salvation
and redemption quiets both my soul and my mind. He is able to do for
me and those I love what I cannot.

This morning I read Psalm 136. Twenty six times in twenty six verses it
states, "His love endures forever." This is the chorus of my song in the
night. Hearing it again and again, I am able to find rest for my mind and
my soul.

A Desperate Plea!

Yes! I hear in my prayer an echo of his prayer. "O my God, incline your ear and hear. Open your eyes and see our desolations, and the city that is called by your name. For we do not present our pleas before you because of our righteousness, but because of your great mercy. O Lord, hear; O Lord, forgive. O Lord, pay attention and act." This is Daniel's prayer; this is his plea for mercy when he sees his own sin and the sin of those around him. All I can say is, Yes!

How should a Holy God respond to a people who so blatantly sin against Him again and again? Really, what I want to know is how God will respond to me. It's me; I'm the one again and again coming before Him. I want to be righteous, but I'm painfully aware of my failures. But it's not just me, it's the people I love. I want them all to be perfect. I can't come before God because I'm righteous, I can only come because He is merciful. Most of the time I'm more aware of my sinfulness and the sinfulness of the ones I love than I am of the mercy of God, and it keep me from praying and just makes me sad.

When I see the passion of Daniel's prayer, it gives me the courage to use his words as my own, "O Lord, forgive. O Lord, pay attention and act." I want to put an exclamation point at the end of every sentence. Am I praying or screaming at God? God didn't get mad at Daniel; He sent Gabriel in "swift flight," like a father who comes to the aid of a frightened child. What was the message that God sent by His messenger? "O Daniel, I have now come to give you insight and understanding. At the beginning of your pleas for mercy a word went out, and I have come to tell it to you, for you are greatly loved."

So what did Gabriel say? In Daniel 9:24-27, God gave a prophecy that showed His plan, "to finish the transgression, to put an end to sin, and to atone for iniquity, to bring everlasting righteousness...." Within these four verses comes the comfort that the God of Mercy forgives and is paying attention and has a plan. Who did God send with this message of salvation?

There were 400 years of silence between the Old and New Testament, but when the silence was broken, Gabriel was there again proclaiming good news; God had a plan. First he spoke to Zechariah, "I am Gabriel, who stands in the presence of God, and I was sent to speak to you and bring you this good news." The good news was that Zechariah's prayers had been heard and that his wife Elizabeth would bear a son. Six months later, Gabriel was sent from God to a city of Galilee named Nazareth with a message to a virgin named Mary.

Lord Jesus, thank You that when I cry out to You for mercy, You open my eyes to the truth. You have a plan to "finish the transgression, to put an end to sin, and to atone for iniquity, to bring in everlasting righteousness." Thank You for hearing and forgiving. Thank You for not only sending Gabriel, but for coming Yourself to be our Savior.

In the Presence of A Holy God

How are unholy people supposed to come before a holy God? I always feel like I should begin my prayers by telling God I'm sorry. I know in many cultures, when they think of coming into God's presence, they do penance. This sometimes involves things like processions, crawling on your knees to church, or walking barefoot on the cobblestone streets, in some cases with faces covered. There are those who carry heavy stalks covered in thorns through the street. These men walk in agony through the streets trying to purify themselves of sin and longing to come before God. I understand their desire to do penance. It's the same as my desire to begin my prayers telling God I am so sorry for my sin. But when I look at Scripture I see a different way.

"Come into his presence with singing! Know that the Lord, he is God! It is he who made us, and we are his; we are his people, and the sheep of his pasture. Enter his gates with thanksgiving, and his courts with praise! Give thanks to him; bless his name!" What I see in Psalm 100 is an invitation not to do penance, not to stare at my sin and shame, but to enter into the loving presence of God. I always have to be careful not to use too many exclamation marks when I write, but there are six exclamation marks in the first four verses of this psalm! How are unholy people to come into the presence of a holy God? With joy and gladness and singing and thanksgiving and praise; blessing His name; focused on His love and not our unworthiness.

Surely this would be enough, but there is more. In Psalm 100 it says that we are the sheep of His pasture. But sometimes sheep stray. What then? Jesus told us, "If a man has a hundred sheep, and one of them has gone astray, does he not leave the ninety-nine on the mountains and go in search of the one that went astray? And if he finds it, truly, I say to you, he rejoices over it more than over the ninety-nine that never went astray" (Matt. 18:12-13 ESV). Again, the terms of fellowship are not based on the straying sheep, but the faithful shepherd, and there is joy and rejoicing.

"For the Lord is good; his steadfast love endures forever, and his faithfulness to all generation" (Psa. 100). I am a mother and a grandmother. How wonderful to know that the love of God is steadfast and unfailing even when I, or the ones I love, fail. My heart is full of joy and gladness and thanksgiving because I am welcomed in His presence, and His faithfulness extends through the generation.

Lord Jesus, thank You that You didn't wait for us to be good enough to come to You. You came to us, and announced Your coming by angels who spoke to the shepherds saying, "Fear not, for behold, I bring you good news of a great joy that will be for all the people. For unto you is born this day in the city of David a Savior, who is Christ the Lord."

When Darkness Hides His Face

Prayers offered in the night when darkness consumes the sky represent the spiritual struggle against darkness. Again and again as I read the Scriptures, I see an invitation to anchor my confidence in the promises and person of Jesus Christ, and not to give up, but to be faithful in prayer. "I've lost all hope in life," I have heard people say. Hope can be lost only if you place it in the wrong thing. Hope placed in God will not leave me ashamed, because "God's love has been poured out into our hearts through the Holy Spirit who has been given to us" (Rom. 5:5 ESV). Because of this hope, I continue to pray in the night.

I have pictures on my refrigerator of children in whose lives I've invested. I hear reports of what they are doing now, and it makes me sad. Should I give up and stop praying? Have I given up all hope in them? Is that the right question? I don't think so. What I see in Scripture is that hope involves patience and endurance; because I don't hope for what I see, but for what I believe. Hope is bound up in faith, and faith gives me an assurance of what I cannot see. Because of my hope I choose to pray, not because of what I see, but because of the One in whom I believe.

I think two of my enemy's favorite tactics are discouragement and anxiety. When I read the book of Ezra, I see the enemy using these two weapons. God had told to His people through His prophets that if they did not obey His word they would go into captivity for 70 years. When the 70 years was up and they were back in their land rebuilding the temple, they became discouraged. They were being threatened constantly by their enemy. The ones among them who remembered the former glory of the temple that had been destroyed
were disappointed that Zerubbabel's temple did not compare with it in size or in beauty. Because of their discouragement, they stopped the work.

Isn't this the way it works? When the darkness of doubt and difficulty cloud my spiritual vision I want to give up and just live in the moment. Hope calls me to base my actions not on what I see, but what I believe. When the people in Ezra's day stopped work on the temple and just focused on their own houses and their own comfort, God sent them two prophets. Haggai and Zechariah, through their prophecies, pull back the curtains of heaven. The people were given an eternal perspective and hope was reborn.

There was a song written by Edward Mote in 1834. One of the verses says, "When darkness seems to hide His face, I rest on His unchanging grace. In every high and stormy gale, my anchor holds within the veil." [Edward Mote, *The Solid Rock*, Public domain.] And so I continue to offer my prayers in the night. When the darkness of doubt or fear hides His face, I choose to persevere; because I believe in the end the love of God will be poured out.

Your Epidermis Is Showing

I was a self conscious first grader on the bus the first time I heard the word. A much older child looked at me and said, "Your epidermis is showing!" I had no idea what it meant, but I was sure it couldn't be good. Because I didn't know what it was, I didn't know how to fix it. I got off the bus and went running into the house crying. I found my mother, lifted my tear-stained face and whispered to her the horrible truth that my epidermis was showing, and I didn't know what to do about it. Mother wrapped her arms around me and choking back the laughter as she explained that epidermis means skin.

I thought about this expression recently in relation to the "flesh." When the Bible speaks of the "flesh," it speaks of natural desires that have become warped or twisted. I was under a lot of pressure, and my response was to become angry and unkind. After my emotional explosion, I sat there feeling very exposed, and the words came back to me, "Your epidermis is showing!" Not just my skin, but also my "flesh."

One analogy I heard for the "flesh" was a scar on the landscape of your soul. I like this analogy, because as I consider my fleshly patterns that are contrary to walking according to the Spirit of God, I can sometimes trace it back to a scar on my soul. A scar is a place where once there was a wound. When I was a little girl I used food to comfort myself. There is nothing wrong with food, but when I turn to food for comfort instead to God, it is a fleshly response to pain and not a spiritual response. When life gets stressful, sometimes I revert back to this fleshly response to pain, and "my epidermis shows."

So what should I do to deal with this? If I go to a bookstore I can find countless number of self-help books. I have bought many myself. However, I have never been able to bring healing by self-effort. There is always suppression; I determine that I will suppress my "flesh," but the more I think about suppressing my "flesh," the greater the desire becomes to give into it. In this struggle I identify with Paul who said, "For I know that nothing good dwells in me, that is, in my flesh. For I have the desire to do what is right, but not the ability to carry it out" (Rom. 7:18 ESV).

Is there a solution for this problem? Oh, yes! "There is therefore now no condemnation for those who are in Christ Jesus. For the law of the Spirit of life has set you free in Christ Jesus from the law of sin and death. For God has done what the law, weakened by the flesh, could not do" (Rom. 8:1-3 ESV). It is not by suppression or human effort that I deal with these scars on the landscape of my soul, it is a matter of walking by the spirit. "But I say, walk by the Spirit, and you will not gratify the desires of the flesh" (Gal. 5:16 ESV).

Lord Jesus, I come humbly before You. Thank You coming to earth to be my Savior. Thank You for setting me free from the law of sin and death. Thank You for setting me free by the power of Your Spirit. Help me today to walk in the freedom of Your Spirit and not in my flesh.

When the Sunrise Visits Us From On High

One of the things I enjoy about working in the café is hearing people's stories. Sometimes I don't know their name, only their story revealed little by little each time they come. It happened recently with a lady who was having lunch with her sister. As they were leaving, the woman mention her sister had been very near death nine months earlier. Her sister came back the next week and told me more of her story.

She told me she had spent 23 days in intensive care. She was in and out of consciousness and was not expected to live. She told me how helpless she had been, unable to do anything for herself. She had been a Christian for many years, yet while she was in ICU, not only was she unable to physically do anything for herself, she was not even able to pray. As she was coming back into consciousness, she heard God speaking to her. He said, "I am for you, even when you cannot be for yourself." She told how the realization of God's tender mercy had changed her life and brought her a great deal of peace.

I have been thinking about her experience for days. I think it is a beautiful picture of what God did for us at Christmas when He sent His Son. Zechariah's prophecy after the birth of John the Baptist reflects this. "And you, child, will be called the prophet of the Most High; for you will go before the Lord to prepare his ways, to give knowledge of salvation to his people in the forgiveness of their sins, because of the tender mercy of our God, whereby the sunrise shall visit us from on high to give light to those who sit in darkness and the shadow of death, to guide our feet into the way of peace" (Luke 1:76-79 ESV).

She spoke of her illness as a gift that showed her God's mercy and had brought her to a place of peace she had never known before. We talked about how God gives us grace, in that He gives us what we don't deserve; and how, in His mercy, He withholds the punishment our sins deserve. But there is so much more to His mercy. Another translation for God's mercy is lovingkindness. God's lovingkindness offers us a place of rest. "How excellent is thy lovingkindness, O God! therefore the children of men put their trust under the shadow of thy wings" (Psa. 36:7 KJV).

The truth of God's mercy and grace don't change, but I think my understanding changes as I go through different experiences. When I was a little girl, I was filled with wonder that God would become a baby and be born in a manger. Now as I think of God's lovingkindness towards me, I am filled with awe. Though I haven't been through a life-threatening illness, the message that He is for me, even when I cannot be for myself, fills me with gratitude.

Lord Jesus, truly You are the sunrise from on high who has shone on us in our darkness. Thank You for guiding us in the way of peace and letting us rest under the shadow of Your wings. Oh, yes, and thank You that even when we could do nothing to bring about our salvation, You came and did for us what we could not do for ourselves.

A Detailed Plan

I was in high school and discussing the mysteries of the universe with my friends. It was an interesting discussion, because we had all heard different theories and we were comparing notes. One boy spoke with more authority than the rest of us because his brother was in seminary. He explained to us that the world was like a big clock that God wound up. After God set things in motion, He stepped out of the picture and was just going to watch to see how things turned out.

This picture of an indifferent God was interesting to me, but not comforting. Was my friend right? Was I, along with all of creation, left to chance? How did what I believe about God's caring or not caring affect anything anyway? As I thought about this, I realized my belief about the nature of God was foundational, not only in the way I viewed the world, but also in the way I saw myself.

When I read the book of Jonah, I saw a very different picture of God than the clockwork God my friend had told me about. In Jonah I found a God who had boundless compassion for the people He had created. Not just compassion on the Jews who were considered His chosen people, but also on the pagan sailors and the Ninevites. In this story of redemption and compassion, God used all of His creation to carry out His plan.

The story of Jonah is full of divine appointments. First, God appointed His prophet Jonah to go to his enemies the Ninevites. Next, God appointed a storm to get Jonah's attention when Jonah decided to go in a direction different from God's. God appoint a great fish to keep Jonah from drowning and give him time to think about the direction he was headed. God appointed a plant to grow and give Jonah shade and save him from discomfort while Jonah was waiting for God to destroy Nineveh. Finally, God appointed a worm to attack the plant and make it wither. This made Jonah very angry. God used it as an illustration that, although Jonah had compassion on the plant because it gave him comfort from the heat, he had no compassion on the city of Nineveh.

Lord Jesus, in this story of the redemptive love of God I see a picture of You. "For God so loved the world, that he sent his only Son, that whoever believes in him should not perish but have eternal life. For God didn't send his Son into the world to condemn the world, but in order that the world might be saved through him" (John 3:16-17). Thank You for not being an indifferent God but a God of love and compassion. When I see my life reflected in Your love, it has meaning.

A Deeper Surrender

When I was a little girl I used to think that I could be a better person if only I was in a different setting. I wanted to be good, I really did; but I was constantly failing. Focusing on my failures often led to depression. I was reminded of this recently as I talked to a young man who told me that he would be a different person if only he had a different set of circumstances. I shared with him what I learned from the Lord through my constant prayer about my own struggle with sin.

Both this young man and I had received justification by faith in Jesus. He and I both understood that Jesus Himself bore our sins in His body on the tree, that we might die to sin and live to righteousness. We both understood that it wasn't our own good works that brought salvation. We understood that by Jesus' wounds we were healed. The question we had both struggled with was, how? How do we die to sin and live to righteousness?

I shared with my young friend what I am still in the process of learning: a deeper surrender to the love of God. The first step in this surrender is to agree with God when He points out sin. What I usually do when my sin is exposed is focus on the sin. I either try to justify it or I feel guilty about it. When I choose to surrender to God's love, I lift my eyes away from my sin and look into my Savior's face. Then my heart is full of gratitude instead of self-loathing.

"We are at war," I told my friend. "We are at war with the world, the flesh and the devil. No matter where you are or what your circumstances of life are, this is simply true." In this war the goal is to die to sin and live to righteousness, but how? Again I believe the answer is a deeper surrender to the love of God.

A deeper surrender to the love of God is to be filled with His spirit. Surrendering to His love, we rejoice in hope, anchoring our expectations in His promise that He has set us free from the bondage of sin. Surrendering to His love, we choose to be patient in affliction; we don't give up. Surrendering to His love, we choose to not surrender to our flesh, the world or the devil, but stand our ground and fight. Often, standing our ground is done on our knees, being faithful in prayer. Refusing to give up or give in, but being sure of what we hope for and confident about what we do not see, we continue to come to the throne of the Almighty and pour out our hearts.

Something happens in this struggle. I want my Christian life to be easy. I want to be good. I don't want to sin, but I don't want it to be a struggle. However, I see a different pattern in Romans 12:1-2, "I appeal to you, therefore, brothers, by the mercies of God, to present your bodies as a living sacrifice, holy and acceptable to God, which is your spiritual worship. Do not be conformed to this world, but be transformed by the renewal of your mind, that by testing you may discern what is the will of God, what is good and acceptable and perfect." Somewhere in this struggle transformation takes place. Surrendering to God's love and offering my body as a living sacrifice is worship.

Lord Jesus, You did for me what I could not do for myself. You took my sin and gave me Your righteousness. You also gave me Your Holy Spirit. Your word tells me to fight the good fight and to finish the race. Lord Jesus, You are my High Priest, always making intercession for me before the throne of God. Please let the only thing I surrender to in this life be Your love! Please let me be an encouragement to those around me not to give up. Because You won the war, let us claim the victory.

Between the Years

I call it the hallway between the years. This week between Christmas and the New Year is when I look back and read the journal I've been keeping. Looking at where I have been helps me gain perspective and see where I am going.

This hasn't been an easy year. There have been a lot of changes in my life, and I have never found change easy. However, there have been some wonderful blessings as well. Because of the difficulties of this year, the blessings seem to shine like stars in the night. I look at my blessings of this year in the same way a sailor looks to the stars to navigate. I choose to record my journey through the past year not based on the darkness, but on the point of light.

When I look at the prophecies in Scripture, I see stars by which to navigate my life. In addition to looking back and seeing where God has led me, I look forward and gain insight to where He is leading. "We have something more sure, the prophetic word, to which you will do well to pay attention as to a lamp shining in a dark place, until the day dawns and the morning star rises in your hearts" (2 Pet. 1:19 ESV).

Every year when I read through the Bible I trace God's faithfulness to fulfill the promises He made. I can see many of the prophecies that Isaiah, Jeremiah, Daniel and the rest of the prophets accepted by faith already fulfilled. These fulfilled prophecies have become the foundation stones I stand on as I gaze at the stars in the night sky, looking forward to the prophecies yet to be fulfilled.

Lord Jesus, You are the sun of righteousness who has risen with healing in Your wings that the prophets foretold. When I reflect on the blessings of this past year, I see the lamp of Your love guiding me. As I look to this coming year, please help me pay attention to Your guiding light until the day dawns and Your morning star rises in my heart.

Don't Be Afraid To Ask

She had only been a Christian for seven months when I met her, but during those months she had read through the Bible twice and the New Testament six times. She had been raised in a Communist country, and for the first 30 years of her life she had been told there was no God. She was taught all things could be accomplished through human effort. Now her eyes were open to a new world she had never known before, a spiritual world. She had experienced the spiritual birth Jesus talked to Nicodemus about in the third chapter of John.

As I listened to her talk I was reminded of two scriptures, "Therefore, if anyone is in Christ, he is a new creation; the old has gone, the new has come" (2 Cor. 5:17 NIV), and "I will give you a new heart and put a new spirit in you; I will remove from you your heart of stone and give you a heart of flesh" (Ezek. 36:26 NIV). Her eyes shone with the excitement of this new life.

I was impressed with the enthusiastic way she was reading through the Scripture. It was all new to her, and she could not get enough of it. However, she had many questions. What she had been taught and what she was learning in God's word were two very different ways of thinking. When she asked me her questions, I was impressed at how different they were from the questions I ask. Her questions were formed in part by the culture she had born into and the things she had been taught from her youth.

To be honest, I didn't have an answer to all her questions. But I shared with her what I have learned as a Christian seeking to understand God's word. I believe this is part of God's plan to draw us closer to Him. Jesus said, "Ask and it will be given to you; seek and you will find; knock and the door will be opened to you" (Matt. 7:7 NIV). Jeremiah 29:13 says, "You will seek me and find me when you seek me with all your heart." Our questions are as different as our experiences, but as we ask our questions we are draw deeper and deeper into our relation with God.

Lord Jesus, after all these years of being a Christian I still have so many questions. Please help me take the time to formulate them so that I can ask, seek and knock. Please help me to be as enthusiastic as this young Christian so that I seek You with all my heart.

The Choice Is Mine

Sometimes I am afraid. I look into the future, and I look at myself, and I am filled with a sense of inadequacy. I can often push the feeling down by staying busy during the day, but at night when my defenses are down, the fear is awaken. So then what?

"Why are you cast down, O my soul, and why are you in turmoil within me? Hope in God; for I shall yet praise him, my salvation and my God" (Psa. 43:5 ESV). This is where I start; I start with the truth that I am struggling. If I were to stop at that point, it would begin a downward spiral; but I have the option of hope. In my prayers I match the thing I am concerned about with an attribute of God. It is a purposeful choice to praise God.

"When I am afraid, I put my trust in you. In God, whose word I praise, in God I trust; I shall not be afraid" (Psa. 56:3-4 ESV). This is the psalm David wrote when the Philistines seized him in Gath. Goliath had been from Gath. I understand why David would have experienced fear. Fear is paralyzing because its focus is on the things I cannot control—the giants in my life that block the sun. However, when I make the conscious choice to praise God I am able to walk by faith. The last verse of Psalm 56 reflects David's deliverance, not only from the circumstances, but also from the fear. "For you have delivered my soul from death, yes, my feet from falling, that I may walk before God in the light of life" (Psa. 56:13 ESV).

"Fear not, little flock, for it is your Father's good pleasure to give you the kingdom" (Luke 12:32 ESV). Jesus had told them before this that they were not to be anxious, but instead they were to consider how God provided for the ravens. Anxiety often causes me, like the disciples, to focus on the wrong thing. Jesus invites me to rest in God's love and turn my focus to seeking His kingdom.

Lord Jesus, help me take my eyes off of myself and the things that cause my heart to be downcast and anxious. Help me instead to rest in Your love and the Father's provision. I choose to praise You for all you have done. Today let my energy not be spent in fear but, by faith, let me seek Your kingdom.

Divine Perspective

When I read through the stories of Old Testament people, I feel as if God has invited me to see through His eyes. Having this omniscient view of their life, I can see how the choices they make affect both them and their descendants. I saw this recently when I was reading the story of King Asa.

At the beginning of his reign he did what was good and right in the eyes of the Lord his God, and things went well for him. When the Ethiopians came out against him, he cried out to God and said, "O Lord, there is none like you to help, between the mighty and the weak. Help us, O Lord our God, for we rely on you, and in your name we have come against this multitude" (2 Chron. 14:11 ESV). God did help him. When the prophet Azariah came to him and said, "Take courage! Do not let your hands be weak, for your work shall be rewarded," he responded by putting away the detestable idols from the land. Unfortunately, this was not the end of Asa's story.

When Asa had been king for 36 years, Baasha king of Israel, went to war with him. But this time, instead of calling on the Lord to help him, he took the treasures out of the house of the Lord to hire the king of Syria to help him. Again he was visited by a prophet. This is the divine perspective the prophet gave: "The eyes of the Lord run to and fro throughout the whole earth, to give strong support to those whose heart is blameless toward him." Asa became angry and put the prophet in the stocks in prison.

Unlike when I read about King Asa's life, I can only see the past chapters of my life and the one I am in the process of living. However, like King Asa, I also encounter threatening circumstances and have to choose where I will turn for help. God invites me to trust Him and rely on His strength; but there is also the pull to trust in myself, to find escape in other ways from the pressures of life. The pressure is real; the choice is mine to make.

Lord Jesus, I want to be someone who chooses to turn to You. Thank You for inviting me day by day to have divine perspective. Please grant me the grace to put my faith in You. When Your eyes are on me, let me put my hope in You and Your unfailing love.

Bon Courage

When she stepped on board the ship that would take her to America, she was leaving behind her father and brother and the tiny grave of her firstborn son. She was sick for most of the voyage across the ocean. There was nothing solid under her feet, only the pitching and swaying of the waves. At the end of her journey she would be a foreigner living among people whose language and culture were different from her own. What was the basis that gave this young woman the courage to leave all that was familiar? She had the hope that her future and the future of her family would be more secure in this new nation. This was my grandmother.

When I was a little girl I would get frightened. I didn't like to try new things, but my grandmother would say to me, "Bon courage." I didn't realize until I was much older how much courage my grandmother had. It can be hard to leave what is familiar for the unknown, even if you know that what you are going towards is better than what you are leaving behind. The courageous choices my grandmother made not only affected her destiny, but mine as well.

I am no longer a child, yet I still have to deal with fear and anxiety when I face the unknown. In times like this I remember my Grandmother and God's faithfulness to her. I also remember the message given to Israel as they were entering the Promised Land. "Be strong and courageous. Do not fear or be in dread of them, for it is the Lord your God who goes with you. He will not leave you or forsake you" (Deut. 31:6 ESV). The courage to leave what is familiar and take hold of what is unknown comes from the belief that I am not alone. I can be courageous like my grandmother when I hold onto the truth that God goes with me and will not leave me or forsake me.

Life is constantly changing. Some stages in life seem to last longer than others, but change is inevitable. I have known people who, during certain times of transitions, have simply gone to bed. The fear of the unknown brought depression and a desire to hide. I feel very compassionate towards those who have this struggle. I find myself going back again and again to the verses that remind me not to be afraid because God is with me.

Lord Jesus, what is not known to me is known to You. You have given me Your spirit. These are the truths I hold by faith. Because I believe that You are with me I will be courageous. Thank You for giving me examples of those who were courageous not only in Your word, but also those who have been part of my family.

Peace or a Lack of Comprehension?

"I'm afraid you have failed to comprehend the magnitude of the situation." This was a phrase we taught my little brother when he was about three years old. He used it when confronted by adults with several situations, and the results were comical. What three-year-old can comprehend the magnitude of any situation?

I thought about this phrase recently when the circumstances of life felt totally overwhelming. I questioned myself, "If, in the midst of the chaos I am experiencing peace, is it because I am failing to comprehend the magnitude of the situation?" As I considered this possibility, I thought about the prophet Daniel. When I read the account of him being put into the lions' den, he seems to be experiencing peace while King Darius is in turmoil. So which one of these men has a true comprehension of the magnitude of the situation?

King Darius had a factual understanding of what it meant to be thrown into the lions' den. First, Daniel was an old man. Second, the purpose of throwing a man into the lions' den was for the man to be overpowered by the lions and killed. The King had been tricked into doing this to Daniel by those who were jealous of Daniel. Darius knew Daniel was a righteous man, but he also knew that no injunction or ordinance established by the Medes and Persians could be changed. All of this weighed heavily upon King Darius, and he was filled with anxiety.

There is a quietness of peace that surrounds Daniel in this story. Daniel knew the doctrine had been signed with the injunction that anyone who petitioned a god or man other than King Darius for the next 30 days was to be cast into the lions' den. He understood the law of the Medes and the Persians, but he continued to pray and give thanks as he had done previously. Did Daniel experience this peace because he failed to comprehend the magnitude of the situation, or was it because he did comprehend the magnitude of the situation?

Lord Jesus, You gave Daniel a vision of the Ancient of Days as He took His seat on His throne of fiery flames. You showed him the One whom a thousand thousands served and the One before whom ten thousand times ten thousand stood. Daniel was given Your peace when he saw You in the night visions. He saw that You were given dominion and glory and a kingdom. Please help me, when I am faced with situations I cannot comprehend, to not let my heart be troubled or afraid because You have given me Your peace.

Where Are You?

The book came from a used bookstore with an inscription on the first page. The message was from a father to his son, "I believe in you and all that you can become." The father had told the son to start reading the book on a certain page. When I turned to the page I found a quote by Philip Yancey underlined. "The most important hurdle an addicted person must surmount is to acknowledge deep in the soul that he is not God. You must recognize individual helplessness and fall back in the arms of the Higher Power. 'First of all, we had to quit playing God,' concluded the founders of AA; and then allow God himself to 'play God' in the addict's life, which involves daily, even moment-by-moment, surrender."

In the father's handwriting underneath the quote was written, "You choose where your heart dwells. God is calling." "God is calling." In the cool of the day Adam and Eve heard the sound of God walking in the garden and they hid themselves. "But the Lord God called to the man and said to him, 'Where are you?'" (Gen. 3:9 ESV). Adam had made the choice to be like God, knowing good and evil. But when he took and ate what was forbidden, his heart lost its home. Fear was introduced, and he was driven out from the Garden of Eden.

"Where are you?" This is the first question asked by God when He came seeking fellowship with the ones He had created. I think back to what the father wrote on the front page of the book, "I believe in you and all that you can become." I see this as a journey, the journey of becoming. Before you can know how to get someplace, you must first determine where you are on the map and where you are going.

Where am I, where is my heart? This is a question I ask myself as I seek to have fellowship with God. The truth is, I don't always know. "The heart is deceitful above all things and desperately sick; who can understand it? 'I the Lord search the heart and test the mind'" (Jer. 17:9-10 ESV). There are places in my life where I have "played god" so often I've become blind to them. The only thing I know to do is to say with the psalmist, "Search me, O God, and know my heart! Try me and know my thoughts! And see if there be any grievous way in me and lead me in the way everlasting!" (Psa. 139:23-24 ESV).

Father, thank You that You did not wait for me to come seeking You, but You came seeking me. Show me where I am, show me where my heart is. Playing god in my life has only lead to fear and bondage. I desire to surrender to You moment-by-moment. I want my heart to find its home in You alone.

Dealing with Scars

When I was seven years old, I had a teacher who would regularly call on the class with this question, "Class, isn't Sarah stupid." The reason she did this was that I had learning difficulties. That was over 50 years ago, but I still feel the effects of it today. I think of it as a scar on my soul. We all have scars. Some scars were inflicted on us by others; some scars we put there ourselves by poor choices. My question is, what do I do with these scars as a Christian?

Scars on the soul are reflected by how I see myself. Some scars threaten to hold me back from being everything God created me to be. Other scars open me up to strongholds that drain my energy and can hold me captive. As a Christian, God offers me a transformed life. "Do not be conformed to this world, but be transformed by the renewal of your mind" (Rom. 12:2 ESV). I am not a victim; instead, because of Christ, I am victorious. However, I have to take hold of that victory.

I would like a quick fix. I would like to do something one time and forever after be changed. However, what I am finding out is that the transformation that is taking place is a lifelong journey. Not only is it a lifelong journey, but it is also a daily one. "Let the words of my mouth and the meditations of my heart be acceptable in your sight, O Lord, my rock and my redeemer" (Psa. 19:14 ESV). Prayer by prayer, word by word, thought by thought, I choose to no longer be controlled by the scars on my soul.

This transformation is taking place, not because of my own determination, but because I have a Redeemer. My Redeemer is the rock I go to when dealing with the effects of past pain or sin. The scars from my past cause me to feel I will never succeed; they whisper messages of hopelessness in my ear. But Jesus said, "I came that you might have life and that you might have it abundantly." By God's grace, I choose to line my thoughts up with the message of hope.

Lord Jesus, by Your scars I am healed. You have given me access to the throne of Heaven and invited me to bring all my brokenness into Your healing presence. Thank You for being my Redeemer and for providing the transforming power of Your grace.

The Missing Verse

I finally found the missing verse!

I was just a little girl when I memorized the 23rd psalm. Maybe it would more correct to say "tried" to memorize the 23rd psalm. I didn't have any problem with the first two verses, but I always seemed to lie down in the green pastures, take a nap, and wake up in the valley of the shadow of death. I knew something else happened in between, but I could never remember what it was. Yesterday I found the missing pieces to the puzzle, or verse to the psalm.

At work we have a calendar that gives a Bible verse for each day. I use that verse for daily meditation. Yesterday's verse was Psalm 23:2, "He restores my soul. He guides me along the right path for his name's sake." *Restores* was in italics, so it stuck in my mind. So that's the order of the verses! He is my shepherd so I don't need to want; He makes me lie down in green pastures and leads me by still waters. The word restore means "to repair, renovate, or return to a former condition." As I meditated on this verse, it became a prayer for my soul and the souls of those I love.

"He guides me along the right path for his name's sake." What a relief! I am really not good at following a map. I often have trouble finding my way, and at times, in total frustration, have just given up and gone home. This verse tells me that I have a guide who is leading me the right way. For someone like me who knows how it feels to get lost, this is just plain good news. I always experience such great relief when, after complicated directions, someone takes pity on me and says, "Do you want me to lead you there?" "Yes!" is my immediate response.

I'm almost glad I've struggled all these years trying to remember the correct order of the verses in Psalm 23, because the blessing of finally seeing this picture of the Shepherd's care for me has been so comforting. In the course of life I often find my soul in need of repair and restoration. I don't know how to restore my soul, but the Shepherd does. It's during times like this that I lose my way. When I get turned around and can't find my way, how precious it is to find that the Shepherd is there to lead me. He leads me for His name's sake because I belong to Him.

Lord Jesus, thank You. Thank You for giving me rest. In the rush and hurry of life, thank You for still waters where I can be refreshed. Oh, Lord, You know how, during the course of life, my soul needs to be returned to it's the former condition. I am so grateful for a Shepherd who is able to do this for me. Thank You for letting me belong to You and for guiding me in the direction I need to go.

Found

Hide-and-Go-Seek. Now that was a game I was good at. In fact, I was so good at that game that one time I hid so well I was never found. I could see them seeking me, I could hear them calling, but they did not find me. Then it became quiet, but I kept hiding. The shadows began to gather, but I kept hiding. I began to get hungry, but I kept hiding. Finally, cold, cramped and hungry, I came out of hiding only to find everyone inside eating dinner. The game had ended for everyone else. My victory at not being found was a hollow one.

I have realized recently that I developed a habit of hiding when life got unpleasant. It seemed innocent enough. When I was afraid, I went to my hiding place to feel safe. When I my feelings were hurt, I went to my hiding place to comfort myself. When life seemed overwhelming, I would go to my hiding place and, well, I hid until I felt safe again. It seemed harmless enough until I realized that my hiding place was really a shrine where I worshiped at the altar of a false god.

I realized this because my hiding place began to feel more like a prison than a safe place. I began to have a sense of being lost. I felt cold, cramped and hungry. The problem was, I couldn't figure out how to stop hiding. I was so very good at it. So I did the only thing I knew to do—I called out for help! To my relief, unlike when I was a child, there was still someone seeking me.

My hidden shrine had become such a habit that I didn't recognize it for what it really was. I thought of it as simply a natural place to go when life got hard. When Jesus found me, suddenly the hiding place was illumined and I could see clearly the idol I was bowing before. The empty security was replaced by His peace.

Lord Jesus, thank You for not giving up on me. Thank You that You are the Good Shepherd. Thank You because You are my true hiding place, and whenever I am afraid I can trust in You.

It's Possible

Do some things seem impossible to you? They do to me. If I can't figure out a solution to a situation then it's hard for me to believe there is one. If the problem has gone on for a long time the hope of resolving it becomes dimmer. If I have tried solving the problem to no avail; I just want to give up.

I hate to admit it, but sometimes it's people I want to give up on. That's why I love the story of Jesus healing the demon-possessed man in the country of the Gerasenes. Talk about an impossible situation! I can't even imagine what it was like to live where there was a demon-possessed man who lived among the tombs and was crying out night and day, bruising himself with stones.

The people around him tried to deal with the problem. They bound him with chains and shackles, but he wrenched the chains apart and he broke the shackles in pieces. No one had the strength to subdue him. It would be very hard to ignore something like this happening in your neighborhood. I think at this point I would be having a conversation with a real estate person.

Jesus is introduced to the scene. When this man saw Jesus from afar, he ran and fell down before Him. Does that sound like worship, to fall at the feet of Jesus? He then cried out with a loud voice and said, "What have you to do with me, Jesus, Son of the Most High God? I adjure you by God, do not torment me" (Mark 5:1-20 ESV). Jesus sent the legion of demons out of the man. When the people who'd been living with this man heard what Jesus did they came to see what happened. What they found was the man who had been tormenting them and had himself been tormented by a legion of demons sitting there, clothed and in his right mind. The Bible says that it made the people afraid and they begged Jesus to leave. It seems to me they should have been afraid of what the man had been like and grateful to Jesus for changing him.

Lord Jesus, sometimes when I am faced with situations that seem impossible I lose sight of You. I forget that with You all things are possible. I am humbled by the picture of this demon-possessed man bowing before You because he recognizes Your power and I do not. Help me remember that, though there are things that are impossible for me, there is nothing impossible for You.

The Wrong Time?

The phone rang. It was my daughter calling, "Mom, can you tell me what time it is?" This was a strange question for her to ask, because she is in a different time zone from me. When I told her the time, she told me why she had asked. The time on her phone was an hour early. She had gotten to her classes before the doors were unlocked.

This began our discussion about the Sovereignty of God. I suggested that, if she really believed that God was Sovereign, instead of being angry and frustrated, perhaps she could pray and ask God why He wanted her at school an hour early. I told her how we all thought we trusted God until what we planned or expected was altered. When our plans change without our permission, how we respond shows whether we really trust a Sovereign God or not.

I also shared with her that one way we learn to trust God is when He leads us into situations where we have no control. We learn to trust when we humble ourselves and submit to His Lordship. I don't think it's a natural thing to trust God. I think we trust more in the clock on our cell phone than we trust in the Sovereignty of God; but we don't know that until the clock gives us the wrong time.

My daughter called me later that morning. I could hear the excitement in her voice. She had been introduced to a man and a concept that could be life-changing to her. I asked her if she thought that was why she had gotten to school an hour early. I was surprised by her response. She told me, "No." She thought she had gotten there early so that she could be reminded of God's Sovereignty.

Lord Jesus, You and You alone are the Sovereign Lord. With You there are no accidents. Thank You for teaching how to trust You. Thank You for inviting me to find rest for my soul by trusting in Your Sovereignty.

wRESTling

I remember when we got our first television. Looking back, I can see how it affected my view of life. Some of my favorite shows were family sitcoms. Every problem worked itself out within thirty minutes, and at the end of the show everyone was smiling. As a child I thought my life would reflect this "reality." Boy, was I in for a surprise!

I have just finished reading about the life of Jacob in Genesis. Here I get a very different picture of family life than the one portrayed in the sitcoms. From the beginning, before he was even born, Jacob is wrestling with his brother Esau. He was given the name Jacob because he was grasping his brother's heel when he came out of the womb. All through Jacob's life I see this wrestling, a striving to gain control of situations and people.

Today I read the last chapter of Jacob's life. Hebrews 11:21 says he worshiped while resting on his staff. I think this is significant, because Jacob's life is so marked by the different wrestling matches he had. However, the most significant one was when he spent the night wrestling with God. He was told that Esau, from whom he had taken both the birthright and their father's blessing by deceit, was on his way to meet him with 400 men. With this threat on the horizon, Jacob encounters a man with whom he wrestles until the breaking of the day. Finally, the man touches Jacob's hip socket and puts it out of joint. Still Jacob held on and said, "I will not let you go until you bless me."

For the rest of his life Jacob walked with a limp. The blessing he received that night was this, "Your name shall no longer be called Jacob, but Israel, for you have striven with God and with men, and have prevailed" (Gen. 32:28 ESV). The picture of Jacob resting on his staff and worshiping God seems very symbolic to me. At the end of Jacob's life he no longer has the strength to make things happen his way. He has something far better; he has faith. As he blesses his sons, he is sure of what he hopes for and confident about what he doesn't see. He is no longer wrestling but instead is resting in the promises of God.

Heavenly Father, I realize that life is hard and life's struggles can seldom be solved in 30 minutes with everyone smiling. Thank You for the life of Jacob. Thank You for showing me what it means to wrestle with You until I find rest in You. Help me face every difficulty being sure of what I hope for and confident about what I don't see. Let my life be a life of worship.

I Washed Her Feet

She asked if she could talk to me. Then, with her eyes downcast, she told me about her struggles. As I listened, a thought came to my mind, "You should wash her feet." Because it was such an unusual idea, I decided to pray about it. The idea wouldn't go away. Not much was said afterward, and I had no idea how what I had done impacted her life until after her death when I found her journal.

June 28

Amazing things happened to me today. This afternoon Sarah and I sat in the swing talking and sharing, and I shared, risking our friendship. I wanted to share these things with someone other than a therapist. Was there someone I could share my heart with who I wasn't paying who wouldn't reject me? Sarah listened, comforted, and shared some things of her own. I cried and then we went on with our activity. Later she said there was something she wanted to do after everyone went to bed.

After supper I asked her what it was. She said, "In response to what you told me, I'm going to wash your feet." I was flabbergasted, totally, and then so touched by her that I began to cry. It was an act of love I have never experienced before, and I was totally humbled by the experience. There, on her knees, my dear sweet friend washed my feet. It was an experience I will never forget. It reached in and crumbled a wall of distrust I never expected to end in this life. I went to bed in tears and awed by such an act. But God blessed it, because I saw a person loving me, honoring me, caring as no one ever had. It softened my resistance and broke my heart towards God. I went to bed praying, praising and thanking God.

I didn't know the impact my washing her feet would have on my friend's life, but God did. I didn't know that when she talking to me, in her heart she had been questioning if anyone would accept her if they really knew her; but God did. I didn't know that when I chose to prayerfully do something that might make me look foolish it would help set her free; but God did.

Lord Jesus, thank You for leading me by Your example. Lord, You are the only one who fully knows me and You have chosen to accept me. Help me to represent You well in a world full of hurting people by humble acts of kindness.

Winter's Garden

If I were to show you my garden right now, what you would see would be a collection of dry, brittle sticks. In the Spring, Summer and even in the Fall there is color and life. There is still life, but you can't see it; it looks barren and dead. God created every season for a purpose. The Winter season in life is a time to live by faith. It is an opportunity to experience hope. In the Winter many people who have gardens sit by the fireplace on cold dark nights and look at seed catalogs and plan for the flowers of Spring.

God allows Winter seasons to come into my life as well. When I was younger I viewed this very differently than I do today. When all I could see was a season that felt cold and lifeless, I would let the chill penetrate my being. However, through the years I experienced again and again the truth that everything God has created is beautiful in its own way.

In the Winter times of my life I find that, like the plants whose roots are seeking nourishment deep within the soil, so my soul is seeking nourishment from God. The beauty of this season is not often found in gay colors and music like it is in the other seasons. The beauty of Winter is in its call to quiet contemplation. In the Winter season of my soul, I look at the promises of God and warm my spirit by His fire. I look no longer at what I can see with earthly vision, but instead open my eyes of faith to see His word fulfilled.

When the days are short and cold, it drives me inward I find myself opening the books of the Prophets. Yesterday I look at Ezekiel 36. The final siege had taken place. Jerusalem, once a city of great rejoicing, had become barren and desolate. All her inhabitants were taken captive. What message did God have for His people in this Winter of their soul? It was not a message of despair but a message of hope: "I will take you from the nations, gather you from all the lands and bring you into your own land. Then I will sprinkle clean water on you, and you will be clean; I will cleanse you from all your filthiness and from all your idols. Moreover, I will give you a new heart and put a new spirit within you; I will remove the heart of stone from your flesh and give you a heart of flesh. I will put my Spirit within you..." (Ezek. 36:24-27 NASB).

Heavenly Father, in this Winter season, when I cannot see beyond the barrenness, help me look at life with eyes of faith. Thank You for the promises that I see in Ezekiel. You are the one who brings the cleansing, You are the one who gives a new heart. You are the one who has put Your Spirit within me. You are the gardener of my soul.

Transformation from Larvae to Dragonfly?

As I was walking along the creek bank, I noticed a cocoon. It had no external beauty, but I knew it held life. I watched as the life within struggled to emerge. It would have been an easy thing for me to simply tear open the cocoon and let its prisoner free, but in doing so I would have also caused its death. So instead I watched the struggle for life. Finally, a dragonfly emerged; but what an odd looking creature with its fat body and tiny wings. The struggle was not over, but the struggle was not in vain. The wings became transparent, beautiful and detailed in their design. As the wings increased in strength and beauty, the body changed into an elegant slender shape. Suddenly the crusade for freedom was over; the dragonfly took flight and was gone.

I have been meditating on, memorizing, and puzzling over Romans 6. What does it mean that I have been baptized into Christ Jesus' death? How can I walk in newness of life? What does it look like to be united with Him in a resurrection like His? When I was a little girl, I would hear fairy tales; and there would be the wave of a magic wand or the sprinkle of fairy dust and poof!—a pumpkin was transformed into a carriage. God calls us to walk in newness of life, but there is no fairy dust or magic wand.

So is my next option to follow a strict list of "Do this" and "Don't do that"? In my imagination I can see an ugly larvae deciding that it's time for him to morph into an elegant dragonfly. What rules does he have to follow to make this happen? Does metamorphosis occur because of the strong determination of the larvae? I think not. Nor do I believe that our transformation into the likeness of the risen Christ is because we have followed a list of rules and regulations.

No magic fairy dust, no strict adherence to the law. What then will bring about identification with the risen Christ? I find in Romans 6 that I am to consider myself as dead to sin and alive to God in Christ Jesus. Because of this I am to present my members to God as instruments for righteousness and not to let sin reign in my mortal body and obey its passions. The struggle that I have is a struggle to surrender and to obey the Spirit of the Living God. This wrestling to no longer obey the passions of my flesh, but instead to become slave of God, becomes my act of worship. I feel this struggle will never end, but I know by faith that the end result is strength and beauty and a transformed life.

Lord Jesus, You came that I might have abundant life. By faith I take hold of the grace You offer to surrender my will to You and to be transformed into your likeness. Your word says that strength and beauty are in your sanctuary. Please, Lord Jesus, may You find both strength and beauty within the sanctuary of my heart.

The Breath of Life

The pain became so intense that it consumed all my thoughts. Then, in the haze, I heard the nurse say, "Breathe, you must breathe, your baby needs the oxygen." Obediently I took a deep cleansing breath and it was time to push. Moments later I heard the breath of life sounding in my newborn infant's cry.

I have been tracing this breath of life throughout the Scriptures. The first place it is mentioned is in the story of creation. "Then the Lord God formed the man of dust from the ground and breathed into his nostrils the breath of life, and the man became a living creature" (Gen. 2:7 ESV). This idea of the breath of life is repeated in Job 33:4, "The Spirit of God has made me, and the breath of the Almighty gives me life." The Hebrew word for breath is *ruah*. *Ruah* can be translated as breath, air, wind, spirit.

I am a very visual person, and one of the most dramatic pictures I can think of in connection with the breath of God is in the valley of dry bones found in Ezekiel 37. The hand of God was upon Ezekiel and the Spirit of the Lord took him to a valley filled with very dry bones. God told him to prophesy to the bones, and when he did the bones came together, but they had no breath. Finally, God said, "Prophesy to the breath; prophesy, son of man, and say to the breath, Thus says the Lord God: come from the four winds, O breath, and breathe on these slain, that they may live." So, by the breath of God, those who were dead became alive.

I see this picture of the breath of God in the New Testament as well. Jesus said in the third chapter of John, "That which is born of the flesh is flesh, and that which is born of the Spirit is spirit. Do not marvel that I said to you 'You must be born again.' The wind blows where it wishes, and you hear its sound, but you do not know where it comes from or where it goes. So it is with everyone who is born of the Spirit." The Greek word *pneuma* means a current of air, breath, or breeze; by analogy it means a spirit. Jesus shows this again at the end of His time with His disciples when He says, "Peace be with you. As the Father has sent me, even so I am sending you." and when He had said this, He breathed on them and said to them, "Receive the Holy Spirit."

Oh, Lord, with every breathe I take today remind me that You are the air I breathe. Twice born I come to You. Breath of Heaven, fill me with Your holy presence today. As I breathe in, may I inhale the deep cleansing breath of Your presence, and may I exhale praise. "Let everything that has breath praise the Lord! Praise the Lord!" (Psalm 150:6).

The Muddy Feet of Faith

"I don't know how to do this." "Sarah, do you know how often you say that," my husband replied. "Do you have any idea how often I feel that," I thought to myself. It seems life is always taking me in directions I've never been before. I find myself confronted with situations that I didn't expect and that I feel unequipped to handle.

The children of Israel were confused. Moses was dead and a swollen Jordan River lay between them and the Promised Land. What were they supposed to do? "As soon as you see the Ark of the Covenant of the Lord your God being carried by the Levitical priests, then you shall set out from your place and follow it.... Do not come near it, in order that you may know the way you shall go, for you have not passed this way before" (Josh. 3:3-4 ESV).

The Ark of the Covenant represented the Lord's presence with them. They were to follow, simply to follow where they were led. Sometimes I see where the Lord is leading me and I am afraid. Even though I know it is the right way to go, I still feel afraid. The children of Israel already knew that there were giants in the land; they knew there were walled cities; and yet they were told to follow the Ark of the Covenant and the presence of the Lord would be with them.

"You have not passed this way before." I identify with this statement. I have not passed this way before; I am unsure of where this path is leading me. I am faced with the same question the children of Israel faced, "Dare I trust the Lord who is leading me?" I find I must do what I'm sure the children of Israel did: I must remember. I must remember

His faithfulness to me in the past when He led me through unfamiliar places.

Lord Jesus, You promised that You would never leave me or forsake me. Please help me not to forsake the way You have chosen for me because my faith is weak. When the priest who were carrying the Ark of the Covenant came to the Jordan it didn't divide until the soles of their feet were wet and they were standing in the muddy water. So, Lord, today help me not to be afraid to get my feet wet and muddy by following where You lead.

The emPHAsis Is On The Wrong syLLAble

You have your emPHAsis on the wrong syLLAble. This is a phrase my husband taught me. When you emphasis the wrong syllable, the word ends up sounding strange or just plain wrong. That's not only true with the spoken word, that's true in life. I often emphasis the wrong thing and the result is confusion.

There is a war going on. It is a clash of the Spirit against the flesh. Sometimes I just want to give in and say, "I just can't help myself." When I do that I am putting the emPHAsis on the wrong syLLAble. This battle of flesh and Spirit is fought first in the mind. According to the fourth chapter of Ephesians, before I was a Christian I had no choice. I was callous and given up to sensuality, greed and practices of impurity. In other words, I was dead spiritually. When I became a Christian I became alive spiritually. Now I can have the mind of Christ. So, which will it be, which will it be? Shall I let the emphasis be on my fleshly desires or shall I obey the Spirit?

Hebrew 11:25 speaks of the fleeting pleasures of sin. If there was no pleasure in sin then there would be no clash between flesh and Spirit. What begins in the mind doesn't stay there; it moves to my actions. Romans 6 goes on to say that I become a slave of the one I obey. I either become a slave of sin that leads to death, or of obedience that leads to righteousness.

Something makes me angry. Now I'm faced with a choice. Do I place the emPhasis on the offense and become angry and let strife grow, possibly causing divisions and dissension? Or do I choose to walk in the Spirit and be forgiving? To be honest, my flesh wants to simply give full vent to my anger. Where I place the emphasis will go beyond my thoughts and affect my actions. Galatians 5 tells me, "If we live by the Spirit, let us also walk by the Spirit."

Lord Jesus, I am faced with this pull between my flesh and Spirit every day in so many ways. You have invited me to walk in Your Spirit and experience love, joy, peace, patience, kindness, goodness, faithfulness, gentleness, and self-control. Please let my first response be to turn my face to You and ask for mercy, and take hold the grace by faith that You have assured me is available.

A Kite with No Strings Attached

"Let's Go Fly a Kite" [Richard and Robert Sherman, *Let's Go Fly a Kite*, © 1963, Wonderland Music Co., Inc.] was a song from my childhood, and it represented a pure sense of freedom. Yet even though there is freedom seen as the kite soars in the atmosphere, there is a certain tension as well and that can be seen in the string. Oh, but don't loosen your grip on that string. You cannot trust the wind.

Lately I've been studying what it means to walk in the Spirit. Looking up the Greek word for Spirit, I found one of them means wind. I must confess that this has not been a purely academic study. I want my life to be one of walking in the Spirit, but I am aware of the truth: In my battle to choose Spirit over my flesh, my flesh often wins. WHY? I've been reading the Scriptures, meditating, praying and simply not understanding. However, I have always found that when I struggle with something like this, if I don't give up prematurely God always meets with me to give me understanding. Once again I have experienced the truth of the verse which says God works in us "both to will and to do His good pleasure" (Phil. 2:13 ESV).

When the children of Israel came out of the Egypt they were free from slavery, yet their heart kept seeking idols. Why? I believe it is the same reason that my heart keeps turning to my flesh and why gripping the kite string is so important. It's a matter of trust. Do I really trust God to meet all my needs? Can I really surrender to His love and be like a kite without a string?

There is this tension of fear. The children of Israel had it; that's why they wanted some kind of idol they could control. Sure, God had delivered them from the slavery of Egypt, but could they really trust Him? Wouldn't they be better off to have God *and* having an idol just in case. For me it's not a whole lot different. Sure, Jesus came and died for my sins and set me free, but can I really trust Him? I am a lot like Eve when Satan tempted her and asked, "Do you really believe God loves you and has your best interest at heart? Just take a look at what He is saying you can't have. Come on, be honest; don't you want a bite?" I don't want to let go of control; that fruit looks so good. Is God holding out on me? Can I trust Him? He can still be my God, but I've got to have just one bite.

Oh, Lord Jesus, You have called me to freedom. You have told me to trust in You with my whole heart. You have told me that friendship with this world is to be Your enemy, and yet I still want to be a friend of this world. So I come to You today with my hands open wide. May I be a kite without strings, free to soar wherever the will of the wind takes me!

The Journey

If I close my eyes I can see exactly where I was when I prayed this prayer: "Lord, I don't really want a free will. I want Your will." I'm not sure what I expected. Perhaps I thought it was the right prayer and after I prayed it I would no longer have any struggles with my sinful nature. I can't remember what I was expecting because it was over 30 years ago; but I can tell you how I have seen God answer that prayer. What I have discovered is that that prayer was not a destination but a starting point for a journey to know God.

As I read through the Bible this year I am looking again at the life of Moses. I can so clearly see from my vantage point how God uniquely put Moses' life together so that he could fulfill God's plan. I can see this because I can read his story from birth to death. He, however, had to live his life the same way I live my life—from day to day. That's why, when God sent him back to Egypt after he had been a shepherd for so many years, he complained of not being eloquent. God's response to Moses' complaint makes me pause and look at my own life and journey to know God. "The Lord said to him, 'Who has made man's mouth? Who makes him mute, or deaf, or seeing, or blind? Is it not I, the Lord? Now therefore go, and I will be with your mouth and teach you what you shall speak'" (Ex. 4:11-12 ESV).

God worked in such a powerful way to deliver His people from Pharaoh, and yet when they were in the wilderness on their way to the Promised Land, they began to long for the food of Egypt. God told Moses that He had heard the wailing of the people and He was going to send them meat for a whole month. Moses' response was, "Would they have enough if flocks and herds were slaughtered for them? Would they have enough if all the fish in the sea were caught for them?" (Num. 11:22 NIV). In my journey with God I have often wondered how He would provide for the needs I faced. I have often gone back to what God told Moses, because I think it's the same thing He tells me. "Is the Lord's arm too short? You will now see whether or not what I say will come true for you" (Num. 11:23 NIV).

I have found this to be true. As a young woman I wanted to surrender my will to God's will. What I discovered in doing so was a journey, a journey much like the one God took Moses and the Children of Israel on: a journey of faith.

Lord Jesus, thank You so much for inviting me on this journey to know you. Even though I know I cannot physically hold your hand, I reach out to You. Guide me on this journey as You guided Moses. Again today I surrender my will for Yours.

The Impossible Made Possible In the Valley of Dead Dry Bones

Have you ever looked across the landscape of your live and seen barrenness? You see no signs of life in the situations you find yourself in. If hope is a confident expectation for good, the opposite of hope must be despair. When God took Ezekiel into the valley full of dry bones he was showing Ezekiel a picture of despair. It was as if God was saying to Ezekiel, "No more pretending things are better than they seem. Look around you. On the whole surface of the valley there is nothing but very dry bones." What a depressing picture!

One of the things I look for when I read the Scriptures is when God asks man a question. In my mind's eye I can see Ezekiel looking with despair at all these dry bones and trying to process the hopelessness that they represent when God asks him a question. "Son of man, can these bones live?" (Ezek. 37). Ezekiel's response was humble and wise. He said, "O Lord God, you know." First, he acknowledged Him as Lord, then he addressed Him as God. From the perspective of a man there was no hope, but Ezekiel was not addressing his answer to a man but to the Lord God. His response showed that he understood that the things that were impossible for him were not impossible for God.

There are situations in my life where God has invited me to participate in the work He is doing of making the impossible possible. This was one of those times in Ezekiel's life. God told him to prophesy over the dead dry bones, and when he did he heard the rattling as he watched the bones come together. Then he watched as the sinews covered the bones and then flesh covered the sinews. Now he was in a valley of corpses, because there was no breath in any of these bodies. I've been there. Places where I've walked with God, believing He could do what I could not, only to find myself surrounded by corpses. There was the promise of life, but not the evidence of it; and all I knew was that I am surrounded by corpses. God, however, was not finished. And in the fullness of time He brought forth breath.

In those places of my life where all hope was lost, God opened the grave and raised my dreams to life again. He did for me what I could not do for myself. "Without faith it is impossible to please him, for whoever would draw near to God must believe that he exists and that he rewards those who seek him" (Heb. 11:6 ESV). Ezekiel believed; why else would he be speaking to dry bones? His faith was not a feeling; instead it was evidenced by his response to who he believed God to be. Because God was the Lord, he did as he was told; he prophesied to the bones and then to the wind. He was rewarded for his faith by being part of God's miracle of taking a valley filled with dead dry bones and causing them to become an exceedingly great army.

O Lord Jesus, help me to see my life through the lens of faith. You are the Lord of life. You are the Redeemer. With You nothing is impossible. You have invited me to be part of the work You are doing in my generation. Your word has told me that You have prepared good works in advance for me to do, but they can only be accomplished by faith.

God Appointed a Worm

"God appointed a worm" (Jonah 4:7). I can remember the first time I heard this taught. I was well aware of my worm status, but was hoping to be promoted to the butterfly position. In the book of Jonah I found that God could use me even if I never got my wings. Over the years I have learned again and again that it's not about my plans and fitting God into them; it's about God's plans and my surrendering to Him.

One of the beautiful things in the book of Jonah is the list of divine appointments. First, God appointed a prophet; but he was a reluctant prophet, and he chose to go the opposite direction of where God told him to go. So God appointed a storm to get his attention. When Jonah found himself drowning, God appointed a fish for transportation. When Jonah had finally obeyed God, He appointed a plant to give his prophet shade and save him from discomfort. God had more He wanted to teach Jonah, so He appointed a worm to attack the plant so that it withered. Last of all, God appointed a scorching east wind and the sun to beat down on the head of Jonah to make him faint and show him the hardness of his heart.

Everyone knows the value of a prophet, but it's easy to overlook the value of a storm, a fish, a plant, a worm, and a scorching east wind. The reason God was sending His prophet to Nineveh was because God is a God of compassion. He wanted the people of Nineveh to hear the message of salvation. God wanted Nineveh to repent. He wanted to have pity on them. Jonah had no pity for Nineveh, so God showed him his heart by taking away something Jonah valued, a shade plant. Then God said to Jonah, "You had pity on the plant, for which you did not labor, nor did you make it grow, which came into being in the night and perished in a night. And should I not pity Nineveh?"

There is so much about this story I identify with. Sometimes God has sent me to share His love with people that I don't really care to share His love with. They have been unkind to me and I want to be unkind back, or at least pretend they don't exist. And then again there is my longing for wings. If I'm going to be part of this story, can't I at least have a pair of beautiful wings? The worm in this story is simply that—a worm, not a butterfly. However, this worm was an appointed worm, who was part of God's story of redemption.

Lord Jesus, when I consider all these things, my mind goes to the second chapter of Philippians, "Do nothing from rivalry or conceit, but in humility count others more significant than yourselves.... Have this mind among yourselves, which is yours in Christ Jesus, who, though he was in the form of God, did not count equality with God a thing to be grasped, but made himself nothing, taking the form of a servant." Lord, I want to be like You, I want the mind of Christ.

God's Celestial Navigation System

Sometimes I find myself praying a certain prayer that I feel sure God initiated. "Lord, please let me honor You," is one of those prayers. Sometimes it takes different forms, such as, "Show me how to bring You glory," or "Help me magnify Your name." But all these prayers have the same focus. Philippians 2:13 says, "For it is God who works in you both to will and to work for his good pleasure." What has been interesting to me is to see how these prayers and God's answering them have impacted my life.

When God chose Moses to be His spokesman, Moses objected because he felt inadequate. "O Lord, I'm not very good with words. I never have been, and I'm not now, even though you've spoken to me. I get tongue-tied, and my words get tangled." God didn't respond, "Oh, that's right. I forgot you have trouble speaking clearly!" What He said instead was, "Who has made man's mouth? Who makes him mute, or deaf, or seeing, or blind? Is it not I, the LORD?" (Ex. 4:11 ESV). How does God glorify Himself? I believe He takes the things I consider to be my weakness and turns them around so that they become the very thing He chooses to make Himself known to those around me. This can be a bit scary, because it means I have to trust that, when God takes me places I don't want to go, it's for a good purpose.

The stars are always shining, but they can be seen best at night. God has answered my desire to bring Him glory by allowing me to experience some difficult days and long nights. As I have walked in the darkness, my vision often blurred by tears, I have been blessed by the sweetness of His presence. I have found joy and wonder in the midnight blackness, because I have found a purpose beyond myself. "The heavens declare the glory of God; the sky above proclaims his handiwork. Day to day pours out speech, night to night reveals knowledge" (Psa. 19:1-2 ESV).

I have found in these difficult periods of my life that I have experienced the glory of God, my understanding of His love for me has been magnified. God is so economical in His ways; because while He is using my weakness to show me who He really is, He is also redeeming my pain and using it to help navigate others into His presence. In doing this, He allows me to become part of His celestial navigation plan. He breathes meaning into the dark night of my soul; and by infusing my life with His presence and grace, I become a star in the night that others can see to lead them into His glorious presence.

O Lord, thank You for the privilege of belonging to You. Thank You for giving meaning to my life, my weakness and even my sorrow. Life is hard with or without You as Lord, but when You are Lord You redeem all the suffering and pain. Thank You that You not only magnify Yourself to me, but allow me to be part of Your celestial navigation system so that I can magnify You to others.

Love Your Neighbor?

I was simply going for a walk. I passed my neighbor's house; she was in her front yard and seemed angry. I'd never really met her, but every time I walked by her house she would say something negative that let me know she was not happy to be there. I would smile and keep on walking. Suddenly, somewhere in my mind I heard the words, "Love your neighbor."

"Love your neighbor." Now, what exactly does that mean? This particular neighbor showed no signs of friendliness and, in fact, totally intimidated me. Yet every time I passed the house I would hear the same directive "Love your neighbor." I wanted to obey what I believed was the Holy Spirit's directive, so I began to pray for my neighbors as I passed their house, hoping that that would fulfill my duty to "love."

"Love your neighbor." It just wouldn't go away. God seemed neither satisfied nor impressed with my prayers. "Go knock on the door and introduce yourself." "But I don't want to! She intimidates me." I responded to what I believed was the directive of the Holy Spirit. "Love your neighbor," was all I could hear, so I hesitantly went up to the door.

On our first meeting, she told me much about the difficulties she had experienced, "No wonder she seemed so angry," I thought to myself. I also found out she was a Christian. She asked me to go to a prayer meeting with her. I was amazed at how she was transformed during her time of prayer and worship. It was as if a heavy weight fell off her. I was able to see her in a completely different light.

I had finally obeyed God prompting to "Love my neighbor" in the Spring. She died in the Fall of that same year. She had adopted four children who were left without a mother. By the next year, three of them were living with me. These children have taken permanent residence in my heart. "Love your neighbor." I had no idea what that would mean.

Lord Jesus, Your word tells me that I am God's workmanship, and that I have been created in You for good works which God prepared in advance for me to do. Help me to be sensitive to the leading of your Spirit. When You tell me to "Love my neighbor," help me to simply obey.

"What Time Is It?"

"Mom, what time is it?" Although this is not an unusual question for one of my children to ask me, this time it was. My daughter was calling me from a different time zone. She was sitting in her car wondering why everything was dark and all the buildings were locked. When I told her the time, she figured out what had happened. Her cell phone had picked up the wrong signal and had given her the wrong time. Now what was she supposed to do?

I could hear the frustration growing in her voice, so I asked her a question. "Do you believe God is sovereign?" I paused for her to think about it. Then I asked my next question. "Is it possible He might have a reason for allowing you to get to school an hour early? Since you have access to His throne by prayer, why don't you talk to Him and ask Him why you're there early." I heard a long sigh as the tension was released. How you see God affects how you respond to the circumstances of your life.

I believe that God is sovereign and that He loves me, but I still struggle when I am faced with unexpected situations. My initial response is to get angry. I get angry because things are not going the way I planned for them to go. Things don't always go the way I planned because I am not sovereign. I am not sovereign, but God is. When I humble myself and acknowledge that God is in control and I am not, then I can ask, "Lord, what do You want me to do?"

Later that day my daughter called me, and I asked her if she had discovered why God allowed her to get to school an hour early, this is what she told me. "It was the first class of a new semester, an 8:00 class. We were all tired. Our teacher is from China, so English is his second language. At first I struggled to pay attention, but I kept thinking about our conversation this morning and asking myself and then asking God, 'What do You have for me, Lord?' As I listened to the lecture, I realized what I was hearing could change the direction of my life." "So do you think that was why God had you get to class an hour early," I asked. "No Mom," she said, "I think I needed to be reminded again the God loves me and that He is in control."

Ah, Sovereign Lord, I know You love me. I know You are in control, yet still I struggle. Today please help me to relinquish my will and humbly accept the things You allow into my life. Thank You for giving me access to Your throne. But, most of all, thank You for loving me.

Whose List?

"Plan your work, and work your plan." I really like this way of doing things. I like the sense of control it gives me. When I can look back over my list at the end of the day and see a check mark beside every item, it's been a good day. I don't really like to have my plans interrupted. I plan into my day the good deeds I intend to do; after all, I am a good person. I don't mind doing things for others as long as I have them written ahead of time on my list. Isn't this the right way to do things?

This morning I read about a farmer who said instead of doing a lot of planning each year, he had opted for a different way of doing things. He said instead of spending all his time planning, he chose to listen. What he discovered was that, when he spent time listening for guidance instead of planning, he was more relaxed and had more fun. He even said that in the end he achieved more than he could otherwise.

I think one of the reasons my lists can be an enemy of peace is that, when I make my list, I often am presuming on the future. The Lord has promised me a daily portion; do I really need more? Sometimes when I make a list of all the things I want to accomplish in a day, I am putting myself in a position I do not posses. I am not the master of my own fate. What I do have is a sweet assurance that a daily portion of grace has been provided for me.

I don't see Jesus having the same irritation I do when people interrupted what He was doing. Why? I find the answer in Philippians 2:4-7: "Let each of you look not only to his own interests, but also to the interests of others. Have this mind among yourselves, which is yours in Christ Jesus, who, though he was in the form of God, did not count equality with God a thing to be grasped, but made himself nothing, taking the form of a servant." No servant comes to his master with a list and says, "This is what I am doing today." However, I do think he listens with humility as his master gives him a list for the day. The master also gives him all the provisions necessary to complete the tasks.

Lord Jesus, help me to humbly listen for Your guidance today. Help me to rest in the assurance that, with every task You give me to do today, You will also provide the grace necessary for me to accomplish it. I want to follow Your example and not only look out for my own interests but also the interests of others, even if I don't have it written ahead of time on my list.

Smelting Furnace?

It often happens this way: I read something in my daily Bible reading and start wondering, "What does that mean?" Yesterday I read, "The Lord took you and brought you out of the iron-smelting furnace, out of Egypt...." The phrase "iron-smelting" caught my attention, so I did a little research and found it used several times in connection with Israel being the Lord's treasured possession. I found in Isaiah 48:10, "See, I have refined you, though not as silver; I have tested you in the furnace of affliction."

The purpose of smelting is to remove dross from the metal by putting it into a furnace that has been strongly heated. The purpose I see in the "furnace of affliction" in my life is so that I can be purged, purified, and refined. This doesn't really sound like something I would choose to participate in. In fact, the only way anyone would want to go through this is if they really trusted God. So perhaps another thing the "iron-smelting" process exposes is what I am trusting in.

Since "iron-smelting furnaces" was what caught my attention yesterday, you might think I had a day of intense testing, but I didn't. What I had was a day of slight frustration, just enough to make me irritable and uncomfortable. So how did I handle it? First, I found myself wanting to eat something. I wasn't hungry, I just wanted to dull the feeling of discomfort. Next, I wanted to grumble and complain. I simply wanted to give vent to my irritability. Sometimes I think can see God using the obvious afflictions in my life to purify me easier than I can see Him using the daily discomforts.

My son is a *Calvin and Hobbs* fan. Calvin made a "transmogrifier" out of a collection of boxes. Calvin would enter the transmogrifier (by crawling under a box) and emerge as a tiger or toad or a duplicate of himself. Sometimes I wish I could be transformed by just crawling into a transmogrifier. What I find instead is that God is calling me to trust Him to purge, purify and refine me daily as I turn to Him for help, not only in the afflictions of life but also the irritations of life.

Lord Jesus, please help me be patient in affliction, even when the affliction is just a daily inconvenience. Help me cooperate with what You are doing in my life by humbly coming to You in prayer instead of seeking my comfort in other things. Your word teaches me that You want to humble and to test me so that, in the end, it might go well with me; yet my flesh doesn't want to be humbled. Thank You for Your promise that, if I ask anything according to Your will, I have the assurance that I will receive what I'm asking for.

Free To Laugh

While sitting in the local coffee shop, with my hands wrapped around a warm mug, I listened to my friend share about the struggles she was having. She spoke about the emotional prison that caused her to feel separated from her family and loved ones. As I listened to her talk, my mind was drawn back to a time in my life I had experienced similar struggles.

I was 18 years old, and I felt I had the weight of the world on my shoulders. My depression was smothering me, and even though I was on a vacation with my family, I felt locked away and unable to engage with anyone. One day we came upon a local fair. My father bought me a ticket for the Ferris wheel. As the wheel went round and round, something happened, I began to laugh. It was such a relief, a relief I had not felt in a very long time. I noticed my Father giving the man who operated the Ferris wheel another dollar every time I went around. I laughed until the tears flowed from my eyes. That was the day I began to heal.

The Bible says, "A cheerful heart does good like medicine, but a broken spirit makes one sick" (Prov. 17:22). I think laughter is a gift God gave us that does some amazing things. I have heard that laughter boosts the immune system. I read that, for every minute of laughter, you produce somewhere around $10,000 worth of healthy body chemistry. These chemicals have positive healing affects on both your body and mind.

An article on aging healthy, happy and youthful said that the average four-year-old laughed 300 times a day, while a 40 year old would only average four times. I don't know if their numbers are right, but I do know the gift of laughter seems lost for many adults. I think there is something about the humility of a child that frees them to laugh. Jesus invites us to enter the Kingdom as little children. In 1 Peter 5 it says that we are to humble ourselves before the Lord. Then he tells us how, by casting all of our cares on Him because He cares for us.

Lord Jesus, You have set me free in so many ways. Help me cast my cares on You and rest in Your love with childlike trust. Help me to lift my face to You and know the joy of a cheerful heart. I have heard the saying "laugh and the world laughs with you." Let my life be a life that draws people into to joy of belonging to You.

Encountering Sacred Moments

I didn't know when I walked into my brother's art studio I was about to encounter a sacred moment. On the pedestal was a mother sitting in a chair. Across her lap her adult handicapped son was draped. The man was not able to speak; he had a palsy that contorted his face and body. My brother was sculpting him. My brother is an artist who not only was looking at the bone structure of this man, but seeing the value of his soul. However, it was the mother's face that forever touched my heart. She was glowing because my brother, the artist, had really seen her son.

Yesterday I took my 91 year old mother-in-law to have her hair washed. She was unable to walk from the handicapped parking to the hair salon, so I got a wheelchair. When I got to the salon I was grateful that I had gotten the wheelchair, because there were no seats available. A van of mentally handicapped adults filled the room. On every wall was a poster of a beautiful smiling model. Beneath the posters sat an assortment of beautiful souls trapped in bodies that the world would never see as beautiful. Their caregiver, however, did see their beauty. She spoke to them with kindness and respect, and I felt again I had encountered a sacred moment.

Many years ago a friend and I led the youth group for our church. My friend worked in the mental health department for our county, and she thought of a wonderful project for our youth group. We planned a dinner for the mentally handicapped adults in our community. The youth group planned a puppet show and a dinner. During the preparations we also educated them about how to relate to people who were different from themselves. Not long before the event was to take place, a beautiful 13-year-old girl's mother died. She still wanted to be included in the activity. I watched in amazement as she tenderly cared for others. I saw healing happen both for her and the adults she shared with.

My daughter has begun working in a local jail. She is working with women who are much older than she is and many who have been in and out of jail for most of their lives. When she talks about them, her face shines. I asked her what she sees when she looks at them, and then I smiled when she told me. She said she tries to see beyond where they are so that she can see who they are.

Thank You, Lord, for loving me. Thank You, Lord, for knowing who I am. Thank You, Lord, for seeing me. It's so easy to get lost these days in the shuffle and the noise. Lord, help me to take the time to see the people You place in my life. Help me not to just look at the external, but to look at who You made them to be. Thank You for the sacred moments of my life when You bless me with the gift of seeing others through Your eyes.

Sweeter Than Candy

I work at the Chocolate Therapy Café where there are many delicious homemade candies and other goodies. But there is something else there too. On top of the candy counter is a perpetual calendar. Every day there is a Bible verse for that day. I read it when I first come to work and then I think about it throughout the day. It's like candy for my soul.

"May God himself, the God of peace, sanctify you through and through" (1 Thess. 5:23 NIV). It seems to me that every day in one way or another I struggle with my sinful nature. When I found this verse in Thessalonians and meditated on it all day at work, the truth of what was being said permeated my mind and spirit. Thessalonians goes on to say, "May your whole spirit, soul and body be kept blameless at the coming of our Lord Jesus Christ. The one who calls you is faithful and he will do it."

I read an account of John Newton recently, about his own struggle after he had become a Christian. He spoke of how he valued the Word of God. He was no longer a drunk, given over to every evil, but he still had a problem. As he put it, "My soul still loved dirt." He found himself in Guinea living a life that would make anyone think that he had forgotten about the Lord's mercies. He said, "Sin first deceives, and then it hardens. I was not tightly chained, but I had no power to free myself— and little desire to. Sometimes I would think about the fix I had gotten into; if I tried to change my ways, I would just sink deeper." So the question is, can Jesus really sanctify us through and through? Is He able to keep our whole spirit, soul and body blameless until He comes? Is He faithful, can He do it?

John Newton went on to say, "Weak and almost delirious, I got out of bed and crept to a secluded part of the island where I had the freedom in prayer I had never had before. I made no more resolutions to be a better man. I simply cast myself on the Lord to do with me whatever He wanted. I did not have a shred of power to do anything right. All I could do was throw myself at His feet, receiving the good of Christ's death for me in a way I had never done before.... I began to wait on the Lord in prayer as I had never done before. I am humbly trusting in His mercy and His promises to be with me as my Guide and Guard till the end of my life."

Lord Jesus, when I read this account of John Newton, I am reminded that You are able to sanctify me through and through. Forgive me for spending so much of my life acting like the weight of the burden to be blameless rests on my shoulders, forgetting that You are faithful and You can do what You've promised to do. Help me do instead what John Newton did and humble myself by casting myself and all my anxieties on You, believing you care for me. Then let me sing the song John Newton wrote, "Amazing grace, how sweet the sound that saved a wretch like me. I once was lost but now I'm found, was blind but now I see." [John Newton, *Amazing Grace*, Public domain.]

Ah! I See Myself

I watched a documentary yesterday about babies. There were no words spoken, just observation. I watched the babies' births. At first, the babies are simply held and loved and nursed, but then I watched as these little ones were introduced to the world around them. I watched the parents as they taught the infants to speak by holding the child on their lap and looking into their faces and slowly forming sounds and then words. The parents would also hold the baby on their lap and show them books that opened up a bigger world then they had yet experienced.

As I considered these things I saw a parallel to my spiritual birth and growth. Like the infant who was nursing at its mother's breast, so I craved the comfort and nourishment of the gospel. I needed to know God as El Shaddai, the All Sufficient God. "Like newborn babies, crave pure spiritual milk, so that by it you may grow up in your salvation" (1 Pet. 2:2 NIV). After birth, in order to grow up, there has to be nourishment.

When I looked at the infant face to face with its parent, learning to understand and then to speak, I thought of 2 Timothy 3:16-17, "All Scripture is God-breathed and is useful for teaching, rebuking, correcting and training in righteousness, so that the man of God may be thoroughly equipped for every good work." Just as these babies were taught and rebuked and corrected by their parents, so I am as I read God's word.

The parents I observed enjoyed their infants, but didn't want them to stay infants. As the child grew older, the parents would begin to expose their children to the world around them. Sometimes this frustrated the child and he would cry, but the parent was always nearby. I feel this frustration sometimes when I am trying to understand what has been prophesied in Scripture. I like things to be comforting, or at least easy; but that's not always true when God is teaching me the things He wants to reveal to me in His word. "The secret things belong to the Lord our God, but the things that are revealed belong to us" (Deut. 29:29 ESV). Even though these things belong to me I must work hard to present myself as "a worker who has no need to be ashamed, rightly handling the word of truth" (2 Tim. 2:15 ESV).

Dear Heavenly Father, I marvel as You who are God Almighty, Eternal, and Omnipotent, stoop down to teach me to understand Your voice and open my spiritual eyes to worlds my earthly eyes cannot see. "For the Lord God does nothing without revealing his secret to his servants the prophets" (Amos 3:7 ESV). Father, sometimes I am like the apostle John who "wept much" when you showed him the marvels in Revelations; or I am like Daniel who fell asleep he was so overwhelmed. This is my prayer as I come to You like a young child comes to her Father, please let me be "filled with the knowledge of God's will in all wisdom and spiritual understanding."

Because I'm Not Always "Fine"

This was something I had to be taught; I didn't understand; it wasn't automatic for me. When I was younger and people asked, "How are you?" I thought they really wanted to know, so I would tell them. Finally someone sat me down and explained that I was supposed to say "Fine" regardless of how I really felt. I learned my lesson well, perhaps too well.

It isn't that I am trying to be fake as much as I'm trying to be safe. Now when I hear "How are you," in my heart I ask myself a question, "Are you a safe person to tell? Do you really care?" When I met my husband almost 40 years ago, I felt secure in his love. Because I felt secure and safe, he came to know not only the public me but the private me. The public me is the one I present to people who ask "How are you," but don't really want to know. The private me is the one that needs a safe secure place to be exposed, because that me isn't always "fine."

I bring this understanding of how I relate to people with me when I read the story of Martha talking to Jesus. I think it was because she saw Jesus as her friend, and someone with whom she was safe, that she could reveal her honest frustration with him. "Lord, don't you care that my sister has left me to serve alone? Tell her to help me" (Luke 10:40). Sometimes my prayers are like that too. I'm not always "fine;" sometimes my prayers reflect the messy me, the confused me, the frustrated me. I can't always get it sorted out before I come to the Lord in prayer. Sometimes I hear Him say to me, "Sarah, Sarah, you are anxious and troubled about so many things. You have forgotten the one thing that is necessary." I need Him to tell me again what that is.

When I gave birth to my first child I did it in a stoic fashion. I focused on breathing techniques so that I would not cry out in pain. However, after the birth I saw my father's face and the dam burst and the tears flowed freely. Why? Although I was a grown woman and a mother, I was still my father's little girl, and I felt safe to release the tears. I feel this same freedom when I pray. There have been seasons in my life when I couldn't find proper words to express the depth of emotion I felt, so I simply wept before my Heavenly Father. These are intimate prayers prayed in the presence of a God I call Abba.

Oh, Heavenly Father, thank You that I don't have to pretend to be "fine" before I come into Your presence. Thank You that I can come just as I am. Thank You that I don't have to wait until I can get everything right; instead I can come to You confused, frustrated, and even at times afraid. Thank You that I can find in Your presence a safe place to reveal who I really am. But, O Lord, thank You for not leaving me just as I am, but instead reminding me what really is necessary, and for breathing peace into my sometimes troubled soul.

It's Not Multiple Choice

"It's not a multiple choice question!" My sister was describing how she had prayed for her children when they were younger. She would go before the Throne of Grace and then present God with a multiple choice of ways He could answer her petition. She felt since she was down here and she was the mother, it might be helpful to God if she gave Him a bit of help.

What she discovered as they grew older was that she was no longer able to help God out as much as she had when her children were younger. The problems grew as her children grew. Life became more and more complex, and she felt she just could no longer supply God with a multiple choice answer to her prayers as she had been able to do when they were younger. That was when she began to give God a blank sheet of paper. She would simply call out the name of her children and let God do the rest.

Yesterday I read a story Edith Schaeffer told about a man from the Lisu tribe in China. This man had been longing for a God he did not know. He found a page torn from a Lisu catechism. He read, "Are there more gods than One? No, there is only One God." "Should we worship idols? No..." the rest was torn away. But he had all he needed; he went home and

245

destroyed his altars.

Not long afterward his daughter became very ill. Everyone accused him of bringing this suffering on his child because he had made the demons angry by destroying their altars. The man believed that he could reach the one true God with his voice. The man knew nothing about prayer. Making a multiple choice for God did not occur to him. He climbed to the highest peak in the vicinity and began to shout out, "Oh, God, if You really are there and You are the One I am to worship, please make my little girl well again." He came home to find his daughter completely healed.

Oh, Lord, there was a time I thought You needed my help, but now I am so grateful that I can come before you and simply call to You for help. Your word tells me I am to walk humbly before You. I humbly bow before Your throne, knowing that what is hidden from me is not hidden from You. I call out the names of those I love. Thank You for hearing me and loving me. And thank You that You don't need me to tell You what to do.

Sometimes...

Sometimes I'm so painfully ashamed. I know who I want to be, but then I am confronted with who I really am. I see my faults and failures and they isolate me and make me want to hide. Then I hear His voice calling, "Where are you?" I think sometimes I know how Adam and Eve felt. I also wonder if the garment of skins God clothed them with was a lamb.

Sometimes I see the haunting look of shame on the faces of those I love. They have lost their sense of dignity. They have lost their way. I want to shout to them, "Behold the lamb of God who takes away the sins of the world!" I want them to understand who this Lamb of God is. "He was despised and forsaken of men, a man of sorrows and acquainted with grief; and like one from whom men hide their face He was despised, and we did not esteem Him. Surely our griefs He Himself bore, and our sorrows He carried; yet we ourselves esteemed Him stricken, smitten of God, and afflicted. But he was pierced through for our transgressions; He was crushed for our iniquities; the chastening for our wellbeing fell upon him, and by his scourging we are healed" (Isa. 55:3-5 NASB).

Sometimes I feel like I am in the middle of a terrible storm. The winds and rain assault me; I feel battered and confused. I cry out for help! In times like these I hear again God's invitation to make Him my hiding place. I run to Him and find again that He protects me from all my trouble and surrounds me with songs of deliverance. Though I have no strength of my own, I rest beneath the shadow of the Almighty.

Sometimes when I am feeling safe because I have put my hope in God's word and have found Him to be my refuge and my shield, I suddenly am aware that someone dear to me has wandered away. I hear their cries, but can do nothing to save them. What good is it if I am safe and secure if the ones I love are in danger! Then I remember the words of Jesus. He came "to seek and to save the lost." He is the Good Shepherd who will leave the 99 and go look for the one lost sheep. Just as God went looking for Adam and Eve and clothed the nakedness of their sins, so Jesus Himself is seeking to save the lost and to take away the sins of the world.

Lord Jesus, I want to be like the virtuous woman in Proverbs 31 who clothed herself with dignity and strength. I am aware that in myself I have no dignity, no strength; but you have made provision to cover my shame with your righteousness my weakness with Your strength. So, once again I come, "Just as I am, without one plea, But that Thy blood was shed for me,... O Lamb of God, I come, I come.... Just as I am, poor, wretched, blind; Sight, riches, healing of the mind, Yea, all I need in Thee to find, O Lamb of God, I come, I come. [Charlotte Elliott, *Just As I Am*, Public domain.]

Finding Rest For Both Body And Soul

"Bong, bong, bong, bong, bong." I was listening to the clock announce the time with a sense a relief that I had been able to sleep through the night. But it didn't stop at five bongs. It went on to bong seven more times. Midnight. It wasn't time to get up, but I was wide awake!

I have always had a love/hate relationship with sleep. I respect the fact that God gave me a body that needs sleep in order to function correctly. I see sleep as a practical act of humility. I think it's very interesting that when the Bible describes a day in Genesis, it says, "And there was evening and there was morning, the first day." What I see in that order is that the day begins as I'm getting ready to be asleep. This is humbling. I guess God can run the universe without my help. Why then do I wake at midnight with a heavy concern about things over which I have no control?

John was in prison. Jesus was at the height of His earthly ministry, but John, who had announced His coming, was in prison. This was confusing, so John sent word by his disciples, "Are you the one who is to come, or shall we look for another?" (Matt. 11). I understand John's confusion. I don't always understand what God is doing in my life either. Sometimes I think, "Lord, if I'm following You, shouldn't my life be easier than this?" Usually I'm thinking this at midnight when I can't sleep.

The chapter in Matthew begins with John's question and it ends with an invitation from Jesus, "Come to me, all who labor and are heavy laden, and I will give you rest. Take my yoke upon you, and learn from me, for I am gentle and humble in heart, and you will find rest for your soul." Jesus always offers more than I ask for. I want to sleep uninterrupted through the night; He offers me rest for my soul. But then, if I have rest for my soul, I will be able to sleep through the night.

Lord Jesus, I, like John, do not always understand what is happening in my life and in the lives of those I love. But You invite me to trust You. I am reminded by Your invitation in Matthew of what I read last night at midnight. "Cast your burden on the Lord, and he will sustain you" (Psa. 55:22 ESV). Lord Jesus, I find again and again as I humble myself in the night, bringing to You the burden I cannot bear, that You not only carry my burden, You carry me as well. And I find rest for my soul as well as for my body.

Following the Cues

I was trying to buy something at a yard sale, and every time I tried, the woman who was selling raised the price. Finally I got it. She didn't want me to buy the item, and instead of saying that, she just kept raising the price out of my range. Sometimes I'm slow picking up on the cues people give me. One of the Scriptures on guidance says, "The mind of man plans his way, but the Lord directs his steps" (Prov. 16:9 NASB).

Sometimes I find myself pushing on doors that will not open. In my mind I must get through the door to reach my destination. However, if it's true that the Lord is directing my steps, I think it's always a good idea when I cannot make a door open to ask the Lord if He has other plans for me. This is what I see in the story of Balaam and the talking donkey. Balaam was furious with the donkey for not going in the direction that Balaam wanted him to go, until God allowed the donkey to speak. It was only then that Balaam became aware of the angel who was standing in the middle of the road with a flaming sword (Numbers 22).

Once I was walking on the country road. Suddenly I felt like I had encountered a wall of fear. I have never been a fearful person, so my first instinct was to ignore this feeling and keep going. The problem was, the feeling of fear became almost a tangible presence. Finally, I stopped and prayed. I realized that it was possible that God was using this feeling of fear to cause me to turn around. Later I found out that a murder had occurred on that road about the same time I was on my walk.

Sometimes the plans that we have for ourselves and the direction God has for us match. Still, God calls for us to pursue our plans with a heart that is surrendered to Him. From the time my father-in-law was a young man, he wanted a farm. For years he and his wife spent all their weekends searching for a place that would fulfill that dream, but finding nothing. Finally, he prayed and told the Lord that he would give up his search if he hadn't found a farm by the time he was 35. He signed the papers for a farm on his 35th birthday.

Lord Jesus, help me humble myself and surrender my plans to You. Please help me be sensitive to the leading of Your Holy Spirit. Give me wisdom to know when to keep going and when to turn around and go in a different direction. By faith, Lord, let me be led by the hand I cannot hold.

The Spinning Has a Purpose

Have you ever felt dizzy, like you were spinning round and round and round? Have you ever felt like you were not only spinning round and round, but that some outside force was applying pressure on you while you were spinning? Me too. I don't think it's our imagination. "But now, O Lord, you are our Father; we are the clay, and you are our potter; we are all the work of your hand" (Isa. 64:8 ESV). So, round and round we go while we are being shaped by the hands of the potter.

So here I am a lump of clay, spinning round and round; and if I only focus on that, it is a very blurry picture. The fact is that this is often how it seems to me: blurry. I am grateful for the perspective I gain in Isaiah. Without this perspective I would feel my life was simply spinning out of control. However, seeing myself on the potter's wheel gives me a completely different picture. The spinning of a potter's wheel is controlled by the potter. The pressure applied by the potter's skilled hand is for a purpose. I, as the lump of clay, can only feel the pressure and the dizzying whirl of the wheel; but it is not what I feel that determines what this process produces. The end product comes from the potter's mind.

Who is this potter? First, Isaiah calls him Lord. This word means master or owner. That would give him permission to do with the clay whatever he wanted. That would give him permission. But that is not as comforting to me as the next name, Father. Knowing that my Heavenly Father's foot is controlling the spin and His hand is responsible for the pressure gives me comfort.

I have children. While I was raising them I often brought pressure to bear upon them. My love for them caused me to be actively involved in their life. Sometimes my children would rebel against the pressure I was placing on them. However, I loved them far too much to simply give up and walk away. This is the same picture I see when God told Jeremiah to go to the potter's house and watch. The clay was spoiled in the potter's hand. He didn't throw the clay away, he reworked it into another vessel, as it seemed good to the potter to do. What a comfort to me to know that the one who does the reworking is also the loving Father.

I come to You today O Lord. You are my Father, you are also the potter. You alone know the plans You have for me. What I know is the pressure and confusion I often feel. Thank You that I can rest in Your love. Thank You that even when the hardness and rebellion of my heart causes You to rework the clay, it can never change the goodness of Your heart or Your kind intentions towards me. I saw this in the Garden when the lump of clay into which You breathed life rebelled against You, and You responded by promising a Redeemer!

A Lesson Learned

I was seven years old when my mother had her ninth child. My oldest brother was ten. It would not be an understatement to say that my mother had her hands full. Something else happened when I was seven years old. That was the year I learned a very important lesson about love.

I was in the second grade, and that was the year I was supposed to learn to read. But I didn't. My teacher had a huge class and no one to assist her. And if that wasn't bad enough, she had me for a student. It wasn't that I didn't try. I tried, I really did; but I still couldn't seem to learn to read. I became a target for her frustration. All through the day she would call attention to the fact that I was failing to read or spell, which meant I wasn't doing well at writing either. Sometimes I would forget to be on my guard and I would suck my fingers in an effort to find comfort. That never worked very well, because then she would have the class look at me, and that brought no comfort, only more ridicule.

Some people have asked me, "Where was your mother?" My mother was at home with a new baby and a two-year-old and a three-year-old and a four-year-old,... need I say more? Not only that, but it never occurred to me to even tell my mother what was going on. I was only seven, and this was only my second year in school. I thought this was just the way life was. It was my teacher who called mother. She just couldn't take my ignorance any longer!

I remember sitting in the hallway when my mother was talking to the teacher. I was swinging my feet because they didn't touch the floor. And, yes, I was sucking my fingers. When mother came out of the office her face was very sad. She was silent for a long time. Finally, Mother looked at me and began to speak. "Sarah, I want you to pay very close attention to what I am about to say." I leaned a little closer to my mother. "Sarah, I know you want everyone to like you, and you try really hard to make that happen." I shook my head, yes. "Your teacher doesn't like you, and it's not your fault, and you can't make her like you." This information set me free. But the next thing she said gave me an anchor. "Although your teacher doesn't like you, I love you. Nothing you do will ever make me love you more. Nothing you do will ever make me love you less. My love for you isn't based on your performance."

Dear Heavenly Father, thank You for giving my mother the wisdom and the words she needed. She did what she could, and it was enough. Thank You for giving me a mother who showed me what Your love looks like. "How great is the love the Father lavished on us, that we should be called children of God!" (1 John 3:1 NIV). And to think I did nothing to deserve that lavish love.

How I Relate To God's Will

In Sunday School we were talking about how we related to God's will. The teacher spoke about dealing with the will of God on three levels. The first was acceptance; the second was surrender; and the third was contentment. I thought about my relationship to the will of God. I think in pictures, so this was what I saw. When I recognized God's will, I accepted it like an assignment.

I saw acceptance like a high ladder that I was to climb. Once I had climbed the ladder, I was on the high dive. Surrender meant walking to the edge of the plank and looking down into a small pool of water and then diving headlong into it. But that was as far as I could go with my mental picture. I could not see contentment, I tried, but I couldn't. The reason I couldn't see a mental picture of contentment was because I wasn't experiencing it. I felt like I was accepting and surrendering to God's will, but I wasn't content.

One thing I learned long ago was that when I don't have the answers to my questions, I need to ask. So I began asking God in prayer to show me how to be content with His will. My lack of contentment made me so miserable that I also began seeking the answer. When my children were little and I would be in my room and they needed me, they would knock persistently on my bedroom door, because they knew I would respond to their need. In this same way, I was asking, seeking, and knocking; because I knew my Heavenly Father had the answer and would give it to me. What does it look like to be content with the will of God?

This is the understanding I have come to about the will of God. Before accepting, or surrendering, or finding contentment in His will, I need to identify it. I believe that the will of God and the love of God are inseparable. "I have loved you with an everlasting love; I have drawn you with loving-kindness" (Jer. 31:3 NIV). My first picture of dealing with God's will looked more like a slave obeying orders. When I began to see His will as His love, the picture changed to that of a bride receiving the love of her groom.

Lord Jesus, I want to accept Your love and believe the words of love I find in Your word. I want to surrender to Your love as a bride surrenders to her beloved. I want to find all my contentment and my identity in Your love for me. "The Lord will fulfill his purpose for me; your love, O Lord, endures forever..." (Psa. 138:8 ESV).

A Calm and Stress Free Life?!?

She stood behind me talking on the phone. I'm sure she didn't mean to be talking so loudly, but still I heard every word of her part of the conversation. "You know I can't handle any stress. I need for my life to be calm." All I could think of were the words of Job 5:7, "Yet man is born to trouble as the sparks fly upward."

Not long ago I was asked to speak at a church. The topic they gave me to speak on was "How to keep your balance in an unbalanced world." I smiled when I heard what they wanted me to speak about, not because I'm so totally balanced, but because I so desperately want to be. Like the young woman on the phone, I too would like to proclaim, "You know I can't handle any stress. I need for my life to be calm."

I read in 1 Peter 3:4 that a gentle and quiet spirit is precious in the sight of God. I think having this kind of spirit might be the answer to the question about how to have a balanced life. Now I have to ask myself, "How do I develop a gentle and quiet spirit?" The fact that life is both stressful and lacking in calm is not conducive to gentleness or quietness.

What does "quiet" mean anyway? I did a little research and found words like tranquil and still. I am not by nature tranquil or still, and my life is full of stress. So how can someone like me, living the life I'm living, develop this quiet spirit? In my mind's eye I saw a pastoral setting and thought about the words to the twenty third Psalm, "The Lord is my shepherd, I shall not want. He makes me lie down in green pastures, he leads me beside quiet waters, he restores my soul." Sheep are animals of prey, and because of this they are very fearful. They have real enemies, and the only way they can be at rest, tranquil or quiet is to have a good shepherd. Only when they have a relationship with the shepherd can they lie down, rest, drink at the still waters, and find their soul restored.

Lord Jesus, my world is not balanced. I often find myself stressed out and fearful. But in You I find peace. You are my balance; You are my tranquility; You are my resting place. You are my shepherd.

The Potentate of Time

I didn't want to be late for work, so I kept checking the time. When I realized the time was drawing near for me to leave, I put my cell phone on the table to help me keep track of the time. I gave myself a full hour to get to work even though I knew it was only a forty five minute drive. When I got to work, my boss pointed out that I was an hour late. My phone had switched time zones. It had the strangest effect on me. I almost felt dizzy, as if I had been time traveling.

The Sunday following this event we sang "Crown Him with Many Crowns." The last verse of the song says, "Crown Him the Lord of years, the Potentate of time." [Matthew Bridges, *Crown Him with Many Crowns,* Public domain.] I was fascinated by the idea of God being the Lord of the years and the Potentate of time. So what does potentate mean? It means one who has supreme power and position to rule over others. God is eternal, and time is a tool in His hand. But how does that affect my life?

Daniel was a godly man who lived his life in the confines of time. He lived during the time of the Babylonian captivity. God, who is not bound by time, showed Daniel through visions many mysteries things that were to take place in the future. The first time this happened Daniel responded, "Praise be to the name of God for ever and ever; wisdom and power are his. He changes times and seasons; he sets up kings and deposes them. He gives wisdom to the wise and knowledge to the discerning" (Dan. 2:20-21 NIV). In Daniel I find a man who was bold and brave because, although he was bound by time, the God he served was not.

"As I looked, thrones were set in place, and the Ancient of Days took his seat" (Dan. 7:9 NIV). Daniel saw this picture of God as the Ancient of Days in the same dream in which he received night vision from God showing him the scope and sequence of kingdoms and empires that were to rise and fall throughout the course of history. Again, I ask the question, how does this affect my life?

Lord Jesus, it is in You that I find understanding because, though I am a prisoner of time, You are not. Yet You entered time and set me free. "In the beginning was the Word, and the Word was with God, and the Word was God. He was with God in the beginning.... The Word became flesh and made his dwelling among us" (John 1:1-2, 14). Thank You, Lord Jesus, for, though You were the Creator, You entered time and became my Redeemer.

With a Strong Hand and an Outstretched Arm

A sheep that has rolled over onto its back and is unable to right itself is a "downcast" sheep. In this position a sheep is very vulnerable and doomed to death either by predators or dehydration if left alone. Shepherds search for sheep in this position, and when they find them, they put them back on their feet. If they are too weak to stand, the shepherd will carry the sheep until it regains its strength. I know what it feels like to be "downcast." Sometimes I just can't seem to right myself and I find myself calling out for help.

When I call out for help, God responds "with a strong hand and an outstretched arm, for his steadfast love endures forever" (Psa. 136:12 ESV). Another word for steadfast is unfailing. I am so grateful for His steadfast and unfailing love and that He responds to my weakness with a strong hand and an outstretched arm instead of by saying, "Get up on your own! I can't believe you can't get this right after all this time!"

I was at work the other day and the verse on the calendar read, "Ah, Lord God! It is you who has made the heavens and the earth by your great power and by your outstretched arm! Nothing is too hard for you" (Jer. 32:17 ESV). What a comfort it is to me to think that this same great power and outstretched arm that made the heavens and the earth is outstretched to me. When life seems too hard for me, I need to close my eyes and see this picture of steadfast love reaching out in my direction.

Sometimes, when I am in this vulnerable downcast position, I feel like the predators are about to come in for the kill. In times like this I am grateful that I have a shepherd. I am so grateful for the pictures I get in the Scriptures that give me a divine perspective of what is going on. "Their own arm did not save them, but your right hand and your arm, and the light of your face, for you delighted in them." When I am vulnerable and weak and find you coming to my rescue, it is not out of duty that you come, but out of love.

Lord Jesus, I would choose to always be strong, but I am not. Thank You for finding me when I have lost my way. Thank You for Your strong outstretched arm that comes to my defense. I am so grateful that nothing is too hard for You. But I am even more grateful for Your unfailing love.

Remembering That I Am a Sojourner and a Guest

Sometimes I forget this truth, and when I do it's like trying to put a puzzle together without all the pieces. I get angry, frustrated, and discouraged if I try to put a puzzle together without all the pieces. And I get angry, frustrated, and discouraged when I forget that I am an alien, stranger and a sojourner on this earth. If I have the understanding that I am a sojourner and a guest and not a permanent resident, then things make more sense to me.

"I am a sojourner on the earth; hide not your commandments from me!" (Psa. 119:19 ESV). Because I am a sojourner, I need God to give me directions! I often lose my way and become confused. Sometimes I get so confused that I think this is my permanent residence. I think this is my permanent home, and yet my heart is filled with a sense that something is missing. When I read God's Word, it's as if I'm looking at the picture that the puzzle is supposed to look like. When I compare the "home" I see described in Scripture to the "home" I have on earth, I realize that I am a stranger here.

One piece of the puzzle that I often forget is that I am not only a sojourner, but a guest. "For I am a sojourner with you, a guest, like all my fathers" (Psa. 39:12 ESV). When my daughter was two, a friend came to visit. She brought with her two-year-old daughter. Faith was worried that the little girl would take her toys. I assured her that the little girl would understand that they didn't belong to her because she was the guest. I was wrong. The first thing the child did was to walk into my daughter's room and lay claim to everything she saw. I am a lot like that little girl. I forget I am a guest and only God is the true owner.

When I find myself staring at this puzzling life, filled with angry frustration, there is only one remedy. I cry out with the psalmist, "I am a sojourner on the earth; hide not your commandments from me!" When I do this, He opens my eyes by faith so that I can see the missing pieces. He does for me what He did for the heroes of faith listed in Hebrews 11. "They did not receive the things promised; they only saw them and welcomed them from a distance. And they admitted that they were aliens and strangers on earth."

Lord Jesus, please help me to remember that I am not home yet. Please help me not to grasp the things of this earth with greedy fingers. Remind me again that I am a guest. You promised that You were preparing a place for me and that You would someday come again and take me home to be with You. Until then, show me how to walk by faith in obedience to Your commands as a sojourner and a guest.

"Trees" and "Iron Chariots"

There is a story in the Bible that matches a struggle I often have. It was when the people of Joseph came to Joshua with the question about their inheritance. God had blessed them; He had graciously given them an allotment in the Promised Land. The problem was, there were obstacles to overcome before they could lay claim to what had been given them. I believe that I am a Christian by the grace of God, yet I struggle sometimes to take hold of the promises given to me.

Joshua told them to go up into the forest and clear land for themselves. Then the people of Joseph complained about the Canaanites who lived in the plain and had chariots. Joshua responded, "You are numerous and very powerful. You will have not only one allotment but the forested hill country as well. Clear it, and it's farthest limits will be yours; though the Canaanites have chariots fitted with iron and though they are strong, you can drive them out" (Josh. 17:14-18 NIV) God had given them the land, but they were responsible to take possession of it by faith.

I think the struggle I have with my flesh is like the "trees" that the people of Joseph complained about. The trees kept them from being able to fully utilize the land they had been given. They complained about the trees; Joshua told them to remove them. I complain about my struggle with my flesh; but I find in the Scriptures the admonition to do something about it. "Put on then, as God's chosen ones, holy and beloved, compassionate hearts, kindness, humility, meekness, and patience, bearing with one another and, if one has a complaint against another, forgiving each other; as the Lord has forgiven you, so you also must forgive. And above all these put on love, which binds everything together in perfect harmony" (Col. 3:12-14 ESV). They were to, by faith, use the gifts God had given them and clear out the trees. I am to use, by faith, what God has given me to overcome my flesh.

There weren't just trees on the land, there were iron chariots. I think my "iron chariot" is the fact that there is spiritual warfare going on. "For our struggle is not against flesh and blood, but against the rulers, against the authorities, against the powers of this dark world and against the spiritual forces of evil in the heavenly realms" (Eph. 6:12 NIV). Joshua told the people that, though there were iron chariots in the land and their enemy was strong, still they could drive them out. In a similar way I find in Ephesians, "Finally, be strong in the Lord and in the strength of his might. Put on the whole armor of God, that you may be able to stand against the schemes of the devil" (Eph. 6:10-11 ESV).

Lord Jesus, in You I lack nothing. But sometimes I can't see that because of all these "trees" and "iron chariots." Please help me, by faith, to take hold of the grace You have provided for me. Help me not to live my Christian life in a cramped way because I'm more focused on the "trees" and "iron chariots" than I am on the gifts You've given me.

Different Route, Same Destination

I have always loved hearing people's testimonies. What was it that finally broke them, what finally showed them they needed a Savior? Often it seemed it was some great sin or the consequences of that sin that brought them weeping before the cross of Jesus. For me, however, it looked like a different route. The destination was the same, only the route looked different.

From my earliest memories I have wanted to be good. I wanted to follow the rules. I memorized John 3:16 when I was a little girl so that I could get a sticker. "For God so loved the world, that he gave his only Son, that whoever believes in him should not perish but have eternal life." I got my sticker, but that verse really bothered me. It bothered me because I didn't just want to be good, I wanted to be good enough for God. This verse wasn't about my loving God, it was about God's loving me; it wasn't about what I did for God, it was about what God had done for me. And I was bothered by it.

What finally broke me? What finally showed me my need for a Savior? It was my sin and the consequences of my sin that brought me weeping before the cross of Jesus. My sin was my pride. I didn't want to need a Savior, I wanted to be the Savior. Time and time again I would attempt to do great things "for God," only to find my heart exposed. What was exposed was a lack of compassion, kindness, humility, meekness, and patience. I was miserable. The only thing my "good deeds" produced was a revelation that I wasn't as good as I thought I was.

At first I was unaware of my need. I was unaware that I had been using the Bible as a guideline of how I could be good enough for God. Then I came face to face with the biblical definition of love in 1 Corinthians 13. From the very first part of the definition I felt condemned. "Love is patient and kind." I wasn't patient or kind, not even with the people I should be loving the most, my husband and my children. The chapter begins by saying, "If I speak in the tongues of men and of angels, but have not love, I am a noisy gong or a clanging cymbal. And if I have prophetic powers, and understand all mysteries and all knowledge, and if I have all faith, so as to remove mountains, but have not love, I am nothing. If I give all I have and if I deliver up my body to be burned, but have not love, I gain nothing." I finally saw myself, a noisy gong, a clanging cymbal, someone who was nothing and had gained nothing by all my good deeds. I found myself weeping at the foot of the cross.

Lord Jesus, thank You for not giving up on me! Thank You for showing me what love really is: "God is love." "In this is love, not that we have loved God but that he loved us and sent his Son to be the propitiation for our sins" (1 John 4:10 ESV). The reality of who You are and what You've done for me because You love me brings me to the foot of the cross.

Tell Me Again That You Love Me

Perhaps it began because the house was so full. There were 14 of us at one time, all living together as a family. Fourteen stories being told, sometimes being shouted, trying to be heard. Sometimes I would feel lost in all the confusion, but that was when it began. I would wake up early and find a quiet place to be with God, and then I'd make my request. "Tell me again that You love me." I opened His book. I'd read His word then I opened my heart and received the gift of grace. Peace always followed.

There have been seasons of great pressure: Deadlines I didn't think I could meet; more was asked of me than I thought I was able to give. Life seemed rushing towards me at a frenzied pace. I didn't feel I had time to breathe. But early in the morning I would wake and slip away and find a quiet place, and then I'd make my request. "Tell me again that You love me." I opened His book. I'd read His word, then I opened my heart and received the gift of grace. Peace like a calming breeze followed.

I walked in the woods and found the place. I closed my eyes and remembered. Twenty five years ago I had stood there weeping before a mound of freshly dug earth. My heart was touched again with the exquisite pain of seeing my baby's coffin covered by dirt. I stood there now as I had then, and made my request, "Tell me again that You love me." I remembered His word, then I opened my heart and received the gift of grace. Peace like a gentle presence followed.

I sit with her. Her eyes are dim, her hearing dull. Few are left who share the memories of her childhood. Her memory of the past is clearer than that of the present. Her feeble frame sits lightly in the chair. With a voice etched with time she makes her request. "Tell me again about His love for me." I open His book; I read His word. Her face softens as she once more opens her heart and receives again the gift of grace. Her eyes are closed, but I can see that peace, as always, has followed.

Lord Jesus, I come today as I do every day. I open Your Word and make my request. "Tell me again that You love me." In the quiet comfort of Your presence I open again my heart to You to receive this gift of grace. I feel again Your peace that passes all understanding. It has once again followed.

The Composition of a Life

Tomorrow is my birthday, and as I look back over the years it seems to me that my life has been like a musical composition. Sometimes the music has been light; sometimes it has been written in minor keys; and sometimes it has been written with dissonant chords. Sometimes I wonder what this composition will sound like when it is finished.

I recently read about Johann Sebastian Bach. At the beginning of most of his compositions Bach wrote the abbreviation *JJ* for the Latin phrase *Jesu juva,* which means "Jesus help," and ended with *SDG* (*Soli Deo Gloria*), which is Latin for "To God Alone the Glory." I want to write that on the composition of my life. For the beginning of each movement I want to write "Jesus help." When the music of my life fades away, I want to be able to say "To God Alone the Glory."

I read that Bach wrote each note as though God Himself was scrutinizing every musical bar and phrase. I think that is a good way to live my life as well: Letting the music of my life play before the courts of Heaven for an audience of one.

One of Bach's most acclaimed works is *The Passion According to St. Matthew,* which has been called one of the greatest choral works ever written. It was only played once while Bach was alive. It wasn't received well at all. One hundred years later Felix Mendelssohn obtained a copy and performed it using the original score. It was met with appreciation and love that has only grown with time. I think that if you begin your work with "Jesus help" and end it with "To God Alone the Glory," you don't need to worry about being "successful."

Lord Jesus, as I live my life before You as a musical composition, I ask for Your help. I cannot hear the music clearly from where I am, but my prayer is that You will scrutinize every musical bar and phrase. Please, Lord, let it be that as the last chords fade away into silence it can be said "To God Alone the Glory."

Finding the Way in the Maze

In the Fall there are several places that invite you to try to find your way through the "Maze." In a maze, a path has been cut through the tall stalks of corn. There is a starting point and an ending point, and plenty of places to get lost in the middle. There are times in life when it feels like I am walking through a maze.

In the middle of the maze sometimes the path splits. One way will lead your toward your goal, the other will cause you to walk in circles. Often when I have made the wrong choice a sense of panic grips me, and I wonder if I will ever be able to find my way out. Usually about that point someone comes along who has a map and together we figure out the direction that leads us to our destination.

The reason it's so easy to get lost in a maze is that all I can see are the tall stalks of corn that surround me; everything else is blocked from view. Because I'm not omniscient, sometimes all I can see are the facts that surround me; and without unlimited knowledge I get confused about with way to go. I do, however, have access to the One who is omniscient. And when I call out to Him in prayer I hear, "I will instruct you and teach you in the way you should go; I will counsel you and watch over you" (Psa. 32:8 NIV).

The thought that God is watching over me is very comforting. It's comforting because I believe He loves me. And even though my path is hidden from me it isn't hidden from Him. A promise in His word is that He makes the simple wise as He teaches them the way they should go. In the midst of my confusion I can call out to Him and I find counsel from the Wonderful Counselor.

Lord Jesus, as I find my way on this often confusing path, thank You that I can put my hand in Your scarred hand and be reminded of Your unfailing love. My hope and my confidence are in Your love as You teach and counsel me along the way.

"Would You Like To Experience A Miracle?"

His eyes flashed with anger, "I will never forgive him." It was a strong and powerful statement for a little boy not yet ten to make, but I knew he meant it. I respected his anger, because I respected the pain that had caused it. You don't have to be an adult to know deep sorrow and hurt. As I sat on his bed, I first listened to him as he poured out the grief that was in his soul. And then I asked him, "Would you like to experience a miracle?"

We looked at each other in silence for a while. He knew I was offering him a light to help him find his way out of the dark place of hurt and pain. His face softened. A warm glow replaced the hot embers of hatred I had seen earlier. He took a deep breath then let it out in a long slow sigh as he said, "Yes." "You have been hurt and wounded and it wasn't your fault," I said, "but, you don't have to carry that heavy load of hate. I know someone who will carry it away for you and leave love in its place." That was the night I told him about the miracle of forgiveness.

I didn't reprimand him for his anger, because I understood it. I also understood that, although throughout the Scriptures we are told to forgive, it isn't something that has ever come naturally to me. In fact, I believe that one of the greatest challenges to human nature is God's command to forgive. That is why I believe that when I am put into a position where I need to forgive someone, God has also lined me up to be able to experience a miracle. This is when I come to God in prayer and say, "I want to obey You and be forgiving, but it is creating a war in my heart. Lord, I am desperate for You. Please come to my aid. Take away my fleshly desire to hold a grudge and to hurt the one who has hurt me. Take away the bitterness in my soul. Please grant me the miracle of a forgiving heart. Do divine surgery in my soul and replace with love where now there is only anger and hate."

What I have found in this mandate to forgive is an invitation from God to humble myself before Him and, through a divine encounter with His Holy Spirit, to have my human nature transformed. I have never experienced the need to forgive someone without first experiencing the humbling of my own heart. With the offense comes the pride rising up in me with the declaration, "You will not treat me this way! I will make you sorry, I will make you pay!" My eyes flash with anger as my heart says, "I will never forgive!" Suddenly I am aware of a loving presence, and I hear Jesus' invitation. "Would you like to experience a miracle?" Only then do I remember all that I have been forgiven of and I bow before Him and pray, "Lord, please do for me what I can't do for myself." That's when the burden is lifted and the fire is quenched. I take a deep breath and let out a long slow sigh as the burden of an unforgiving spirit is replaces by the presence of Love incarnate.

Lord Jesus, You have taught me what is like to be forgiven. You have redeemed my life, forgiven all my iniquities and healed the disease of my heart by crowning my life with Your steadfast love and mercy. Because You have been merciful and gracious, slow to anger and abounding in steadfast love, my sins have been removed as far as the East is from the West, yet this was not the end of your mercies. You have invited me share in Your nature by inviting me to experience the miracle of not only being forgiven but to be forgiving. Help me to share this miracle with others so they too can know this divine encounter with Your Holy Spirit.

The Power of a Mindset

Last night I read about a woman named Lori Schneider. She was 52 years old when she climbed Mount Everest. That in itself is an amazing feat, but there is more to the story. She had MS. Multiple sclerosis is a baffling autoimmune disorder that attacks the central nervous system and can lead to paralysis, vision loss, dementia and death. So how could someone with MS climb Mount Everest? As I read her story I discovered her secret. It was her mindset. "I stopped thinking of myself as a victim of MS," Lori said, "I was a person with MS, a person first; the disease was not me."

All day I had been meditating on Romans 8:6, "To set the mind on the flesh is death, but to set the mind on the Spirit is life and peace." I was intrigued by the power of a mindset, so I looked up the Greek word for mind and found the word *phronema*. It means, "the innermost, personal level of opinion; inner perspective as it determines... outward behavior, especially as it bears on the outward results" [http://biblesuite.com/greek/5427.htm]. One mindset leads to death, the other to life and peace.

As I read through the whole chapter, I understand better why a mind that is set on the flesh is death. Having a mind set on the flesh comes from a life that is being lived according to the flesh. The chapter goes onto say that "the mind that is set on the flesh is hostile to God." So, if I live my life according to my basic carnal desires, then not only do I have a fleshly mindset, but I also have a mind that is alien to God. The trajectory of a mind like this is death.

Lori was able to climb Mount Everest when she stopped thinking of herself as a victim of MS. She had to see herself not as the disease but as a person. MS creates a battlefield in the body. I often have a battlefield in my mind. "For I delight in the law of God in my inner being, but I see in my members another law waging war against the law of my mind...." I can have my mind set on the Spirit because the Spirit of life set me free in Christ Jesus. I recognize I am weak but my weakness does not define me. My relationship to the Spirit of life defines me.

Lord Jesus, thank You for people like Lori who help me understand that I don't have to be limited by my flesh. Thank You because, when I can't change my mind, the Spirit Himself intercedes for me with groaning too deep for words. "And He who searches hearts knows what is the mind of the Spirit."

"Not a Mumbling Word"

"Do you really think you can do that," my daughter asked incredulously. To be honest, I wasn't really sure myself. Was it possible for me to go through this difficult season of my life without saying a mumbling, grumbling word? I got the idea when I heard the old spiritual *"He Never Said a Mumbalin' Word."* As I listened to the song being beautifully sung, I could almost see Jesus standing before Pilate, silent like a lamb before its shearers.

"He was oppressed, and he was afflicted, yet he opened not his mouth; like a lamb that is led to the slaughter, and like a sheep that before its shearers is silent, so he opened not his mouth" (Isa. 53:7 ESV). Why was Jesus silent when He stood before His accusers? Why was the Son of God on trial in the first place? It all started in the Garden when Adam and Eve rebelled against the love of God and decided they would be their own god. That's when death first made its entrance onto the scene, that's also when the promise of love was made. Sin and rebellion brought with it death; love promised a Savior and life. This life was given in surrendered silence.

The Children of Israel cried out because of their slavery in Egypt, and with a strong hand and an outstretched arm God set them free from their oppressors. God led them through the wilderness to show them that they could trust Him to teach them He was able to provide for all their need; to bring not only rest for their bodies in the Promised Land, but rest for their souls in His love. How did they respond? They mumbled and grumbled in rebellion against God's will for them. They fought against what they could not see; they rebelled against the One who led them. With their mumbling grumbling words they rebelled against the God of love who had come to set them free.

"They all cried, 'Crucify Him.'"... "They nailed Him to the tree."... "They pierced him in the side."... "He hung His head and died." After each of these statements the choir sang, "not a word, not a word, not a word." Finally the song ends with, "He never said a mumbalin' word." [Author unknown, *Never Said a Mumbalin' Word*, Public domain.] Jesus was the promise of love made in the Garden. He came to set me free from the slavery of rebellion and sin. He came in silence because He came willingly. He came in silence because He came in love. He did not rebel against the price He had to pay to purchase my freedom.

Lord Jesus, I am so much more like the Children of Israel than like You. My mouth is often filled with mumbling and grumbling words, words of rebellion against situations I find myself in, words of rebellion against the God who led me here. Forgive me because for doubting Your love. Forgive me for longing for the comfort of Egypt instead of silently learning to rest in Your love. Thank You for Your promise that, if I ask anything according to Your will, You will give me what I ask. Lord Jesus, I ask that You would change my heart and make it more like Yours so that I can face my life without a mumbling, grumbling word.

Essence

One of the definitions for the word essence is "the real or ultimate nature of a thing". When making perfume, you find the essence of the flower by crushing the petals and adding oil. I think the essence of the human heart is often known when the circumstances are crushing and the tears flow freely. But what about the oil that is added? In the Bible, oil is often regarded as a symbol of the Person and ministry of the Holy Spirit.

Sometimes in the night I find myself unable to sleep. The person I thought I was collides with the person I see exposed by the struggles of the day, and the tears flow freely. It is during nights like these that my real and ultimate nature is exposed. It is during nights like this I call out for God to be gracious to me. As I seek to praise the Lord through the watches of the night, longing to trust the God I do not see, I find my soul anointed by the oil of His Spirit

"You have kept count of my tossing; put my tears in your bottle" (Psa. 56:8 ESV). When I read this verse I thought about the making of perfume. This psalm begins with David calling on God because, "my enemies trample on me all day long." This trampling caused David's heart to cry out for someone who was bigger than he was. "This I know, that God is for me. In God, whose word I praise, in God I trust; I shall not be afraid." It is only when you add the oil of the presence of God to the crushing circumstances of life that perfume is made.

Isn't this the picture of redemption where God enters into our suffering and takes our grief and puts in its place joy? Who but God could take the essence of human suffering by bottling our tear and create a sweet aroma with it? Without this oil of the presence of God the crushing simply produces suffering and the trampling simply produces grief.

Lord Jesus, You shared our grief and carried our sorrows. Your tears mingled with the tears of mankind. Because of You, the tears that represent the essence of our human suffering have been redeemed.

There Is a Place of Welcome

There is a place of welcome. When I feel lost, cold and afraid, there is a place of welcome. When I am tired and the questions I can't answer seem to be screaming in my head, there is a place of quiet rest, there is a place of welcome. When my heart is hurting for myself and those I love, there is a place of sweet comfort, there is a place of welcome. There is place where I am safe a place of full release, there is a place of welcome.

She needed a place of welcome. She sat weeping by the well. She was alone; well, not really alone. She was pregnant. She had been rejected and sent away. She could see nothing through her tears. But that was when she received her welcome. She didn't go to Him; He came to her. He came to her with comfort, direction and the promise of His blessing. She had felt invisible in her pain, unwanted, unseen, uncared for. He showed her she was wrong. After her encounter she named Him "The God who really sees." Her name was Hagar.

She needed a place of welcome. She didn't understand; she thought she'd understood, but she didn't. She thought He loved her, that He would come to her in her darkest hour, but He didn't. She had asked Him to come. She had waited for Him to come, looking, longing through the dark nights, until it was too late. Her brother died. He was buried and all that was left were the memories and the question, "Why didn't He come?" But He did come. He came with the promise of resurrection. There was welcome, there was joy, there was hope, there was promise. Her name was Martha.

He needed a place of welcome. He thought he was better than he was, but he had failed. When he had been needed most, he had not been there. He had always seen himself as a strong man, one on whom others could lean. But when he had been put to the test, he wavered and hid in the shadows. He heard the cry of pain, but did not go to his friend's rescue. He was lost in his sense of unworthiness. That's where

Jesus found him. Jesus welcomed him, forgave him, restored him to a position of leadership. His name was Peter.

Lord Jesus, You are the door that leads to the place of welcome; the place of welcome where we find a quiet rest; the place of welcome where there is sweet comfort; the place of welcome where our heart at last finds full release. Lord Jesus, You are the door through which we find welcome, near to the heart of God.

With My Knee Bent and My Heart Lifted

There is something I learned to do as a little girl that I don't think my granddaughters have been taught to do. When I was a little girl I learned to genuflect. I learned to genuflect when I entered the church and saw the flickering lamp that represented the presence of God. My heart would swell with a sense of awe as I bent my knee to the ground in worship and as a sign of respect.

When I was a child my world was loud, but there was no talking at church. When I would walk into the church it was as if I were walking into another world. The silence, the candle to remind me of God's presence, and the genuflecting all prepared me for a holy encounter with God. Lately, I have been thinking about how I come into the presence of a Holy God today.

Sometimes when I pray I kneel. I think about who God is; I think about who I am. I feel like I should begin every prayer with, "Oh, God, I am so sorry!" In the presence of a Holy God I see my sins so clearly. Then I think about how Jesus taught His disciples to pray, "When you pray, say, 'Father'."

When I think about calling the God of the Universe "Father," once more my heart swells with a sense of awe and wonder. My inclination is to come before Him with my head bent low; but because He invites me to call Him "Father," with a gentle hand He lifts my head to behold His eyes of love. I am invited to focus not on my unworthiness but on His love.

Father, how great is this love You have lavished on me, that I should be called a child of God! Help me today to live my life in a way that will bring You honor. Your great love humbles my heart and fills it at the same time with the wonder of Your love.

Find the Dove

There is a game that I used to play with my children. It is called "Find the hidden object." Hidden within the picture were several objects. As we found them, we would check them off the list. I have been playing a similar game lately. I call it "Find the Dove." I am looking daily for the Holy Spirit. The Holy Spirit is like the wind. I cannot see the wind, but I see the effects of it; and so it is with the Holy Spirit.

To "Find the Dove" I must look for more than I can see. When I looked with eyes of flesh, I saw someone who was old and bent with age. Their windows to the world were dimmed, and the sound of singing birds was not heard. Often, as the world goes hurrying on, they were forgotten. Yet in them I "Find the Dove." As I sought to minister to this weakened vessel I found within her "love, joy, peace, patience, kindness, goodness, faithfulness, gentleness, and self control." I smiled and said, "Ah, yes, I found the dove."

Over 60 years ago they made a promise to each other. They were young when they looked into each other's eyes and vowed that from that day forward, for better or for worse, for richer, for poorer, in sickness and in health, they would love each other and cherish each other. Sixty years is a long time to keep a promise like that, but it has been more than 60 years, and they continue to look lovingly at one another and say, "I still do." Ah, yes, I found the dove!

I was inadequate for the job. My heart wanted to do so much, but I was lacking. Throughout the week I have been surrounded by others who have made up for what I couldn't do. They have come to give their time, to lend a hand, to clean, to cook, to sing. I have heard the sound of mighty wings. Ah, yes, I found the dove!

Lord Jesus, You promised that You would send the Holy Spirit. So often my eyes are blinded by the things I look at. Please open the eyes of my heart so that I can see the Dove today.

By a Charcoal Fire...

"A smell can bring on a flood of memories, influence people's moods and even affect their work performance. Because the olfactory bulb is part of the brain's limbic system, an area so closely associated with memory and feeling, it's sometimes called the 'emotional brain,' smell can call up memories and powerful responses almost instantaneously"[http://science.howstuffworks.com/life/human-biology/smell.htm]. I found this in an article written by Sarah Dowdey on "How Smell Works." Do you think Jesus knew that when He chose to make a charcoal fire to cook the fish on for His disciples after His resurrection?

The word for charcoal is only used twice in the New Testament. The other time it is used was when Peter was warming himself by a charcoal fire. He was warming himself by the charcoal fire when he denied that he knew Jesus. The rooster crowed. It was early morning on the day Jesus was to be crucified. The smell of charcoal burning would forever awaken in Peter's "emotional brain" that he failed.

I wonder if a rooster crowed just as the day was breaking and Jesus stood on the shore by the Sea of Tiberias? It was after Jesus had risen from the dead. His disciples had decided to go fishing when He appeared on the shore. Peter had rushed to greet Him. Jesus had prepared a charcoal fire with fish laid out on it. I wonder if He was warming Himself by the fire on that early morning? Surely, since Peter had jumped into the water, he too would need the warmth of that charcoal fire.

The last time they had eaten together Jesus had told Peter that he would deny Him. The last time Peter had warmed himself by a charcoal fire he had denied Jesus, not once but three times. Now with Peter's "emotional brain" screaming "FAILURE!"Jesus asks him a question three times. "Simon, son of John, do you love me?" Three times by a charcoal fire he had denied his Lord early in the morning. Three times by a charcoal fire Jesus invited him to affirm his love early in the morning.

Lord Jesus, You are my Redeemer. You came and bore my griefs and carried my sorrows. You were wounded for my transgressions, you were bruised for my iniquities; the chastisement for my peace was upon You, and by Your stripes I am healed. You heal the brokenhearted. Just like Peter I have failed You. Just like Peter I have found in You a Redeemer.

What Difference Does It Make?

She lay in bed and reached out her hand, "Sarah, who they?" she whispered. I saw no one, but I was suddenly struck by the memory of my first night after moving to her home to care for her.

I had exchanged my spacious home for a room. However, when I woke in the night I felt confused. I stood in the hallway and watched as the walls pushed back. Suddenly I was no longer in a narrow hallway but instead in a spacious room filled with light. There was a great deal of activity going on that I didn't understand.

When I went into the bedroom my husband and I were sharing, I once more saw the walls pushed back. I stood there staring and trying to understand, when suddenly it all made sense. I remembered the story of Jacob's Ladder. Jacob had left Beersheba and was on his way to Haran when he came to a place to sleep. He dreamed there was a ladder set up on the earth; the top of it reached to heaven. As I blinked my eyes I thought, "I am living in a physical and spiritual world simultaneously."

What difference does it make if I believe that I not only live in the physical world that I can see, but that I also live in a spiritual world? How does that affect the choices I make, the things I choose to do or not do? I believe because of what Christ did for me that I have experienced a spiritual birth. "Truly, truly, I say to you, unless one is born of water and the Spirit, he cannot enter the kingdom of God. That which is born of the flesh is flesh, and that which is born of the Spirit is spirit. Do not marvel that I said to you, 'You must be born again'"(John 3:5-7 ESV).

Lord Jesus, let me walk in the truth and in newness of life. Let me base my choices of what I do or not do not on just the physical reality of what I see, but on the spiritual reality of what You did for me on Calvary.

Trusting the One Who Is In Control

I heard her crying out in the night. I hurried down the hall to where my little girl lay crying, stepping on toys and knocking the pictures askew in my flight. When I got to her, I wrapped my arms around her and whispered, "It's okay now, Mommy is here." Her eyes were wide in terror as she told me her nightmare. My five-year-old daughter had dreamed she had been driving a car but she didn't know how to steer it and she couldn't reach the brakes. As I stilled my frightened child I remembered similar dreams of not being in control from my own childhood. But I remembered sometime else too, the words of a song "Jesus, Savior, Pilot Me."

> Jesus, Savior, pilot me
>
> Over life's tempestuous sea;
>
> Unknown waves before me roll,
>
> Hiding rock and treacherous shoal.
>
> Chart and compass come from Thee;
>
> Jesus, Savior, pilot me.

I heard her calling in the night. She was calling out in pain, but not in fright. Long ago she had surrendered her will to her Savior. "Mom, I'm here," I said. She patted my hand comfortingly, "It's alright, Sarah, go back to sleep. I'll be alright." She had walked many years being guided by her Savior. Again I was reminded of the words of the song:

> When at last I near the shore,
>
> And the fearful breakers roar
>
> 'Twixt me and the peaceful rest,
>
> Then, while leaning on Thy breast,
>
> May I hear Thee say to me,
>
> "Fear not, I will pilot thee."
>
> [Edward Hopper, *Jesus, Savior, Pilot Me*, Public domain.]

Lord Jesus, when I was young I heard of Your steadfast love. I have seen those who trust in Your unfailing love walk their last steps in peace. Cause me to know the way that I should go, for to You I lift up my soul.

Be Kind

It was one of the first Bible verses I taught my children. I taught it to them in self defense. "Be kind" (Eph. 4:32). I often shouted it at my children from the driver's seat of the car when they were behind me fighting, "BE KIND!" Lately, our family has been going through a difficult time and I have found myself going to Ephesians 4 over and over to remind myself to "Be kind." I have also had to stop and think, "What does kindness really mean?"

How elementary is kindness really? It was always my starting place in teaching my children I wanted them to be kind. I find in Proverbs that what is desirable in a man is his kindness. Kindness is also translated as unfailing love, steadfast love, and loyalty. Having demanded kindness of my children, I have a confession: I am not by nature a kind person.

When life becomes difficult or I am hurting, my natural inclination is to be selfish and to want others to focus on my needs. This is a problem when everyone is going through a hard time. Where can I go to find the kindness that I need? How can I change my natural inclination to be selfish and have instead a sweet temper that focuses on easing the pain of those around me?

Kindness is a fruit of the Holy Spirit. Jesus told me that, if I wanted to be His disciple, I needed to deny myself, take up my cross, and follow Him. What I see is that this difficult time is an opportunity to do just that. I want to be a disciple of Jesus, therefore I choose to deny my selfish tenancy and instead surrender my will to the will of the Holy Spirit. I want to clothe myself with kindness.

Lord Jesus, You came because of the tender mercy of God. You have shown me by example what kindness looks like. I have been comforted by Your love. I have known Your tenderness and compassion. Thank You for giving me an opportunity to extend this kindness to others. Please let me represent You well.

Judgment

When I was a little girl I had no trouble at all judging him. From the first time I heard the story, I condemned him with all the self-righteousness that was in my young heart. Jesus stood before Pilate and even told him that His kingdom was not of this world. Then Pilate had to form a critical opinion and pronounce judgment. Pilate was afraid: If he chose to believe the incarnate word of God who stood before him, he would be at enmity with those who had power over his position of authority. Was it Jesus who stood on trial before Pilate, or Pilate who stood on trial before Jesus? Pilate pronounced his judgment; he chose to side with the world.

"All Scripture is breathed out by God and profitable for teaching, for reproof, for correction, and for training in righteousness, that the man of God may be competent, equipped for every good work" (2 Tim. 3:16-17 ESV). When I was an untested child, it was easy for me to condemn Pilate; but I, like him, have failed at times when I have had to judge between what the Word of God says and what the world says. If I take my stand with God's word I will place myself at enmity with those who disagree with God's judgment. What shall I do? I can either stand in judgment of God's Word or let God's Word judge me?

When I was a little girl I had no trouble at all judging her. From the first time I heard the story I condemned her with all the self-righteousness that was in my young heart. Eve stood in the garden before the serpent. God had placed her in Paradise and had given her permission to eat the fruit of any tree in the Garden but one. Now the serpent was before her, forcing her to form a critical opinion and pronounce judgment. Did God really love her and have her best interest at heart? Could she trust Him? Eve chose to be deceived because of the lust of her flesh. Eve pronounced her judgment; she listened to the serpent and took what God had forbidden.

"For the word of God is living and active, sharper than any two-edged sword, piecing to the division of soul and of spirit, of joints and of marrow, and discerning the thoughts and intentions of the heart. And no creature is hidden from his sight, but all are naked and exposed to the eyes of him to whom we must give account" (Heb. 4:12-13 ESV). When I was an untested child it was easy for me to condemn Eve; but I, like her, have failed when I have been tempted by the serpent to take what God has forbidden. I have stood before God's Word with both my hands and mouth stained by what I judged to be good. It was the living, active word of God that exposed my thoughts and the intentions of my heart. Standing before Him, all the sin of my heart was exposed.

Lord Jesus, You told me that I have a threefold enemy, the world, the flesh, and the Devil. I have fallen before each one of them. In the Garden, You promised a Savior. When Jesus stood before Pilate, He was condemned to die, but it was not for His guilt but mine. Thank You, Jesus, that when I come before the court of Heaven to be judged, you have taken away my sin so that I can be pronounced righteous.

From Raging to Rest

She asked me to speak for a luncheon at her house. I asked her what she wanted me to talk about, and she said, "Pray about it and then talk about whatever the Lord puts on your heart." Every time I prayed I came up with only one idea *"When Jesus Invites You into a Storm."* It was beautiful and sunny the day of the luncheon; it didn't seem to match at all what I would be talking about. I didn't know that in within a few short months a tornado would hit that same neighborhood, causing what the governor called "utter devastation."

Storms come, and with them comes confusion. As the sky darkens, anxiety can flood my heart like the waters flood the earth. When I read in Luke 8 about the storm Jesus' disciples encountered on the lake, it adds another dimension of helplessness. "They were filling with water and were in danger." Why were they out in their boat on the lake in the storm? It was because Jesus had said, "Let us go to the other side of the lake," and then, as they sailed, He fell asleep.

Storms expose my helplessness. When all around me is calm and peaceful, I have the illusion of being in control. However, when the tempest comes, I am often jolted and find myself off balance. I feel sick when it seems that even what I'm standing on is being tossed by the waves of a squall. The darkness of the sky causes me to lose my direction. The darkness, the confusion, the loss of balance also cause me to feel very isolated and cut off from any who could help. Storms expose my helplessness, but they also expose what I really believe and what I put my faith in—or don't put my faith in.

"When it is dark enough, you can see the stars" (Ralph Waldo Emerson). When my life is assaulted with the darkness of the storm, I begin to recognize my weakness; and it is then that I begin to understand who God really is. When Jesus' disciples woke Him because they felt they would drown, they found out who this man really was. Did He care? This is a question that has come unbidden to my mind as well when the darkness comes. Can He help? Jesus "rebuked the wind and the raging waves and they ceased, and there was a calm." When it's dark enough and all around me I hear the raging wind, it is then I come to know the one who can command even the wind and the waters. And I experience within my soul a supernatural calm that can only come when He calms the storm.

Lord Jesus, You not only rebuked the storm You rebuked Your disciples. "Where is your faith?" Help me, when I become aware of my helplessness and am afraid, to put my trust in You. Thank You for the storms, because it is in the midst of them I discover again that you care and are able to bring calm to my soul. When it is dark enough, I see Your light.

A Prayer of the Brokenhearted

There was a prayer request for someone's mother who had congestive heart failure. We also prayed for someone's friend who was having heart surgery. Then came one of the strangest prayer requests I've ever heard. Someone asked for prayer concerning their own heart: "Please pray that I would have a broken and contrite heart."

I knew the reference from Psalms. It was David's response when Nathan confronted him with his sin concerning Bathsheba. A few verses earlier David had prayed, "Create in me a clean heart, O God, and renew a right spirit within me" (Psa. 51:10 ESV). David had committed adultery with Bathsheba, and then when he found out she was pregnant, he tried to cover his sin by having her husband murdered. David couldn't clean his own heart; he could only offer his broken heart as a sacrifice to God.

Not only that, but it wasn't until God exposed his sin that he was able to repent of it. Until then, he just kept covering it up.

What my friend prayed was that God would make her aware of her sins and then cause her to be able to grieve those sins so that she too could offer God the sacrifice of a broken and contrite heart. This could be a scary prayer, because you open yourself up to be humbled. God sent Nathan to confront David. Sometimes the Holy Spirit uses my husband to point out what I cannot see myself. My heart is often calloused by the sins I have committed, and it can be dangerous to point them out to me.

Why would anyone want to have a broken and contrite heart? Why would anyone pray such a strange prayer? When I pray this prayer it shows I want God more than I want my sin, and that I am willing to be broken over my sin. The opposite is to cling to my sin and continually cover it up. When I bring to God the sacrifice of a broken and contrite heart, according to Psalm 147, "He heals the brokenhearted and binds up their wounds." Psalms 34 says, "The Lord is close to the brokenhearted and saves those who are crushed in spirit." What I am really asking is to be healed.

O Lord, Your word teaches me that You dwell in a high and holy place, but also with him who is contrite and lowly in spirit; to revive the spirit of the lowly and to revive the heart of the contrite. Because I want You to dwell with me, and I want to be revived, I will join my friend and pray, "Lord, please give me a broken and contrite heart."

The Beauty of a Diamond

"Tell me the good news." It's what I want to hear, but sometimes people need permission to tell me more than just the good news. I can share in other people's joy, but what about their sorrows? Yesterday I was talking to a woman who has gone through a great amount of suffering, and she told me how most people were uncomfortable with her pain.

He touched the blind eyes; He made His home with those who were poor and with those who were considered the outcasts. "Though he was in the form of God, he did not count equality with God a thing to be grasped, but made himself nothing, taking the form of a servant, being born in the likeness of men" (Phil. 2). Jesus came to take our griefs and carry our sorrows, and then He invited us to follow His example.

"So if there is any encouragement in Christ, any comfort from love, any participation in the Spirit, any affection and sympathy, complete my joy by being of the same mind, having the same love." When Jesus entered our suffering with His presence and His promises, light overcame the darkness. When we follow His example, we too shine like lights in the world, and there is joy.

When I think about joy that is born from sorrow, I think of the way diamonds are made. To make a diamond there must be a great amount of pressure and a great amount of heat. But in the end you have a jewel that is both strong and beautiful. When a diamond is exposed to the sun it reflects the light and sparkles with the colors of a rainbow. Because Jesus is my Savior, where once there was only grief, now I find a diamond.

Lord Jesus, thank You for the joy of Your promises and Your presence. Thank You for making it possible to find encouragement, comfort from love and participation in Your Spirit. May the joy of my salvation be like a diamond that reflects Your light and causes others to be drawn to the rainbow of the hope I find in You.

In You I Find Grace, In You I Find Peace

I live in a broken world. I live in a broken world where there have been broken promises resulting in broken hearts. Like Eve, whose hands were stained by the fruit of rebellion, my own heart is stained by the sin of disbelief. Into this dark and broken world there is a bright ray of hope. There is grace and there is peace from God, my Father, and the Lord Jesus Christ.

With eyes that often sting with tears I look upon the lives of those who struggle under the weight of sin. If I only saw the world with my physical eyes I would despair; but day after day I look through the spiritual lens of God's word and find hope. I find the blessed God and Father of my

Lord Jesus Christ, who has blessed me in Christ with every spiritual blessing in the heavenly places. What lavish love is this that he should have chosen me in Christ Jesus before the foundation of the world? It is only by His grace and mercy that I could be holy and blameless before Him.

I live in a broken world. I live in a broken world where sin brings isolation, and unforgiving hearts resulting in hate. My own sinful unforgiving heart would be doomed if it had not been conquered by the love of God. I marvel at the love that chose me in Christ before the foundation of the world. Before I knew Him, in love, He predestined me for adoption through Jesus Christ, according to the purpose of His will, to the praise of His glorious grace, with which He has blessed me in the Beloved.

In this broken world where sin has ushered in death, there can be a chill of hopelessness, when death seems to claim dreams and those I love, and leaves behind it only the shadow of what used to be. But the darkness has been overwhelmed by the light, and death has been swallowed up in victory. God has made known the mystery of His will when He sent in His son. Through Jesus I have obtained an inheritance sealed with the promise of His Holy Spirit.

Lord Jesus, You came into this broken world and showed me the love of God when You redeemed me from my sins. You showed me the immeasurable greatness of Your power by not only setting me free from my sins, but by sharing Your inheritance with me. In You I find grace, in You I find peace.

My Greatest Weakness Becomes My Greatest Strength

The Hebrew word carries with it the meaning that darkness or calamity seemed to have covered or enveloped his soul. This is a place I am familiar with; a place where my soul seems covered or enveloped by darkness. Sometimes it is a series of calamities that overwhelm me.

Things begin piling up on me till I begin to feel smothered. But not always. There have also simply been times when sorrow eclipses joy without warning and without a visible cause. This smothering darkness causes me to cry out with the psalmist, "From the ends of the earth I call to you, I call as my heart grows faint; lead me to the rock that is higher than I" (Psa. 61:2 NIV).

When I am in this place where my soul has been enveloped by sorrow, I need help. To whom do I go for help? I confess I have sometimes gone to idols of my own making, thinking they might give me comfort. But they have only taken me deeper into grief and further from the source of light. I reached out to others and found some measure of relief; but I have also taken them by the hand and drawn them down with me.

What I have found is that I need someone who is stronger than I am, who is willing to come to my rescue. I can't find my way to them; I can only call out for help. But help comes. I call as my heart grows faint, and my Savior comes and leads me to a rock that is higher than I. "The Lord is my rock, my fortress and my deliverer; my God is my rock, in whom I take refuge. He is my shield and the horn of my salvation, my stronghold" (Psa. 18:2 NIV).

From my earliest memories I have done battled with a downcast soul, but I don't see it as a disability but as a door that leads me to God's presence. My weakness and inclination towards depression has taught me to cry out. Just as the darkness threatens to overtake me I cry out, and find coming towards me is the Savior who said, "I will never leave you or forsake you." The eyes of my spirit are opened and I experience a joy that far exceeds the sorrow.

Lord Jesus, because You are my Savior, my greatest weakness has become a place of strength, my greatest sorrow a place of joy. You told Moses, "There is a place near me where you may stand on a rock" (Ex. 33:21). Lord Jesus, You are the Rock on which I stand near to the heart of God.

Before the Throne of Unapproachable Light I Cry, "Abba"

It was two in the morning when he came to wake me. My husband and I are caring for his mother during her last days on earth. She was uncomfortable. We worked together until she was resting. I got back in bed and my mind was flooded with anxiety. I would like to say, because the Bible says "Be anxious about nothing," that I am never anxious; but then I would be lying, and the Bible also says "Do not lie." What I can say is that when I am anxious I am drawn irresistibly before the throne of grace.

Have you ever had your heart so full that you felt you just had to talk to someone? But then you notice as you were talking they really weren't listening? Or have you ever been at a counselor's office and you were just beginning to be able to put words to your pain, and they looked at their watch and said, "Times up." That would be the opposite of what I experience when I go to God in prayer. "Let us then with confidence draw near to the throne of grace, that we may receive mercy and find grace in time of need" (Heb. 4:16 ESV).

Sometimes I sit in silence with the things that weigh my heart down. Who could help anyway? But when I go to God in prayer, I picture Him on His throne. "He wraps himself in light as with a garment; he stretches out the heavens like a tent" (Psa. 104:2 NIV). He "dwells in unapproachable light" (1 Tim. 6:16 ESV). His throne is in appearance like sapphire, His voice is like the sound of mighty rushing waters. According to Ezekiel there is brightness all around Him and there is a rainbow that encircles His throne. To this throne of grace I have been invited; to this throne of grace I come. Bathed in His light and love I find the welcome that a father gives to his child. Surrounded by His glory, He invites me to lay my burden down and know His rest. As the light of His glory penetrates my tears, I see the colors of a rainbow, and I find comfort in His promises.

How can someone like me have access to such glory? I am a mere mortal, and stained by sin; and yet I come because I have been invited. I don't have to come; I could sit in the darkness, overwhelmed by grief and sorrow. But because of the sacrificial death of Jesus I come with confidence to this holy place.

I come by the new and living way that He opened for me through the curtain, which is through His flesh. I know, according to the book of Hebrews, that because Jesus is my high priest I can draw near to God with full assurance. I have been invited through grace to come, and by faith I have accepted the invitation.

Lord Jesus, in the middle of my night my heart was full of darkness and anxiety about things I could not control. Thank You for inviting me before the throne of grace to lay my burden down. Thank You for lavishing Your love on me so that when I look at the one who is seated on the throne I can cry, "Abba, Father!"

The Gift I Could Not Earn

My mother came to the café where I am a waitress. It was a very busy day, and I was rushing from table to table serving. When I got to my Mother's table she told me she had a gift for me. I leaned over as she fastened a necklace around my neck. I couldn't see it, but my fingers felt its beauty. Because we were so busy it was quite some time before I could slip away and see this gift my mother had given me. When I looked in the mirror, my breath was taken by the beauty of the sapphire and diamonds on a gold collar. So I spent the rest of the day with my hair pulled back in a ponytail, cap on, apron on, waiting on tables, clearing tables, washing dishes, and all the while wearing the most beautiful sapphire and diamond necklace I have ever seen.

This scene in my mind of wearing this beautiful necklace while being a servant is like a parable of my Christian experience. When I looked up the meaning of sapphires in the Bible I found this quote, "God comforts His people with the promise that, while they are suffering now, He will eventually restore them beyond anything they could ever expect or imagine" (Isa. 54:11). "O thou afflicted with tempest, and not comforted, behold, I will lay thy stones with fair colors, and lay thy foundations with sapphires."

When I am not at the café being a waitress I am at the home of my dear mother-in-law who is in the final days of her life. We sit around her bed surrounding her with love. She is barely able to speak now. She still blesses us with her smile, and every word she utters reminds us that she loves us and knows that we love her. My heart is often squeezed with sorrow. I don't want to say good bye, but I know the curtain is closing on her life here with us. But I also know, because of Jesus, things are not always what they seem. We grieve, but not without hope, not without the promise that to be absent from the body is to be present with the Lord.

"Where, O death, is your victory? Where, O death, is your sting? The sting of death is sin, and the power of sin is the law. But thanks be to God! He gives us the victory through our Lord Jesus Christ" (1 Cor. 15:55-56 NIV). I am the waitress wearing a sapphire and diamond necklace that reminds me the promises that God has given me are more than anything I could ever expect or imagine. I am one who sits with tear-washed eyes watching at the bedside while one whom my heart loves draws her final breath. But with eyes of faith I see beyond the veil, I see the Lord of love standing to greet her with outstretched arms.

Lord Jesus, thank You for the gifts of grace I could never earn.

Finding a Refuge in the Stillness

There are two chair facing west at the top of the hill. As the evening begins to cool and the sun begins to set, he and I make our way out once more to take our place. We sit in companionable silence, each lost in our own thoughts. At first I'm almost worried that my vision might be hurt. The brilliant orb seems shining directly in my eyes. But as we continue watching, the sun slips behind the mountains. The air is cooled, but the beautiful display of colors warms our heart. Darkness begins to blanket the earth, but still we sit, the beauty feeding our souls. I lift my eyes to the heavens. Coming through the darkness now there is the glow of the evening star. Reluctantly we stand to go.

In the stillness and the quiet of those moments our hearts find the strength to continue our vigil at the bedside of his dying wife. We have whispered the words night after night as we watched the sun set, "Be still and know that I am God..." (Psa. 46:10). We have found the beginning words of the psalm to be true as well: "God is our refuge and our strength, a very present help in trouble." The chairs are set side by side; we sit together at the bed and remember. The grief and pain are real, but so is the strength we find in the stillness of the night and the knowledge that we are not alone. Surely our God is a very present help.

This is not a place any of us would ever choose to be, but it's not a place we can escape; death comes to us all. My daughter has dubbed this peculiar time we are in "Heaven's Waiting Room." Many things are happening as we sit and in the stillness and wait. Quietly we are sitting together bound by love, by faith, by hope. Tonight I asked the question, "What is the chief end of man?" Without a pause, my 91-year-old father-in-law responded, "The chief end of man is to glorify God and to enjoy Him forever." So here we sit together, even now praying that God will be glorified, and finding our hearts comforted at the prospects of enjoying Him forever.

Tomorrow morning I will look toward the east and watch the sun rise. I will remind myself of the promise of the resurrection.

Strength Made Perfect in Weakness

"How can I help you?" This was the question she always asked. Ma Belle's vision was gone, and she had difficulty hearing even with her hearing aids. Mom had suffered the effects of several mini strokes, leaving her weak and often unable to remember things that had just taken place. Still, she would ask, "How can I help you?"

Several years ago when Ma Belle was struggling with the loss of her sight, and as a result the loss of her freedom, she told me what she had prayed. "I prayed and told the Lord I was willing to be weak if He could use my weakness to make my family the people He wanted them to be." This was such a prayer of love; this was such a gift of grace. She humbly believed that, if God allowed suffering into her life, He would also be able to redeem that suffering. The gift she asked for as a result of that redeeming love was for her family, not for herself.

I have been both a recipient and an observer of how God answered her prayer. I have read in 2 Corinthians 12:9, "For my strength is made perfect in weakness," but now I have observed it. Ma Belle became weaker and weaker until she could do nothing for herself. As I cared for her, I became more and more aware of the honor and privilege of caring for someone who was willing to sacrifice strength and dignity for the ones she loved. Spurgeon said, "A primary qualification for serving God with any amount of success, and for doing God's work well and triumphantly, is a sense of our own weakness."

It is one thing to give your strength in service to the Lord, but it is another to give your weakness. What a beautiful picture of humility and faith to surrender your weakness, believing that God will use it to bless the people you love. She humbled herself and laid aside her dignity. She considered others more significant than herself. She didn't look to own interests but instead she looked to the interests of others. I watched as this brilliant woman followed her Lord and allowed herself to be made nothing. She, in her total weakness, became a servant of the most high God.

Mom died on Sunday. Mom died quietly. It seemed as if she just slipped away from us, leaving us one of the most precious gifts that can be given. She showed us by example what self-sacrificing love looks like. Now I have to close my eyes to see her; but when I do I think of Psalm 45:13, "The king's daughter is all glorious within; Her clothing is interwoven with gold." Thank you, mom, for showing me what strength made perfect through weakness looks like.

Changing Clothes

It was the most beautiful shirt in the world. A princess wearing a shirt interwoven with gold would have been jealous if she saw it. What was it about this shirt that set it apart? There were two things. The first thing was my imagination, and as a ten-year-old, my imagination was highly exercised. The second thing that set this shirt apart from any other shirt that had ever been made was the amazing fact that I, myself, without the help of any other, had stitched every stitch. I remember walking out into the sunshine wearing this glorious creation for the first time and feeling like light was emanating as much from me as it was from the sun. But there was a problem.

The very thing that had brought me to this summit of pride plummeted me to the pit of humiliation. Yes, my ten-year-old hand had stitched every stitch of that shirt, but the problem was, I really didn't know what I was doing, nor did I realize how easily a hand-sewn seam could come undone. So, having made my grand entrance and making sure that everyone on the playground had been informed that I was not just any child, I was the seamstress of the glorious shirt, I joined in the playing with abandonment. That's when it happened. The stitches just seemed to suddenly unravel. And with head bent and hands clutching what was left of my shirt, I ran all the way home.

A frequent answer to the question, "If you were to die tonight and stand before the gates of Heaven, why should they let you in?" has something to do with the person being good or trying to be good. When I hear that, I think about my glorious shirt and how it fell apart when put to the test. I'm also reminded of what I read in Galatians 3:27, "And all who have been united with Christ in baptism have put on Christ, like putting on new clothes." I can be clothed in Christ's righteousness because of His sacrifice. He put on the robe of flesh so that I could put on the robe of His righteousness.

Sometimes in my life it has taken going through humiliating situations for me to become humble. In my pride I've always wanted to be good enough. I remember hearing about Jesus' sacrifice on the cross for my sins as a young child and thinking, "I still think I could be good enough for God if I try hard enough." What the years have taught me is that I am far more capable of sin than I am of goodness. Again and again I have experienced my best efforts dissolving, leaving me running from situations with my hands clutching what was left of my pride.

Lord Jesus, I bow in the presence of Your love. The truth is, I cannot cloth myself. I've tried and it's only ended in my shame. Thank You for bathing me in Your grace and clothing me in Your righteousness.

I Come

Sometimes I come into His presence like a child on a treasure hunt. I have watched my children this week as they have delighted themselves with hidden family heirlooms. Boxes and boxes of old letters written years ago. Pictures, old coins, trinkets of the past all with meaning that help them to unlock the stories of their ancestors. Sometimes I open God's word and I spend hours seeking to understand all that I find, doing word studies, tracing an idea throughout the Scripture, studying the historical context.

Sometimes I come into His presence like a child who is overwhelmed by life. The world seems so big and I feel so small. Often I will slip away by myself and sit in the stillness and remember that He is God and I am not. I let the beauty of nature speak to me of its Creator. Often this happens at night, and I will sit in the stillness and the quiet of the night and listen because, "The heavens declare the glory of God; the skies proclaim the work of his hands. Day after day they pour forth speech; night after night they reveal knowledge" (Psa. 19:1-2 NIV). I sit in the stillness and listen until I can hear His voice, and my heart becomes quiet and at rest.

Sometimes I come into His presence so aware of my failures that I can barely lift my head. This is when I rest in God's unfailing love. I come into His presence not because of my great love for Him, but because He has loved me with a faithful and steadfast love. God has lavished His love on me and has entered into a covenant of love with me and has called me His child. Though I have often stumbled and failed in my love for Him, I always find in His presence a God of tenderness and compassion, one who is slow to anger and rich in faithful love.

Sometimes I come into His presence to soothe and quiet my soul. "I do not concern myself with great matters or things too wonderful for me. But I have stilled and quieted my soul; like a weaned child with its mother, like a weaned child is my soul within me" (Psa. 131:1-2 NIV). I come knowing that when I am in His presence I am fully known, completely understood, and unconditionally loved.

Lord Jesus, because of Your invitation, I come.

Remembering Life's Brevity

Ma Belle died last Sunday. All week we have been gathered around Papa, her beloved husband of 64 years. There has been an unspoken theme in our shared grief. Boxes were found that contained love letters, love letters written from generations past. We spoke not only about the covenant of love that they had shared, but we also spoke about the unfailing love God has been shown to this family as they have sought to serve God throughout the generations.

Lord, you have been our dwelling place

throughout all generations.

Before the mountains were born

or you brought forth the earth and the world,

from everlasting to everlasting you are God.

Our conversation has often begun with Papa wondering how they could possibly be in their 90s. Last year we had a big celebration for their 90th birthdays. Lots of pictures were taken, pictures that we now cherish. However, Papa never saw himself as an old man; instead he found a picture of his wedding day and put it with the picture of the 90th birthday and said, "This is how I still see myself and Isabelle."

You turn men back to dust,

saying, "Return to dust, O sons of men."

For a thousand years in your sight

are like a day that has just gone by,

or like a watch in the night.

You sweep men away in the sleep of death;

they are like the new grass of the morning-

though in the morning it springs up new,

by evening it is dry and withered.

Both Ma Belle and Papa had one request for their funeral services—they wanted a clear presentation of the gospel. Why? It was because they understood what Jesus had done for them. They understood that, "This is real love—not that we loved God, but that he loved us and sent his Son as a sacrifice to take away our sins" (1 John 4:10).

We are consumed by your anger

and terrified by your indignation.

You have set our iniquities before you,

our secret sins in the light of your wrath;

All our days pass away under your wrath;

we finish our years with a moan.

The length of our days is seventy years-

or eighty, if we have the strength;

yet their span is but trouble and sorrow,

for they quickly pass, and we fly away.

For a week after Ma Belle died we surrounded Papa with our songs of love and listened as he sang his love to us. We wept, we laughed, we cried, we remembered God's faithfulness to us throughout the generations. Then Papa and I shared a quiet moment and he said, "Come Monday, I'm going to need to start learning to live my life without her...but I don't want to." He knew that by Monday we would all need to return to our busy lives, and he would still be here grieving. But Monday never came. Papa died on Sunday. His was a heart full of love a heart full of wisdom and when it stopped beating he was ushered into the presence of God.

Who knows the power of your anger?

For your wrath is as great as the fear that is due you.

Teach us to number our days aright,

that we may gain a heart of wisdom.

"We've been mighty blessed!" This was a statement that Papa often made as he thought back through the years. Both Papa and Ma Belle had been from Christian families. They had been taught from their earliest memories what the chief end of man was. In his 90s, with a tear-choked voice, he would say, "The chief end of man is to glorify God and enjoy Him forever." Then he would add, "Why, why have we been so blessed?" My answer was always the same," Papa, you have been blessed to be a blessing. God has chosen you to be a living parable of what it looks like to know God and have His splendor show throughout the generations."

Relent, O Lord! How long will it be?

Have compassion on your servants.

Satisfy us in the morning with your unfailing love,

that we may sing for joy and be glad all our days.

Make us glad for as many days as you have afflicted us,

for as many years as we have seen trouble.

May your deeds be shown to your servants,

your splendor to their children.

Ma Belle and Papa died one week apart. A week that was filled with stories of love and the faithfulness of a covenant-keeping God. During this week we heard story after story after story about how the ancestors had committed their lives and plans to the Lord and how He had been faithful to establish the plans they had committed to Him. The day before Papa died, I read Psalm 90 to him, the same Psalm I have quoted here. He wept and spoke through his tears, "It is so; yes, it is so."

May the favor of the Lord our God rest upon us;

establish the work of our hands for us—

yes, establish the work of our hands.

Grieve? We Grieve, But Not Without Hope!

I got the message. It was from my nine-year-old grandson, "Mimi, come quick I need you!" I rushed to his side and found him sobbing uncontrollably on his bed. With a broken voice washed in tears he cried out, "I want to hear her voice again! I want to hold her! I want her to hold my hand!" My heart broke and my tears mingled with his as we lay there holding each other. No words, only shared grief, because grief is real, and grief is painful.

Tears must flow because death is an enemy, the last enemy. I am gently and slowly telling Jack the truth. "The last enemy that will be abolished is death." I have more to share with this precious child who, it seems to me, has known more than his share of grief. I softly whisper a mystery into his ear, hoping that it will take root in both his heart and his soul. "Behold! I tell you a mystery. We shall not all sleep, but we shall all be changed" (1 Cor. 15:51 ESV).

There is another grief I am aware of. Although we speak of the joy of this Christian couple who shared in a Marriage Covenant that lasted 64 years, not everyone has had this blessing. There is the grief of the broken home, the broken promises, the broken hearts. There is the grief of broken parents from generations of brokenness, those who have not known the love of the Savior. My heart grieves with them as well; my eyes are not dry when I think of their pain.

But I know a secret. "God sets the lonely in families" (Psa. 68:6 NIV). Our family has always had an open door policy. We have always sought to be inclusive. For years the question has been asked, "Do you know anyone who will be alone that we can invite to join us?" Oh, but there is something far better than being included in our family. Jesus said, "In my Father's house are many rooms. If it were not so, would I have told you that I go to prepare a place for you?" (John 14). Jesus has invited us to share His home. In that same chapter he said, "I will not leave you as orphans; I will come to you."

Lord Jesus, because You came to bear our grief and carry our sorrows we have hope. We still grieve on this side of eternity because of empty chairs and empty places, but we don't grieve like those who have no hope.

Broken By Love

I thought it would be a good idea, that it would make me a better person. And so I began. I began by memorizing 1 Corinthians 13 first in the King James Version, "Love suffers long, and is kind." I tried it in another version, "Love is patient, love is kind." I tried it in still another version, "Love is always patient, love is always kind." But it didn't make me a better person, it just pointed out—again and again—that I wasn't really loving.

"Love is not jealous; love does not brag and is not arrogant, does not insist on its own way, is not provoked, does not keep a record of wrongs," I memorized, I meditated, I became convicted that what I thought was love wasn't. As I looked at this picture of perfect love, it became a mirror into which I could look and see God more clearly, as well as myself. I was jealous; I found many creative ways to brag; I knew how often I insisted on my own way in my relationship to my husband.

But what really broke me was that love is not provoked and does not keep a record of wrongs. "Love does not rejoice in unrighteousness, but rejoices with the truth."

Conviction. Then came the crescendo of impossibilities: "Love bears all things, believes all things, hopes all things." What breaks you and brings you to your knees? For me it was memorizing, and meditating on 1 Corinthians 13. I wanted to use it to make me a better person; God used it to show me that I wasn't even good in the first place. The crescendo built until at last I heard the truth, "Love never fails."

Broken shattered fragments of who I thought I was lay all about me. But then I remembered something else, "For this is what the high and lofty One says—he who lives forever, whose name is holy: 'I live in the high and holy place, but also with him who is contrite and lowly in spirit, to revive the spirit of the lowly and to revive the heart of the contrite'" (Isa. 57:15 NIV). Then I knew the truth—this love was the love God has for me.

Lord Jesus, thank You for showing me what the love of God looks like, "This is love, not that we have loved God, but that he loved us, and sent his Son to be the propitiation for our sins" (1 John 4:10).

The Promise of the Resurrection

It was the day before he died, I walked into the house and found him bent down with sorrow. "Papa, would you like to walk with me and then share another sunset?" He lifted his head and offered me his gentle smile and said, "Yes."

We walked slowly stopping often and then took our seats facing West, facing the setting of the sun. "Sarah, what do you think Isabelle is doing now?" A few years ago I had taught a study on what the Bible tells us about Heaven, earlier that week his beloved wife of 64 years had died. I looked into his dear face and my heart was touched by his great grief. Our hearts were heavy, but we comforted ourselves with the promises of God.

I did not know then what I know now. That would be the last evening I would ever share with him this side of eternity. We talked about the promise that, "He will wipe away every tear from their eyes, and death shall be no more, neither shall there be mourning, nor crying, nor pain anymore, for the former things have passed away" (Rev. 21:4 ESV). We shared our grief, we shared our hope, we shared the comfort of the word of God. We sat and talked about the love of God. And while we watched the sun set behind the mountain we also watched as two butterflies flitted about, and our hearts were gladdened by the beauty of God's gift of nature.

The next morning he died, and that evening I sat alone and watched the sun set. Yet I wasn't alone; the two butterflies that had blessed Papa and I the night before returned. I watched them again, and my heart was gladdened. But this time it was not only their beauty that comforted me but the reality they were a picture of the resurrection. I heard once that the Christian view of death is like a group of mourning caterpillars carrying a cocoon like a casket. Above there is a beautiful butterfly staring down in disbelief. The butterfly reminded me that there is the promise of new life even in the midst of my grief.

Both Papa and Ma Belle had requested that their memorial service focus on the gift of salvation. They wanted the good news of eternal life to be told as we gathered to grieve their death. "For God so loved the world, that he gave his only Son, that whoever believes in him should not perish but have eternal life" (John 3:16). On the last night of Papa's life he told me, "I love this month, I love this season of Spring because it reminds me of new birth." How fitting that God should choose to take both Papa and Ma Belle into His eternal presents during this time of new birth.

Please Turn the Light On

For the last three months, ever since my husband and I moved in to take care of his aging parents, I have had Philippians 2 on my mind. It is a chapter about following Christ's example of humility. "Do nothing from rivalry or conceit, but in humility count others more significant than yourselves." I always think in pictures, and the picture is see of humility is this. I cut two pieces of pie; one piece is slightly bigger than the other. If I serve you the larger piece without calling attention to my sacrifice that is humility. "Oh, Lord, You know that I would much rather pretend the pieces were cut identical so that I could have the larger piece! Please grant me Your Spirit so that I can count others more significant than myself."

"Let each of you look not only to his own interests, but also to the interests of others." I have gotten up early and have been enjoying solitude when I hear footsteps approaching. I am confronted with a choice: shall I choose to pretend I don't notice that someone else is awake and would like my company, or do I continue to enjoy my solitude? "Dear Lord, help me to practice what You're teaching me! Help me not only to look to my own interests but to the interests of others."

"Have this mind among yourselves, which is yours in Christ Jesus, who, though he was in the form of God, did not count equality with God a thing to be grasped, but made himself nothing, taking the form of a servant...." If I take on the form of a servant that means I will be willing to do the menial job without calling attention to myself. I will be looking for ways I can meet the needs of others instead of how they can serve me. "Oh, Lord, I don't want to that! I'm tired. I want someone to be meeting my needs. The contrast of what comes natural to me and what you ask of me is glaring."

"Do all things without grumbling or questioning...." I've heard that "grumbling and questioning" come from an attitude of rebellion against what the Sovereign Lord has chosen for you to do. I am guilty. I don't want to grumble and complain and question the reasonableness of what He has for me to do. But if I said, "I've never grumbled," I'd be lying and my children would tell on me. "Oh, Lord, let me focus more on You than the task set before me!"

I have read through this chapter repeatedly for three month and for three months I have found in my own strength I cannot do this. However, in this second chapter of Philippians I read, "It is God who works in you, both to will and to work for his good pleasure."

Dear Lord, please, please grant that I might be blameless and innocent, a child of God without blemish in the midst of a crooked and twisted generation. Please let me shine as a light in the world, holding fast to the word of life. Amen.

A Birthday with Heaven in View

In the home of Samuel and Zenna Jones, May 4, 1921 was a day of great celebration. It was the day they welcome John William Jones into their family. As they held their firstborn child their hearts were filled with hopes and dreams about the man he would one day be. Today, 91 years later, it is May 4, 2012. Today we will gather for his memorial service. Those of us who knew and loved him will celebrate the man we knew him to be.

Ecclesiastes 7 says, "A good name is better than precious ointment." When Samuel and Zenna chose the name John William for their son, that name held the dreams of who they hoped he would one day become. As we gather together 91 years later, we recognize that he gave his name the sweet fragrance we gather to enjoy. John William was a man of character, with a godly mind and life. The fragrance of his reputation was not only with men but with the God he served.

"And the day of death is better than the day of birth." This seems like an odd verse. Papa and I talked about many things the day before he died. We talked about his age, the chief end of man, and Heaven. When we spoke of his age it was in the context of Psalm 90, "The length of our days is seventy years—or eighty, if we have the strength; yet their span is but trouble and sorrow, for they quickly pass, and we fly away." When he was a very young child, Papa's mother had taught him to memorize the catechism. He never forgot, deeply rooted in his soul and life was the truth that "the chief end of man is to glorify God and enjoy Him forever." It was the driving force of his life. The day of his death marked an end to the trouble and sorrow of life when God called him home.

"It is better to go to the house of mourning than to go to the house of feasting, for this is the end of all mankind, and the living will lay it to heart." It is so easy to get caught up in the moment and lose the perspective of eternity. However, when I go to the house of mourning as I will today, it gives me a chance to think, to ponder, and consider the question, "When everything has been said and done, will my life be one that has brought God glory. Will I have made the choice to enjoy God forever?"

Lord, Your word says that the heart of the wise is in the house of mourning. As I prepare once more to go the house of mourning, give me understanding, grant me wisdom. Help me to remember that even 91 years, when it is past, is but a breath of time. Please help me to live each day of my life with eternity in view. Today, on Papa's 91st birthday, Heaven is no longer a vision, it is a view.

The Meditations of a Sojourner

There were two things that woke me last night. One was the grief of having lost two people I loved in a week, and the other was the pinched nerve in my neck. Both the physical and emotion pain made sleep seem impossible. I came into the living room to sit, think and pray. At the heart of my prayer was this verse, "I am a sojourner on the earth; hide not your commandments from me!" (Psa. 119:19 ESV).

I realized that in many ways I want and even expect life to be easy. But that is not what Jesus taught when He invited me to be part of His Kingdom. In fact, he never said that I would have peace in this world. He said, "I have said these things to you, that in me you may have peace. In the world you will have tribulation. But take heart; I have overcome the world" (John 16:33 ESV).

As I sat and prayed and meditated on the truths of scripture I was reminded of something my friend told me about the painting by Rembrandt called "Christ in the Storm." The picture depicted what I felt: A small fishing boat caught in a life-threatening storm. She told me to look at the picture and identify which figure represented me. I saw the disciples straining to keep the boat afloat. I saw some, with fear-filled faces, trying to wake the sleeping Savior. Then there was the one who seemed to be simply sitting passively in the storm-tossed boat. With my pinched nerve and grief-stricken heart, it was the picture as a whole I identified with.

Another verse came to mind as I meditated on my truth that I am a sojourner on this earth and that I have been promised tribulation in this world and not peace. The words that came were the words of Jesus, "Peace I leave with you; my peace I give to you. Not as the world gives do I give to you. Let not your hearts be troubled, neither let them be afraid" (John 14:27 ESV).

Lord Jesus, I confess I seek comfort in this world and am surprised that instead I find tribulation, just as You said I would. Thank You for the storms that teach me the truth that I belong to Your Kingdom, and in You I will always find peace.

My Payer to a God Who Is Near

I was awakened by the chiming of the clock in the den. Could it be it was only a week ago that I had been awaken at that very same hour by Papa complaining of chest pains? When the paramedics came they did an EKG which did not show a problem; his blood pressure was good, his oxygen level was normal, and yet Papa died when he got the hospital later that morning. Are all things left to chance, or is there a God who is in control?

I find the same comfort in thinking about the many days of Papa's life that I found when pondering the few days of my baby Belle Marie's life. Those days were not a random number chosen by chance, by an uncaring God. "Your eyes saw my unformed substance; in your book were written, every one of them, the days that were formed for me, when as yet there were none of them" (Psa. 139:16 ESV).

When I read this psalm I am reminded that the Lord I serve has an intimate concern for me. "O Lord, you have searched me and known me! You know when I sit down and when I rise up; you discern my thoughts from afar. You search out my path and my lying down and are acquainted with all my ways" (Psa. 139:1-3). The fabric of my life has been ripped by the loss of two people I love within the span of a week. There is a feeling of not only loss but vulnerability; yet I take the comfort that is offered to me in the psalm. Though I don't know the path that lies before me, the Lord does.

"If I say, 'Surely the darkness shall cover me, and the light about me be night,' even the darkness is not dark to you; the night is bright as the day, for darkness is as light with you" (Psa. 139:11-12 ESV). One of the things I am discovering about grief is that it makes it hard to think clearly. How comforting to know that I serve a God who is not only intimate with all my ways but that there is no darkness with Him. It is not only that there is not darkness with Him but He shares His light with me. "How precious to me are your thoughts, O God! How vast is the sum of them!" (Psa. 139:17 ESV).

Lord, I am comforted in knowing that You are not a God who is far off. You are not an indifferent God, but one who has hemmed me in, behind and before. You have laid Your hand upon me. "Search me, O God, and know my heart! Try me and know my thoughts! And see if there be any grievous way in me, and lead me in the way everlasting" (Psa. 139:23-24 ESV).

A Blessing for Those Gathered Around the Table

I have heard this prayer many times over the last 38 years, but I had never heard it prayed in this way before. Like many people, Papa had a prayer he would say before meals. "May Thy blessings rest upon this table and all who are gathered around it. Fill our hearts with grateful love. In Christ's name we pray. Amen." Sometimes I have to admit that I was so familiar with the prayer that I participated more out of habit. That changed the week following Ma Belle's death.

All the family gathered together. They came to grieve together, to support Papa in his loss. Many friends brought meals, and as we gathered around the table holding hands, Papa would begin to pray: "May Thy blessings rest upon this table and all who are gathered around it." Then he would pause, everyone there could feel his love and gratitude for their presence. Yet we were also aware that someone was missing. Some lessons are taught in a classroom and some are taught holding hands around a table and joining in a prayer of gratitude. While grieving his loss, he chose to recognize the gift that surrounded him.

Sometimes during this week Papa's voice broke and he would ask someone else to pray. The words would be different but the presence of the one who heard the prayer could be sensed. When Papa was able to pray, he said each word tenderly and with great emotion. I not only heard the words, I felt them, "Fill our hearts with grateful love." When your heart is full of sorrow it can be hard to find room for grateful love.

Papa brought not only his heart but ours as well, and we experienced the miracle of answered prayer together.

We didn't know then that that was to be the last week of Papa's life. It was a beautiful week full of love, memories and tenderness. Each of us were not only blessed by the fellowship we had around the table, we were blessed because Papa had requested it. "May Thy blessings rest upon this table and all who are gathered around it. Fill our hearts with grateful love. In Christ's name we pray. Amen"

Lord Jesus, thank You for Your many blessings. Thank You that there is a table that extends into the Heavens. Thank You for the sweet communion we have experienced as a family and for the communion that we look forward too. Surely Your blessings will rest upon that table and all who will be reunited around it. My heart is filled with grateful love as I wait in anticipation.

Come and Magnify the Lord with Me

We found her prayer book. These were the prayers she had written 21 years ago when she first began to lose her vision and recognized that she was beginning to have trouble with her memory. Ma Belle had come from a long line of "worriers." Being anxious about the people she loved often plagued her. Opening the pages of her prayer book was like stepping into a conversation she was having with her Heavenly Father.

"Do not be anxious about anything, but in everything by prayer and supplication with thanksgiving let your requests be made to God" (Phil. 4:6 ESV). The pages began with her neat and concise handwriting. Her words exposed the fullness of her heart, but the focus of her prayers was not the problem that was facing her or her family; the focus of her prayer was the God to whom she brought her petition.

"I will praise the name of God with a song. I will magnify him with thanksgiving" (Psa. 69:30 ESV). Ma Belle's prayers were like a telescope that searched the Heavens and found the throne of God. As she filled page after page with her prayers, based on who He is and not on what she was experiencing at the moment, I saw God magnified. Though she was bound by time, she prayed to a God who was not hemmed in by time. Her earthly vision was fading, but her prayers, so full of praise and thanksgiving, showed someone who had keen spiritual insight.

By the end of the prayer book the words were no longer touching the lines because she could no longer see them. She had filled the book with prayers for herself and those she loved. She had come before an all-sufficient God and had humbled herself before Him, not with arrogance but with the heart of a child. She brought Him the only thing she had to give—her brokenness, her worries and concerns for those she loved. "The sacrifice acceptable to God is a broken spirit. A broken and a contrite heart, O God thou wilt not despise" (Psa. 51:17). Yes, she brought her brokenness before Him, but she magnified Him with her praise and thanksgiving.

Oh, Heavenly Father, thank You for helping me see You more clearly through the praise and thanksgiving I find in this prayer book. Please let the legacy I leave to those I love be like the legacy Ma Belle left us. May I too live my life in humble dependence on an all-sufficient God. As I humbling come before You in my brokenness and dependence on Your love and mercy, may my prayers magnify You and not my anxieties.

The Prayer Book

It was the last entry of her prayer book. It had taken her several years to complete this book, and the last page showed the difficulty she had writing with her loss of vision. She had chosen Philippians 2 as the theme of her last recorded prayer. "Do nothing from rivalry or conceit, but in humility count others more significant than yourselves. Let each of you look not only to his own interests, but also to the interests of others." These verses not only reflected how she chose to pray but how she lived her life as well.

Three months before she died, my husband and I recognized that she and Papa needed help. So we moved out of our home and into a spare bedroom in their house. I saw the need; I wanted to meet it. I didn't want to be selfish, but not wanting to be selfish didn't change the reality that I am a selfish person. Daily I turned to Philippians 2 and prayed through it verse by verse. Day after day I asked God to allow me to have the same attitude that Christ Jesus did when He made Himself nothing and took on the form of a servant. I believed that God could change my heart to match my actions.

We didn't find the prayer book until after Ma Belle had died. I couldn't help but marvel as I read page after page of how she struggled in the same way I did. "All Scripture is God-breathed and is useful for teaching, rebuking, correcting and training in righteousness" (2 Tim. 3:16 NIV). Ma Belle's prayers were often based on the scripture she was reading. Her prayers reflected how God's word was teaching her, rebuking her, but also correcting her. I was encouraged to know I was not alone in my struggles to be the person God was calling me to be.

One of the difficulties Ma Belle prayed about was that she was going blind and losing her memory. She had always been a highly intelligent, independent women. In the middle of her prayer book is a prayer of surrender, "Lord, if you can use my weakness in the lives of those I love, I am willing to be weak!" This was her prayer response to Philippians' admonition to count others more significant than yourself. How I marveled as I read this and recognized that God had called Ma Belle to use her weakness to serve me, using the same verses He had used to call me to serve her!

Lord Jesus, thank You for Your example of humility. Thank You for the encouragement that both Ma Belle and I found in You. Thank You for giving me examples, like Ma Belle, of those who shine like lights in a dark world. Help me to continue to obey You and work out my own salvation with fear and trembling, always remembering that it is You who works in me, both to will and work for Your good pleasure.

The One Who Wants To Be Healed

I opened my eyes and looked at their faces. It was obvious that they were stunned at the words that had just come out of my mouth. But then so was I. I had been in the middle of a prayer when my heart was exposed. The prayer had gone something like this, "Lord help me with my sin, but I thank You that at least my sin isn't____."

Even if I'd never said it out loud, the fact that I thought my sin was less offensive to God than someone else' sin put me in good standing with the Pharisees of Jesus' time. The Pharisees saw themselves as being righteous before God because they kept the law. They missed the point. The law wasn't given to expose their holiness but the holiness of God. It wasn't given to show them how well they were doing, but instead to show them their need for a physician so that when the physician came they could be healed.

Jesus said, "Those who are well have no need of a physician, but those who are sick. Go and learn what this means, 'I desire mercy, and not sacrifice.' For I came not to call the righteous, but sinners" (Matt. 9:12-13 ESV). The problem with not fully recognizing my lack of righteousness, and how sick my sin really is, is that I also miss how great the love of God is. Creating my own righteousness is like using artificial lights so that I can't see the true light of the stars.

Here is another odd thing about my sin comparison. The thing I found most irritating about "them" was that "they" didn't see that what "they" did was a sin. When God graciously shed a light on my sinful attitude I began to daily ask God for the gift of humility. I also began to ask that He would show me how offensive my sin was. What I found was that by humbly acknowledging my sin before a holy God, I also encountered both the grace and the lavish love of God that I neither earned nor deserved.

Lord Jesus, I get so confused sometimes, tangled up in my sin and pride. Please help me today to come into Your holy presence aware that my only access is because of Your love and sacrifice for my sin. Help me to humbly extend my hand to other sinners who are in need of You, the Great Physician.

"If"

The words just seem to be highlighted on the page when I read them this morning. "If my people, who are called by my name, will humble themselves and pray and seek my face and turn from their wicked ways, then will I hear from heaven and will forgive their sins and will heal their land" (2 Chron. 7:14 NIV). When I got up to go about the my day the words seemed to follow me, asking me the question, "Have you humble yourself? Are you bringing you concerns to God in prayer or trying to work things out on your own? Are you turning your face to God seeking Him, or have you turned your face toward other things, seeking comfort, approval, control and power elsewhere?"

The idea of humility is one I have been thinking of for some time. I have seen in the Scriptures where, "God opposes the proud but gives grace to the humble" (James 4:6 NIV). I don't want to be someone who God is in opposition with. I see humility coupled with prayer: "Humble yourselves, therefore, under the mighty hand of God that at the proper time he may exalt you, casting all your anxieties on him, because he cares for you" (1 Pet. 5:6-7 ESV). So when I am humble, I don't try to work out everything on my own. I really believe that God cares about me, so I come to Him with all the cares that weigh down my spirit.

The next thing I see is God inviting me to seek His face. What does it mean to seek God's face? The illustration that comes to my mind is that of my nephew when he was nine months old. He was sitting across the room from his father. When his father smiled, he smiled; if his father frowned, he cried. He was so bonded to his father, and so intent on studying his father's face, that what he read there was the main influence on this young life. I want to know my Heavenly Father's face with that same passion.

The last directive I see in the "If my people" passage is that they are to turn from their wicked ways. My friend and I were having a very honest discussion about this the other day. We were talking about the things in our life that we turn to, other than God. Sometimes it's something that we turn to that brings us comfort; and although we are willing to say it's a sin and we are wrong to do it, we really don't want to give it up. Sometimes it's power or control we seek; and even though we've made a public confession that it is wrong, we still go back to it in a habitual way. In other words, I find it very hard to give up the thought that I have the power to do whatever I want, when I want, and how I want. This is why I so desperately need to humble myself and pray and seek God's face.

Lord Jesus, I want to turn my face to You and not away from You. I cannot live the life I see You calling me to live in Your word without Your help. I see the statement "if my people" and my heart responses with, "Please grant me the grace to humble myself and pray; help me seek Your face and turn from my wicked ways." Oh yes, and thank You, because I've also read in Your word that "if" I ask anything according to Your word, I would be given the thing I asked for.

A Wedding Gift

They gave me the gift so quietly that it took me years before I realized I'd been given a gift at all. In fact, I didn't understand what they had done for me until it was my turn to do it for someone else.

"Love is not jealous" (1 Cor. 13:4 NLT). This was one of the wedding gifts my parents gave me. My parents encouraged me to become part of my husband's family. They taught me to call my husband's parents the same names that had uniquely applied to them—Mom and Dad. They gave me permission to love and be loved by another family.

If my parents had shown jealousy, I would have been torn; but they didn't. Instead they took a step back and allowed me to bond to my husband and his family. This was done so quietly and without any fanfare that it was only when it was my turn to love someone so much that I was willing to step back that I began to understand this sacrificial gift of love.

When love is not jealous it shows that the focus is more on the one being loved than the one loving. True love seeks what it best for the recipient. When it was my turn to love someone enough to step back so that someone else could step forward, I discovered that it wasn't easy. When I was confronted by my selfish jealous heart I suddenly remembered my parents. They never spoke about their gift, they simply gave it.

Lord Jesus, thank You for giving me parents who have taught me so much by example! Please let me live my life in a way that shows sacrificial love.

In Spirit and in Truth

"But the hour is coming, and is now here, when true worshipers will worship the Father in spirit and truth, for the Father is seeking such people to worship him" (John 4: 23 ESV). What does that mean? What does it mean that, "the father is seeking those who will worship Him in spirit and truth?" And aren't we the one seeking God? What does it mean that the Father is seeking? Is there someone's life I can see these things in?

I have been comforted so many times when I think about Jesus' parables about the shepherd who went looking for his lost sheep, and the woman who searched until she found her lost coin, and finally the parable of the father who longed to have his relationship restored with his sons. This is a comfort to me—that it is the father who does the seeking. I know the horrible feeling of being lost and not knowing where I am, and I also know the peace of being found and finding myself safe. I think this must be what Jesus was talking about when He said "The Father is seeking."

How do we worship in spirit and in truth? I think this comes from understanding the gospel. I see the truth of the gospel is that, "God sent forth his Son, born of a woman, born under the law, to redeem those who were under the law, so that we might receive adoption as sons" (Gal. 4:4-5 ESV). According to Roman adoption, the adoptee was taken out of his previous state and placed in a new relationship to his new father. All his old debt are canceled, and the adoptee started a new life as part of his new family (Francis Lyall, "Roman Law in the Writings of Paul—Adoption." *JBL* [*Journal of Biblical Literature*] 88:466). That would be the truth of the adoption.

What part does the Spirit play? When I think about this I think about Jesus telling Mary, "Don't you know I must be about my Father's business?" "God has sent the Spirit of his Son into our hearts, crying 'Abba! Father!'" (Gal. 4:6 ESV). Because we have been adopted into God's family, we too must be about our Father's business, but not in our own strength. Because of our adoption we have the same access to the throne room Jesus has. The work of the Father is to be done with the resources that the Father provides. When I worship the Father in Spirit and in truth, I acknowledge I am His child, called to do His work with His resources.

Yesterday I was listening to the radio and I heard Chris Fabry [Moody Radio, "Chris Fabry Live!"] ask a question about what made Chuck Colson stand out. I remember meeting Chuck Colson when he came to town after writing his first book, *Born Again*. He spoke about how God had found him in his brokenness and how he had been born again into the family of God. Over the years I watched as he went about his Father's business. It was inspiring to watch as he not only received God's pardon and release from the debt of his sins, but also lived his life in the power of the Spirit. What I saw in Chuck was a man who was worshiping the Father in Spirit and in truth.

Lord Jesus, Thank You for finding me. I want to worship You in Spirit and in truth. Thank You that I can come before Your throne and call on You as "Abba," confident that you hear me because I am Your child. And Lord, when my life become a memory of those I love, please let the memory be that I worshiped You well!

Learning to Trust

I saw her tears. I sat with my friend as she wept. She was so full of love for her children. She had adopted her children and loved them from the beginning, yet the children suffered with an attachment disorder. This is not uncommon for children who have suffered early experiences of neglect and abuse. Children who suffered these things early in life have trouble learning to trust.

I saw her tears. My friend Laraine had suffered from both neglect and abuse in her childhood. She became a Christian as an adult and was adopted into the family of God. But there was a problem—she had an attachment disorder. She didn't know how to trust God because of the abuse of her childhood. She discussed this with me often with tears in her eyes.

When my friend Laraine died, I found her journal. What I found there gave me hope for others who share this difficulty in trusting. In this journal I learned how God uses us in the lives of other.

> *December 6, 1990*
>
> *I see that my fear of trusting God is rooted in my fear of trusting*

anyone because it might turn out to be a lie. I'm afraid to relax and enjoy my life, afraid to be happy, afraid to really live, because it has hurt so bad to have believed the lies of the past and find out the truth. The truth has healing, but it's so very painful, and the more I see the more there is to deal with. I'm afraid I won't make it. I feel so alone, so far from God. Who am I? Who is Laraine? Who am I? What can come of this quest for healing? Is healing really possible for someone questioning the power that heals? Oh God, I don't know what I believe and what I don't believe in my heart where it counts. I want to know how I can learn to really trust You!

June 28, 1991

Amazing things happened to me today. This afternoon Sarah and I sat in the swing talking and sharing; and I shared, risking our friendship (in my mind.) I needed to have someone else, besides my therapist, that I could say these things to and not be rejected by them. Sarah listened, comforted and shared some things of her own. I cried, and then we went on with our activity. Later she said there was something she wanted to do after everyone went to bed. After supper I asked her what it was. She said, "In response to what you told me, I'm going to wash your feet." I was flabbergasted, totally, and then so touched by her that I began to cry. It was an act of love I have never experienced before, and I was totally humbled by the experience. There, on her knees, my dear sweet friend washed my feet. It was an experience I will never forget. It reached in and crumbled a wall of distrust I never expected to end in this life. I went to bed in tears and awed by such an act. But God blessed it, because I saw a person loving me, honoring me, caring as no one ever had. It softened my resistance and broke my heart toward God. I went to bed praying, praising, and thanking God.

I read these words over ten years after Laraine had written them. I had no idea the impact washing her feet had on her. Do any of us ever know the impact we have on another person? If God used something as simple as what I did to impact my friend, just imagine what He will do with the love that parents give their adopted children!

Father, thank You for using me in the life of my friend. Thank You for those who have opened their home and hearts to children through adoption. Father, You see their tears, both the tears of the children and those who love them. Please bless the efforts of these parents as they try to bring healing to the hearts of these wounded children. Help, Father, both parent and child to trust You.

Listening to the Song

The song came out all wrong. I must have scratched the record. The more I tried to fix it the worse it sounded. I kept gently lifting the needle and repositioning it, but no matter how many times I tried, the results were always the same. This was not music, this was simply noise, irritating, teeth-gritting noise!

I lay in bed drifting off to sleep, my mind reviewing the events of the day. A record began to play in my head, "What is wrong with you? Do you always have to talk so much? How many times are you going to make the same mistakes? You are hopeless; you are never going to get this right!" I turned on my right side; I turned on my left side; the needle seemed to be stuck. The message was magnified by its repetition. Finally I gave up; I couldn't fix this song it needed to be changed.

There seem to be some sins that I struggle with, and no matter how hard I try I just can't seem to get it right. The more I focus on them the more I magnify them. Finally it dawns on me that I'm trying to be my own savior, again.

"The Lord your God is in your midst, a mighty one who will save; he will rejoice over you with gladness; he will quiet you by his love; he will exult over you with loud singing" (Zeph. 3:17 ESV). The songs of deliverance do not come from my trying harder; they come from the Lord who is in my midst. When I tune my ear in the night to hear his love songs of salvation, my heart is at last quieted by his love. He puts a new song in my heart.

Lord Jesus, help me to stop trying to fix my broken record. Help me to stop focusing on myself and listen to the song You are singing over me. Let my life's song be the one You sing to me—unbroken filled with love and gladness.

Comfort Beneath a Terebinth Tree

It's funny how things will sometimes catch my attention. The terebinth tree is one of those things. I kept seeing it referred to in Scripture and wondered what it was. To my knowledge it doesn't grow in North Georgia. One of the places I found it in Scripture was when Abraham showed hospitality to the angel of the Lord. Yesterday when we were at the Elah Valley, our guide pointed one out and told us about it.

She told us about the extensive root system and that it could grow quite large. It was a very hot day and the sun was beating down. I was amazed at the comfort I found in the shade of that tree. As I stood there, cooled by the shade of its branches, I understood why the terebinth tree would be known as a hospitality tree.

"Reach out and touch the branches and then touch it to your tongue." I did as she suggested, and was surprised by the taste of salt. That taste of salt on my tongue reminded me of the taste of tears. I stood there sheltered from the scorching heat, enjoying the hospitality of this ancient tree, and remembering other times I have found comfort while also experiencing a taste of tears.

I have often found that those who have endured many hardships have also developed an extensive root system. The hardships of life have caused them to go deep into the word of God to find comfort and strength. When they share the comfort they have found, it is an oasis for my soul.

Lord Jesus, may life's difficulties cause me also to sink my roots deep into Your promises. When I have a taste of tears on my tongue, remind me of the terebinth tree and change my sorrows into a place of welcome and comfort for my fellow pilgrims.

Beneath the Protective Wing

A cacophony of sights and sounds, places and people flood my mind. "Tell us about Israel!" I try to speak, but find myself unable to sort out all the images that rush to present themselves. My family waits for me to speak. The stories I tell are about the people I have met; about my friend who gave me this amazing gift, a trip to Israel. "She's gone all the way to Israel and all she can tell us is about the people she's encountered!" My family smiles and shakes their head. Oh, but I have so much more I want to say, I just don't know how to sort it all out.

I awake. Is it 2 A.M. or 9 A.M.? It's jet lag, a confusion of time and place. I become fully awake and recognize my surroundings, I am back home on our farm in Georgia. It's 2 A.M. In a sleepy fog, my mind is travelling back to Jerusalem. I am standing again on the temple mount. I hear the guide saying, "This is where Jesus said, 'Jerusalem, Jerusalem, who kills the prophets and stones those who are sent to her! How often I wanted to gather your children together, the way a hen gathers her chicks under her wings, and you were unwilling'" (Matt. 23:37 NASB).

Now mixed with the images of Jerusalem I see in my mind my grandson Jack standing before me, wanting to share his sense of wonder. He gently spreads the wing of the hen and says with an awed filled voice, "Mimi, isn't this beautiful!" He loving holds the bird, wanting to share with me the beauty he has found.

As I drift off once more to sleep, I find the softness of my pillow resembles the downy feathers of a mother hen; my comforter is it's protective wing. I hear an invitation in this early morning waking to rest, to sleep, to know a deep comfort of a loving God.

Oh Lord Jesus, just as Jack longed to share the wonder and beauty he has found in Your creation, so I long to share the wonders that I found in Israel. Help me unwind the stories in my mind. And may I also share with others the peace I find beneath Your protective wing.

Chosen

I stood in Israel listening to the guide, feeling the hot sun. I was physically there, and while I listened, I saw with the inner eye of my spirit two stories playing themselves out on the geography of the land. It reminded me somewhat of watching television. When my father has the remote, you never end up watching just one program. The story I saw on the screen of my soul was of two men, two kings chosen by God.

First, I saw Saul hiding himself among the baggage when he was proclaimed king. When I first heard that story of Saul, I thought to myself, "Now, that is a picture of humility!" But was it? Was it really humility that made Saul hide, or was it pride at the core of his being? The scene in my mind changes to a youth who has also been anointed to be king. I see him in the Elah Valley facing Goliath. He does not hide from the challenge but instead rushes to do battle with the champion of the Philistines. Is this pride or humility? As I stand on the ground that they once stood on, I ask myself, how does humility play itself out in my life—with boldness or timidity?

Both Saul and David were anointed to be king. Each were chosen by God. They had their victories, but they also had their time of failure. I am reminded of the Scripture, "All have sinned and fall short of the glory of God" (Rom. 3:23 NASB). When confronted with the failure, how did they each respond? Saul responded to Samuel by denying he had done anything wrong. When Nathan the prophet confronts David with his sin, David responded with, "I have sinned against the Lord" (2 Sam. 12:13 NASB). I have heard that true confession is to agree with God. I think perhaps this is also a picture of true humility.

Standing on the real land where these real people lived out their lives, I asked myself the question, "What am I to do with the Scripture that says I too have been chosen, chosen before the foundation of the world?" Like Saul and David, I have been chosen to be holy and blameless before Him. Like them I face situations that make me want to run and hide. How shall I face the challenges of my life, with timidity or humble boldness? I too have failed—often.
When confronted with my sin do I defend myself, or like David simply say, "I have sinned against God"?

Lord Jesus, I am quick to stand in judgment of Saul and to see my life reflected in David's choices. And yet the truth is I am often afraid and hide from the challenges You place before me. When I am confronted with my sin I am quick to explain that it is not really my fault and seek to place the guilt with someone else. As my mind travels back from where I have been and what I have seen in Israel, let me live my today as one who has been chosen. Help me to be humble and bold and quick to repent. Show me how to sink my roots deep into Your promises as one who has been chosen to bring You glory. May both my identity and strength come from You.

A Spiritual Geography Lesson

I was in the fourth grade when I was introduced to geography. I hated it. Because of my learning disabilities, the maps looked like someone spilled colored spaghetti on them. I had trouble visualizing or imaging the places I was told about. I am amazed at how things have changed. Now I am fascinated by maps and find that I can learn spiritual truths from geography.

It's in Deuteronomy 11 that God teaches His people a spiritual geography lesson. He does it by comparing Egypt to Israel. In Egypt the people sowed their seeds and irrigated it. The land was dependent on the Nile for water. When God lead His people into the Promise Land, the geography was different. Now the land was a land of hills and valleys. This land would not receive its water from irrigation, but instead, "drink water by the rain from heaven."

This is where I find the spiritual lesson in what God had to say about the land. "The eyes of the Lord your God are always upon it, from the beginning of the year to the end of the year. And if you will indeed obey my commandments that I command you today, to love the Lord your God, and to serve him with all your heart and with all your soul, he will give the rain for your land in its season, the early rain and the later rain, that you may gather in your grain and your wine and your oil" (Deut. 11:12-14 ESV).

Sometimes in life I experience spiritual drought. When this happens, and life seems dry and unpleasant, I am faced with the choice of what to do about it. Do I go back to "Egypt" where, although I experienced slavery, I had some control over getting what I wanted by my own efforts? Or do I lift my face to the heavens and call out for mercy?

Lord Jesus, I am dependent on You. When times of spiritual drought come, let my prayer be, "Search me, O God, and know my heart! Try me and know my thoughts! And see if there be any grievous way in me, and lead me in the way everlasting!" (Psa. 139:23-24).

In the Valley of Elah

I was standing there with the rest of the group that had come on the tour to the Valley of Elah. Together we had listened to the story of David and Goliath. Our guide pointed out the place where David had picked up the five smooth stones for his slingshot. I too bent down and selected five smooth stones. That is when it happened.

I stood up, and I no longer saw an empty field. I was no long surrounded by silence, but instead by an enemy that was taunting me and mocking the power of the God I had professed to trust in. The enemy stood before me mocking. Behind me were my kin, paralyzed by the taunts of the enemy.

In this Valley of Elah, only one champion had been chosen to battle a giant; defeat him and the victory was yours. Before him was a large shield that covered his whole body. He wore a coat of mail, and in his hand he held a huge bronze spear. I had seen him before with the eyes of my imagination when I was a child. Then, like David, I imaged myself running to the battle. slaying him. and leading those behind me into a great victory. Today I held my five smooth stones and wept.

Suddenly I was back in the present and saw the sympathetic gaze of one of my fellow sojourners. "Sarah, why are you crying?" I humbly told him that, though I wanted to be brave like David, I realized I had allowed the enemy's "champions" to mock God's power in my life. There were areas where I stood immobilized because, though I wanted to believe, I saw failure far more clearly than I saw victory. If that were not enough, I also realized that I had passed my doubts and fears on to those I love. I had taught them by my example that there were giants of the enemy that must be respected.

Lord, You are the same yesterday, today and forever. You gave David victory over the giant who mocked Your power, and I believe that that same power is available for me today. Please help me fill my mind with who You are so much that when the enemy sends the champion of fear to paralyze me, I will be able to conquer him by faith. Oh yes, and let my victory be multiplied in the lives of those I love.

Finding Balance in an Unbalanced World

Maybe I should have disqualified myself as soon as I heard the title. I was asked to speak at a church, and when I asked what they wanted me to speak about, they told me, "Finding Your Balance in an Unbalanced World." I accepted the challenge.

Where should I begin? The pressures of my own life made me feel like an animal of prey surrounded by predators. So I began by looking at my own unbalanced self, and tried to find someone in the Bible who matched how I felt. I found her; her name was Martha. I could see her coming into focus. Her house was filled with people, and she was filled with frustration. So what did she do? She went and complained to Jesus.

Now, that doesn't really sound very spiritual, and yet I think perhaps it is a starting place. Sometimes that's what my prayers look like. I go to God and pour out my confusion, my frustration, my complaint. I bring to Him the things I can't fix. Jesus was Martha's friend, and because of that she felt safe to be real. It's the same with me; because I believe I am loved and accepted, I can let down my guard and expose my heart to the only one who can help.

Jesus meets me where I am. I don't learn balance in spite of my unbalanced world but in the midst of it. Jesus meets me where I am and invites me to come to Him, seek Him and open up to Him. It's in times of intense stress I recognize my intense need for a Savior.

Lord Jesus, thank You for Your invitation to come to You when I am weary and heavy laden with the stress of this world. You are the Prince of Peace and in You I find balance in an unbalanced world.

A Song of Ascent

I don't know why it always takes me by surprise when difficult things happen. It shouldn't, but it does. I was thinking about that when I was on the tour bus in Israel going through the Judean Wilderness. I looked out the window, and all I could see for miles and miles were barren hills. Three times a year the people of God were required to go on a pilgrimage to Jerusalem that would take them through this wilderness.

What happens in a wilderness when there is no food or water except what you bring yourself? What would it be like in the summer time when the heat could reach up to 120F or in the winter when there might be snow along the route? If that wasn't enough, there were bandits and killers hiding along the wayside to take advantage of the pilgrim. Was God aware of this when He set up these times for His people to come to Jerusalem to worship?

I am often surprised by the wilderness experiences in my life, but I shouldn't be because I think they are preludes to worship. The psalmist said, "I lift up my eyes to the hills" (Psalm 121:1 NIV). It was very possible that the hills were in this Judean wilderness. The hills could be harboring bandits and murderers or wild beasts so he asks, "Where does my help come from?" There is nothing like going through a wilderness experience to expose your vulnerability; it also exposes what you believe or don't believe. It was in the midst of this uncomfortable journey that the psalmist declares, "My help comes from the Lord, who made heaven and earth."

The other day I was going through an emotional wilderness. It was both uncomfortable and unpleasant, but I found comfort in meditating on Psalm 121 because I knew it was a Song of Ascent, a song the pilgrims would have sung on their way up to Jerusalem. Wilderness experiences are part of the journey to worship. Every time I'm in the wilderness I see again my need for God. The pressures of the wilderness and the discomfort cause me to call out to God for help. When I cry out to God I find again that it is the Lord who is my keeper, and that He is worthy of my trust.

Lord, You know that if life was always easy I would be very independent, trusting my own ability. Thank You for the prelude to worship which includes wilderness experiences because when I am put in situations that expose my vulnerability I am at the same time given an opportunity to see Your strength.

Paying the Debt You Do Not Owe

Why is this so hard? Sometimes I just gloss over it and say, "Never mind, it's okay," because I don't want to take the emotion energy to deal with it. It never seems to come at a convenient time, and sometimes I have been held hostage for days by it, unable to escape. And why was it the only conditional part of the prayer that Jesus taught His disciples, "Forgive us our debts *as* we forgive our debtors"?

I had a group of friends over at my house yesterday, and as we were talking about this several things came up. First, we looked at humility when there is the need to forgive someone. This really comes out in the story Jesus used to illustrate forgiveness. He told how a servant was forgiven a debt of 10,000 talents—that would translate to the equivalent of about $300,000,000—who then refuses to forgive the debt of a few dollars. My friend pointed out that the man who had been forgiven the large sum had initially said, "Be patient with me, I'm planning to pay you back."

To be able to truly forgive someone I need to understand how much I have been forgiven. When the wicked servant said, "I'll pay you back," it showed he really didn't understand how much he owed and there was no way he could pay it back. When I have been filled with angry resentment towards someone, I also feel superior to them. From my position of superiority I am right in both judging and condemning them. If I don't compare my debt to God with what others owe me, then my pride doesn't allow me to forgive.

In the Lord's Prayer we have a definition of forgiveness. If someone has wronged me, they owe me a debt; something has been taken away from me. It could be tangible or emotional. Either way it is a debt that must be paid. So in forgiveness, who pays this debt? The person who forgives absorbs the debt! That's not all! Sometimes the thing I have forgiven has many ramifications and it's not a one-time payment. And what if I pay this debt from my own resources and the person who wronged me doesn't appreciate the sacrifice I've made? It's no wonder forgiveness is so hard!

Lord Jesus, please help me to humble my heart and recognize the gift of grace You gave me when You paid the debt I could not pay. Lord, thank You for giving me the grace to forgive those who are in my debt. Help me make payment on their debt to me by not punishing them, avoiding them, or trying to make them seem small in the eyes of others. Lord, You said, "Be kind and compassionate to one another, forgiving each other, just as in Christ God forgave you" (Eph. 4:32 NIV). Please help me remember the grace You extended to me when You paid the debt You did not owe so that I can follow Your example.

"Remember and Do Not Forget"

The children must have found it when they were playing "library" upstairs with my book shelves. I found the two-year-old journal waiting for me this morning. I picked it up and began reading. I was amazed at how the memories I had written about came to life.

I began the habit of keeping a journal when I was nine years old. I would begin my day by taking the essence of the day before and writing it down. I have heard that what you remember isn't as important as how you remember it. I think that how I choose to remember my days has been influenced by the fact that this practice of capturing the day that has just past is part of my quiet time with God. Sometimes I wake feeling like I've heard my name being called. I sit in silence enjoying the presence of God. Then I reflect on what happened the day before.

The Bible is full of Scriptures that tell us to remember what God has done. "Remember and do not forget," this is an admonition given several times in the book of Deuteronomy. "Praise the Lord, O my soul, and forget not all his benefits—" (Psa. 103:2 NIV). "I will remember the deeds of the Lord; yes, I will remember your miracles of long ago" (Psa. 77:11 NIV). "Remember His wonders which He has done, His marvels and the judgments uttered by His mouth" (Psa. 105:5 NASB).

This past week a friend who had become a widow when her children were still very young came by. When her husband died she also lost her home and her income. It was a very frightful time in her life. She smiled, however, as she remembered how God had taken care of her. "I always get goose bumps when I remember how fully God has met my needs." Her memories were not dominated by the difficulties she had encountered, but by how she had encountered God in the midst of her difficulties.

Lord Jesus, the truth is, sometimes my memories can be very dark. But if

I look for You, even in the darkest times I can find You. Help me as I reflect on my yesterdays to see Your hand of protection. Let the memories of Your faithfulness to me in the past become the courage I need to face the future.

A Risky Prayer?

I thought I had found the perfect prayer for me to pray. I had studied the book of Ezekiel earlier this year, and I had read where God caused Ezekiel's tongue to cleave to the roof of his mouth unless he was speaking for God. When I was asked by my prayer group what they could pray for me, I shared this idea with them. One of the women in the group cocked her head and said, "That's a pretty risky prayer for a speaker to pray, isn't it?"

I was a keynote speaker at a family camp when I made this prayer request. I didn't think it was risky at the time, because I had prayed over all the talks I was going to give. I felt fairly secure. That is when it happened. God answered my prayer.

I was speaking that night about how to find your balance in a unbalanced world. I talked about facing your fears and letting the love of God bring you to a place where you have rest for your soul. Every time I went over my notes I kept hearing the Lord ask, "Sarah, do you believe what you are saying?"

The time came for me to speak. I stood before the crowd, and all I was able to do was give them the outline of what I had planned to say. Then I found I could say nothing else. I told everyone to go to the place they feared the most and ask God to meet them there. I don't know how long I stood there, unable to say anything but "For the eyes of the Lord move to and fro throughout the earth that He may strongly support those whose heart is completely His" (2 Chron. 16:9 NASB). So many people came to me later to tell me what they had heard. What they had heard had not come from my mouth.

Lord Jesus, thank You for showing me what I should already know: You don't need my mouth to speak Your message to Your children. Thank You for meeting me in my own fearful place as I stood before a room full of people, unable to speak.

I Don't Have To Keep That Record

I begin my day by choosing what to remember about the day that has just past. I make a conscious choice not to record the hurtful or offensive things that happen. Twenty four hours in a day can hold a variety of experiences, and I don't want to keep a record of everything. My memories will be shaped by the records I keep, so I choose to discard the hurtful ones. "Love keeps no record of wrongs" (1 Cor. 13:5 NIV).

I've been uncluttering my house getting ready for my daughter's wedding. She wanted to have the reception at home. The first thing I had to do before I could even start cleaning was to get rid of things that were just taking up space. My friend told me that if it didn't have beauty, if it wasn't valuable or useful, if it didn't have sentimental value, to get rid of it. I used this guideline, and when I finished a room I felt like prisoner that had been released. "Love isn't irritable and it keeps no record of being wronged" (1 Cor. 13:5 NLT).

One of the byproducts of getting rid of the clutter in my home was that I was able to see the things I have that are beautiful, valuable, useful and have deep sentimental value. They had gotten lost under the pile of clutter. My memories are like that too. "Love does not take into an account a wrong suffered" (1 Cor. 13:5 NASB).

I saved a lot of time when I got rid of the things I'd been holding onto that weren't beautiful, valuable useful. I hadn't realized how much time it took to maintain all those things, cleaning them, moving them around, tripping over them. I know this same freedom in my spirit when I choose to not hold on to things that cripple me emotionally. "Love does not insist on its own way; it is not irritable or resentful" (1 Cor. 1:5 ESV).

Father, thank You for freeing me from the burden of keeping a record of the hurtful things that happen in life. Thank You for providing me the grace that is necessary to be set free from the web of offensive memories that would entangle me. And, Father, let this freedom from holding on to wrongs that are suffered be a blessing my daughter and her new husband take with them into their married life.

"Who are YOU?"

"Who are YOU?" said the Caterpillar.

This was not an encouraging opening for a conversation. Alice replied, rather shyly, "I—I hardly know, sir, just at present—at least I know who I WAS when I got up this morning, but I think I must have been changed several times since then" (Lewis Carroll, *Alice's Adventures in Wonderland,* 1865).

I realize that often I have attempted to understand who I am in relationship with others: "I am the third of nine children, and the oldest girl in my family." That was who I saw myself as as a little girl. But I have changed several times since then.

Sometimes I introduce myself by the difficulties I have known. Everyone has difficulties of some kind, but if I only let people see me through that lens, it is far too limiting. The hard things I have encountered in life are not who I am, they are simply tools that have been used to shape who I am.

I remember the day my son brought the girl who was to become his wife home to introduce her to the family. I was intensely interested in knowing who she was. I spent the whole morning finding work I could do in the front yard so I would be there when they drove up. My understanding of who she was began with the understanding that this was someone whom my son had come to love.

"Who are YOU?" I understand how Alice in Wonderland would have a hard time with this question. I have found that the only way I can truly understand who I am is to see my reflection in my Heavenly Father's eyes. Every morning when I look into His word I see my relationship to Him. I find healing for my soul. But most of all, I realize that my identity is that I am loved.

Lord Jesus, thank You that I can find my identity in You. Thank You for Your redeeming love and that I am not who I was. Morning after morning as I with an unveiled face behold Your glory, I am being transformed into Your image by the power of Your Spirit.

Untethered

All they knew was that they were to protect the tree they were tethered to. I listened as the group of young people described what they had learned from the game they had played the night before. One girl spoke and said that she finally realized that she wasn't really protecting the tree, she was protecting the rope that bound her. Once she realized she was being held captive, she was able to be set free.

I've been thinking about that picture of protecting the thing that binds you. I realize that I do that too. There are some sins that are pet sins. The Scripture says that there can be pleasure in sin for a short time; just enough time for the enemy of my soul to bind me. Often I don't even recognize that I have lost my freedom, and I will fight for the right to be a slave.

Unforgiveness can keep me captive as well. I find when I choose to not forgive someone that I become bound to the offense. I have a hard time not thinking about the wrong that has been done to me. I become a prisoner in my thoughts and my mind goes involuntarily back to the person who wronged me.

Then there is also the binding power of anxiety. How can I know what freedom feels like if I am tied to the things over which I have no control? I've heard people say that they felt that if they worried about something then it wouldn't happen. I think if I did that I would forever be held captive to negative thinking.

Lord, I want to be free! I don't want to be bound by my sins, my forgiving heart, or by fear. Your word says, "So if the Son sets you free, you are free indeed" (John 8:36). Thank You for doing for me what I could not do for myself. Help me to walk in the freedom You have given me.

Perspective, Perspective, Perspective

"I'm just not feeling it." I have heard this expression used when talking about someone's spiritual walk, and I can identify with them. There have been times when I have been emotionally bankrupt; and yet, because of what I've learned from studying the Scripture, I keep going.

Having the eternal perspective that I gain through reading the Bible makes all the difference when I encounter spiritual dry times in my life. For instance, I read that in the life of Hezekiah, "God left him to test him and to know everything that was in his heart" (2 Chron. 32:31 NIV). I confess that during difficult times I have been appalled at what has been revealed. I see that God uses these times as part of His work in transforming my heart.

When John the Baptist was locked up in prison he sent word to Jesus and asked, "Are you the One we've been expecting, or are we still waiting?" Jesus responded by pointing John to the prophecies of Isaiah that He was fulfilling. The prophecies pointed to the fact that the wretched of the earth had been given a Savior. John remained in prison and was beheaded. The truth of the gospel was not diminished by the things John suffered.

The disciples were on the Sea of Galilee in a storm. The little boat they were in was being tossed back and forth by the waves. They were fighting for their lives and Jesus was asleep in the boat. When they woke Him with their cry, "Don't you care that we are about to perish!" they discovered His power over the storm. They had to recognize their weakness before they could recognize His strength. Their panic became an opportunity to know peace.

Lord Jesus, help me see my life through the lens of faith. When "I'm just not feeling it," help me remember You're still at work. When my heart is tested and sin is exposed, help me to humble myself. Lord, help me to live my life based on Your promises and not according to my circumstances. Please let the storms of life, while exposing my weakness, reveal Your strength.

Like the Rocks in My Garden

My garden had become overgrown with weeds, and I decided to clean it up. I got the hoe and started to work. There were lots of hidden rocks in my garden, but one in particular was buried deep and hidden not only by the weeds but by the dirt. When the metal of my hoe hit the stone,

sparks flew. When at last I was able to pry up the stone I
was attacked by fire ants that were living beneath it. The fire ants
furiously swarmed my legs, curling their bodies into a C-shape as they
bit with their mandibles and stung with their stingers. I had to stop and
ask myself, "How badly do I want flowers instead of rocks and weeds? Is
this worth it?"

In my life pride is buried deep like the rocks in my garden; so deep I
don't even realize it's there. Sometimes this hidden rock is exposed by
confrontation. When that happens, the sparks fly. The rock or pride is so
much a part of the landscape of my life it's hard to get rid of it even
when it's been exposed. My anger is often like a fire ant attack. This
process can be so unpleasant that sometimes, I confess, I just walk away
and leave the stone in place.

I have been reading through the book of Isaiah, and I see Isaiah's word
causing sparks to fly as God used him to confront
the Israelites about their sin. As long as their pride was intact,
the response to Isaiah's word would be bitter anger. The antidote to
both the pride and the anger was humility. "For thus says the One who
is high and lifted up, who inhabits eternity, whose name is Holy: 'I dwell
in the high and holy place, and also with him who is of a contrite and
lowly spirit, to revive the spirit of the lowly, and to revive the heart of
the contrite'" (Isa. 57:15).

The only cure for pride is humility; the only hope when the fire ants of
anger attack is to call on the one God sent to deliver me. "Do you not
know? Have you not heard? The Lord is the everlasting God, the Creator
of the ends of the earth. He will not grow tired or weary, and his
understanding no one can fathom. He gives strength to the weary
and increases the power of the weak" (Isa. 40:28-29 NIV). When I have
humbled myself before Him and the painful work of removing my pride
has been accomplished, only then am I ready for the flowers to be
planted in my garden.

Lord Jesus, I can only know where these hidden places of pride are in
my heart when You expose them. This process is not pleasant, but I
would rather have the flower of grace than the stone of pride in my
heart. Please do for me what I cannot do for myself as I humble myself
before You. Thank You for being my Redeemer and the gardener of my
soul.

The Voices I Hear In the Wilderness

When all the world is right and filled with light, life swirls round and round about me. There is no time to stop and take note of all that is going on. I am caught up and filled with the music of the dance of life. But then, suddenly, the music stops; the light turns to darkness; and I am led into the wilderness.

In the wilderness there is a deep silence. In the silence there is time to think, there is time to reflect. My enemy comes into this barren wasteland to fill it with accusations: "Do you see your failure? Do you see how you have hurt the ones you love? You are inadequate, you have no hope!" In this desolate place I can see what I am shown. I see the truth that I have failed, I have missed to mark. What I thought was a masterpiece I now see for what it really is, just scribbles on a page. In my attempt to escape the grasp of my enemy who tells me I have no hope, I cry out, "Where does my hope come from?"

At first I only hear a whisper, but it is enough to break the hold my enemy has on my heart. "I am your hope, I am 'your Redeemer, who formed you in the womb: I am the Lord, who made all things, who alone stretched out the heavens, who spread out the earth by myself' (Isa. 44:24 NIV). Though you have failed I have not." These words are whispered to me in the night, but they are enough to silence my enemy.

Again I hear the words of my Redeemer, but this time it is no longer in a whisper. This time the words are given in command and in a promise. "Forget the former things; do not dwell on the past. See, I am doing a new thing! Now it springs up; do you not perceive it? I am making a way in the desert and streams in the wasteland" (Isa. 43:18-19 NIV).

Lord, You form the light and create the darkness. You are Lord when all the world seems right and filled with light and laughter, but You are also Lord when darkness comes and I am led into the wilderness. When my heart feels crushed within me, and I am made aware of all my faults and failures, by Your mercy let me put my hand into the hand of my Redeemer and turn a deaf ear to the one who says I have no hope.

Thistles and Angels

It's such a royal looking plant growing out in the field, its purple head raised high. But to my husband, the farmer, it is the enemy. This spring my husband became the "Thistle Hunter." Why is this beautiful, regal plant considered an enemy? To understand the problem, I had understand the root system and how the thistle multiplies. When the thistle invades the land above, it also invades the earth beneath and blankets it with a root system that expands and resembles concrete. Woe unto the farmer who lets the thistle flower, because now not only will you be at war with the roots, but with the seeds.

For a while I was just an observer, watching my husband fight for dominion over the thistle. But it got personal when I found one trying to invade my flower bed. "Oh, no you don't," I said, as I reached out and grabbed it by the stem. That was the day I gained a new respect for this weed. Not only is it beautiful with its purple flower, well-rooted and prolific, it also it covered with thorns. My hand still remembers its first encounter with the thistle's poisoned thorns.

While reading *The Message* by Eugene Peterson, I gained a new appreciation for the parable Jesus told about God's Kingdom. This is what I read, "God's kingdom is like a farmer who planted good seed in his field. That night, while his hired men were asleep, his enemy sowed thistle all through the wheat and slipped away before dawn. When the first green shoots appeared and the grain began to form, the thistle showed up too" (Matt. 13:23). Since Jesus was telling this parable to farmers, they would understand how this act could sabotage the whole field!

The farmhands wanted to know if they should try to weed the field, but the farmer told them to wait till harvest and let the harvesters separate the wheat from the grain. When Jesus explained the parable to His disciples, He told them that the harvest hands were the angels who were assigned to do this job at the end of the age.

Lord, thank You for this parable that helps me understand
spiritual struggle by comparing it to the physical world I live in. Lord,
You know how frustrated and panicked I get when I see "spiritual
thistles." I want to to get rid of them, now. Thank You for showing me
Your plan so that I don't spend my life doing what You
have assigned angels to do at the end of the age.

Unaware

He was physically alive but spiritually dead; however, he was unaware
of his condition. That could be the only explanation for his actions.
Because of his spiritual condition he was unable to see the Ancient of
Days whose clothing was as white as snow and hair like pure wool. He
couldn't see the throne with its fiery flames, nor did he see the stream
of fire issued that came out before that throne. Unaware of the ten
thousands time ten thousands that stood ready to serve the Most High
God, this man mocked the one who had everlasting dominion.

Like a physical corpse that cannot hear physical sound, so it was with
this man who stood before the High and Holy One unable to hear with
spiritual ears. If only he had heard the thundering sound of the mighty
rushing waters he would not have made such a fool of himself in the
courts of Heaven. All he could hear was the sound of his own voice
mocking the glory; because, since he was blind and deaf to the reality of
the Eternal One, of course that meant that the God of Glory did not
exist.

"The fool says in his heart, 'There is no God.' They are corrupt, they do
abominable deeds, there is none who does good. The Lord looks down
from heaven on the children of man, to see if there are any who
understand, who seek after God" (Psa. 14:1-2 ESV). I would imagine at
this time that the Cherubim, whose bodies sparkle like the color of
bronze and whose appearance is like coals of fire, would be standing
ready to annihilate this fool who says there is no God. But God had
another plan. Because He is not only the God of glory but also the God
of love, He sent His Son to bring sight to the blind, open the ears of the
deaf and bring the dead to life. He sent His Son so that the wretched of
the earth would learn that they were no longer alone but that God was

on their side.

Here I see another mystery, when God's son came to earth He was not cloaked in His glory. Instead, "He had no beauty or majesty to attract us to him, nothing in his appearance that we should desire him. He was despised and rejected by men, a man of sorrows, and familiar with suffering. Surely he took up our infirmaries and carried our sorrows,... He was pierced for our transgressions, he was crushed for our iniquities; the punishment that brought us peace was upon him, and by his wounds we are healed. We all, like sheep, have gone astray, each of us has turned to his own way; and the Lord has laid on him the iniquity of us all" (Isa. 53:2-6 NIV).

The only explanation for their behavior could be that they were spiritually dead. That is why they didn't see the one who hung before them dying was the Son of God. All of His suffering took place as it had been prophesied, yet those who considered themselves wise were really fools. They stood mocking Him as He died just as other fools had mocked God as He sat on His throne. How did He respond? He said, "Father, forgive them, for they know not what they do." God had not sent His son to condemn the world but that the world through him might be saved.

Shaking Off the Shadows

Sometimes in the morning I have trouble shaking off the shadows and I wake up with gloomy thoughts. When this happens I have to take some time to tell myself the truth and turn my face to the light.

Regrets can often take sleep awake. When this happens I open my eyes in the light but only see darkness. It's time to tell myself the truth: "The steadfast love of the Lord never ceases; his mercies never come to an end; they are new every morning; great is your faithfulness" (Lam. 3:22-23 ESV). When I think about this verse I am reminded that no matter how much I may fail, God's love doesn't fail. His love is unwavering and immovable it is a safe place for my heart to find rest.

I can never use up His compassion because it is new every morning. This is an important truth to focus on when my first thoughts upon waking are my failures. Because I want to fill my mind in the morning with light instead of darkness, I choose to receive this precious gift of mercy. I think of this as I sit on my front porch watching the sun rise and the morning-glories unfolding their petals.

This reassuring verse is found in the book of Lamentations. A lament is a cry of sorrow and grief. In the middle of this book of laments, God comforts His people with the promise that even if they are unfaithful, He will always be faithful. And so my day begins with choosing to turn my face towards the light while bathing my mind with the truth of God's unfailing love and His fresh mercy. Because of His great faithfulness, today will unfold like the petals of a flower.

Lord, today I open my eyes and find You are already there. You are the author of this day and You have filled it with unconditional love. As I begin this day I am reminded that I can never use up
Your compassion, because new mercy awaits me every morning. Your faithfulness is great. You are my portion and I will put my hope in You.

Harmony

"A man's steps are directed by the Lord. How then can anyone understand his own way," Proverbs 20:24 NIV.

"Allemande left with your left hand, here we go with a right and left grand." The square dancers are going one way when suddenly the caller tells them to change directions. A good square dancer has two characteristics: First, he learns each part of the dance; second, he learns to listen to the caller who tells him what to do next.

If a dancer doesn't learn each part, he will stand there unsure of what to do next while everyone else bumps into him. If he learns each part but doesn't learn to listen, he might do the right thing but at the wrong time. Without the two components working together, the square breaks down and the dance comes to a stop.

Sometimes I think about this when I think about the Christian life. First, I have to learn how to walk with Christ. I read and meditate on God's word and in doing so I gain understanding. Second, I must have faith. God is the one who directs my steps, and to be honest, I just don't always understand the direction He is leading me in. Faith is when I consider God worthy of my trust and therefore go when He says go— even if I don't understand.

Just like in the dance, if these two parts aren't working together there is chaos. However, when I practice both listening to the Lord and obeying Him, my life flows in harmony with His plans.

Father, give me the determination to learn Your word and the humility to listen to Your way. Please help me live my life in harmony with Your will.

Move On

Sometimes my faith grows when I am faced with an impossible situation and God comes to my rescue, doing for me what I could never do for myself. Then there are those other times when I am faced with a hopeless situation and, while I'm waiting for God to come to my aid, He tells me to move on.

This is how I imagine it happening with the Children of Israel: There they were, boldly walking out of Egypt. Fresh on their mind was the power they had seen displayed by their God. All was right with the world— until they turned around and saw that they were being pursued by Pharaoh's chariots and horsemen. Pharaoh was behind them, and the Red Sea was in front of them. They were trapped.

Moses responded to their cry by telling them to "Be still." God responded to Moses' cry by saying, "Why are you crying out to me? Tell the Israelites to move on" (Ex. 14:15 NIV). Moses assumed God would work now as He had before with the Israelites. He expected to watch as God sent one more plague on Egypt. This time, however, God required that they trust Him and that they take a step of faith onto the dry path across the Red Sea.

Sometimes God asks this of me as well. Sometimes He calls me to walk by faith on an impossible pathway that He has made possible.

Father, as You open up the path You have chosen for me, enable me to follow You one step at a time.

The Stone of Remembrance

Diane was discouraged when she got to our house. Her present and her future seemed dismal. During the two weeks she stayed with us, I gently questioned her about how God had directed her in the past. She and I were both blessed as she recounted God's faithfulness time and time again in her life. Remembering God's past blessing, she was encouraged for the future.

Samuel took a stone and set it up between Mizpah, which in Hebrew means "a military observation point," and Shem, which means "to teach diligently." The name of the stone was Ebenezer, meaning, "thus far has the Lord helped us."

God had won a mighty victory for the children of Israel. The Ebenezer stone was to be a reminder to them of His faithfulness. As a military observation point, this memory would give them courage. As they diligently taught it to their children, it would teach them that they too could put their faith in God.

I often find myself like Diane: discouraged. God has done great things for me; He has been very faithful; but my mind can sometimes just dwell on negative thoughts. How interesting to me that this stone of remembrance was set up between a "military observation point" and a place whose name meant "to teach diligently." This reminds me that not only do I need to remind myself about what God has done for me, but I also need to share it with others.

Father, when my enemy whispers discouragement to my soul, help me to counter his attacks by remembering all the places in my life where You have blessed me.

When the Landscape of Life Changes

I looked up Psalm 46:2 in several translations and this is what I found:

> Therefore we will not fear, though the earth give way and the mountains fall into the heart of the sea. NIV

> So we will not fear when earthquakes come and the mountains crumble into the sea. NLT

> Therefore we will not fear, though the earth should change And though the mountains slip into the heart of the sea. NASB

Honestly, how would I feel if the earth should give way, quake or change? When what I am standing on is no longer stable? And what about when mountains fall, crumble or slip into the sea? When the landscape of my life changes and the things I thought were stable are simply no longer there, how would I respond? Panic is a word that comes to mind. Panic, by definition, is a sudden overwhelming fear that produces hysterical or irrational behavior. When what I'm standing on is no longer solid, panic would be a good word to define how I would feel.

It is interesting to me that the verse that precedes this is, "God is our refuge and strength, a very present help in trouble." God is the one I flee to for safety. The truth is, I do get afraid and there are times when I feel very vulnerable. When this happens, I go to God as my place of safety. He is my source of strength when I am in danger. Even when what I am standing on gives way, quakes and changes, the God I have put my trust in remains secure.

Mountains are an earthly picture of strength, so when they fall, crumble or slip into the sea it is terrifying! When my heart panics because what I thought was stable begins to shake, I also find that God comes to my rescue. He is a very present help in time of need. God is my strength. I sometimes think I'm strong, but take away all my props and the truth is made evident: I need a source of strength outside myself. In times like this I do not turn to God, I RUN to Him.

Oh, Father, because I have found You to be my source of strength in times of danger, I will not fear. Because You are the high tower, the fort the fortress where I have always found safety in times of danger, I will not fear. I am weak and defenseless, but You have opened wide Your arms and invited me to find refuge in Your strength. And so when the landscape of my life changes I will not fear.

Sure Footing

My son Andrew was three years old, and was determined that he was able to go by himself. That was a problem, because where he was going was an ice-covered hill. I too was going up the hill, but I had chosen a path that still had unfrozen grass, so I had traction. Andrew chose solid ice.

Soon he began to slip, and because he had no traction, he continued slipping. Seeing him in distress, I went to help him. I firmly took his hand and together we made it to the top of the hill.

There have been several times in my life when I have felt myself slipping; times when I have felt I had no traction under my feet. And I have been grateful for the verse that says, "The steps of a man are established by the Lord, when he delights in his way; though he fall, he shall not be cast headlong, for the Lord upholds his hand" (Psa. 37:23-24 ESV).

If my confidence were only in my ability, I would be like my three-year-old son trying to walk up an ice-covered hill. When I put my trust in God, He establishes my steps. Because He holds my hand, even when I stumble—and I do stumble—I am not cast headlong.

Father, I do slip. I often find myself stumbling along the path. Sometimes on this journey I fall; but my confidence is not in my own ability, but in Your promise to hold my hand. Thank You for letting this journey not be based on my strength but on Your faithfulness.

The Only Thing That Counts

"The only thing that counts is faith expressing itself through love" (Gal. 5:6 NIV). I'm trying to understand this. So, what is faith? "Now faith is the assurance of things hoped for, the conviction of things not seen" (Heb. 11:1 ESV). I also know from that chapter that "without faith it is impossible to please God." But faith without love is nothing. "If I have prophetic powers, and understand all mysteries and all knowledge, and if I have all faith, so as to remove mountains, but have not love, I am nothing" (1 Cor. 13:2 ESV).

The night before Jesus died He gave an illustration of what love looks like: "When Jesus knew that his hour had come to depart out of this world to the Father, having loved his own who were in the world, he loved them to the end" (John 13:1 ESV) He laid aside His outer garments, tied a towel around His waist, and began to wash their feet. He told them that night that people would know who belonged to Him because His disciples would be the ones loving each other.

I've always been struck by the parallel between these two verses. "For God so loved the world, that he gave his only Son, that whoever believes in him should not perish but have eternal life" (John 3:16 ESV). "Believing in him" is what faith is all about. "By this we know love, that he laid down his life for us, and we ought to lay down our lives for the brothers" (1 John 3:16 ESV). If by faith I accept the love of God, it means by faith I must also lay aside my pride and love others the way Jesus showed me.

Now my question is this: What does faith have to do with love? By faith I believe that I am no longer a slave to my flesh but instead I am free to obey the law of love. So when I read that the works of the flesh are evident and that they include selfish ambition, desiring what other people have, being argumentative and outbursts of anger, just to name a few, I feel a bit sick realizing that I have myself displayed all of these traits just yesterday. Where faith comes in is that, although I sin, sin no longer has dominion over me. So when I sin I confess it and by faith lay claim to the grace of God and seek to once more lay aside my pride and love others.

Lord Jesus, You have taught me that faith without love is nothing. You said that the only thing that really counts is faith expressing itself through love. I want to be Your follower; I want to love others; but the truth is I often fail. Thank You that by faith I can be sure of what I hope for and confident about what I don't see; that because of Your grace I can love others.

Stinky Feet

"Would you please get your stinking feet out of my face!"

I have seen pictures of what the table for the Last Supper might have looked like, and it seemed to me that the dirty feet of the person next to you would be a real problem. The day must have been exhausting for everyone. A lot had taken place that day, and now they were tired. They didn't feel like washing their own feet, much less anyone else's. I've had days when I felt like that too.

This was to be Jesus' last meal with them, and I am so touched by the words, "having loved his own who were in the world, he loved them to the end" (John 13:1 ESV). How did He express this love? He got up, took off His outer clothing, and wrapped a towel around His waist and started washing their stinking feet.

I find that this happens when I live in community with others. They become familiar my "stinky feet" and I with theirs. "Stinky feet" happen because, although I am a Christian, I still walk everyday in the world, and I get dirty in the process. In community, that dirt is exposed.

It is an act of humility to wash someone else's feet; not just humility, it is love. It is also an act of humility to have someone else wash my dirty feet. I'm not sure which I struggle with the most: having to confront someone else's "dirt," or having someone confront me with mine.

Lord Jesus, You showed me how to live in community. You showed me by example how to love others. Please help me to humbly love others by not ignoring their need to have their "feet washed." And help me to be humble when someone confronts me.

"I hate this!"

I don't know who pinned the note to the ceiling above the chair in the dentist office, but I agreed with what it said. As the chair leaned back and the dentist would begin to insert the needle filled with Novocain into my gums, I read, "I hate this!" Then I continued to hate it as I sat there opening my mouth so that he could proceed to take a drill to my tooth. I didn't fight against this. I didn't get up and run. The fact is, I paid him to do it!

Just as decay needs to be dealt with in my teeth, sin needs to be dealt with in my life. But I don't like it. Before I can go to the dentist, I have to admit I have a problem and call to make an appointment. The same is true with the sin in my life; before I can deal with it I have to admit it's there. "If we confess our sins, he is faithful and just to forgive us our sins and to cleanse us from all unrighteousness" (1 John 1:9 ESV).
To confess is to agree with God.

I have never once gone to the dentist and asked to be given the drill so that I could use it on myself. In the same way I can't, by any action of my own, deal with the sin in my life. What is required of me is humility. "Humble yourselves, therefore, under the mighty hand of God so that at the proper time he may exalt you, casting all your anxieties on him, because he cares for you" (1 Pet. 5:6-7 ESV).

Sometimes I just don't want to admit I have a problem. I'd rather ignore the pain than humble myself. If I can only stay busy enough it won't bother me anyway. At the heart of my problem is this question, "Do I really trust the Lord? Can I rest in His love for me? Does He love me enough that if I come to Him, having failed again, He can bring healing?"

Lord Jesus, here I am again. I want to be perfect on my own, but the truth is I can't be. I would like to be able to fix myself without any help and without any pain, but I can't do that either. Over and over You showed me Your faithfulness. Thank You.

What's the Purpose?

He was born in the spring of 1921. His mother took her job to "raise him up in the nurture and admonition of the Lord" very seriously. She taught him from his earliest memories that "the chief end of man is to glorify God and enjoy Him forever." He spent the rest of his life discovering what that meant.

What does a man that glorifies God look like? This was a question that he and I often talked about. He was a quiet man, a farmer. But this morning I read something that reminded me of him, "Blessed is the man who trusts in the Lord, whose confidence is in him. They will be like a tree planted by the stream. It does not fear when the heat comes; its leaves are always green. It has no worries in a year of drought and never fails to bear fruit" (Jer. 17:7-8 NIV)

When you live to be in your 90s you are bound to know days of drought as well as days of plenty, so it was for my father-in-law. But he was a humble man whose trust was in the Lord. In good times and bad he placed his confidence in God and not in himself or the circumstances he found himself in. He had been shown as a young child where the stream of living water was and that is where he sank his roots.

The night before last I sat watching the sunset remembering the conversation he and I had the day before he died. I remembered asking him the question his mother had asked him so many years ago, "What is the chief end of man?" Without hesitation but with a smile he said, "The chief end of man is to glorify God and enjoy Him forever." He died the next morning. We had his memorial on what would have been his 91st birthday had he lived. As I sat in that room full of people who had been touched by his life I remembered another verse, "Now when David had served God's purpose in his own generation, he fell asleep" (Acts 13:36 NIV).

Father, when my life has ended, may it be said of me that I brought Your glory and that mine was a life marked by the joy that belongs to someone who belongs to You.

Where Mercy Found Me

"What did he say!?!" I had asked my pastor to pray for me before I went to be a speaker for a week at camp. As I stood before the congregation I heard him pray, "Lord, as You sent the Gadarene demoniac back to his hometown to tell of Your mercy to him, we send Sarah to tell of Your mercies to her." It was a humbling prayer, but it made me stop and think about the mercies I have received.

When I was 18 and all my friends were leaving home to go off to college I was in a mental hospital. When I was released I was deeply confused and terribly frightened that I would have no future. That's where mercy found me. At first it is was only a small flicker of light, but I

337

followed that light and found hope. Hope that taught me to put my trust and confidence in a God who loves me.

I also remember watching as the small coffin that contained my baby was lowered into the earth. The dark cloud of grief threatened to smother me. That's where mercy found me. At first it was only a small flicker of light, but I followed that light and found hope. Hope that taught me to put my trust and confidence in a God who loves me.

There were times when the consequences of my failures seemed far too great a burden to bear. All I wanted to do was to give up. I wanted to find a place to hide. That's where mercy found me. At first it was only a small flicker of light, but I followed that light and found hope. Hope that taught me to put my trust and confidence in a God who loves me.

Lord, my life has been filled with Your mercy and grace. Thank You for the reminder that the only thing I have to give is what You've given me. Please allow me to be someone who shares Your mercy with others. Let me go into the dark places of life holding high Your light so that I might share with others the hope I have found in You.

Learning to Fly With a Broken Wing

"It isn't fair that some people get everything while other people have nothing." A young woman said this to me while I was sitting in my mother's living room holding my infant daughter. She and I had had similar mental struggles, but I had gone on to marry and now had a beautiful baby she was still struggling. But her perception of my perfect life was faulty. While she had just come back from a trip to Israel I had gone to visit my mother because the mobile home I was living in had become rat infested and I was staying with my mother until the rats were gone.

The next year that young woman committed suicide. When I think about my friend it makes me sad. When she died I wondered, how can you learn to fly with a broken wing? She and I had both gone through experiences that in some ways crippled us. As I look back over the 30 years of my life since her death I realize that life can be very hard. I also realize that I have learned the secret of flying with a broken wing.

I often struggle with depression. For me it's not always just the situations of life that can cause this heaviness that keeps me earthbound, it is also a chemical imbalance. Yet I believe that I do not have to give up without a fight. Every morning I start my day by setting my mind on things above. I read in Psalm 100 that we are to, "Enter his gates with thanksgiving, and his courts with praise! Give thanks to him and praise his name." Often my choice to obey this verse does not match my feelings.

Now here is the secret to flying with a broken wing: it's faith. Every day I am invited to be sure of what I hope for and confident about what I do not see or feel. Each new day I wake and wait on the Lord, watching as the sun comes up on the horizon. I offer my sacrifice of praise and thanksgiving believing that He who has promised is faithful. As I wait I gain strength for the day and hope for tomorrow. And then it happens—my heart is no longer earthbound; I am mounting up on the wings of an eagle.

Father, thank You for never leaving me or forsaking me. You told me that I am not to base my life on what I see or feel but on Your love and promises. In You I find everything I need to face the challenges of this life. In You I have renewed strength. I can run and not grow weary, walk and not faint. I can even fly with a broken wing.

When I Cry, Abba! Father!

When they talk to me they do not use my given name. When they speak to me they speak to me in terms of our relationship. Mother, Mommy, Mom; all these names unlock my heart. Because I have this relationship with my children, it help me understand how Jesus taught His disciples to pray.

I'm really glad Jesus' disciples asked Him how to pray because prayer is such a mystery to me. The fact that Jesus told them to begin by calling the God of the Universe Father is significant. "See what great love the Father has lavished on us, that we should be called the children of God" (1 John 3:1 NIV). So my prayer begins with a reminder that the love of

God has been lavished on me because He has chosen me to be His child.

When Jesus was encouraging His disciples to relate to God as their father He said, "Which one of you, if his son asks him for bread, will give him a stone? Or if he asks for a fish, will give him a serpent? If you, then, who are evil, know how to give good gifts to your children, how much more will your Father who is in heaven give good things to those who ask him!" (Matt. 7:9-11 ESV). When I begin my prayer with "Father" I am reminded I am not only speaking to God's ear, I'm speaking to His heart.

Sometimes my children call me Mother, but sometimes they call me Mommy. The term Mommy is very tender and intimate. It's like calling my father "daddy". Because I have been adopted into God's family, He "has sent the Spirit of his Son" into my heart. His spirit cries, "Abba! Father!" (Gal. 4:6). Sometimes life crushes me so hard I don't know what to say. When this happens the same Spirit that cries "Abba! Father!" helps me in my weakness. "The Spirit himself intercedes for us with groaning too deep for words." (Rom. 8:26 ESV)

Father, I come before Your throne, not like a slave to her master, but like a child to her Father. And when the world comes crushing down on me and I cry, "Abba! Father!" I know that you not only hear me with Your heart, You even give me the words to say.

Untangling Weedy Thoughts

Sometimes I have to talk to myself and tell myself the truth. I have to do this because my mind becomes entangled with negative thoughts like a garden overgrown by weeds. Yesterday was one of those days. As I tried to free my flowers from their weedy prison I was also trying to free my mind from dark oppressive thoughts.

Sometimes while I talking to myself saying, "Why, my soul, are you downcast? Why so disturbed within me? Put your hope in God, for I will yet praise him, my Savior and my God" (Psa. 43:5 NIV), I find other people listening in. Yesterday, my grandson joined me in my weedy garden. I was sitting on a little stool, dripping sweat, with both my hands wrapped around the weeds I was yanking out of the garden. But our conversation was about hope.

I refuse to surrender my garden to the weeds and I refuse to surrender my mind to the discouraging thoughts that bring sadness with them. Sometimes it helps me to have someone listen as I choose to talk about my hope in God. Psalm 22:3 says that God inhabits the praises of His people. I told Jack that the stem that bears thorns produces a rose. It amazes me sometimes how talking to children can help me refocus on the truth.

Jack left me for a little while, but when he returned he brought with him a cup of cool water, an umbrella and an electric fan he had plugged into an extension cord. He sat beside me again, holding the umbrella, and ready to hear more about the goodness of God. When my heart is filled with praise I can see God more clearly and I find others who want to see Him too.

Thank You, Father, for being my Savior. Thank You because even when my heart feels bound by negative thoughts You come to my rescue. I can put my hope in You and share that hope with others. Oh, yes, and thank You for grandchildren who come with cool water and umbrellas.

Nothing to Fear

Even though I sometimes feel like I'm in control the truth is I'm not. I think that is one of the reasons why this verse is so comforting to me, "Count it all joy, my brothers, when you meet trials of various kinds" (Jas. 1:2). I find this comforting because I see in the trial an invitation to know God on a deeper level. Every time I've encountered God in my suffering or trial I have been changed.

Not only am I not in control but when I am faced with trials I wasn't expecting I realize how little I know. In James, after we are told to consider our trials joy, we are also told that if we lack wisdom we can ask God for it. Part of the reason I can face uncertainty is because I have an invitation to draw on God's wisdom. When I encounter God's wisdom in the midst of my trial my faith deepens.

I see this in the life of Daniel when Nebuchadnezzar ordered the execution of all the wise men of Babylon. Daniel's response was to ask for time to pray. When God gave Daniel the wisdom he asked for this was his response, "He reveals deep and hidden things; he knows what lies in darkness, and light dwells with him. I thank and praise you, O God of my ancestors: You have given me wisdom and power" (Dan. 2:22-23 NIV).

When I look through the Bible at where people encountered God I see that it was most often during times of trials and testing. When Joseph spoke to his brothers who had sold him into slavery he said, "As for you, you meant evil against me, but God meant it for good" (Gen. 50:20 ESV) I am not in control but God is and He invites me to count my trials as joy, when I do my faith grows and I know a peace that passes understanding.

I thank You, Father, because you reveal the deep and hidden things, You know what lies in darkness, and light dwells with You. I thank You, Father, because whenever I face a trial You give me the wisdom that I seek.

Finding Security in an Insecure World

The first time I heard this definition of hope was at Grandmother Ruth's funeral. The preacher said the word he felt represented her life best was the word hope. He then went on to define hope as a confident expectation of good. As he spoke I thought about Grandmother Ruth. I remembered her ever-present smile, but I also remembered the stories she had told me of her life.

The smile she gave the people she encountered didn't come from a life of ease but from a heart at rest. Grandmother Ruth had known many difficult times. She knew what it was to be tossed on the sea of life with no visible means of rescue. She also knew what it meant in those times to let her anchor grip a solid rock. Her confidence and her expectations were not in herself or in the situations she found herself in. Her confidence and her expectations were in person and the promises of Jesus Christ.

It's been many years since I have seen Grandmother Ruth's smile, but the memory of her smile and her hope lingers with me to this day. The memory of how she ran the race of faith causes me to have the courage to run with endurance the race that is set before me looking to Jesus who is the founder and perfecter of my faith. Grandmother Ruth was sure of what she hoped for she was confident about what she didn't see and that confidence gave her the courage to smile.

Now it's my turn to give to my children and my grandchildren the gift of my smile when I face uncertain times. I want them to know what I have learned about finding security in an insecure world. Though often my boat feels storm tossed I know my anchor holds secure. My confidence and my expectations are in the unfailing love of God, my heart is at rest and I can smile.

Father, thank You for the people You have given me who taught me deep lessons about life, not with words but by example. Father, let me share with others what has been shared with me, a smile and the gift of hope.

I Choose to Rejoice

Sometimes I become discouraged. Doubts begin to haunt me. I see my failures and they seem to blot out everything else on the horizon. When I feel this blanket of despair beginning to smother me I talk to myself using God's words, "Rejoice in the Lord always; again I will say, Rejoice" (Phil. 4:4 ESV).

This is how I choose to rejoice: I stop focusing on how I feel and I tell myself the truth. "Don't be afraid, for I am with you. Don't be discouraged, for I am your God. I will strengthen you and help you. I will uphold you with my victorious right hand" (Isa. 41:10 NLT).

The passage in Philippians that issues the command to "Rejoice," also issues the command, "Do not be anxious about anything, but in everything let your requests be made known to God." When I walk in God's truth and not according to my feeling I make the choice to believe the promises of God. I reach out my hand and by faith take hold of the hand extended to me. I pour out all that is in my heart. I do not just rehash why I am discouraged, I accept the strength that is not my own with a thankful heart.

This process is one of the ways I experience God. When I choose to walk in the truth the peace comes. This peace then guards both my heart and my mind in Christ Jesus. Because I can only think about one thing at a time, I choose to think about "whatever is true,… whatever is pure, whatever is lovely, whatever is admirable—if anything is excellent or praiseworthy" (Phil. 4:8), these are things I choose to fill my mind with.

Father, thank You for the invitation to Rejoice in You. Thank You for the truth than You are with me and You give me Your strength. Thank You for the gift of prayer and for the gift of Your Spirit that enables me to know peace.

I Know I Will be Given What I Asked For!

I'd read about it, heard about it, prayed about it, but never understood it. This summer I heard a sermon about it and suddenly a light went on. The funny thing is that the answer was there all along, but it wasn't until the preacher pointed it out to me that I saw it.

One of the first things I'd memorized as a child was the Lord's Prayer. I regularly asked, "Give us each day our daily bread," but I was never really sure just what "daily bread" was. The answer was hidden from me even though it was there in plain view. In Luke 11 where Jesus teaches His disciples this prayer He goes on to explain to them a little more about this principle of asking.

The preacher talked about how in the culture of Jesus' time bread was baked daily. Jesus audience would therefore understand why the man had no bread for his unexpected guests who came at midnight, but the man knew someone who did have what he needed and he wasn't shy about asking for help. Jesus also referred to a child asking his father for food. Jesus made the comment, "If you then, who are evil, know how to give good gifts to your children, how much more will the heavenly Father give the Holy Spirit to those who ask him!" (Luke 11:13 ESV).

I heard this sermon at the beginning of the summer and I have been meditating on it ever since. Not one day goes by that I, like the man who had the midnight visitors, am not faced with situations where I feel like I need to give more than I have. I am comforted that if I ask God for my basic needs He is not going to substitute something harmful. But most of all I have spent the summer pondering what this means, "how much more will the heavenly Father give the Holy Spirit to those who ask him!" Oh yes, and I do love it when I find an exclamation point in the Scripture.

Father, I need this daily bread. I do not know what this day holds, but You do. I see in Your word that it pleases You for me to ask, to seek and to knock, so here I am asking, seeking and knocking. I recognize that I do not posses in myself all I need, but I believe You do. But most of all please, please fill me with Your Spirit!

A Place of Safety

I remember the first time I heard the preacher talk about the fear of the Lord. He explained that the fear of the Lord is to have reverence and respect for who God is. When I have a fear of the Lord it is because I understand my relationship to Him. He is the Creator and I am the created. He is the Lord and I am His servant. He is the Father and I am His child.

Oswald Chambers said, "The remarkable thing about fearing God is that, when you fear God, you fear nothing else; whereas, if you do not fear God, you fear everything else." *Webster's Dictionary* defines fear as "a feeling of anxiety and agitation produced by the presence or nearness of danger, evil, pain, etc." I often feel this since of fear when I am in situations I have no control over. Since I have little or no control over most situations, I could experience this constantly if it weren't for my relationship with the only one who is in control.

"Oh, how abundant is your goodness, which you have stored up for those who fear you and worked for those who take refuge in you, in the sight of the children of mankind!" (Psa. 31:19 ESV). This reminds me of something that happened this week. My daughter got a trampoline for her children to play on. It was a surprise. She told them to go clean their rooms while it was being assembled. One of her children disobeyed her; there was a lack of reverence and respect. Because of the disobedience she had to discipline the child. Instead of letting that child play on the new trampoline, that child could only watch as the other children enjoyed the gift that had been given them. What I see is that when I fear the Lord there is both obedience and blessing. When I don't fear the Lord there is anxiety and agitation.

When I am afraid I have to do inventory and figure out where I am failing to trust God or relating to Him properly. When I truly humble myself and seek refuge in who He is I find both protection and blessing. Living on a farm I sometimes see the baby chicks finding refuge under the wing of their mother. This reminds me of Psalm 5:11, "But let all who take refuge in you be glad; let them ever sing for joy. Spread your protection over them, that those who love your name may rejoice in you" (NIV).

Heavenly Father, when I am afraid, help me to put my trust in You. Thank You that when I seek refuge in You I am never turned away. Thank You for the good plans You have for my life. Help me to always relate to You with reverence and respect.

A Deeper Understanding

All week long he worked and worked hard, but when Sunday came he belonged to us. Some of my favorite childhood memories were made on Sunday afternoons when my Daddy would change from his business suit into his casual clothes and get down on the floor and play with us. When I became a teenager I recognized my Father as a man who was strict and had very high standards for his children. However, whether I was playing with my Daddy on the floor, or being disciplined by my Father as a teenager, I knew he loved me.

I wonder what it sounded like to hear God walking in the garden in the cool of the day. The fellowship Adam and Eve had known with their creator in the beginning must have been like the relationship I had with my Daddy when I was a little girl. Then I read about this same God— who walked in the garden in the cool of the day to meet with Adam and Eve—described in Daniel: "As I looked, thrones were placed, and the Ancient of Days took his seat; his clothing was white as snow, and the hair of his head like pure wool; his throne was fiery flames; its wheels were burning fire" (Dan. 7:9 ESV).

I have always loved the picture of John leaning on Jesus at the last

Supper. John describes himself as "the one whom Jesus loved." I can see how he would feel this way, though I also believe that each of the disciples would see themselves in that description. Later in John's life he gives us a different picture of Jesus: "in the midst of the lampstands one like a son of man, clothed with a long robe and a golden sash around his chest. The hairs of his head were white, like white wool, like snow, His eyes were like a flame of fire, his feet were like burnished bronze, refined in a furnace, and his voice was like the roar of many waters" (Rev. 1:13-15 ESV).

When the Bible describes love in 1 Corinthians 13 it says, "When I was a child, I spoke like a child, I thought like a child, I reasoned like a child. When I became a man, I gave up childish ways. For now we see in a mirror dimly, but then face to face. Now I know in part; then I shall know fully, even as I have been fully known" (1 Cor. 13:11-12 ESV). Ever since I was 13 I have been reading the Bible year after year what I have seen from Genesis to Revelation is the love of God being revealed in a deeper and deeper way.

Heavenly Father, thank You for Your love whether I experience it in the cool of the evening in a garden like a child who plays with her father, or as a woman awed by Your holiness. Year after year I have seen the truth of the Scripture that says, "God is love."

The Cure

Grumble. Mumble. Grumble, mumble, grumble. Every thought I had when I woke up this morning produced a negative emotion. That's when I remembered what Grandma Frizzy taught me.

When I was a teenager I became part of a group that adopted grandparents. I thought at the time I was doing a good deed by going to visit a lonely elderly lady who had no family. Every week I would go visit her in her room. That's all she had was a room; a room and the lessons she had learned in life. Her room was filled with old pictures, old furniture and a sense of peace that made me want to visit her week after week.

One foggy autumn day I went to visit Grandma Frizzy. I felt sad and depressed. She noticed my emotional state and started telling me stories. Her stories opened a window into her life that I could look through. She had gone through many difficulties and yet each trial had brought her deeper and deeper in this peace that I experienced each time I walked into her room. Then she looked directly into my eyes and asked if I would like to know her secret.

"Sarah, when the sorrows of life tie a loop around my ankle and begin to drag me down to the dungeon of despair, I fight!" Slowly she got up from her chair and walked over to her bedside table and got a slip of paper. She handed me the paper with these words printed on it, "By him therefore let us offer the sacrifice of praise to God continually, that is, the fruit of our lips giving thanks to His name" (Heb. 13:15 KJV). So she taught me her secret.

Father, thank You for the people who shared their life and examples with me. Thank You for the truth that when I offer the sacrifice of praise, regardless of how I feel, You come to me with peace.

And thank You for Grandma Frizzy who gave me more than I could have ever given her. Please let me share with others the lessons of life that I have learned by walking with You.

Tomorrow is Already Taken Care of

"Does anyone have a praise they would like to share?" There was silence and for a minute or two and I wondered if anyone was going to share anything. Then she stood up and told about her Bible study on the names of God. She told about her study of Jehovah Jireh. This wasn't her first time to study the name, she knew it meant "The Lord will provide," but this time it held a special meaning for her. This time she realized that the name Jehovah Jireh carried with it the idea that God had already provided for her need before she even knew about it. She was bound by time but God is not.

Abraham gave God the name Jehovah Jireh when he was ready to sacrifice his son Isaac and God stayed his hand and showed him a ram caught in the thicket by his horns. In James 2:23 it says that Abraham was called a friend of God. Why? Abraham was God's friend because he trusted Him. He came to know God as the one who would provide because he walked in obedience.

Jesus invited His followers to enter into this kind of friendship with God. Having this kind of friendship means that I believe the literal meaning of Jehovah Jireh, that the "Lord Who Provides" will take care of my needs. Jesus invited His followers to consider the lilies of the field and the birds of the air. He pointed out how God provided for the needs of all His creation, and then He told His listeners not to be anxious. I don't know what I will need tomorrow, but God not only knows the need He has already provided for it.

This truth is one that I need to be reminded of regularly. God has promised to "supply every need of yours according to His riches in glory in Christ Jesus" (Phil. 4:19). I know the name Jehovah Jireh; I know Abraham was called a friend of God because he trusted God to provide; I know that Jesus told His followers not to be anxious because God has tomorrow already taken care of; yet still I sometimes struggle. So today I choose to join my friend and praise God because, although I am bound by time, God is not.

Meeting Challenges

She handed me a slip of paper and said, "I thought maybe you could use this in your talk." I was getting ready to speak at a woman's retreat. I don't remember what I had to say so many years ago, but what was written on that paper has stayed with me. It said, "I'm living the life God has given me to live and by His grace I'm meeting every challenge."

Every season of life has its challenges, but I find a deep sense of comfort in knowing that the details of my life are not by chance. Psalm 139 says, "Your eyes saw my unformed body; all the days ordained for me were written in your book before one of them came to be." God knew before I was born where He would place me in history and what challenges I would face.

"I'm living the life God has given me to live and by His grace I'm meeting every challenge." I see this in the life of King David. He was anointed king as a boy, yet his life was filled with challenges where he had to learn to trust God's provision. Living the life God has given me to live means that my goal is to fulfill God's purposes in my generation. The only way I can do that is to do it by the grace He has made available to me.

God told the prophet Jeremiah, "Before I formed you in the womb I knew you, before you were born I set you apart." The life God had chosen for Jeremiah was a difficult one. Jeremiah's assignment was to be a prophet to the nations. The message God spoke using Jeremiah's lips was not a popular message. Jeremiah served the purpose of God in his generation relying on the grace and power of God.

Father, I don't know what today will bring, but You do. Thank You for the peace that comes from knowing that what is unknown to me is known to You. Thank You also in advance for the grace that You will provide for each challenge I have yet to face.

On the Other Side

"That day when evening came, he said to his disciples, 'Let us go over to the other side" (Mark 4:35 NIV). It was already beginning to get dark when they got in the boat, but then the storm hit. They couldn't see to navigate. The wind and waves tossed their boat; they had no control. They were already tired before they got on the boat, but the strain of both anxiety and muscle was more than they could stand. Although they were together in the boat, the fear they felt caused each to feel alone. And where was He—the one who invited them to go with them to the other side? He was asleep in the boat.

On the other side a madman waited, hiding among the tombs. He screamed at the rain that pelted him. No one was strong enough to tame him or bind him. Many had tried but he broke the chains and snapped the ropes. Tonight was the same as all nights. He was roaming through the graveyard screaming and slashing himself with sharp stones. No one was strong enough to bind him, no one was strong enough to set him free. Or so it was thought.

"Teacher, is it nothing to you that we're going down?" When Jesus awoke He spoke to the wind and the waves and the sea became as

smooth as glass. When they got to the other side the madman saw
Jesus he ran to Him and cried, "What have you to do with me, Jesus,
Son of the Most High God? Do not torment me." With a word Jesus
released the man from the demons who had tormented him. With a
word Jesus brought peace to the storm without and the storm within.

Getting to the "other side" often involves a storm. I don't think the
disciples would have been able to understand the peace and the power
that having Jesus with them could bring unless they
had experienced the storm; the storm that showed them the contrast
between who they were and who He is. The man who had
been possessed would have never known the peace and the mercy
Jesus had to give if he had not known the power of his madness.

Lord Jesus, I often hear You inviting me to go with You to the other side.
Help me not to be afraid of the storms in my life but instead by faith to
consider them joy because in the storms of life I come to know You
better, whether the storm is internal of external. And, Lord Jesus, when
the storm is passed, let me share with others my story of Your mercy.
The mercy I have found by being invited to go with You to the other
side.

The Secret Things Belong to the Lord

"The secret things belong to the Lord our God, but the things revealed
belong to us and to our children forever, that we may follow all the
words of this law" (Deut. 29:29 NIV). It's a holy habit I formed years ago,
to begin the day by reading God's Word. A habit is an action that is
repeated day after day so that after a while you don't even think about
it, you just do it. So when I wake up, I start my day by I look for the
things God has revealed in His word.

"It is the glory of God to conceal a matter; to search out a matter is the
glory of kings" (Prov. 25:2 NIV). Every year I try to read through the Bible
from Genesis to Revelation. Today my reading was in Ezekiel. I have to
confess that's some heavy reading. Last year I did an inductive study in
the book of Ezekiel and it helped me understand what I'm reading a
little better. Why do I keep reading even when it's hard to understand?

Not just because it's a holy habit, but also because I believe
that searching out what God has said gives me understanding I could get
no other way.

"Surely the Sovereign Lord does nothing without revealing his plan to
his servants the prophets" (Amos 3:7 NIV). I am fascinated by this verse.
To think that the plans of God have been revealed in the prophets and I
have access to those books fills me with wonder. In my life the
byproduct of reading the prophets year after year has been perspective.
When I read the prophets I feel like I am looking at a globe and I can
understand a little better how everything fits together in the bigger
story of God's love that is being told.

"All Scripture is breathed out by God and profitable for teaching, for
reproof, for correction, and for training in righteousness" (2 Tim. 3:16
ESV) It's not just the big picture I need, I also need to know how to
navigate my way in this world. What is right? What is wrong?
Sometimes I can get very confused. But when I turn to the words God
breathed, I find myself being taught, often rebuked and then corrected.
I find a deep sense of security in the truth that I can go to the words
God inspired and be instructed in how to live a righteous life.

Father, I know the secret things belong to You, but I come to You today
because You have given me an invitation to come. You have not only
given me Your word, You have also given me Your Holy Spirit to teach
me. Morning by morning I am invited to come into Your presence to
receive what You have given. Father, never let me lose the wonder of
this invitation.

When Plans Change

One week from the wedding the Bride, my daughter, realized they'd
forgotten to make reservations for the night of the wedding. Every place
she called was booked because it was Labor Day weekend. That day she
also found out that the people from whom she was buying the lace for
her wedding dress forgot to order it. Four days before the wedding our
friends who were providing music called to tell us that there was a
family emergency and they would be unable to come. That was also the

day I, the mother of the Bride, had to have an MRI.

I talked to my sister on the phone and told her everything going on. Later that day she sent me this text: "God deals wonderfully in weddings. He allows—brings—crises then turns water to exquisite wine! Praise Him. He is awesome in power and mighty to save! 'Bless the Lord, O my soul! And forget none of his benefits!'"

I talked to my daughter about all the challenges she was facing as her plans were being rearranged. I told her one of the beautiful symbols that a marriage represents is that Jesus identified Himself as the Bridegroom of the church. As a wife is to rest in her husband's love, so we are to rest in the love of Jesus. The way I see life is that the challenges I face are opportunities to encounter the love and provision of Jesus.

A friend found a beautiful room at a Bed and Breakfast where the Bride and Groom will go on their wedding night. It was more beautiful than she could have ever planned. Another friend drove to Atlanta and found material to replace the lace that wasn't ordered. She liked it better than the lace she had chosen in the first place. A friend of ours will play the cello for us and we are hoping to be a blessing to him. Concerning the MRI, I am resting in the love and provision of Jesus.

Lord Jesus, You turn the water in wine. I rest in You as I meet the challenges of life, waiting with expectation to see Your loving provision.

When He Calls Your Name

I was tucking my grandchildren into bed. I could tell they were tired by their big yawns and the way they were rubbing their eyes. As I got ready to pray for them, I told them about when Samuel was a little boy laying down in the temple of the Lord where the Ark of God was. I told them how God had called his name, but because he didn't yet know the Lord and because the word of the Lord hadn't been revealed to him yet, he didn't know who was calling him. Then I prayed that God would call their names and that they would know Him and that God would reveal His word to them.

Have you ever heard God call your name? Someone shyly told me this summer that he had heard God call his name. I think that he was afraid of how I would respond. He had been pursuing God and longing for a deeper relationship. I wasn't surprised, nor did I think it strange that God had called his name. The question I asked him was, "Well, how did you respond?"

Samuel, however, wasn't pursuing God when he heard his name called. The Scripture says that he didn't yet know the Lord. The message God gave this young man was a hard one. Eli told Samuel to say, "Speak, for your servant hears" (1 Sam. 3:9), but the message God gave Samuel was about how Eli had not been listening to the Lord and how God was going to bring punishment on his house forever. Now that's a heavy message to wake a young man up with in the middle of the night!

"This is the confidence we have in approaching God: that if we ask anything according to his will, he hears us. And if we know he hears us—whatever we ask—we know that we have what we asked of him" (1 John 5:14-15 NIV). With this confidence I lay my hands on the heads of my grandchildren and I ask that God will wake them up by calling them by name. I ask that He will reveal Himself to them through His Word. I also ask that God will take these children and give them the courage to speak the truth.

Lord Jesus, I too want to hear You call my name. Open my ears to hear, my eyes to see, and please give me the courage to obey. Let my life be an example to my children and grandchildren of one who hears and obeys Your voice.

I Saw Jesus at the Wedding

My little girl got married yesterday. All throughout the preparations I had a prayer that was as constant as the beating of my heart. "Lord Jesus, come to the wedding feast. Make your presence known."
This morning I can't stop crying, not because He didn't come but because He did. My tears are tears of joy not sorrow.

I saw Jesus at the wedding. His reflection was on all the faces of our friends and family who surrounded us as we prepared to celebrate. Again and again I felt my inadequacy. "Oh Jesus, I have no more strength." In the midst of my weakness I felt His loving presence by those who came to my aid. Every crisis became an opportunity for Him to turn the water into wine and bring joy.

I saw Jesus at the wedding. Today my mind is filled with the memory of the smiling faces of the Bride and Groom. I watched as my little girl walked down the aisle, her face glowed with the love that filled her heart. Her groom was waiting. The Bride had made herself ready for this moment. The preacher spoke of Jesus waiting to receive His bride. I saw His love reflected in their faces.

I saw Jesus at the wedding. We had prayed it wouldn't rain, but it did. With the rain came the humidity. I always want life to be perfect. My plan was there would NOT be rain! Jesus' plan was to penetrate the raindrops with the light of His presence. He sent not one but two rainbows. The rain lasted but a moment, the rainbows lingered.

Lord Jesus, thank You for coming to the wedding! Just as You did at Cana of Galilee, You took the ordinary and made it extraordinary.

Wrapped Up in Perfect Peace

The day has been long and I am so very tired. Finally, I get to go to bed. Then it happens, just as my head is sinking into the pillow and my mind is blanketed with unconsciousness, the "guilts" come. With a harsh voice they begin to whisper in my mind. "Why did you...?" "How could you have forgotten to...?" "You are so selfish and self centered!"

No matter how weary I may be the "guilts" have the ability to chase away sleep and replace it with shame. I would be an insomniac if it were not for my secret weapon. Long ago I hung a calligraphic Bible verse above my bed. It reads, "Thou wilt keep him in perfect peace, whose mind is stayed on thee: because he trusteth in thee" (Isa. 26:3 KJV).

So how guilty am I? The thing that wakes me is the fact that there is truth in all the accusations that the "guilts" hurl at me. However, there is a deeper truth that I see when my mind is steadfast and I choose to trust God. Every scene of guilt and shame becomes a backdrop for me to see more clearly the love of God. I make a choice to fix my thoughts on my Savior, my Redeemer and the lover of my soul.

So the place where I have been attached for my failures becomes a place of worship. The contrast of who I am and who God is causes me to bow before Him and worship Him in the beauty of His holiness. My mind is blanketed with perfect peace; my heart finds it's resting place in the unfailing love of God.

Lord Jesus, when the darkness of my sin matches the darkness of the night help me to seek Your comfort. Thank You for inviting me to worship You in the beauty of Your holiness. Thank You for wrapping me in Your perfect peace.

When I Am Afraid

Sometimes I feel afraid. I feel overwhelmed by the things I have no control over. I see the effects of a broken world on the lives of the people I love. I know the Bible says not to be anxious but to pray, so I choose to pray. If I pray with my mind wrapped around the thing I fear, it anchors me to that fear. I choose instead, as my starting point, to fill my mind with the pictures I find painted by the prophets.

I think one of my favorite ways to picture God is in Daniel: "As I looked, thrones were placed, and the Ancient of Days took his seat; his clothing was white as snow, and the hair of his head like pure wool; his throne was fiery flames; its wheels were burning fire" (Dan. 7:9 ESV). I live my life confined by time, but the one to whom I pray is not confined to time; instead He is the Ancient of Days. He knows the end from the beginning.

When I pray I like to think about what Ezekiel saw when he saw the Lord: "Like the appearance of a rainbow in the clouds on a rainy day, so was the radiance around him. This was the appearance of the likeness of the glory of the Lord" (Ezek. 1:28 NIV). On rainy days the beauty of a rainbow gives me hope.

If this was the only way I pictured God I would never have the courage to pray. But I also read, "And because you are sons, God has sent the Spirit of his Son into our hearts, crying, 'Abba! Father!'" (Gal. 4:6 ESV). Sometimes my prayer is very short and its goes something like this, "Help!" Whether my prayer is long or short I direct it to my Father who is in Heaven.

Father, I don't really understand prayer, but I see again and again this invitation in Your word to come before You and to bring with me the things that cause me anxiety. So I come. When I am afraid I will come, and I will lift my eyes, I will lift my voice, I will lift my heart to the Ancient of Days whose radiance is like a rainbow on a rainy day and who has invited me to call Him Abba.

I Can See a Rainbow!

Yesterday I went to the doctor and heard, "You have a brain tumor." I'm really glad my sister was with me, because once I found out there was a tumor growing in my brain, it was hard to focus on anything else. My sister has a nursing degree so she was able to ask the right questions and listen to the answers with understanding.

The doctor said it was the good kind of tumor because it grew slowly and 90% of the time this type tumor is benign. In some cases brain surgery is needed. Because the tumor is on the auditory nerve sometimes hearing can be lost when the surgery is done. So this is the physical reality in which I now live. But I also live in a spiritual reality.

The day before I found out about my tumor I was visiting with a very dear friend who is an atheist. Because I love her so much I wanted to share with her not only my physical life experiences but my spiritual life as well. I failed miserably and simply came across as being "preachy."

I thought about what I had wanted to communicate. This morning, sitting here knowing that there is a tumor growing in my brain, I know exactly what I was trying to tell her. I wanted to share with her the rainbow that I see. My daughter got married Saturday and at the reception there was a double rainbow. I wasn't satisfied to just look at it, I wanted everyone around me to see it too: "Look up! Can you see the rainbow?!"

Thank You so much, Father, for filling my cloudy sky with the beauty of a rainbow! Your loving presence fills my physical and spiritual reality. Please help me to share what I believe without being "preachy." I want others to know the joy and hope I feel in You that cannot be disturbed by the presence of a brain tumor.

My Journey of Faith

When I was a little girl I loved to go to church. The door to the church opened to a spiritual world that was as real to me as the physical world. When I spent the night with my grandmother I would cuddle in bed with her as she read the Bible out loud with a voice full of wonder. It seemed like a foreign language to me, but I found it to be the language of peace. When I was young I saw a picture of a little girl resting her head on Jesus' lap. When I would go to bed at night I pretended I was the little girl in the picture and my pillow was Jesus' lap.

When I became a teenager I began to read the Bible for myself. I was very blessed to have exciting Bible teachers. I met Kay Arthur when she had only been a Christian for five years. Every week I would look forward to learning more of the mysteries from Bible. Every day began with my mother, sister and I reading and sharing together the treasures we found in God's Word.

When I turned the corner from being a child to becoming an adult the tests of faith began. At 18 I had a life altering illness. When I married my husband he had cancer and began chemo therapy the month after our wedding. There were times during our first year of marriage I wasn't sure if he would live. I have known the grief of standing at the graveside of one of my babies. I have known the wounds that cause the question, "God are You there?"

What I have found true in my life is in the dark times God's light shines the brightest. One of my favorite Scriptures is found in Lamentations, "The steadfast love of the Lord never ceases; his mercies never come to an end; they are new every morning; great is your faithfulness" (Lam. 3:22-23 ESV). To lament is to express grief or sorrow, and in the places of my life where I have experienced this kind of grief I have also experienced God's mercy.

Father, thank You for today. I do not know what I will encounter today, but I know Your steadfastness love will be there. I thank You in advance for the new mercies I will find.

The Initiation

I want to share a secret with you. There are mysteries that are learned not by studying but by applying God's word in the midst of a trial. It's as if the very thing I fear becomes an initiation to a place of peace. If God has allowed a difficulty into my life, He has with that difficulty issued me an invitation to know Him better.

I find this world a beautiful place filled with many good things. I would have no problem being content with its simple pleasures; however, I can't ignore the suffering that I have seen. This awareness of suffering has caused me to be aware of not just time but eternity.

I have noticed the effect of suffering on different people. I have watched some people who seemed to know and love God encounter a grief, a disappointment, something that didn't match their expectation of how God should operate. I have seen the light go out as they walked away. I wanted to scream, "Don't give up! Don't just look at what your physical eyes can see."

I am old enough to have known disappointments on many levels. I have known hurt and sorrow. But I have walked long enough with my Lord to know the secret; a secret that I will now share. Whenever I walk among the charred ruins of my plans and dreams I look intently for the invitation. The invitation reads, "Come and know me better, Child."

Oh Father, I thank You for the good times, and I thank You for the hard times. Thank You for teaching me how to rejoice in You with tears in my eyes. Thank You for initiating me into the mystery of faith by allowing me to find joy in You regardless of the circumstances. Thank You for teaching me the secret of contentment that I can do all things through You.

Walking in The Truth

I was standing in line when the woman in front of me said, "Do you know what today is? It's Tuesday, September 11, the eleventh anniversary of the Tuesday America was attacked. Does that bother you?" I guess she thought it might bother me because we were standing in line to get on a plane. Her question caused me to remember what I was doing 11 years ago.

I was preparing to go to a church and speak when someone called and told me about the airplanes crashing into the Twin Towers. The talk I gave that morning was from 3 John 1:4, "I have no greater joy than to hear that my children are walking in the truth." What is the truth you walk in when your world seems so uncertain? Is it the truth that was shown repeatedly on the television—that we were under attack?

The truth I choose to walk in is not found on the nightly news; the truth I choose to walk in is not based on negative test results. The truth I choose to walk in is found in God's Word. "I have loved you with an everlasting love: I have drawn you with unfailing kindness" (Jer. 31:3 NIV). If I based my life on negative things I would be shrouded by fear. When I base my life on the truth that I am loved by God I am wrapped in a deep sense of peace.

When I walk in this truth of God's love I am choosing to walk by faith. "And without faith it is impossible to please God, because anyone who comes to him must believe that he exists and that he rewards those who earnestly seek him" (Heb. 11:6 NIV). How can I live a life that brings God joy and pleases Him? I can do that by walking in the truth that He exists, He loves me, and that He rewards those who earnestly seek Him. I can walk in this truth even in a world that can sometimes be scary.

Father, thank You that in You I find peace regardless of what the news is. Help me to walk in Your truth today and share that truth with others.

A Friend of God

This morning I woke up with a jumble of thoughts, but they all they all had the same theme. This has been a very eventful year in my life and I guess my subconscious mind was working to understand all that is going on even when I sleep. The theme of the night was being a friend of God.

I thought about Abraham and the journey of faith God took him on. I thought about how the Lord told Abraham to leave what was familiar and to follow Him. Abraham was promised a son yet had to wait till he old to have that promise fulfilled. I thought about how God told Abraham His plans and how Abraham interceded for Sodom saying, "Shall not the Judge of all the earth do what is just?"(Gen. 18:25 ESV). Abraham's faith in who God is was seen in his hope, in his patience and in his prayers. Abraham was called a friend of God.

When Jesus was about to leave His disciples He told them that they were not just His servants they were His friends. The disciples had gone on a journey with Jesus, and in the process they had learned to trust Him. Because they believed what He told them after His resurrection, they were able to be joyful in hope, patient in affliction and faithful in prayer.

My journey with God began many years ago. Every difficult situation I have encountered has been like an invitation to experiences God's faithfulness. Because I have experienced God's faithfulness in the past I find I can rejoice in hope today. It's easier to be patient in affliction since I have encountered His comfort in past difficulties. I have also been invited to participate in what God is doing in my life through prayer.

Father, my life has been a journey of coming to know You. Please help me to abide in Your love and share that love with others. Thank You for being my friend.

A Living Hope vs. A Temporary Life

This has been a hard week. I had several doctor's appointments; each one reminded me that I am getting older and my body is wearing out. I went upstairs to work in my daughter's room, but had to stop because I couldn't quit crying. I am happy for her, but it brought into focus how the roles in my life are changing. I woke up this morning thinking about this verse, "All flesh is like grass and all its glory like the flower of the grass. The grass withers, and the flower falls, but the word of the Lord remains forever" (1 Pet. 1:24-25 ESV).

When I talked to my friend who is an atheist this was the view she held: life is beautiful but when it's over, it's over. Personally, I find no comfort in that at all. The Bible has much to say about how temporary life is. "They spring up like flowers and wither away; like fleeting shadows, they do not endure" (Job 14:2 NIV). "As for man, his days are like grass, he flourishes like a flower of the field: for the wind passes over it, and it is gone, and its place knows it no more" (Psa. 103:15-16 ESV). "A voice says, 'Cry!' And I said, 'What shall I cry?' 'All flesh is grass, and all its beauty is like the flowers of the field. The grass withers, the flower fades when the breath of the Lord blows on it; surely the people are grass. The grass withers, the flower fades, but the word of our God will stand forever" (Isa. 40:6-8 ESV).

Because of what I am experiencing I see the truth in what my atheist friend says about how beautiful and temporary life is, but that's not all I see. The same psalm that speaks of the days of our life being like the flower of the field speaks of God's steadfast love: "But the steadfast love of the Lord is from everlasting to everlasting on those who fear him,...The Lord has established his throne in the heavens, and his kingdom rules over all" (Psa. 103:17-19 ESV). I believe what my physical eyes can see, the beauty of a morning glory that blooms in early in the day will by noon be withered. I also, however, believe what I see through eyes of faith: that the steadfast love of God is from everlasting to everlasting.

I woke up thinking about the verse in 1 Peter that says all flesh is like grass. That was all I could remember, so I read the whole chapter to put it in context: "Blessed be the God and Father of our Lord Jesus Christ! According to his great mercy, he has caused us to be born again to a living hope through the resurrection of Jesus Christ from the dead, to an inheritance that is imperishable, undefiled, and unfading, kept in heaven for you" (1 Pet. 1:3-4 ESV). This is my living hope; because of God's great mercy He sent His Son to give me eternal life.

Meditations in the Morning

I like to wake up before the sun does. I start my day in the early morning silence. The silence is replaced by the sound of birds. I watch as the morning light chases away the shadows of the night. I have read that God's mercy is new every morning, so I approach the new day with anticipation.

I don't know what the new day will bring, but I know who brings the day. "But God, being rich in mercy, because of the great love with which he loved us, even when we were dead in our trespasses, made us alive together with Christ" (Eph. 2:4-5 ESV). As the light exposes the colors of the world around me, God's word brings into focus the "immeasurable riches of his grace in kindness toward us in Christ Jesus." I will look for rich mercy, great love and the immeasurable riches of His kindness as I go through this day.

From my earliest memories I have fought with depression, but I learned to fight. Sometimes when the day is beginning my mind awakens to the negative thoughts. Just as the light of the sun replaces the darkness of the night. the truth of God's word reveals His great mercy to me, and living hope replaces despair.

When I begin my day I start by writing in my diary. I look back over the day that is past and look for God's grace to me. Often during the day I'm too busy to notice. I trace in my memory the places I have received mercy. When I have acknowledged the grace and mercy that I have already received, it gives me peace. When the day is filled with light and my heart is filled with peace, I have the courage to face whatever the day may bring.

Father, thank You for Your grace, mercy and peace. I will look for You today. Thank You for Your promise that when I seek You I will find You. Thank You that I can begin each day with Your promise that Your mercy is new and fresh every morning; great is Your faithfulness!

"Clear off Your Desk and Get Out a Clean Sheet of Paper"

"Clean off your desk and get out a clean sheet of paper." Even now so many years later those words that indicated a test was about to take place make me uncomfortable. That cleared-off desk and clean sheet of paper was preparation for finding out what I knew and what I didn't know.

I think tests get rid of clutter in my life. Like that cleaned-off desk and clean sheet of paper a test forces me to focus. I just finished reading the book of Job and there seemed to be a lot of cluttered thinking going on. Everyone was trying to explain God, and in the end they failed. I, however, have a little bit of an advantage when I read Job. I have a bit of a cheat sheet, because I have the first 12 verses that show me a divine perspective of what's taking place on earth.

When Job is put to the test he doesn't pretend he's not suffering. He doesn't understand what is happening any more than the people around him. None of them had access to the first 12 verses like I do. Job suffered, he struggled and he complained; but when everything was stripped away, Job showed what real worship looks like. He said, "The Lord gave, and the Lord has take away; blessed be the name of the Lord" (Job 1:21 ESV). It seems like the main question on this test was, "Do you believe God is good and that you can trust Him?" Job answered, "Yes."

Job was a very righteous man, but he couldn't understand why God allowed him to be so thoroughly tested. Even reading those first 12 verse of Job I don't understand either. I think the point of Job and the test wasn't so that Job, his friends, or anyone else could walk away and say, "Oh, okay, now I understand God." I think in the end the lesson learned by the test was that, though I can't understand God, I can trust Him. At the end of the test God revealed Himself to Job in such a way that Job responded, "My ears had heard of you but now my eyes have seen you" (Job 42:5 NIV).

Father, the tests in my life reveal how little I really know. I'm afraid it also reveals how weak my faith is. But sometimes I wonder if the real reason for the test isn't to expose my lack, but so that I can experience You in an uncluttered way. And I wonder sometimes if the test isn't more of an invitation for me to know You in a deeper and richer way. Maybe that's why the book of James says to count it all joy when my faith is tested.

Borrowing Words

Sometimes I have a hard time finding the words that express how I feel. I remember when my sister came back from France, and she would often use a French word that expressed what she wanted to say better than an English word. To be able to verbalize my thoughts, feelings and beliefs is a very basic need. It is the need to be known, and that's why it's so frustrating when I can't find the right words.

Sometimes I turn to the Psalms to find the words that express what I want to say. Then again, sometimes I read the Psalms and am amazed at how honest the psalmist is about his struggle. When I read the Psalms I see someone who comes before God without a veneer. In the Psalms I find honest emotion, pain and sometimes anger. I also find permission to borrow these words to express how I really feel.

One particular Psalm makes me wonder, "Who borrowed whose words?" This is the Psalm that begins, "My God, my God, why have you forsaken me? Why are you so far from saving me, from the words of my groaning? O my God, I cry by day, but you do not answer, and by night, but I find no rest" (Psa. 22:1-2 ESV). Jesus borrowed these words from David when He was hanging on the cross. Psalm 22 goes on to describe the pain and suffering Jesus experienced on the cross. David wrote the psalm to express the depth of his suffering to God, and Jesus used the words and showed how He had entered into that suffering.

The words of Psalm 22 always make me think of Isaiah 53: "He was despised and rejected by men; a man of sorrows, and acquainted with grief; and as one from whom men hide their faces he was despised, and we esteemed him not. Surely he has bore our griefs and carried our sorrows; yet we esteemed him stricken, smitten by God, and afflicted. But he was wounded for our transgressions; he was crushed for our iniquities; upon him was the chastisement that brought us peace, and with his stripes we are healed" (Isa. 53:3-5 ESV). So what I see when I look at the borrowed words of Psalm 22 is that, because Jesus was forsaken, I never will be.

Lord Jesus, emotions can be a deceitful. Thank You for showing me how to come before You and be completely honest with how I feel. Thank You for giving me the Psalms to guide me in how I can be completely honest in prayer. Thank You also for using the Psalms to point me back to the truth of Your great love.

Keeping Balanced in an Unbalanced World

I was asked to speak on the topic "How to Keep Your Balance in an Unbalanced World." I've been thinking about that lately. When I think of someone who did this well I think of Daniel. As a young man he was taken from his homeland and given a different name. When all that was familiar was stripped away from him, Daniel resolved not to defile himself. I think this is the first clue in his ability to find balance when everything around him was changing. He didn't just look at his world with physical eyes, he used the spiritual eyes as well.

There was so much upheaval during Daniel's life. Soon after he was made a wise man in Nebuchadnezzar's court he was told he was to be killed if he couldn't interpret a dream the king had had, even though the king refused to tell what the dream was. Daniel wasn't destroyed, because he and his friends sought mercy from the God of heaven concerning this mystery. Here is another clue to the way he kept his balance, he trusted God to reveal to him what he needed to know.

When Daniel blessed the God of heaven he said, "He changes times and seasons; he removes kings and sets up kings; he gives wisdom to the wise and knowledge to those who have understanding" (Dan. 2:21 ESV) How many kings did Daniel see rise and fall? First there was Nebuchadnezzar, then his son Evil-Merocach, who only reigned about two years before he was assassinated by his brother-in-law Neriglissar. Neriglissar only reigned for four years when he was replaced by Labashi-Marduk. Then a usurper named Nabonidus took the throne, but removed himself to northern Arabia, and his son Belshazzar became a co-regent. All the time this upheaval was taking place Daniel kept his balance by continuing to worship the God of heaven.

One of the ways I keep my balance in my own unbalanced world is to open my spiritual eyes and look at what Daniel saw. "As I looked, thrones were set in place, and the Ancient of Days took his seat.... In my vision at night I looked, and there before me was one like the son of man, coming with the clouds of heaven. He approached the Ancient of

Days and was led into his presence. He was given authority, glory and sovereign power; all nations and people of every language worshiped him. His dominion is an everlasting dominion that will not pass away, and his kingdom is one that will never be destroyed" (Dan. 7:9, 13-14 NIV). Because Daniel had a spiritual view and not just a physical view he was able to keep his balance no matter what he faced.

Oh, Ancient of Days, I too come before Your throne with the prayer that Jesus taught me to pray, "Father, who art in heaven hallowed be thy name, thy kingdom come, thy will be done, on earth as it is in heaven." Help me to keep my balance by keeping my heart, my mind and my spirit focused on You and Your kingdom.

The Choice

I watched the child sit, with arms crossed, determined to be in a bad mood. It was a beautiful day; we were at a party and a choice had to be made to participate in the fun or not to participate. I thought about that scene as I woke up this morning. The verse that came to mind was, "This is the day the Lord has made. We will rejoice and be glad in it" (Psa. 118:24 NLT)

I first learned this verse as a teenager. I remember the difference it began to make in my life when I woke up recognizing that the Lord had made each day and I could choose to rejoice. It made a difference because before I knew that verse I would wake up with a sense of dread, not knowing what the day would hold.

Choosing to begin the day by rejoicing is choosing to walk by faith. Who can know for certain when a day begins what will happen? "All Scripture is breathed out by God and profitable for teaching, for reproof, for correction, and for training in righteousness" (2 Tim. 3:16 ESV). What Scripture teaches me is that I can rejoice at the beginning of each new day.

The truth is, however, that sometimes I wake up in a bad mood, like the child at the party. Often I feel like I have some pretty good reasons for my dark mood. So what do I do then? That's when I am reminded that to rejoice is an act of faith. I find God's word rebuking me and correcting my thoughts. Like a child that needs to be disciplined or trained, I too need to be disciplined. The correction of my thinking causes me to recognize that I can rejoice and be glad because I can trust the one who made this day.

O Lord, You know that I tend by nature to more negative than positive. Thank You for giving me Your word that day by day points me in the right direction. Today I will look for You and the good things You have provided. I choose to rejoice and be glad in this day because I trust the one who made this day.

Habitual Thanksgiving

I read something yesterday morning that stayed with me. I read about Daniel in the lions' den. Such a familiar story, but this time something caught my attention that I hadn't noticed before. The men who were jealous of Daniel set a trap for him involving his prayer life: that if anyone prayed to any god or man other than the king for 30 days he would be thrown into the lion's den.

"Now when Daniel learned that the decree had been published, he went home to his upstairs room where the windows opened toward Jerusalem. Three times a day he got down on his knees and prayed, giving thanks to his God, just as he had done before" (Dan. 6:10 NIV). What got my attention was the content of his prayer. He gave thanks three times a day. He was giving thanks even though he knew the decree had been published and it could cost him his life.

By this time in history Daniel is an old man. He is an old man, yet three times a day he got down on his knees to pray to give thanks to his God. I know that scripture is given to teach, rebuke, correct and train in righteousness, and this picture of Daniel as an old man on his knees praying and thanking God at the risk of his life does all of that.

Ever since I was a child and I first heard the story of Daniel I saw him as a quiet man. I saw him as a quiet man in the midst of turmoil. Every time I read his story I saw him as one who experienced peace no matter what situation he was put in. When I thought about how he humbled himself and prayed with thanksgiving, I understood where the peace came from.

Lord, I want to learn this lesson from Daniel. I want my life to be marked by humility toward you. I also want to pray with thanksgiving three times a day. I have been around people who habitually complain and I don't want to be one of them. Lord, please let my life be marked by habitual thanksgiving.

Choices

I see a question being asked throughout the Scriptures. It began in the Garden and continues throughout every generation. How this question in answered determines much about how we live our lives. The question was first posed by God's enemy to Eve, and yet I think everyone who has ever lived has had to decide how to answer it. The question is, "Does God really have your best interest at heart, and can you trust Him?"

When God delivered the children of Israel from Egypt with a mighty hand and an outstretched arm, there was a problem. The problem was they didn't really trust Him. They were delivered from slavery and promised a land of their own, but on the way to that Promised Land they had to go through a wilderness. In the wilderness they murmured and complained. They murmured and complained because they didn't really believe that God had their best interest at heart; nor did they believe that they could trust Him.

Daniel was in captivity. His enemies were looking for a fault in him, a way to bring a complaint against him to the king. And the only thing they could find was his devotion to God. They appealed to the king's pride: that if anyone made a petition to a god or man other than the king for 30 days he would be thrown into the lions' den. But Daniel believed that God had his best interest at heart, and he believed that he could trust him. So he continued to go to his upper chamber to kneel and pray with thanksgiving towards Jerusalem. He was praying towards Jerusalem even though it had been destroyed by Nebuchadnezzar. His prayers were marked by thanksgiving and not by murmuring and complaining because he was trusting in what he believed about God and not what he was experiencing.

I asked my friend to choose one word to describe Daniel. After a short pause she said, "Steadfast." I thought about that, and then I thought about James 1:2-4: "Count it all joy, my brothers, when you meet trails of various kinds, for you know that the testing of your faith produces steadfastness. And let steadfastness have its full effect, that you may be perfect and complete, lacking nothing." Daniel was firmly loyal and constant in his belief that God is good and he could trust Him. His unshakable faith caused him to offer prayers of thanksgiving, just as the children of Israel's doubt of God's goodness caused them to murmur and complain when their faith was tested.

Father, Your word is filled with stories of how You have shown Yourself faithful in the lives of Your people. Long ago I learned that faith comes by hearing and hearing by the word of God. Thank You for letting me see Your faithfulness in the lives of others. But thank You also that when I face trials I am being invited to see Your faithfulness firsthand in my own life.

The Gift

I don't know who that gift was for. Maybe it was just part of my mother's decorating scheme. Mother kept a beautifully wrapped gift on the dresser of the guest bedroom. Whenever I came to spend the night with her I would look at that wrapped gift and smile. I think of hope like a beautifully wrapped gift. Hope is the confident expectation of good.

The joy in gift giving is not only for the one who receives the gift but for the one who gives it. I was with my sisters this weekend, and I had chosen birthday gifts for two of them. I delighted in watching as my sisters open their presents. I saw my pleasure reflected in what I read this morning: "The Lord delights in those who fear him, who put their hope in his unfailing love" (Psa. 147:11 NIV). What a gift! Unfailing love that is given to me even when I fail.

In the book of Romans it talks about "rejoicing in hope." This kind of rejoicing happens because, no matter what I may be experiencing at the time, I know that this hope I have in the unfailing love of God will not put me to shame. In fact, even now God's love has been poured into my heart through the Holy Spirit, and the Holy Spirit is only a taste of what is to come.

There is not only joy that comes as I live my life aware of this beautifully wrapped gift, there is also peace. "May the God of hope fill you with all joy and peace in believing, so that by the power of the Holy Spirit you may abound in hope" (Rom. 15:13 ESV). This peace and joy gives me not only hope for the future but courage and strength to face the challenges I meet each day.

Dear Heavenly Father, You have filled my life with gifts I did not earn and that I do not deserve. Please help me be someone who delights you by putting my hope in Your unfailing love. As You pour out Your love into my heart through Your Holy Spirit, help me live this day with courage, empowered by the gift of Your love.

Standing in the Courts of Heaven

"Use your imagination and see yourself sitting in a room full of people. Everyone has gathered to listen to your deepest darkest secrets exposed. There is no place for you to hide; there is nothing you can do but lower your eyes as all eyes focus knowingly on you." This is how my daughter began her creative Bible Study class. Her assignment had been to choose a group of people where she would bring the message of hope. Because she was ministering at a local jail, she chose them as her audience. When she described the courtroom I was reminded of a scene from Heaven I'd read about.

My friend stood before me with her eyes cast down. "Please pray for me," she said. She was being smothered by a mantle of guilt. She told me how she wanted to be free but that she just couldn't get past her crippling sense of guilt. I shared a scene from Heaven with her and asked if it sounded familiar.

"Then he showed me Joshua the high priest standing before the angel of the Lord, and Satan standing at his right hand to accuse him. And the Lord said to Satan, 'The Lord rebuke you, O Satan! The Lord who has chosen Jerusalem rebuke you! Is not this a brand plucked from the fire?'

Now Joshua was standing before the angel, clothed in filthy garments. And the angel said to those who were standing before him, 'Remove the filthy garments from him.' And to him he said, 'Behold, I have taken your iniquity away from you, and I will clothe you with pure vestments'" (Zech. 3:1-5 ESV).

I have felt the crippling effects of guilt. Sometimes it has even felt noble to focus on my guilt. Yet, when I look at this picture of Satan standing on one side accusing and the angel of the Lord pronouncing that the iniquity has been removed, I get another picture. This is a picture of what Jesus did for me. Even though Jesus has pronounced me pure, Satan still retains his role as accuser. The question is, to whom do I listen?

Father, because Jesus took the punishment that I deserved I have been like a brand plucked from the fire. Jesus wore the robe of flesh so that I could wear a robe of righteousness. Please help me to walk in this truth and honor You. Please help me not to honor the accuser by letting him cover me with the filthy garments that You removed.

"Made Strong Out of Weakness"

I don't remember waking up; I just know I wasn't sleeping. Parading through my mind was a long list of things that needed to be done, and lying there only half conscience I felt defeated. Finally I drifted off to sleep, but when I woke up I was reminded of the command given to Joshua, "Be strong and very courageous." I woke up thinking about the connection between faith and action.

Faith that is real invokes action. What that means to me is that instead of standing still dreading the tasks that are before me because I feel inadequate, I move towards them, believing that if God has given me the task He will provide the means to do it. Joshua was told seven times to be strong and courageous. He had seen the Promised Land, but he had also seen the giants and the walled cities. If my faith is real it means that I have the same strength and courage available to me that was available to Joshua.

Joshua remembered what he had seen when he spied out the land 40 years earlier. It would have been natural to be afraid or terrified— except that God promised to go with him. He promised that He would never leave Joshua or forsake him. When I was tossing and turning in my bed last night all I could see was how inadequate I was for the tasks that awaited me. When I woke up I was reminded that, like Joshua, God has also promised me that I am not alone.

Since I was thinking about how faith and actions fit together I looked up Hebrews 11. I reviewed again how people who had put their faith in God had responded to the challenges they faced. What I saw in each life was courage and strength. I saw people of action and then I saw that they were "made strong out of weakness."

Father, thank You for reminding me again that I never have to be afraid of the jobs that seem impossible for me to do, because You've promised that if You called me to do it You'll equip me as well. Thank You for the encouragement I find in seeing Your faithfulness to those who trust You. Please let my life be an encouragement to others as I choose to trust You. Please let Your strength be seen in my weakness.

"What do You Want?"

When I was a little girl and I first heard about how God had told Solomon that he could ask for anything he wanted and it would be granted to him, I began to wonder what I would ask for if God told me that. Even today I can imagine myself standing like Isaiah in the courts of Heaven and seeing the Lord high and lifted up on a golden throne and the train of His robe filling the temple. I see Him as Daniel described Him, as the Ancient of Days with His clothing white as snow, His throne like fiery flames. The book of Revelation says that His throne is encircled with a rainbow. I have heard His voice described as the sound of a mighty rushing wind, a mighty voice. In Revelation His voice is described as the sound of mighty waters, but Elijah heard Him as a still small voice. Now, with all this in mind, I approach the one who sits on this throne of glory with my request and I am in too much awe to say a word.

There is another story of someone to whom it was said, "What do you want me to do for you?" (Mark 10:51). Unlike King Solomon this man had not just finished building a grand temple. In fact, this man was simply a blind beggar. When Jesus asked this blind beggar named Bartimaeus, "What do you want me to do for you?" he answered, "Rabbi, I want to see." When Jesus opened his eyes, I wonder what he really saw.

I wonder if, when this blind man opened his eyes, he saw, "the image of the invisible God, the firstborn of all creation. For by him all things were created, in heaven and on earth, visible and invisible, whether thrones or dominions or rulers or authorities—all things were created through him and for him. And he is before all things, and in him all things hold together. And he is the head of the body, the church. He is the beginning, the firstborn from the dead, that in everything he might be preeminent. For in him all the fullness of God was pleased to dwell..." (Col. 1:15-20 ESV). What I do know from reading his story in the book of Mark is that Bartimaeus received his sight and followed Jesus.

I have discovered through reading the Scriptures that the same God who invited Solomon to ask something of Him has given me this same invitation! The prayer that I bring mirrors both Solomon's request and Bartimaeus'. This is what I'm asking for, "that the God of our Lord Jesus Christ, the Father of glory, may give *me* a spirit of wisdom and of revelation in knowledge of him, having the eyes of *my* heart enlightened, that *I* may know what is the hope to which he has called *me,* what are the riches of his glorious inheritance in the saints, and what is the immeasurable greatness of his power toward *me* who believes, according to the working of his great might..." (taken from Eph. 1:17-23 ESV).

Father, in the book of James You said that I didn't have because I didn't ask. Now I have made my request and I am also thanking you for giving me what I have asked of You. Because You promised that if I asked anything according to Your word I could be assured I would receive what I asked for.

"I have loved you," says the Lord

"I have loved you," says the Lord. "But you ask, 'How have you loved us?'" These are the words I began my day with yesterday, out of first chapter of Malachi. I was still thinking about them when my husband invited me to go with him for a ride in the mountains.

Steve had taken the windows off the Jeep so I could see the colors of the leaves, feel the wind and smell the fall air. "I have loved you," says the Lord. Thinking about these words in Malachi I began to pray a prayer I often pray: "Lord, please help me to look until I can see; touch until I can feel; listen until I can understand."

"But you ask, 'How have you loved us?'" This question that follows God pronouncement of His love I think began in the Garden, when sin caused a veil to be placed over the eyes of the first man and woman who chose to believe the lie that God wasn't really good and He didn't really love them and He could not be trusted. The taste of the fruit of disobedience was the beginning of the loss of ability to be satisfied with the taste of what was good. They could no longer enjoy the fragrance of worship.

"I have loved you," says the Lord. "But you ask, 'How have you loved us?" It is a humbling thing to believe that I am loved. If I receive a gift I want to be somehow be worthy of it. But to receive this gift of love from the Lord means I take my eyes off myself and I begin to see Him. Being in the mountains, experiencing the beauty of autumn with all my senses, I acknowledge God's love for me and respond with the worship of a grateful heart.

O Lord, so many times I read in Your word that You love me. Please fill my heart with grateful wonder so that I can enjoy the gifts that surround me. In the receiving of Your love let me give to You the gift of worship.

Waiting...

This has been a month of waiting for me. The kind of waiting that you do when you go from one doctor to another and then wait for the results of all the tests. During this waiting what I believe or don't believe can come to the surface. Fears can bubble up in the night and ask the haunting question, "What if...?"

I am also experiencing another kind of waiting. It's the kind of waiting

Isaiah 40 talks about. This is the waiting that is done when you savor the promises of God. This is the waiting that is done with confidence and expectation that God is real and His promises are true. This is the waiting that Isaiah says will cause you to mount up on wings like eagles. This kind of waiting causes me to wake up and gaze at the stars, believing that the one who created them can hear me when I cry.

To be honest, I am experiencing both kinds of waiting at the same time. It's like having a wrestling match going on inside my head. I want to be honest and real and deal with life in an honest and real way. I think my wrestling is a reflection of what Jacob did. He wrestled with the angel all night after he heard that Esau and 400 men were coming toward him. On one hand he knew God had told him to return home; on the other hand he knew when he left home his brother had threatened to kill him. In the real world, wrestling is part of life.

Both kinds of waiting are real; the wrestling is real; and in the process I become real. There is something else that is happening as I wait upon the Lord, bringing my concerns to Him, remembering His promises as my mind meditates on Him in the watches of the night. My heart begins to soar. As I stretch out and spread my wings of faith I find myself being lifted and soaring on the promises I believe. Carried by the winds of the Holy Spirit my soul finds its rest in Him.

Father, thank you for inviting me to know the wonder of trusting You. May it be that as I learn to stretch out and reach towards You in faith my strength will be renewed. I want to be real and I want to "mount up with wings like eagles" (Isa. 40:31).

"Come now, and let us reason together."

The phone rang in the middle of the night and jolted me awake. It didn't take long for me to realize what kind of phone call this was. Suddenly, out of my mouth came words my Grandmother had had me memorize many, many years before. "Come now, and let us reason together, saith the Lord: though your sins be as scarlet, they shall be as white as snow; though they be red like crimson, they shall be as wool" (Isa. 1:18 KJV). Before he could respond I added, "All we like sheep have gone astray;

we have turned every one to his own way; and the Lord has laid on him the iniquity of us all" (Isa. 53:6 KJV). There was silence and then he said, "Please tell me those things again." After I repeated the verses a second time he said quietly, "Thank you," and hung up. "You shall know the truth and the truth shall set you free" (John 8:32 KJV).

"Did Mommy tell you what happened last night?" There was a haunted look in his eyes. I assured him I had heard nothing, and we went about having a good time together, reading the next chapter in our book, planting a tree in the back yard. Then it was bed time and we were having the kind of quiet talk that happens at twilight when he asked me again, "Are you sure you don't know what happened last night?" "Why, don't you tell me," I said. His heart and voice broke at the same time as he told me about the burden of guilt he was carrying. I told him what my Grandmother had told me: "We've all done wrong. Every one of us has messed up, that's why Jesus came." I told him about my struggle with guilt. "We have both an Accuser and a Savior. Which one are you going to pay attention to?" He gave me a sweet little boy hug and said, "Thank you, Mimi." "You will know the truth and the truth will set you free" (John 8:32).

What is the truth that sets us free? I think about what John the Baptist said when he saw Jesus coming toward him. "Behold, the Lamb of God, who takes away the sin of the world!" (John 1:29 ESV). From the very beginning of His ministry Jesus was identified as the one who had come bear our griefs and carry our sorrows. "He was wounded for our transgressions; he was crushed for our inquiries; upon him was the chastisement that brought us peace, and with his strips we are healed. All we like sheep have gone astray; we have turned—everyone—to his own way; and the Lord has laid on him the iniquity of us all" (Isa. 53:5-6 ESV). I believe knowing this truth sets the prisoner free from guilt and shame.

The Accuser, however, is always at hand to draw attention away from the Truth that brings freedom so that my focus will not be on the one who has come to take away my sins, but instead my attention will be on my sins. "Do you think you can be free from your failure? Just look at what you've done! You are guilty!" This also is true; I am guilty. What am I to do? Again the words my Grandmother taught me so many years ago return. "Come now, and let us reason together, saith the Lord: though your sins be as scarlet, they shall be as white as snow; though they be red like crimson, they shall be as wool." This Truth brings with it both peace and freedom.

Lord Jesus, the truth is I have sinned. I have not only failed to do the good I wanted to do, I have also done the wrong things I didn't want to do. I hear and feel the condemnation of the Accuser. I would be at his mercy except I, like John, have seen and known the Lamb of God who has come to take away my sins. I hear both the voices of the Accuser and of the Savior. I choose to listen to Your voice, Jesus. I choose to base my life on the Truth that You are the Lamb of God who has taken away my sins.

Soul Surgery

"All Scripture is God-breathed and is useful for teaching, rebuking, correcting and training in righteousness" (2 Tim. 3:16 NIV).
I experienced the truth of this verse when I decided I would memorize 1 Corinthians 13 in several versions at the same time.

I've heard people ask the question, "Does anyone really know what *love* means?" Well, I think God gives a good definition in His word. When I started my memorization project I began with, "Love is patient and kind" I couldn't get much farther than that because I found God's word not only teaching me what love is, but I also felt rebuked because of my lack of patience and kindness. The fact that I was homeschooling my four children at the time brought my lack into clear view. So I began to pray that God would also correct my lack of patience and kindness.

"For the word of God is living and active, sharper than any two-edged sword, piercing to the division of soul and of spirit, of joints and of marrow, and discerning the thoughts and intentions of the heart" (Heb. 4:12 ESV). As I continued memorizing, I came to the part that said, "love does not boast, it is not proud." Since I was memorizing this in several versions simultaneously this is what was in my mind, "love is not arrogant, it's not puffed up, it doesn't brag, it's not conceited, and doesn't sing its own praise." The sword hit its mark. I hit my knees and prayed, "Lord, have mercy on me, a sinner. I am everything love is not! Lord, please take Your word and do surgery on my soul."

I also decided that any time I got into a fight with my husband I would think through what these verses had to say about love and apply them to myself. Again I was convicted by the words "love is not irritable or resentful, not easily angered, it keeps no record of wrong, it doesn't seek its own, it takes no account of evil." I can only say how grateful I am for Isaiah 55:11 "So shall my word be that goes out from my mouth;... it shall accomplish that which I purpose, and shall succeed in the thing for which I sent it." I am so grateful that God's word not only brings with it conviction but it also brings with it the gift of repentance.

Lord, thank You for the gift of Your word. As I memorize what love is I am always reminded that at the heart of the definition is the truth that "God is love." As I meditate on Your word, please do soul surgery so that I can represent You better.

The True Artist

"The earth was without form and void, and darkness was over the face of the deep. And the Spirit of God was hovering over the face of the waters" (Gen. 1:2 ESV). I think that the first artist, the true artist, is the Spirit of God. I think it's interesting that the first place He chose to display His creative spirit was in a place that was, "without form and void," a place where there was darkness.

I see this same Spirit at work with the backdrop of the wilderness when God announced that He wanted His people to build a sanctuary for Him. How could this be done in a wilderness, with a people who have just come out of slavery? "I have called by name Bezalel, son of Uri, the son of Hur, of the tribe of Judah. I have filled him with the Spirit of God in wisdom, in understanding, in knowledge, and in all kinds of craftsmanship, to make artistic designs for work in gold, in silver, and in bronze, and in the cutting of stones for settings, and in the carving of wood, that he may work in all kinds of craftsmanship" (Ex. 31:2-5 NASB) In the wilderness the Spirit of God entered into a man so that he could provide a place for God to dwell among His people.

This sanctuary was a copy and shadow of what is in heaven according to the book of Hebrews. The man chosen to be the artist was Bezalel. His name means "in the shadow of God." This is what I see: the Spirit of God overshadowed him and he became saturated with creative skill. I think it's also interesting that he was from the tribe of Judah. That can be translated *let God be praised*, the same tribe as King Solomon who built a temple for God.

When I think about how Bezalel, an artist, was filled with the Holy Spirit in order to artistically create a dwelling place for God, my mind is drawn to 1 Corinthians 6:19-20, "Do you not know that your body is a temple of the Holy Spirit within you, whom you have from God? You are not your own, for you were bought with a price. So glorify God in your body" In a world filled with profanity, where there is contempt or irreverence for what is sacred, the Holy Spirit has chosen to dwell within His people so that we can glorify God.

Heavenly Father, Your Spirit is the only true artist. Please change me, remake me, conform me into the image of Your son. Please show me how to glorify You through the power of Your Holy Spirit as I walk through my own wilderness.

Lights on the Runway

I'm looking out the window at a scramble of blue lights. I see no pattern; I have no understanding about how this works. I can see, hear and feel the plane aiming toward those lights, but this is something that is not in my control. I am the passenger and not the pilot. Panic or peace is determined by my trust or lack of trust in the one who pilots the plane.

This is very descriptive of how I feel right now. There is so much happening in my life, and to be honest it's overwhelming. When I think about all the things that have taken place in my life over the last few months I feel like a passenger in a plane descending at a great speed toward the flickering lights of a runway at night. The feeling is one of not being in control; the question is, "How shall I respond to those feelings?"

"O Lord, my heart is not lifted up; my eyes are not raised too high; I do not occupy myself with things too great and too marvelous for me" (Psa. 131:1 ESV). The truth is I don't understand everything that's going on in my life right now, any more than I understand how to safely land an airplane at night on the runway. Morning by morning I make the choice to trust the one who navigates my life. I choose to walk humbly believing that what is not known to me is known to Him.

"But I have calmed and quieted my soul, like a weaned child with its mother; like a weaned child is my soul within me. O Israel, hope in the Lord from this time forth and forevermore" (Psa. 131:2-3 ESV). This is such a picture of comfort and trust. A child that has been weaned is a child that has experienced the comfort of its mother and is willing to be quieted and calmed by her presence. This is also a picture of hope, the confident expectation of good. Like one who sits as a passenger looking out at the flickering blue lights on the runway anticipating a safe landing.

Heavenly Father, I am confused by all that is happening in my life right now but I truth You. Please help me to calm and quiet my soul as I choose to put my hope in You.

It All Depends on Who You Listen To

It was the spirit of intimidation. The Jews had come back from captivity, but what faced them was a broken-down wall and the remains of what once had been a powerful city. It had been destroyed because of their sin. Now they were trying to rebuild. Sanballat heard about what they were doing and surrounded them with jeering taunts, "What are these feeble Jews doing?... Will they revive the stones out of the heaps of rubbish, burned ones at that?" Tobiah the Ammonite joined in the taunt saying, "Yes, what they are building—if a fox goes up on it he will break down their stone wall" (Neh. 4:2-3 ESV). The intimidation was to break the people and produce the fear of failure.

It was the spirit of conviction. The Jews had gathered together to hear the Book of the Law of Moses that the Lord had commanded Israel. They not only read it clearly, the priest gave it sense; and when the people understood they bowed their heads with their faces to the ground. Their hearts were grieved because they understood at last the depth of their sin. When they at last understood what God's word said they were filled with the fear of the Lord. The spirit of conviction broke their hearts and produced a spirit of worship.

The spirit of intimidation versus the spirit of conviction; one produces the fear of failure, the other produces the fear of God. With intimidation comes discouragement; with conviction comes courage. Intimidation points out my faults and failure; conviction points me toward God's holiness. Both produce a form of brokenness.

"For thus says the One who is high and lifted up, who inhabits eternity, whose name is Holy: 'I dwell in the high and holy place, and also with him who is of a contrite and lowly spirit, to revive the spirit of the lowly, and to revive the heart of the contrite" (Isa. 57:15 ESV). This is what happened when the people were convicted of their sin and the fear of God fell on them and they bowed to worship. The next verse is a verse of encouragement, "Do not be grieved, for the joy of the Lord is your strength" (Neh. 8:10 ESV). Conviction opens the door to experience repentance Repentance opens the door for the Savior.

Father, sometimes I hear both the spirit of intimidation and conviction at the same time. Let my fear be the fear of God that brings with it wisdom. Thank You that You dwell with those who have a contrite and lowly spirit. In Your presence there is joy and strength.

Don't Try

Try to be strong and very courageous. *Try* to give thanks to the Lord. *Try* to rejoice in the Lord; I will say it again, *try*. Something is wrong with these sentences. I added a word that I realize I sometimes add without thinking.

When I add the word *try* to something God's word says *do*, it gives me the option of success or failure. I can try to be strong and very courageous, but I can't promise anything. I can try to give thanks in the Lord, but I'm not sure I will. I can try to rejoice in the Lord, but let me say it again, I'm only trying.

Isn't it only reasonable to add the word *try* to these verse? Wouldn't it be foolish to "be strong and very courageous" if you don't know what's coming your way? Shouldn't 1 Thessalonians 5:18 read, *"Try* to give thanks in all circumstances; for this is the will of God in Christ Jesus for you." Difficult things happen, so wouldn't it be more reasonable to say, "*Try* to rejoice in the Lord always; again I will say *Try!*

When I add the word *try* to these verses what I am saying is that I am relying on my own strength to accomplish these things. However, what I see in the Scripture is, "Not by might, nor by power, but by my Spirit, says the Lord of hosts" (Zech. 4:6 ESV). How can I be strong and very courageous? How can I give thanks in all circumstances? How can I rejoice in the Lord? I can do these things, not because I am trying, but because I am trusting in the Spirit of the Lord of hosts!

Father, thank You that with the command You also gave Your Spirit. Thank You for allowing me in my weakness to experience Your Strength. Thank You for Your invitation to rejoice, give thanks and know Your strength and courage, not by trying, but by trusting Your Spirit.

The Choice is Mine to Make

I have been going through a season of major to mild irritations, grieving the loss of people who are dear to me, dealing with health issues, facing change, change and more change. Every morning I wake up and make a decision of how I choose to respond to the challenges of that day. I make my decision before I get out of bed. Before my feet touch the floor I make my declaration, "This is the day that the Lord has made; I will rejoice and be glad in it" (Psa. 118:24).

My decision to rejoice, however, does not eliminate the battle. I have to choose over and over to take every thought captive; because if I don't I begin to feel myself becoming captive to negative thoughts. Although I have a freedom that was purchased with the blood of Jesus Christ, still I must choose daily to walk in that truth.

A man is slave to whatever has mastered him (2 Pet. 2:19). Bombarded by negative thoughts, if I allow them to dictate how I respond to the challenges I face then they will be my master. But I don't have to be their slave. I can choose to be free from the crippling influence of negative thoughts because of the salvation I have received through faith in Jesus Christ.

The real question is, how shall I represent Jesus Christ to a broken world? I am a broken person who lives in a broken world and yet according to 1 Corinthians 3:16 I am also God's temple, and God's Spirit lives in me. My spiritual act of worship morning by morning is to offer my body as a living sacrifice, choosing each day to rejoice and give thanks in the power of the Holy Spirit, taking every thought captive to the obedience of Jesus Christ.

The Wedding Band

My grandmother asked me to bring her her wedding band. She had given it to me for safe keeping when she went to the hospital. When I looked for it, it was nowhere to be found. I was a child deeply aware of my need, so after I looked everywhere I knew to look, I dropped to my knees and prayed.

It was an unsophisticated prayer. It had two elements to it: one, I was aware of my great need; and secondly, I believed I was praying to a God who loved me and was able to answer my prayer. I dropped to my knees and cried with all my heart, "Father, help me!" I opened my eyes and there, tucked in the folds of my grandmother's comforter, was the wedding band.

Many years have passed and many prayers have been said since that day long ago. As I grew up my prayers became more mature. There have been seasons in my life when I didn't feel the great urgency to pray. There have been times when things have been going well and I have felt quite capable of navigating my life.

But then that bubble of self sufficiency bursts. I find myself like a child crying out, "Father, help me!" Again I am aware of two basic facts: my great need, and that I have a great God who loves me. The answers to my prayers are not always as tangible as when I found my grandmother's wedding band, but it is the same peace that invades my heart, mind and soul now as it was when I was a child.

Heavenly Father, thank You that You hear my prayers even if I don't know exactly the right words to say. Thank You for deciding in advance to adopt me into Your own family through Jesus Christ. Thank You for Your peace that passes all understanding.

The Answer

There was something I wanted to say, but I wasn't sure if I should speak or keep silent. I was in France for my nephew Guillaume's wedding. I wanted to share with Guillaume and Amandine something that had profoundly affected my life and my marriage, but I just wasn't sure when or how or if I should do it, so I prayed.

"If any of you lacks wisdom, let him ask God, who gives generously to all without reproach, and it will be given him" (James 1:5 ESV). Part of my lack of wisdom was that I wasn't sure of my motives: was I just wanting to call attention to myself? I also didn't want to be preachy. The truth is, I don't even have the wisdom to understand myself. But I do know a God who has promised to give me the wisdom that I lack, and so I prayed.

On the eve of the wedding I received the answer to my prayer when Guillaume told me he had something he wanted me to say at his wedding. He asked me to read 1 Corinthians 13. It was the same passage I had been praying about sharing with him. Years ago I had memorized this passage in several translations. I began the practice of saying it to myself at different times throughout the day. I felt it was a gift God had given me, and I wanted to pass it on to my nephew and his bride.

I know that "all Scripture is God- breathed" (2 Tim. 3:16), and when I stood to speak I could feel the breath of God. So many people are confused about what love is. When I shared that day I shared not only words but how the power of the Holy Spirit, through Scripture, teaches me what is true, corrects me when I am wrong, and guides me to do what is right.

Lord Jesus, when I'm confused and I don't know what to do, Your Word invites me to ask, with the promise that You are listening. When I am lacking the ability to love, I go to Your Word and Your Spirit speaks to me, teaching , rebuking, correcting and guiding me.

The Gift That Brought Me to My Knees

A gift; an amazing gift that opened my world, that opened my heart, that brought me to my knees. This gift came without instructions, so how was I supposed to decipher what each cry meant? I may not have known what to do, but at least I knew where to find wisdom. The gift of children taught me to appreciate the gift of prayer.

People were bringing little children to Jesus to have Him touch them (Mark 10:13). More than anything in the world I wanted to bring my children to Jesus. I wanted Him to touch them, to open their eyes so they could see the world through eyes of faith. As a mother, my highest goal with my little children was to bring them to Jesus; my deepest prayer was for Him to touch them.

It doesn't take long for a baby to become a little child and a little child to grow into an independent youth. When my little children became youths they discovered that I was not omniscient. At that time in their life I wanted to be all-knowing! I wanted to have a correct answer to all their questions. I wanted to wisely guide them in the decisions they had to make, decisions that would put them on the right path. My children are a gift from God, a gift that makes me want to be more than I am, a gift that brings me to my knees, holding them up to Jesus before the throne. Before the throne I ask the One who is omniscient to guide their steps and to bless them.

The sun rises and the sun sets, and before I know it my house is very quiet. Yet in my heart I hear the echo of their voices. Each voice, each memory is a treasure that is mine to keep. My position is no longer that of authority, it has now changed to that of counselor. I remind myself daily not to be anxious for these children who carry my heart with them wherever they go, but instead to carry them constantly before the throne of God. I carry each one before the throne of mercy with prayers, with supplications and, yes, always, with thanksgiving. I pray with thanksgiving because I know Jesus never turned away the mothers who brought their children to Him.

Oh, Father, what an amazing gift You gave me when You gave me children. They have taught me about love in ways that have humbled me and brought me continually to my knees. When they were young I would place my hands on their heads and pray for them but now they have grown and gone. Still I bring my children to You, Lord Jesus, I know

Your hands can reach them when mine cannot, and I know You hear a mother's prayer for the blessing of her children.

For Everything There is a Season

I knew eventually I was going to have to begin the painful process of letting go. I wanted to hold on to things that were familiar, things that carried with them memories of a time that was now over. Sometimes it's hard to sort through the things that people leave behind, especially if the people are people you have loved dearly and miss terribly. Yet the truth is that in order to move forward in life I know I must be willing to accept change.

Seasons bring with them an understanding of change. Time does not stand still and there is a time for every matter under heaven. According to Solomon God has made everything beautiful in its time. But I also believe that if I am to understand the beauty of all things I must also accept that God has placed eternity into the hearts of every man, even though I do not understand what God has done from the beginning to the end.

How can I find peace in this ever-changing world? In order for me to find peace and stability, I find I must anchor my hope in something that doesn't change. "The steadfast love of the Lord never ceases; his mercies never come to an end; they are new every morning; great is your faithfulness. 'The Lord is my portion,' says my soul. 'therefore I will hope in him'" (Lam. 3:22-24 ESV).

Because the steadfast love of the Lord never ceases, and because I believe in the God of eternity who has loved the world so much that He gave His only Son, that whoever believes in him should not perish but have eternal life, I can accept that there is:

a time to be born, and a time to die;
a time to plant, and a time to pluck up what is planted;
a time to kill, and a time to heal;
a time to break down, and a time to build up;
a time to weep, and a time to laugh;
a time to mourn and a time to dance;

a time to cast away stones, and a time to gather stones together;
a time to embrace, and a time to refrain from embracing;
a time to seek, and a time to lose;
a time to keep, and a time to cast away;
a time to keep silent, and a time to speak;
a time to love, and a time to hate;
a time for war, and a time for peace (Eccl. 3:1-8).

O Lord, I believe Your word, that everything is beautiful in its time. But some seasons are harder that others! Grant me the wisdom to know what season I am in and the courage to do what that season requires.

"NO! I Don't Want That!"

"No thank you, I don't think I want that." There are lots of qualities in the Scripture that I want, but there is one that never appealed to me, never. Every time I read about it there was something in me that would recoil. It reminded me of the story of children who would wake up on Christmas morning and find coal in their Christmas stocking. The coal was a cruel joke, NOT a gift!

Coal is black and dirty. However, when coal is subjected to high temperatures and incredible pressure over a very long period of time, a diamond is born. The beauty of a diamond is found in its relationship to light. When light hits a diamond there is a dazzling dance and it refracts that light into all the colors of the rainbow.

Now, I understand better the gift that God has been offering me all these years. The problem is that I have been viewing this gift with my flesh and not the Spirit. Whenever I look at this gift through my flesh it appears like a dirty black lump of coal. But because God has given me His Holy Spirit, I am now beginning to recognize the diamond instead. I am beginning to understand that what is being offered to me is a gift. Through this gift God can shine His love into my life so that those around me can be bathed in all the colors of the rainbow, the very colors that surround His throne in Heaven. Through this beautiful gift God is inviting me to be part of something that is so much greater than I am. He is inviting me to reflect His glory.

I have been blessed to see God's light reflected in the lives of others as they humbly received this gift from God. I have seen it displayed in a mother whose eyes have been repeatedly washed by tears, and yet she refused to stop loving and believing in her child. I was privileged to overhear the words of love spoken by a husband to his wife as she lay dying. He held her hand and willing entered into her suffering by his love. And I saw a rainbow.

Heavenly Father, Your word has taught me that love suffers long and is kind. Your word has taught me that long suffering is a fruit of Your Holy Spirit. You, Father, are gracious and full of compassion, slow to anger and great in mercy. I understand now that You have invited me, by the power of Your Holy Spirit, to represent Your love to a hurting, broken world through being long suffering. Thank You for being long suffering with me and please, please let my life be more like a diamond than coal. And let the rainbow of hope be seen in me through Your light.

The Prince of Darkness vs. The Prince of Peace

It may have seemed he was alone, but he wasn't. Unseen by human eyes the Prince of Darkness taunted him with questions and accusations that were aimed to cause confusion and doubt. "You were so sure of yourself when you proclaimed to all that you were the voice of one calling in the desert to make straight the way of the Lord. So where is he now? You were making a way for him, why doesn't he make a way for you to be released from this dungeon, if he really is the Messiah, the Lamb of God, who takes away the sins of the world? You testified that this Jesus is the Son of God, so why are you in prison?"

He sent two of his disciples to Jesus with this question, "Are you the one who is to come, or should we expect someone else?" He was humble enough to admit he may have made a mistake. Jesus responded by continuing to cure those who were diseased, casting out evil spirits, and giving sight to many who were blind. Then He said to the messengers, "Go back and report to John what you have seen and heard: The blind receive sight, the lame walk, those who have leprosy are cleansed, the deaf hear, the dead are raised, and the good news is preached to the poor. Blessed is anyone who does not stumble on account of me" (Luke 7:18-23 NIV).

John could understand the message that Jesus was sending him, because John was well versed in Scripture. Jesus was quoting from Isaiah 35. It also says, "Strengthen the weak hands, and make firm the feeble knees. Say to those who have an anxious heart, 'Be strong; fear not! Behold, your God…. He will come and save you. Then the eyes of the blind shall be opened, and the ears of the deaf unstopped; then shall the lame man leap like a deer and the tongue of the mute sing for joy" (Isa. 35:3-6 NIV).

Sometimes I feel like John the Baptist and I find myself in situations that don't fit my ideas of how I thought my life as a Christian would be. At times like these I remind myself of what Jesus said the night before He died, "Peace I leave with you; my peace I give to you. Not as the world gives do I give you. Let not your hearts be troubled, neither let them be afraid" (John 14:27 ESV). This peace that I have received by faith in the Prince of Peace silences the voice of the Prince of Darkness. When I put my faith in Him I am sure of what I hope for and confident about what I cannot see. I am blessed because, like John the Baptist, I have chosen to give my allegiance to the Prince of Peace and I will not fall away on account of him.

Lord Jesus, when I am assaulted by the taunts of the enemy, help me to fix my mind on Your words of truth. Your words silence both confusion and doubt. Your peace lifts me up and helps me see the bigger picture. It gives me a view of Your Kingdom where You reign. I want You to reign in my life and bring tranquility to my soul so Your kingdom can be seen in me.

Release

I don't remember exactly when my fingers went numb, but I kept hoping that if I ignored the problem it would go away. I was wrong. I began not only having numbness but difficulty using my hands, particularly my right hand. Then the pain came, waking me up at night. Finally, I went to the doctor and he explained that the median nerve going through the carpal tunnel in my wrist was being compressed. He said it would require surgery where he would cut into the ligament that was pressing on the nerve. He said if I left it untreated the nerve could be permanently damaged, causing weakness, numbness and tingling. His last words to me where, "I recommend you have release surgery."

"See to it that no one fails to obtain the grace of God; that no 'root of bitterness' springs up and causes trouble, and by it many become defiled" (Heb. 12:15 ESV). Bitterness in my spiritual life is like the ligament that is pressing on the nerve leading to my hand, because bitterness can cause me to fail to receive God's grace. Without God's grace flowing freely in my life I'm as useless as a hand in pain that doesn't work.

I had the surgery done a couple of weeks ago. I was unable to cut through my own wrist and then cut through the tendon to release the nerve. However, I did participate. First, I admitted I had a problem. Then I submitted to the surgery. It was done while I was awake. I did not get off the table but stayed there while the surgeon released my nerve.

I find regularly in my spiritual life that roots of bitterness have begun to get a stranglehold on different areas of my life. I don't always deal with them right away; I really want them to just go away. But when the pain and weakness gets to the place where I can't ignore it anymore, I come to the Great Physician for help. My responsibility is to humble myself and accept the discipline He chooses to bring so that I can be healed.

Oh, Heavenly Father, You are the Great Physician. I humbly come to You today and ask that you would examine my heart and show me where bitterness has gained a stranglehold. I submit myself to Your discipline so that I can know full release.

The Story behind the Fading Pictures

There are boxes filled with pictures all over my living room floor. As I look through these pictures I am aware that most of the people I'm looking at are no longer alive; yet when the pictures was taken they were young and vivacious. I think that's why I woke up this morning thinking about these verses: "A voice says, 'Cry!' And I said, 'What shall I cry?' All flesh is grass, and all beauty is like the flower of the field. The grass withers, the flower fades when the breath of the Lord blows on it; surely the people are grass. The grass withers, the flower fades, but the word of our God will stand forever" (Isa. 40:6-8 ESV).

I have counted at least seven places in the Scriptures where it talks about a man's life being like a fleeting shadow or a mere phantom as he goes to and fro. And yet in these same passages I often find God offering comfort. The comfort is found in the contrast between who we are and who God is. In the same chapter of the Bible that I quoted above I find this description of God: "Have you not known? Have you not heard? The Lord is the everlasting God, the Creator of the ends of the earth. He does not faint or grow weary; His understanding is unsearchable" (Isa. 40:28 ESV).

There is another picture that has always filled me with wonder. This same everlasting God, the Creator of the ends of the earth whose understanding is unsearchable, is spoken of in Ephesians. In Ephesians I see a picture of something that took place before the foundation of the world. "Blessed be the God and Father of our Lord Jesus Christ, who has blessed us in Christ with every spiritual blessing in the heavenly places, even as he chose us in him before the foundation of the world, that we should be holy and blameless before him. In love he predestined us for adoption as sons through Jesus Christ, according to the purpose of his will, to the praise of his glorious grace, with which he has blessed us in the Beloved" (Eph. 1:3-6 ESV).

These pictures of people whom I have loved remind me of how fleeting life is. Their life here on earth is now a memory, very much like the flowers that were blooming in my yard yesterday before the frost came last night. However, the word of God that remains forever shows me a much bigger picture. "For God so loved the world, that he gave his only Son, that whoever believes in him should not perish but have eternal life" (John 3:16). When Ma Belle was alive she told me that the only thing she wanted said at her funeral was the message of eternal life. And so these pictures that fill my living room remind me not only of the brevity of life but also of the eternal life promised in God's word to those who believe.

Father, I have been reminded so much lately that my life here on earth is temporary. And yet I am filled with hope when I read in Your Word about the love You have lavished on me. I grieve for those I can now only see in photographs, but I don't grieve like those who have no hope because I believe in the eternal life given through faith in Your Son.

He Can Come Riding on the Wind or Walking on the Water

Storms come in nature and in life. Though this is not an uncommon thing they often take us by surprise and hold us hostage by their power. This has been a very stormy season in my life. Storms are often accompanied by darkness and strong winds that show me clearly that I am not the one in control. "By now it was dark, and Jesus had not yet joined them. A strong wind was blowing and the waters grew rough" (John 6:17-18 NIV). He saw the disciples straining at the oars, because the wind was against them. It was in the midst of this storm that Jesus came to them walking on the water.

Sometimes God uses the storms in my life to humble me. But with the humbling comes a deeper sense of awe and wonder at who He is and the beauty of His power. This takes away the sting of fear and enables me to come to Him not in my own power but by the power of His invitation. "'Lord, if it's you,' Peter replied, 'tell me to come to you on the water.' 'Come,' he said.'" The storms in my life allow me to see more clearly who this God is that I worship. They allow me to cast off my high view of myself and enter into to an awe filled sense of worship.

One of my favorite hymns was written by a man who lived a very stormy life. His name was William Cowper. His life was filled with mental anguish, which included an 18 month stay in an insane asylum and several attempted suicides. While he was in the asylum he began reading the Bible and as a result he humbled himself and accepted Jesus as his Savior. This was a man who knew what it was to struggle in the darkness, sometimes becoming overwhelmed by the winds of deep depression. However, just as Jesus chose Peter to walk on the water God chose William Cowper to give us the words of the hymn "God moves in a Mysterious Way."

> God moves in a mysterious way
> His wonders to perform;
> He plants His footsteps in the sea,

And rides upon the storm.

Deep in unfathomable mines
Of never failing skill
He treasures up His bright designs
And works His sovereign will.

Ye fearful saints, fresh courage take;
The clouds ye so much dread
Are big with mercy and shall break
In blessings on your head.

Judge not the Lord by feeble sense,
But trust Him for His grace;
Behind a frowning providence
He hides a smiling face.

His purposes will ripen fast,
Unfolding every hour;
The bud may have a bitter taste,
But sweet will be the flower.

Blind unbelief is sure to err
And scan His work in vain;
God is His own interpreter,
And He will make it plain.

[William Cowper, *God Moves in a Mysterious Way*, Public domain.]

And so, Lord, I am aware of the darkness, I feel the wind and the rain, but I also hear Your voice saying, "Come!" Because You are Lord of storm as well as Lord of my life, I choose to come.

When Kingdoms Collide

"My kingdom is not of this world" (John 18:36 ESV). A kingdom that is not of this world? Can you imagine how that sounded to Pilate as Jesus stood before him, bound and bloody from a night spent in the court of the high priest? John the Baptist had declared, "Repent, for the kingdom of heaven is at hand" (Matt. 3:2 ESV). For this kingdom and this king John was willing to die; and he did. Pilate, however, when presented with the truth of the kingdom of heaven washed his hands of it.

"To you it has been given to know the secrets of the kingdom of heaven, but to them it has not been given" (Matt. 13:11 ESV). Jesus proclaimed the kingdom, He spoke about it in parables and what had been prophesied came to pass, "I will open my mouth in parables; I will utter what has been hidden since the foundation of the world" (Matt. 13:35, Psa. 78:2 ESV). So the King spoke of His Kingdom, but not everyone who heard the words understood. There was a problem, "For this people's heart has grown dull, and with their ears they can barely hear, and their eyes they have closed" (Matt. 13:15 ESV). The ones who couldn't hear Jesus had not heard John when he cried, "Repent, for the kingdom of heaven is at hand."

Jesus taught us to pray, "Your kingdom come, your will be done on earth as it is in heaven" (Matt. 6:10). I was thinking about this prayer in connection with Paul praying constantly for the Colossians, that they would be filled with the knowledge of God's will in all spiritual wisdom and understanding, "so as to walk in a manner worthy of the Lord, fully pleasing to him, bearing fruit in every good work and increasing in the knowledge of God" (Col. 1:10 ESV). Why should their life look any different from the lives of those around them? It was because, "He has delivered us from the domain of darkness and transferred us to the kingdom of his beloved Son" (Col. 1:13 ESV). If we have been delivered from the kingdom of darkness and we are now saints in light then we should shine as lights in the world. When I pray that God's kingdom comes and His will is done this is part of what I am asking for.

When I read the Scripture I see that what I believe about the kingdom of heaven should make a difference in how I live. When Jesus taught the mysteries of the kingdom of heaven the people whose hearts had grown dull were unable to hear and understand what he was saying. In Colossians Paul tells those who have accepted Christ as their king to put to death whatever belongs to their earthy nature. What I see is that as I grow in a deeper knowledge of the king and His kingdom, I should represent Him more clearly to the world around me.

Father, let Your kingdom come and Your will be done on earth as it is in heaven.

A Backdrop for His Glory

"Don't cry," he said. I knew he wanted to bring comfort, but I also knew my daughter needed to cry. Crying was the right response that night. We were gathered around the bedside of someone we loved, watching her draw her final labored breaths. The tears flowed, the pain was real, and yet we were all searching for where faith and grief intersect.

In times like this prayers are not elaborate. Martha and Mary were watching their brother die. It was a painful vigil. "So the sisters sent word to Jesus, 'Lord, the one you love is sick'" (John 11:3 NIV). When the pain is deep the words are few. Jesus heard; He understood the grief they were experiencing, but He didn't come right away. He had chosen to paint the glory of the resurrection on the canvas of their life.

Suffering the death of someone you love is a very confusing. When grief comes it is like a cloudy day, you know the sun is shining even though you can't see it or feel its warmth. I see this when I read about Jesus' encounter with Martha after her brother's death. She still believed, she just didn't understand. "Jesus said to her, 'I am the resurrection and the life. He who believes in me will live, even though he dies; and everyone who lives and believes in me will never die. Do you believe this?" (John 11:35-36 NASB). She really did believe, but when they got to the tomb and Jesus said to take the stone away, she warned him that after four days the dead body would stink.

Jesus didn't condemn the deep emotional response that death brought. In fact, "Jesus wept." This reminds me of what it said in Isaiah 53 when it describes Jesus as "a man of sorrows, acquainted with grief." Jesus identified with their pain. He heard them when they told Him that their brother was sick. It was on this dark canvas of human suffering that He chose to display the truth of the resurrection.

Lord Jesus, thank You for hearing my prayers, even when my prayer is a simple telling of what I am experiencing. Thank You for understanding my confusion. And please, take my messy life and let it be a backdrop for Your glory.

Seasons Change

My friend and I were hiking in the North Georgia mountains this week. We have been friends for over 30 years, and for over 30 years we have come to these mountains to hike. Year after year we have watched the seasons change. We have grown to appreciate the beauty of each season. Each year we try to go on a hike to celebrate our birthdays; mine is the first day of spring and hers is in the autumn.

Each season has its own particular beauty; each season also has its own difficulties. Our conversation encompasses both of these. We don't walk as fast as we used to, and it's not only because we are getting older. We take more time to stop and admire the way the sun shines through the leaves as we look up through the branches. We admire the soaring birds and appreciate the view from the north rim of the canyon.

We have walked together long enough to have many shared memories. At one time we hiked while caring our babies in backpacks. When our children were young we were constantly trying to point out the glories of the canyon. They, however, were too busy marveling at the rocks and the insects they were discovering to see the bigger picture.

This year our conversation was about the season of life we were in. Because I was talking to my friend I was able to be honest and say this has been a hard year. Yet, I'm not willing to say it's been a bad year any more than I'd be willing to say there is a bad season. My mind keeps going back to Ecclesiastes where it says "For everything there is a season, and a time for every matter under heaven." I think the key to understanding that everything is beautiful in its time is the fact that God has placed eternity into man's hearts.

Heavenly Father, Your word tells me that, "All are from dust, and to dust all return" (Eccl. 3:20 ESV). As the seasons come and go I am aware of the passing of time. Yet You have placed eternity in my heart. Thank You so much for loving me and sending Your Son into this world so that by believing in Him I have eternal life.

It is a Mystery

It is a mystery, and because it is a mystery I cannot fully understand or explain it. Yet, I am content to live with mystery; to believe in a God that is beyond my ability to completely explain. If I could fully understand the ways of God I would be His equal; I am not. One of the mysteries is this: He has allowed me to be a participant in His plans through prayer.

There are many places I see this in Scripture, but the one I find most intriguing is in Daniel. Daniel was a man who was faithful in prayer. In the tenth chapter of Daniel he tells about a time he was fasting and mourning and seeking to understand the word God had revealed to him. In response to Daniel's prayer God sent an angel. This is what the angel said, "Fear not, Daniel, for from the first day that you set your heart to understand and humble yourself before your God, your words have been heard, and I have come because of your words. The prince of the kingdom of Persia withstood me twenty-one days, but Michael, one of the chief princes, came to help me, for I was left there with the kings of Persia, and came to make you understand what is to happen to your people in the latter days" (Dan. 10:12-14 ESV).

Is there a parallel picture in the New Testament? Yes. "For we do not wrestle against flesh and blood, but against the rulers, against the authorities, against the cosmic powers over this present darkness, against the spiritual forces of evil in the heavenly places" (Eph. 6:12 ESV). We are to enter into the this mystery the same way Daniel did, "praying at all times in the Spirit, with all prayer and supplication" (Eph. 6:-18 ESV).

But I have to ask myself, am I really doing this? Am I really entering into what God is doing by praying at all times in the Spirit, with all prayer and supplication, or am I simply existing in the moment? Jesus' admonition to His followers was to watch and pray. However, I am aware that I often simply watch the events around me unfold without entering into the mystery of God by prayer.

Heavenly Father, forgive me for the lack of faith that keeps me from prayer. You have given the command to not only watch what You are doing in my generation, but to pray. Your word teaches that the prayer of a righteous person has great power. Please grant me the grace to enter into this mystery of prayer.

There is a Goat in the Middle of the Highway

I don't want to be late; I don't want to be early; I just want to be on time. But there is a goat in the middle of the highway. This goat has a name. Her name is Sugar. She's is a LaMancha goat. This means Sugar has no ears. Sugar has no horns. Sugar has no handle for me to grab her by. I live on a farm, but I'm not really a farmer. All I want to do is get to my appointment on time, but there is a goat in the middle of the highway.

I park my car. I have no idea what I'm supposed to do, but I can't pretend I don't notice this goat named Sugar in the highway. This was not part of my plans for today. I'm now standing next to the goat and I'm talking out loud, but not to the goat. "Father, what am I supposed to about this! You know I don't know how to do this sort of thing! This goat has no handle!" I think I'm kind of screaming the prayer as the cars and trucks whiz by.

I guess goats don't understand English, because I'm telling her where she needs to go to be safe, but she keeps going in the opposite direction. I've been chasing that goat for 30 minutes and now I have to call and explain why I'm not going to be there for my appointment. The phone is pressed to my ear by my shoulder because I'm holding a tree branch in each hand. Suddenly, I have an idea. I let the phone drop, grab my good silk scarf from around my neck and tie it around Sugar's neck. At last I can lead drag Sugar to safety.

Now I'm sitting in my car just thinking about what just happened. It's as if I've been given a picture of what this past week was like. I made plans of what I would do, but they didn't happen, because I'm not really the one who is in control. Not only that, but sometimes I'm just like Sugar: standing the middle of harm's way, but not trusting the one who wants to lead me to safety.

Heavenly Father, Your word says to, "Trust in the Lord with all your heart and do not lean on your own understanding" (Prov. 3:5 ESV). That is so hard to do. Please help me to humble myself and believe that You are Lord. When You allow things in my life that I am not expecting, please help me trust You.

The Magnitude of the Situation

My oldest brother was a master of big words; my little brother loved attention. It was the perfect combination for what took place. Nick began to work with Cessna, teaching him to form words that were far beyond his ability to understand. Finally, he was ready. His timing couldn't have been better. He turned to the adult who addressed him and, with his toddler's tongue he proclaimed, "You cannot fully comprehend the magnitude of the situation."

What is the magnitude of my situation? This year has brought with it so many challenges. If I wasn't looking at life through the lens of faith I think the magnitude of the situation would overwhelm me. My faith isn't in myself and it isn't in the belief that everything is going to be alright. My faith doesn't keep me experiencing the storm that rages all around me. But by faith I can see a greater story being told than just the chapter I am experiencing now.

"For I am convinced that neither death nor life, neither angels nor demons, neither the present nor the future, nor any powers, neither height nor depth, nor anything else in all creation, will be able to separate us from the love of God that is in Christ Jesus our Lord" (Rom. 8:38-39 NIV). It is in the magnitude of God's promise that I have put my faith.

Faith is being sure of what I hope for and confident about what I don't see. What I do see is scary. I see broken hurting people; but through eyes of faith I also see a Redeemer. Long ago I put my confidence in the one who said, "Never will I leave you; never will I forsake you" (Heb. 13:5 NIV). Absolute magnitude is a measure of the intrinsic luminosity of a celestial body. The absolute magnitude of God's grace and glory can only be seen through eyes of faith.

Heavenly Father, I am overwhelmed by the greatness of Your love and Your peace that passes understanding. Your love is far beyond my comprehension. Though I do not fully understand the situations I find myself in, I know that I am not alone and that nothing can separate me from Your love.

The Blessing

My granddad was the strongest man that ever lived and he loved me. I loved him too. I loved everything about him: his Italian accent, the way he could grow garlic in the garden, and the way he said my name, "Sadah."

It made me so sad when he had a stroke. After his stroke he couldn't walk anymore, so I would sit by his wheelchair and keep him company. He would tell me stories of his childhood, what it was like to grow up in Italy. He told me about tending to sheep. Though he was confined to a wheelchair, through his stories we traveled back to days of his youth.

Granddad never got tired of hearing me read the Gospels. He would say, "Sadah, I lika all the Bible, but read to me again about Jesus." My granddad was a strong, independent man and it was hard for him when he lost the use of his legs. One day I found a picture in his house of Jesus holding a lamb. "Granddad, when you were younger you were like the sheep in this picture who are running all over the field. But now you're like the lamb that Jesus carries." From then on Granddad kept that picture where he could see it.

Granddad gave me a special gift. Every night as I would climb the stairs to go to bed he would call out, "Sadah, Goda blessa youra good heart!" It's been many years since I was a young girl climbing those stairs. In fact, I am now have grandchildren of my own but sometimes as I'm falling asleep I can still hear my granddad calling out his blessing.

Lord Jesus, thank You for the blessings You have placed in my life.

The Orbit

The path taken by one object as it circles around another object is called an orbit. I have orbited around many things. Sometimes I have been held in the orbit of guilt as my mind has rehearsed again and again my faults and failures. Other times I have been held in the orbit of anger and resentment as the faults and failures of others held me in its gravitational pull. Being trapped in the orbit of either guilt or anger is a miserable place, but I have a secret weapon.

When I wake in the night orbiting around and around faults and failures there is only one thing that break the gravitational pull. "At midnight I rise to praise you" (Psa. 119:62 ESV). When I turn my heart and mind towards God I am drawn into His light and love. Praising God and focusing on who He is sets me free.

"About midnight Paul and Silas were praying and singing hymns of praise to God, and the prisoners were listening to them, and suddenly there was a great earthquake, so that the foundations of the prison were shaken. And immediately all the doors were opened, and everyone's bonds were unfastened" (Acts 16:25-26 ESV). Praise and thanksgiving is so powerful that not only does it set me free from the negative orbit, but it can have an effect on all those around me as well.

Orbiting around faults and failures, either mine or others, always produces sorrow. I am so grateful that I have been set free, ransomed, from the negative gravitational pull of this orbit. Orbiting around the Jesus Christ with songs of praise and thanksgiving I have obtained joy and gladness; and sorrow and sighing have fled away.

Grandmother Embraced Life!

Usually, I had to share her with my eight siblings, but for one glorious year I had her almost all to myself. Grandmother opened up worlds for me. In her backyard she had a wildflower garden. She would show me the different flowers as if they were her friends. Outside the breakfast room window she had a bird feeder. She knew the birds not only by name but by their songs. One time there was a comet passing in the heavens and Grandmother bundled up several of her grandchildren and took us to a bluff where we would be able to see it best. Grandmother embraced life!

With the same passion Grandmother embraced life she embraced God. I would tiptoe into her room in the morning hungry for breakfast and there she was on her knees talking to God. Often she would be praying out loud and I would kneel beside her and join in. Grandmother prayed fervently for all her grandchildren. My Aunt Sally was a missionary in Brazil and Grandmother prayed about everyone Aunt Sally mentioned in her letters.

While I was with Grandmother that year she was preparing her home for when Aunt Sally and her family would be coming home on furlough. Grandmother was so excited because at last she was going to get to meet her grandchildren from Brazil for the first time. I was so jealous! Because talking to God at Grandmother's house was such a natural thing to do, I began to talk to Him about my jealousy. My prayer became a request that God would take away my jealousy and replace it with love. I asked God to give me a special love for my cousins.

God did for me exactly what He promised He would do. "This is the confidence we have in approaching God: that if we ask anything according to his will, he hears us. And if we know he hears us—whatever we ask—we know we have what we asked of him" (1 John 5:14-15 NIV). Grandmother died about five years later, but the special love God gave me for my cousins has continued and now has been extended to their children as well.

Father, thank You for giving me a grandmother who taught me to embrace life. Thank You for teaching me through her that I could embrace You and be embraced by You. Thank You for enriching my world by the people You have given me to love. And, oh yes, thank You for teaching me the cure for jealousy.

A Quiet Moment

It takes time for the stillness to seep into my soul. Sunday I slipped away to a quiet place and watched as one by one the leaves fell. To say the leaves fell is too brief a description. I could not feel the breath of the wind, but I watched as the leaves gently danced their way to earth. The stillness of the scene was not broken as each leaf was gently received to earth in unbroken silence.

"Be still, and know that I am God" (Psa. 46:10). This was the verse I thought of as I sat there in silence. But it was hard to be still when one by one the troubling events of the week came rushing to my mind. Somehow the quietness of the moment had allowed all the things I'd been trying not to think about to come to the surface.

When I looked this verse up in *Barnes' Notes on the Bible* I found that the Hebrew words "be still" mean to properly cast down, to let fall; to let hang down; then to be relaxed. It expresses the attitude of leaving matters with God and not being anxious about the issue. So as I watched the trees around me releasing the leaves that the fluttered to the ground, I began to relax and let go of the troubles I had brought with me.

When I find a solitary place to be still I look around me at all the evidence that God is at work. I look around me and everywhere I look I see His fingerprints. I see the silhouette of the tree whose last leaf has silently found its way to earth. Now the tree looks as if it is raising its arms in praise. Finally, I find both stillness and praise entering my soul as well.

Father, help me to carry this quiet moment back into my busy world.

Hidden In Plain View

"Now, children, remember; these decorations are to be hidden in plain view." These are not only a Christmas decoration but a game we play each year. I have twelve small reindeer and snowmen that the children are to hide, but they are to hide them by making them part of the decorations. Whoever finds one of these reindeer or snowmen then has to find another hiding place where it will be in plain view. Right now I have a snowman riding the camel in my nativity scene and a reindeer hanging from my dining room chandelier.

"I love those who love me, and those who seek me diligently find me" (Prov. 8:17 ESV). I see this throughout the Scriptures as an invitation to seek and an invitation to find. "If you call out for insight and raise your voice for understanding, if you seek it like silver and search for it as for hidden treasures, then you will understand the fear of the Lord and find the knowledge of God" (Prov. 2:3-5 ESV).

There is something about the process of first discovering a longing and a thirst for something that helps me appreciate its value. What I see in these verses is that there is treasure that I am invited, not just to seek, but to find. God placed a yearning in my heart for Him and a desire to find Him.

This imagery of seeking and finding is in the New Testament as well. When Jesus tells us what the Kingdom of Heaven is like He says, "The Kingdom of heaven is like treasure hidden in a field" (Matt. 13:44 NIV); "Again, the kingdom of heaven is like a merchant looking for fine pearls" (Matt. 13:45 NIV). In all these verses I see an invitation with a promise of finding the thing I am longing for.

Father, thank You for giving me this desire to seek for You. Thank You for not only giving me the desire to seek, but also the delight of finding both You and Your Kingdom.

Dealing With What Has Been Left Behind

This has to be the hardest job I've ever been given. I am going through the house Papa built and packing things up. Papa died the week after Ma Belle, and now it's time to deal with things left behind. The family went through and made lists of things they would like, and this is very helpful.

Each list is touching, because the things that are being asked for don't have great monetary value but instead are reminders of the life that was shared with the ones who once owned them. My ten-year-old grandson's list, however, is the most touching of all. He wrote, "I want Papa's brown shoes because they were the ones he wore the most and he touched them all the time. I want one of Papa's hats because he wore it. I want Grandma's mirror because she looked in it and I remember helping her with her hair. I want the ceramic brown cow with the broken tail because I used to give Grandma Belle flowers to put in it. Finally, I want Grandma's hummingbird on the gold wire that always sat on the dining room table because it's beautiful and it reminds me of her."

This job has caused me to think about the things I will leave behind; because the truth is, we take nothing with us, not even our bodies. What will my children and grandchildren choose to remind them of me? As I am working my way through Ma Belle and Papa's home room by room I am finding in each nook and cranny evidence of a couple who loved the Lord and each other.

"Foxes have holes, and birds of the air have nests, but the Son of Man has nowhere to lay his head" (Luke 9:58 ESV). So what did Jesus leave behind? "These things I have spoken to you while I am still with you. But the Helper, the Holy Spirit, whom the Father will send in my name, he will teach you all things and bring to your remembrance all that I have said to you" (John 14:25-26 ESV). Jesus didn't leave things to remind us of Him, He sent His Spirit to dwell in us.

Lord Jesus, as I box up the things that have been left behind, I pause to thank You that You gave me Your Holy Spirit to comfort, counsel and teach. I also thank You because You have also given me the promise of resurrection so that I do not grieve like those who have no hope.

He Called Me by Name

Growing up in a big family I knew that if someone was looking at me they were probably talking to me, even if they called me by the wrong name. I've experienced talking to people who weren't sure how to address me so they didn't use my name. But I also remember when Steve looked into my eyes and spoke the words before a church filled with people, "I, Steve, take you, Sarah, to be my wife." He called me by name.

I was reminded of this yesterday when we read the passage, "Fear not, for I redeemed you; I have called you by name, you are mine" (Isa. 43:1 ESV). In my relationship with God I am more than just one of His creations. I am not simply lost in the sea of humanity; He called me by name.

I live on a cattle farm. When herding the cows shock sticks are used, but when a shepherd is herding his sheep he calls them by name. When Jesus described the kind of shepherd He was He said, "The sheep hear his voice, and he calls his own sheep by name and leads them out" (John 10:3 ESV). This is such a comfort: He not only calls me by name, but he also leads me.

Sometimes I feel lost. I'm not sure where I am, much less where I'm supposed to be going. When I feel insecure and unsure of who I am or where I'm going, I remind myself that my security rests in the fact that I have a good shepherd; a good shepherd who not only leads me but also gives me abundant life. I don't have to be afraid; He doesn't just lead me, He also calls me by name.

A Cure For Drudgery

I've been decorating for Christmas. I do it partly for my grandchildren, because when I put the angels on the mantle and string the lights on the porch it builds a sense of anticipation. But I don't just do it for them, I do it for myself as well. I can get locked into the drudgery of life and only see the day-in/day-out work that is before me. Christmas reminds me that I'm part of a bigger story.

"I am Gabriel. I stand in the presence of God, and I was sent to speak to you and to bring you this good news" (Luke 1:19 ESV). This is part of the wonder of Christmas, this intersection of what happens in the presence of God and here on earth. Gabriel was sent from God's presence to tell Zechariah that the 400 year of silence were over. What was the good news he brought? Zechariah's prayers had been heard and his wife was going to have a baby. This child would be filled with the spirit of Elijah and make ready for the Lord a people prepared.

Next Gabriel was sent from God's presence to a city of Galilee named Nazareth. I have now been to Israel twice and both times the tour guide didn't think Nazareth was significant enough to stop the bus. It may not be significant enough to stop a tour bus, but God choose Nazareth as the place where Gabriel would greet Mary with the news that she had been chosen to be overshadowed by the Most High by the Holy Spirit, and that she would conceive a child.

The lights I have on my porch come on automatically. They remind me that Jesus was born at night. I can just imagine the shepherds keeping watch over their flock by night, trying to stay awake and maybe wishing they were home in bed. In this ordinary setting, to these very ordinary people, an angel of the Lord appeared and the glory of the Lord shown around them. Then came the message that the fullness of time had arrived, a Savior, who is Christ the Lord had been born! "And suddenly there was with the angel a multitude of the heavenly host praising God and saying, 'Glory to God in the highest, and on earth peace among those with whom he is pleased!'" (Luke 2:13-14 ESV).

Father, I am filled with wonder at the message the angels brought on the first advent. But I am filled with anticipation with what the angel said at the resurrection: "Men of Galilee, why do you stand looking into heaven? This Jesus, who was taken up from you into heaven, will come in the same way as you saw him go into heaven" (Acts 1:11 ESV). It's been almost 2,000 years since the angels said these words, but that doesn't diminish my anticipation; it increases it.

Don't Let Your Goals Be a Stumbling Block

I don't remember the exact words she used, but I understood what she was asking. She was one of the callers on a radio program I listen to, and the question she asked had to do with her and her husband of three months making plans about how they would serve God together. The response to her question was rich with wisdom. "You are young and you do not yet know the challenges you will face. It is good to have goals of what you want to do for God, but don't let them become stumbling blocks if your life doesn't turn out the way you planned for it to turn out." I'm not sure if these were his exact words either, but they are what I heard.

I remember the goals I had as a young woman leaving home for the first time. I dreamed of serving God in dramatic ways. The truth is, if I had been the author of my own story it would look far different than it does today. Looking back now I wonder if I was seeking to bring God glory or wanting my own glory by seeking God?

"You are young and you do not yet know the challenges you will face. It is good to have goals of what you want to do for God, but don't let them become stumbling blocks if your life doesn't turn out the way you planned for it to turn out." I had no idea when I was a young woman what the challenges were that I would face. If I had placed my faith in myself or my goals I would have been crushed long ago.

What I have found throughout these years of longing to serve God is that it is both a humbling and a purifying pursuit. The challenges I have faced have been like a refining fire, exposing my prideful heart and desperate need of a Savior. The role that God has given me has not been that of being the author of this story but of trusting the One who is.

Lord Jesus, I am fixing my eyes on You. You alone are the author and perfecter of my faith. I lay on Your alter all my ambitions, hopes and dreams.

"But, Mama, Who Will Light the Christmas Candle?"

The year was 1973. I was young and very much in the love with the man who would become my husband. It was our first Christmas together, and it was at that first celebration that I was introduced to the lighting of the Christmas candle. I didn't know then that this lighting of the Christmas candle would become one of my most cherished Christmas traditions.

Samuel Hardiman Jones Sr. held in his gnarled hands an old brass candleholder. The skin on his hands was as transparent as his heart, and the tears slid unbidden down his wrinkled cheeks. The brass candleholder had once belonged to his mother. As he lit the candle, he was reminded of the Christmases of his childhood when his mother's young hand held the light on those dark December nights of long ago. His mother was now a sweet memory that was awakened every Christmas when he would hold in his hand the same candleholder that she had held in her hand. And he would weep.

I learned that year that tears were part of the Christmas celebration. Samuel Hardiman Jones Sr., with a voice that choked with emotion, explained the significance of the brass candleholder. Then he lit the candle. And as he did he spoke about the tender mercy of God. "This light is to remind us that we have been visited by the sunrise from on high. Jesus has come to give light to those who sit in darkness, and in the shadow of death, to guide our feet into the way of peace."

When Great Granddaddy died I was given the antique brass candleholder. Every year I would ask Papa, Great Granddaddy's son, to light the Christmas candle. He would take the candleholder into his hands that had become twisted by the years, and he would pause as the tears gathered in his eyes. With a voice husky with emotion he would light the candle and remind us that Christmas is about when the light of the world penetrated our darkness.

Earlier this year Papa died. His bride of 64 years had died just six days before him. As Christmas was approaching my daughter broke down and wept. Beside the olive wood nativity I had placed the candleholder. "But, Mama, who will light the Christmas candle?" I knew the pain in her heart because it was in mine as well. "Your Daddy will light the candle and we will all weep. We will remember Papa and Grandma Belle and all the ones we love who are no longer with us, and we will weep. However, we will not grieve like those who have no hope. We will light the candle and we will remember why Jesus came."

"Overshadowed"

Has your life ever been overshadowed by something? The definition of the word overshadow is:
1. to exceed in importance: *"the tragedy overshadowed the couple's happiness"*
2. to cast a shadow over: *"the scandal followed her all her life."*

This year I have had some health issues, and I discovered that via the Internet I could spend hours doing researching if I chose to. However, I chose not to do that, because I was afraid that if I did it would overshadow everything else in my life. I did not want to define who I am by things like that.

Although I chose not be overshadowed by my health issues, there is something I do choose to be overshadowed by. I want to be overshadowed in the same way Mary was when the Gabriel said to her, "The Holy Spirit will come upon you, and the power of the Most High will overshadow you" (Luke 1:35 ESV).

In my life this overshadowing took place when I was baptized into Christ

Jesus. "We were buried therefore with him by baptism into death, in order that, just as Christ was raised from the dead by the glory of the Father, we too might walk in newness of life" (Rom. 6:4 ESV). This new life is lived in the power of the Holy Spirit.

Lord Jesus, I come to You and ask that I might decrease and that You would increase in my life. I want to be alive to You and dead to me. Please fill me today with Your Holy Spirit.

Did I Miss It?

I thought I had plenty of time, but now I find myself sitting in the dark wondering if I'm too late and it has passed me by. Did I miss it?

All these back roads look the same and there is no light. I can hardly see the curve of the road. Where am I? How did I get so lost! I thought I knew where I was going. I thought I knew where this road would take me, but now I don't know where I am. I was wrong. Now I know that I am lost!

Walking on a deserted country road I suddenly feel afraid. I don't know what I'm afraid of, but the fear is almost tangible. It's like a warning to turn and go a different direction. I obey the warning, and find out later that a murderer lived down the road I was about to walk on.

I have a shepherd. There are times in my life when I feel like I have missed out on what I was supposed to do with my life—except that as a child I asked Jesus to be my Savior. Jesus said that He was the Good Shepherd, and ever since I was a child I have asked Him to guide me. So I choose to silence my doubts by trusting my shepherd.

I have a shepherd and this is a good thing, because like sheep I have a tendency to lose my way. One of my favorite psalms is Psalm 119. "With my whole heart I seek you; let me not wander from your commandments! I have stored up your word in my heart, that I might not sin against you.... Open my eyes, that I may behold wondrous things out of your law. I am a sojourner on the earth; hide not your commandment from me!" (Psa. 119:10-11, 18-19 ESV). In this psalm I see a passionate love for God's word. My heart resonates with the psalmist's passion. However, I whisper the last verse of this psalm in prayer as well: "I have gone astray like a lost sheep; seek your servant, for I do not forget your commandments" (Psa. 119:176 ESV).

I have a shepherd. I need a shepherd, because I also have an enemy that comes to steal and kill and destroy. This spiritual enemy is just as real as the murderer who lived down the street. Jesus said, "I have come that they may have life, and have it to the full. I am the good shepherd. The good shepherd lays down his life for the sheep" (John 10:10-11 NIV). I not only have a shepherd, I have a Savior.

Lord Jesus, like a sheep I do not know the path I am to take. Thank You for guiding me. Like a lamb that wanders off, I too have sometimes lost my way. Thank You for seeking me. I have walked in the valley of the shadow of death. Thank You for being my Savior.

The Relationship between Repentance and Peace

"I like your website, but you have to test the spelling on quite a few of your posts. A number of them are rife with spelling issues." This was one of the comments I found on my Blog. I am often concerned not only that I might spell something wrong, but also that I might have run on sentences, comma slices, and even sentence fragments. I do proof read what I write, but still I often find it difficult to see my own mistakes. This would be the benefit of having someone else edit my work.

This is not just a problem with my writing, this is a problem I have in general. I have a very difficult time seeing where I am wrong. The other night I got into a fight with my husband. It began when I did something that hurt his feelings. My response was to justify myself and point out his faults. His faults were obvious to me, but I was blind to my own.

As I was going to sleep I prayed a prayer I often pray, "Search me, O God, and know my heart; test me and know my anxious thoughts" (Psa. 139:23 NLT). God answered that prayer and I was finally able to see where I had offended my husband. The light penetrated my darkness, and only then could I see where I had been self-centered.

This incident made me think about the relationship between repentance and peace. Until I was able to see that I had wronged my husband and that I needed to repent, we didn't have peace between us. Not only that, but I didn't have peace within myself either. When God sent John to prepare the way for the Savior, his message was one of repentance. In order to receive the Peace from Heaven there had to first be the acknowledgement and repentance of sin.

Zechariah said, "And you, child, will be called the prophet of the Most High; for you will go before the Lord to prepare his ways, to give knowledge of salvation to his people in the forgiveness of their sins, because of the tender mercy of our God, whereby the sunrise shall visit us from on high to give light to those who sit in darkness and in the shadow of death, to guide our feet into the way of peace" (Luke 1:76-79 ESV).

The Torch is Lit and I am Waiting

She was my Grandfather's sister. Aunt Ellen had always been a kind and generous presence in my childhood, so when my Mother told me she was on her death bed I went to visit her.

She looked so small and frail in her hospital bed. I wasn't sure if she would know who I was or not, but when our eyes met I knew she did. She told me to pull a chair up next to her bed, then she reached out and took my hand. "Sarah, my mother always hoped that she would live to see the return of Christ. When she died she passed the hope to me. Now I pass this torch of hope to you. Live your life with the anticipation that Jesus may return in your lifetime."

This morning I was reading to my grandson about Simeon. "Now there was a man in Jerusalem, whose name was Simeon, and this man was righteous and devout, waiting for the consolation of Israel, and the Holy Spirit was upon him. And it had been revealed to him by the Holy Spirit that he would not see death before he had seen the Lord's Christ" (Luke 2:25-26 ESV). We read how he had come in the Spirit to the temple on the very day Joseph and Mary had brought Jesus.

I told Jack that when Jesus had ascended into Heaven angels had appeared and had told the disciples that this very same Jesus would return in like fashion. I have carried this torch of anticipation all my life, and now it was my turn to share it with the next generation. "Jack, Jesus is coming back again. Simeon was there is see Him the first time Jesus came. Perhaps you will be alive when Jesus returns. Live your life with this anticipation."

Lord Jesus, as I prepare for Christmas I am reminded of what You said in the last chapter of Revelation, "'Surely I am coming soon.' Amen. Come Lord Jesus!" (Rev. 22:20).

Our Deliverer Has Come

I stood in the middle of the kitchen and wept. The radio was on, and I heard for the first time the details about the shooting that had taken place that day at an elementary school. I felt overwhelmed by sorrow. In my mind I could see the faces of my own children and grandchildren at that young age. I grieved for the children and the families and for all of us, because these children in some ways belong to all of us.

"A voice was heard in Ramah, weeping and loud lamentation, Rachel weeping for her children; she refused to be comforted, because they are no more" (Matt. 2:18 ESV). This too is part of the Christmas story. Why did Jesus come? He came to be the deliverer, to rescue us; "For we do not wrestle against flesh and blood, but against the rulers, against the authorities, against the cosmic powers over this present darkness, against spiritual forces of evil in the heavenly places" (Eph. 6:12 ESV).

Sometimes I feel that at Christmas time everyone should be happy, but this reflects a very shallow understanding of why Jesus came. Jesus came in response to the tender mercy of our God; to be our deliverer, to save us from the Power of Darkness. Jesus came "to give knowledge of salvation to his people in the forgiveness of their sins, because of the tender mercy of our God, whereby the sunrise shall visit us from on high to give light to those who sit in darkness and in the shadow of death, to guide our feet into the way of peace" (Luke 1:77-79 ESV).

Last Sunday we sang *My Deliverer is Coming* by Rich Mullins. The song was particularly touching because we had a small choir of young children who sang these words:

> My deliverer is comin', my deliverer is standin' by

> My deliverer is comin', my deliverer is standin' by
> He will never break His promise
> He has written it upon the sky

[Chad Cates, Tony Wood, Jason Walker, *My Deliverer is Coming*, © Universal Music Publishing Group.]

Father, yesterday the thin membrane that separates us from the evil one was ruptured. I am reminded of that first Christmas when there was the sound of weeping and lamentations; mothers weeping for their children, refusing to be comforted because their children had been taken from them. Two thousand year later the sound of weeping mothers can be heard again. Thank You, for sending Your son into this broken world to be our deliverer.

"Be Ready For the Son of Man is Coming"

When I was a senior in high school I wrote a paper about all the prophecies Jesus fulfilled in His first coming. I can still remember the sense of wonder I was filled with as I explored the scriptures in this way for the first time. It was as if I was discovering arrows of light that pointed to the truth.

One of the prophecies was that men would have eyes but they would not see, and ears but they would not hear. I see this clearly when the wisemen came to Jerusalem saying, "Where is he who has been born king of the Jews? For we saw his star when it rose and have come to worship him" (Matt. 2:2 NIV). This was not done in secret. Herod and all Jerusalem were troubled. This was not the first hint that the Messiah had been born.

When Jesus was eight days old his parents had taken him to the temple to be dedicated. Simeon, who had been waiting for the consolation of Israel, when he saw Jesus proclaimed, "Lord, now you are letting your servant depart in peace, according to your word; for my eyes have seen your salvation that you have prepared in the presence of all peoples, a light for revelation to the Gentiles, and for the glory of your people Israel" (Luke 2:29-32 ESV). The prophetess Anna had recognized who Jesus was, and "she began to give thanks to God and to speak of him to all who were waiting for the redemption of Jerusalem" (Luke 2:38 ESV). These things took place not in a remote place but in the temple at Jerusalem.

Now here they were: a caravan of Gentiles following the light of a star just like Simeon had proclaimed in the temple! Herod assembled all the chief priests and scribes of the peoples, he inquired of them where the Christ was to be born. They told him, "In Bethlehem of Judea, for so it is written by the prophet: 'And you, O Bethlehem, in the land of Judah; are by no means least among the rulers of Judah; for from you shall come a ruler who will shepherd my people Israel'" (Matt. 2:5-6 ESV). They knew what was written by the prophets.

There are prophecies yet to be fulfilled; prophecies about Jesus' second coming. "Tell us, when will these things be, and what will be the sign of your coming and of the end of the age?" Matthew 24 is Jesus' response to His disciples' question. Jesus told them, "But concerning that day and hour no one knows, not even the angels of heaven, nor the Son, but the Father only. As were the days of Noah, so will be the coming of the Son of Man" (Matt 24:36-37 ESV). What were the days of Noah like? "The earth also was corrupt before God, and the earth was filled with violence" (Gen. 6:11 KJV).

Lord Jesus, I do not want to be like those who missed Your first coming. You told Your disciples to, "Be ready, for the Son of Man is coming at an hour you do not expect." Help me to understand the times in which I live. Help me to have eyes that see and a heart that understands. Grant that I might be like Simeon and Anna and live my life with a sense of anticipation.

The Candle is Lit

The candle is lit. It illumines the darkness and I know His presence is in this place. The quiet of the sanctuary fills my being with a sense of awe and wonder. Mother and Daddy woke me from a sound sleep to dress me and bring me to church at midnight. The room is dark except for the flickering light of the candles. The air is filled with the smell of sweet perfume and the sounds of worship. Now I see what I've been waiting for, the Nativity.

The candle is lit. When the light of the world came into our darkness there were shepherds out in the fields, keeping watch over their flocks by night. "Suddenly, an angel of the Lord appeared among them, and the radiance of the Lord's glory surrounded them" (Luke 2:9 NLT). They were common people, yet they had been invited to come and see the baby wrapped in swaddling clothes and lying in a manger. And now here I was, just a common little girl wrapped in the wonder of Jesus' birth.

The candle is lit. I'm sitting, waiting, holding my unlit candle. All through the service the sanctuary has been lit by the flickering lights of the candles, but now the flame is being passed from one candle to another. Now it's my turn. I touch the wick of my candle to the flame. "I am the light of the world. The one who follows me will never walk in darkness" (John 8:12 ISV).

The candle is lit. When I was a little girl the light of the candle reminded me that I had come to worship. At Christmas time when I was entrusted with a burning candle I was reminded that I, like the shepherds, had been invited to participate in celebrating the coming of the Savior.

Lord Jesus, You are the light of the world. The night of your birth the armies of heaven proclaimed, "Glory to God in the highest heaven, and peace on earth to those with whom God is pleased." Lord, You came into our darkness to bring us light. You entered into our chaos to bring us peace. Please let me carry within me Your light.

"Mark My Footsteps, My Dear Child"

Whenever I couldn't remember the exact words to a song I would make them up. This was not really a problem unless I was singing with other people. However, this did make it difficult for my children because they were familiar with the words I put to the song and were confused when others sang the same song in a different way.

Recently I went to a friend's house for a carol sing. One of the songs we sang was, "Good King Wenceslas." It's a fun song to sing. There was one verse in the song that stuck in my head. It stuck in my head slightly altered from its original form.

"Father, the night is darker now
And the wind blows stronger
Fails my heart, I know not how,
 I can go no longer."
"Mark my footsteps, my dear child
 Tread thou in them boldly
Thou shalt find the winter's rage
 Freeze thy blood less coldly."

As I have sung my version of this song I have thought about my parents. When I was a child I thought they simply did what came naturally. I know better now. Now I know that the decisions they made were guided by their choice to follow in Jesus' footsteps. I have been blessed beyond measure by their example and I pray that my children will be able to find shelter from the winter's rage by following me as well.

Lord Jesus, this Christmas I thank You again for humbling Yourself and coming to us in human form. Thank you for leaving us not only footsteps to follow but for giving us Your Holy Spirit.

You Don't Have to Be in Control

The world had become too big for him. He was hiding in my closet. He looked so vulnerable, so scared and small. Quietly I joined him. I didn't come to lecture; I didn't come with answers; I came to listen. I held him as he poured out his fears, his anger, his tears. We sat together in the darkness. I have learned you don't have to have all the answers if you've found a resting place in the one who does.

I looked into the eyes of my beautiful friend and saw a cloud of sorrow there. I listened as she told me about her disappointment. When she opened the door to her heart and began telling me about her broken dreams the tears began to flow. "It's alright to be vulnerable," I said, "You don't have to be in control. You are safe. You are not alone."

It was long ago when the lie was told and then believed. "You can be like God, knowing good and evil." Innocents died and naked vulnerability was clothed with the harsh lie of control. In the cool of the evening God came to garden to invite the created to enter into sweet fellowship with the Creator, but they were hiding and fellowship was broken. Death had come when the lie was believed. Now there would be pain and thorns and thistles to control. But all was not lost. There was also the promise of a Redeemer.

The one who came to set us free was born as a vulnerable infant. There was no power of wealth associated with the parents He chose. When He was born there were whispers of shame that some associated with His birth. He entered into history at a time when there was oppression and bondage. He tasted our tears, carried our grief and bore our sorrows. He came to the thorn-infested garden to show us a way to be free from the bondage of the lie that we were in control.

Jesus, thank You for coming. Thank You for entering into our weakness so that we could enter into Your strength.

When You Get to the End of the Rope...Let Go

"I am totally at the end of my rope." When I read these words that my friend had written me I wanted to whisper in response, "Then let go of the rope."

We live in a broken world. In fact, "the whole world is under the control of the evil one" (1 John 5:19 NIV). We live in a broken world under the control of the evil one and Jesus told us, "In this world you will have tribulation." The word tribulation comes from the Greek word *thlipsis*. When I researched the word in "HELPS Word-Studies" [www.helpsbible.com], I found it meant pressure (what constricts or rubs together), used of a narrow place that "hems someone in;" tribulation, especially internal pressure that causes someone to feel confined (restricted, "without option"). This Greek word carries the challenge of coping with the internal pressure of a tribulation, especially when feeling there is "no way of escape." But Jesus didn't simply tell us that we would have tribulation in this world. He said, "But take heart! I have overcome the world" (John 16:33 NIV).

I understand this desperate feeling of clinging to the end of the rope when the world is pressing in and crying out, "I'm trying as hard as I can!" This is when I hear my Savior whisper, "Let go of the rope." Letting go of my striving I find myself plunged into His grace. As I let go of my desperate hold on the rope I cry out, "I have been crucified with Christ and I no longer live, but Christ lives in me. The life I now live in the body, I live by faith in the Son of God, who loved me and gave himself for me" (Gal. 2:20 NIV). In the process of letting go of the rope and taking hold of the promise, I find peace.

Sometimes when I am feeling hemmed in by the pressures of life I forget the truth. I forget that I have been invited to rest in the love of God, not because of what I have done for Him, but because of what He has done for me. The place I find victory is not in striving but in trusting. When I walk in the truth of His love for me then I am sure of what I hope for and confident about what I don't see.

Lord Jesus, thank You for inviting me into that place of perfect peace. Thank You that I can let go of the rope and find myself safe in Your arms. Please help me share this truth with others.

Beyond the Mist

The phone rang and as soon as I heard his voice I knew the message it carried. He was calling to tell me my friend was dead. I felt a deep sorrow. I spent the rest of the day remembering times I had spent with her as if they were scenes from a movie. I also thought, "What is your life? For you are a mist that appears for a little time and then vanishes" (James 4:14 ESV).

All day I thought about my friend, remembering the first time we met; how we would watch our children play together. I had always enjoyed her artistic approach to everyday things, and her ability to find treasures at yard sales was legendary. But now, like a vapor that floats for a while in the air but which disappears with the heat of the rising sun, my friend was gone.

I had shared many things with my friend, but there was one part of my life she did not want to participate in. She wanted nothing to do with my faith. She was always very kind, and when we were together she would invite me to pray before meals; but she did not join in the prayer. She allowed me to freely talk about my faith with her, because she loved me and understood that what I believed was an intrinsic part of who I was, but always made it clear that she did not share those beliefs. "They are like a breath; their days are like a fleeting shadow" (Psa. 144:4 NIV). Like a fleeting shadow my friend was gone.

That evening I received a second phone call. It was from my friend's brother. He was calling to tell me what had happened on Christmas Eve two days before she had died. "I want you to know this because I know you prayed for my sister, and I do not want you to grieve like those who have no hope." He told me how he had share the gospel with his sister. He told her, "As Moses lifted up the serpent in the wilderness, so must the Son of Man be lifted up, that whoever believed in him may have eternal life. For God so loved the world, that he gave his only Son, that whoever believes in him should not perish but have eternal life" (John 3:14-16 ESV). She lifted her eyes, believed in God's Son, and received eternal life. Her brother and I wept together; but in the midst of sorrow there was the joy that we would see her in eternity.

Father, I do not understand Your love, that though our life here on earth is like a vapor, You have given us Your Son so that whoever believes on Him might not perish but have eternal life. Thank You that even though I grieve the loss of my friend, I am confident that I will see her again.

SCRIPTURE INDEX

ABOUT THE AUTHOR

Sarah Decosimo Jones was raised in a Christian home. From her earliest years she learned to love God's word and to have communion with Him through prayer.

At eighteen she suffered from a serious illness that threatened her future. It was during this time of trial that Sarah began to understand Romans 15:13, "May the God of hope fill you with all joy and peace as you trust in him," (NIV) even if the circumstances tell a different story.

Later, hope deepened as she walked through cancer with her young husband. Again as a young mother, God was her place of refuge as she stood at the graveside of her infant. The sorrow and pain of this life has taught Sarah to anchor her confidence in the character of God and place all of her expectation in His promises, which do not fail.

Sarah hears the cries of a hurting world. She has walked with her husband, her daughter and her friends through their battles with cancer. She has opened her home to the homeless and to those alienated from their family. She has taken in children who were orphaned. Sarah's prayer is that the hope she has been given will overflow to those around her by the power of the Holy Spirit.

Verses that have special meaning to her are Psalm 84:5-6, "Blessed are those whose strength is in you, who have set their hearts on pilgrimage. As they pass through the Valley of Baca, they make it a place of springs;..." (NIV). In Hebrew, *Baca* means "a place of weeping," and Sarah's prayer is that the things God has taught her during the places of weeping will become a place of refreshment to those who follow.

The Gift of Hope